# ROYAL COMMISSION ON THE PRESS

CHAIRMAN: PROFESSOR O R McGREGOR

# Analysis of Newspaper Content

A REPORT BY PROFESSOR DENIS McQUAIL

Research Series 4

*Presented to Parliament by Command of Her Majesty*

*July 1977*

*LONDON*

HER MAJESTY'S STATIONERY OFFICE

£5.25 net

Cmnd. 6810-4

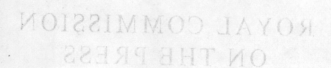

# ROYAL COMMISSION ON THE PRESS

CHAIRMAN: PROFESSOR O R McGREGOR

## Analysis of Newspaper Content

A REPORT BY PROFESSOR DENIS McQUAIL

ISBN 0 10 168104 6

# FOREWORD BY THE CHAIRMAN

1. The present Royal Commission on the Press was set up in 1974 with the following terms of reference:

To inquire into the factors affecting the maintenance of the independence, diversity and editorial standards of newspapers and periodicals, and the public's freedom of choice of newspapers and periodicals, nationally, regionally and locally, with particular reference to:

(a) the economics of newspaper and periodical publishing and distribution;

(b) the interaction of the newspaper and periodical interests held by the companies concerned with their other interests and holdings, within and outside the communications industry;

(c) management and labour practices and relations in the newspaper and periodical industry;

(d) conditions and security of employment in the newspaper and periodical industry;

(e) the distribution and concentration of ownership of the newspaper and periodical industry, and the adequacy of existing law in relation thereto;

(f) the responsibilities, constitution and functioning of the Press Council;

and to make recommendations.

2. The Royal Commission have taken evidence from many organisations and individuals, and have commissioned research from those with special knowledge in relevant fields. This report by Professor Denis McQuail of the University of Southampton is the fourth in the series of research papers which the Royal Commission is publishing with the object of promoting and informing public discussion.

3. We commissioned Professor McQuail to analyse the content of newspapers. He classified the content of newspapers on 24 days in 1975 by a similar method to that used in a research project carried out for the 1947–49 Royal Commission on the Press, so that comparisons could be made. He also made special studies of newspaper coverage of news relating to industrial relations, social welfare and foreign affairs.

4. Professor McQuail's work has been of great value to the Royal Commission and constitutes a major contribution to an understanding of the Press. We are therefore publishing it in full.

O R McGREGOR
June 1977

# Preface

This volume brings together the reports of five separate studies which were carried out for the Royal Commission on the Press. The aims of each are explained at the beginning of each Part and the general purpose of the work is set out in the Chairman's foreword. The broad strategy was to conduct, firstly, several descriptive surveys of the main kinds of newspaper in Britain and, subsequently, to focus in more depth on selected areas of content. Plans for the analysis evolved as the work proceeded, in consultation with the Secretariat and Members of the Commission. Inevitably, the ground covered is far from complete and a number of questions of interest have remained unanswered. The separate studies are related to each other in the following way. The main descriptive survey of content provided the basic sample of national daily newspapers for more detailed analysis. Thus, the three surveys of content relating to industrial relations, to foreign affairs and to social welfare and social policy, respectively, are all based on this sample of twenty-four issues in 1975. The additional study of cases of industrial relations reporting on eight days (Part C of the report), was intended to supplement the survey material on this topic and is also based on issues of newspapers included in the main descriptive survey.

The work described in the Report was carried out in the Department of Sociology and Social Administration at the University of Southampton, in consultation with the Secretariat and Members of the Royal Commission on the Press and their Advisers. It was necessarily completed within a rather short period of time and required the co-operation and assistance of a number of different people. The setting up of an *ad hoc* research group was greatly helped by members of the University, especially Professor J H Smith, who made the allocation of my time possible during 1975–6, and Mr C W Swann who facilitated the recruitment of staff for the purpose. Advice was generously given by Professor P G Richards of the Department of Politics and Professor G Kalton, Dr J Fields and Mr T J Tomberlin of the Department of Social Statistics. Particular thanks are due to members of the research team. Mrs Thelma Payne typed the original work with efficiency and provided organisational and other support which was quite indispensable. Derek Cox, as Research Assistant, carried out the computational work essential to the analysis of the surveys of content with great zeal and was much helped by Mrs Pat Sait. The research would not have been possible without the dedicated work of the coding and analysis team, Janice Grant, Jennifer Weeks, Marylin Ross, Jane Clark and Mary Allan, of whom the last three made an exceptional contribution by their careful and intelligent work on the detailed studies of industrial relations, social welfare and foreign content. Appendix R is largely the individual work of Mary Allan. Amongst the Commission's own staff, particular thanks is due to Mr Paul Starkey for arranging the supply of newspapers for analysis and to Mr Peter Gudgeon for advice on the local press. I would like to express my thanks for generous help and advice from Professor John Eldridge of Glasgow University and members of his research team, and to Peter Golding and Paul Hartmann of Leicester University.

DENIS McQUAIL
University of Southampton

# Contents

# Part A

*General Analysis of Content in five types of newspaper: National Dailies and Sundays; Provincial Mornings and Evenings; Local Weeklies*

# Main Tables

# PART A
# I  Aims and Methods

## 1. Introduction

The research reported below has its origin in the wish to provide some evidence relevant to the question of editorial standards in newspapers. Its main aim has been to provide background descriptions of the contents of the main kinds of British newspapers as they were when the Royal Commission was considering their future. The main precedent for such work lies in the research carried out by Mr R Silverman for the first Royal Commission on the Press (1947–9) although similar analyses have been carried out by others*. The work was expected to make a contribution on three main points: firstly, to assess changes in the broad outlines of the national daily press since 1947; secondly, to gain some insight into the functions of the press at present and to make comparisons between different categories of newspaper and different titles within each category; thirdly, to provide a quantitative background picture of the press to set the context for more detailed qualitative studies of some particular types of content. While the results as reported bear only indirectly on editorial standards, they may be helpful in assessing the diversity of the press and in establishing the main characteristics of different titles and different types of newspaper. While the present research is based on earlier models, it differs also in its extension to new categories of newspaper, especially the provincial and local press.

## 2. Content analysis as a method

The analysis of press content is a long established practice in the social sciences. Although the method embraces a wide range of different techniques, most of these fall within the definition offered by Bernard Berelson†, in writing that it aims at "the objective, systematic and quantitative description of the manifest content of communication". This at least reflects our own intention. A set of categories has been established and the space in chosen newspapers allocated to these categories. A number of assumptions have been made in doing so. Firstly, it is assumed that the categories themselves are distinct, relevant to the purpose of the description and meaningful to those familiar with the press. Secondly, it is assumed that they are mutually exclusive, in that a given section of newspaper space should not fall under more than one of the proposed headings. Thirdly, we assume that the categories are equally applicable to different sorts of newspaper. Fourthly, we assume that the categories can be applied in a systematic way, so that different analysts would achieve the same results with the same task. Fifthly, we assume that space in newspapers can be measured in such a way that comparisons in numerical terms can be made between different categories and different newspapers. Finally, it is common for content analysis to be carried out on a sample of a much larger population of cases (here, newspapers) and to assume that one can generalise from the sample to this population. Indeed, one of the main justifications for undertaking a content analysis of the kind attempted here is that it can provide economically a representative picture of an otherwise unmanageably large universe.

---

* For instance, R Williams in *Communications*, Chatto & Windus, 1966; C Seymour-Ure, *The Press Politics and the Public*, Methuen, 1968.
  † B Berelson *Content Analysis*, Free Press, 1952.

1

Each of these assumptions has weaknesses and can be justified only to a limited degree. A brief comment, at this point, on these weaknesses may be helpful in assessing the general utility of the evidence of this report. On the categories themselves, it should be said they represent only one set out of a range of possibilities. They are somewhat arbitrary, chosen for the purpose at hand in the belief that they can convey something about the press which reflects the way newspapers are put together and read. Their meaningfulness depends entirely on convention and current usage and there is no objective or neutral way of deciding which categories should be used. Here, the wish to maintain comparability with earlier research has been the decisive factor in the selection of particular categories. In this, as in other similar research, the requirement of exclusiveness can rarely be fully met. Rules of precedence can be established which deal with most problems of classification, but there is often nothing intrinsic to the content itself which objectively determines the appropriate classification. Hence judgement is involved as well as the somewhat arbitrary rules. This weakness affects the third and fourth assumption. The rules and definitions appropriate to one title do not always apply equally to another title of a quite different kind and the meaning of categories has to be stretched accordingly to cope with this diversity. By some standards, we might not admit the possibility of classifying very different sorts of newspapers within the same scheme of categories and the assumption that the "newspaper" describes a homogeneous universe of publications is a doubtful one. On the other hand, it may take an analysis of content to establish where the assumption breaks down. The assumption of "measurability" has self-evident weaknesses where newsprint space is used very differently in different papers and perhaps paid attention to very differently. Once one accepts other assumptions about classification, measurement and the homogeneity of what has been measured, the final assumption of "generalisability" presents relatively few problems, since the size of sample errors can be estimated precisely. The newspaper of a given title is sufficiently regular in form and distribution of content between broad categories to make this the least difficult problem.

These points have been made, not in order to reduce confidence in the results, but to explain why some procedures were adopted in the research and to establish realistic expectations of what can and cannot be achieved by research of this kind. In particular, it should have become clear that the validity of the results depend on the validity of the initial classification scheme, and that figures produced are only approximate, subject to some errors of classification and variability of judgement as well as to limitations inherent in any sampling procedure. General cautionary words applicable to all content analysis also apply here: we cannot make inferences about the effects of the press or the way it may be read from a description of content, nor can measurements of space in themselves offer evidence on the quality of the press without some other value judgement being made. Few value judgements are attempted in this report, although the distinctions used in the classification scheme may embody some implicit value judgements.

## 3. Methods of sampling

### (i) *National Dailies*

Since a main purpose of the research was a comparison between the national daily press in 1975 and in 1947, a sampling procedure very similar to that used at the earlier date and described in the 1947–9 Royal Commission Report (Appendix III) was chosen. A representative sample of issues for each newspaper was chosen in a way which would give appropriate weight to each quarter of the year and each day of the week. In practice, the method involved sampling *days* of the year, so that the samples for different titles would carry basically the same news and be more directly comparable. Six days were chosen from each quarter, each of the six being a different week-day, making 24 days in all, or a sample of approximately one day in every 13 of the total week-days for the calendar year 1975. In making this choice, the procedure adopted was to number the weeks of each quarter from 1–13, to choose six of these weeks at random, then to randomly allocate a particular week-day to each of the chosen six weeks. Because 1 January fell on a Wednesday and this was designated as week 1, there was no chance for two week-days to be chosen in that sample week. Correspondingly, the last four dates in 1975 were excluded from the sampling procedure. A further difficulty arose because on two of the dates chosen in the initial sample, one of the nine National Dailies failed to appear. A substitute day was chosen in each case by a similar method. The final sample of days was as follows:

| | | | |
|---|---|---|---|
| 7 January | Tuesday | 7 July | Monday |
| 15 January | Wednesday | 2 August | Saturday |
| 3 February | Monday | 21 August | Thursday |
| 15 February | Saturday | 5 September | Friday |
| 21 February | Friday | 10 September | Wednesday |
| 6 March | Thursday | 23 September | Tuesday |
| 17 April | Thursday | 18 October | Saturday |
| 23 April | Wednesday | 29 October | Wednesday |
| 9 May | Friday | 10 November | Monday |
| 12 May | Monday | 18 November | Tuesday |
| 3 June | Tuesday | 27 November | Thursday |
| 28 June | Saturday | 12 December | Friday |

The sample of dates was drawn before the year was complete and the particular issues analysed were either acquired for the purpose or in some cases obtained in photo-copy from the British Museum Library*. We are aware that editions of newspapers vary in their content and that this limits the direct comparability of newspapers published on the same day. We had no practicable way of controlling for this variation, since some issues had to be found by unusual methods. For the most part, the copies analysed were as supplied in London to the offices of the Royal Commission on the day of issue.

## (ii) *Provincial Morning Newspapers*

The same sample of days was used for the analysis of 17 English, Welsh and Scottish provincial morning newspapers. However, since it was decided to analyse a smaller sample of issues (for reasons of time and resources), only the 12 dates in the second half of the year were used. Direct comparisons could then be made between the half-year figures for the National Dailies and the

---

* We are grateful to the publishers of *The Sun*, *Daily Express* and *The Guardian* for permission to make photo-copies of some issues and to the publishers of the *Financial Times* for supplying several photo-copies.

Provincial Morning samples. The *Scottish Daily News* was included in the study initially but since it ceased publication before the end of the year, the analysis was discontinued. Results based on the analysis of six issues are discussed briefly in Appendix A14.

### (iii) *National Sunday Newspapers*

A small random sample of six issues falling entirely in the second half of the year was chosen for each of seven titles. While the sample is too small for reliable estimation of content, it was expected that the results would have some value for purposes of comparison. The sampling procedure was to choose three dates by a random method from each of the third and fourth quarters. The following six dates provided the issues for the analysis reported in Section III:

| | |
|---|---|
| 20 July | 19 October |
| 7 September | 23 November |
| 12 October | 14 December |

### (iv) *Provincial Evening Newspapers*

The selection of 12 titles for analysis from amongst approximately 82 evening newspapers was not based directly on a random sample. It was guided, on the one hand, by a wish to include titles appearing in the regions which formed sampling points for the survey of Community Influentials* and, on the other hand, by some criteria of intrinsic interest. Consequently, no claim is made that these particular titles are representative of the provincial evening press as a whole, although they do reflect some of the diversity of region and circulation size. Initially, two weeks in the second half of the year were chosen at random and the six issues of each evening paper title acquired for these two weeks (13–18 October and 3–7 November). Subsequently, it was decided to analyse only one week's newspapers and the second of the two weeks was chosen, because one issue of one title in the earlier week failed to appear.

### (v) *Local Weekly Newspapers*

In all, 28 different titles have been studied out of approximately 1,000 weekly newspapers. The same criteria of selection apply as with the evening newspapers and the same remarks about representativeness. Some of the particular reasons for choice are discussed in Section VI. There was, in particular, an interest in different sorts of ownership and in the possible effects of competition. In brief, the titles were chosen to allow certain comparisons to be made, but the selection of titles does generally reflect something of the diversity of ownership, region, size and format of the local newspaper. The initial sampling decision was to choose six weeks, three each surrounding the chosen weeks for analysis of the evening press, since for some purposes evening and weekly papers might be looked at together. Subsequently, it was decided to reduce the scale of the task by analysing only three issues of these titles and the weeks concerned fall in the period 27 October to 15 November 1975. Because of the very small size of the sample, the results can only be regarded as indicative and the reliability of estimates cannot be assessed.

---

* Survey of Attitudes to the Press, SCPR. Royal Commission on the Press, Research Series 3.

## 4. Methods of coding, measurement and analysis

(i) While methods varied slightly for different categories of newspaper, the basic procedure was the same in all cases. A coding frame listing the basic categories for classification was first drawn up. In the case of the National Dailies, the frame used in the 1947 study was taken as a starting point so that direct comparisons could be made with previous content analyses. Some elements of this frame were also used in the analysis of provincial and local newspapers. Each newspaper chosen for analysis was then read or scanned and its entire printed area allocated, item by item, to a category. A measure of item space was calculated so that the sum of individual measurements accorded with the total space of the newspaper. Percentage figures for the different categories for each title were then calculated by summing the total space per category for the 24 issues (in the case of National Dailies) and expressing the result as a percentage of total space (or whatever sub-total was appropriate).

(ii) The coding and measuring was carried out by a team of six workers recruited for the purpose and the work was so organised that the different issues of the same title were allocated to different people. This should have helped to increase overall consistency. In addition, consultation on doubtful points was encouraged and, finally, each coded and measured newspaper was checked in detail by a supervisor. The coding assistants were instructed in the use of the coding frame and a week spent in training and practice. Despite these precautions, it is inevitable that variations of judgement should have occurred and the scale of such variation is indicated in Appendix A1, where a double coding check is reported. At best, the results of such a coding procedure can only be as good as the judgement of those collectively responsible and the aim has been to maximise the consistency of interpretation between the judges. A particular difficulty arises from the variation between newspapers and the tendency to treat the same original "story" or event in different ways. Generally, the same story will be classified similarly in different newspapers, but at some point the difference of treatment is great enough to require a different classification. A source of variation in judgement arises from a tendency to place a particular story in a category to which it had seemed to belong when coding a previous newspaper. As a contribution to increased consistency, a guide was prepared for each newspaper title giving, *inter alia*, an agreed coding for certain regular features which might otherwise have been variably coded.

(iii) The measurement procedure was carried out separately for each item, except in the case of advertising and sports and financial news, where large blocks of similar content appear together. Results were initially recorded in terms of a number of "standard column centimetres". In practice, this is derived by multiplying the column length by the number of columns. For instance a half page article in *The Times* would be measured at 224 col. cms, since the length of a half page is approximately 28 cms and there are normally eight columns to a page. The expression "standard column" is used, because the column width, and number of columns to a page, may vary from one paper to another. Hence a particular measure is standardised for a particular title only. It is necessary and convenient to do this, since column widths do in fact vary *within* a particular newspaper. For instance, the leader page of *The Times* normally has seven columns, instead of eight. In the tabloid newspapers,

5

especially, a mixture of different column widths may occur on the same page. The use of a standard column to express results ensures that all initial column centimetre measures for a *given title* are directly comparable with each other. The percentage figures for each title are based on totals of column centimetres which differ in absolute size from one paper to another. This does not affect the direct comparability of percentage figures for different papers as they appear in the tables, but it does mean that the same percentage figure may indicate a different total amount of space in one paper, compared to another. In order to allow direct comparisons of *absolute space* between papers, a further adjustment has to be made. This has been done by calculating a measure of space in terms of an overall standard column width of 5 cms., which approximates to the size of the widest normal column in a national daily newspaper. This measure has been called an "adjusted standard column centimetre" measure and has been obtained by applying an appropriate multiplier for each different title to convert the different standard columns into one of 5 cms. This is the measure of space given, for comparative purposes, at the foot of all comparison tables in this part of the Report.

(iv) The calculation of percentages was based on the aggregation of space measurements as described above. An alternative method, used in the 1947 study, would have been to calculate percentage distribution for each issue and then average the percentages to give a figure for the paper as a whole. This would give equal weight to issues of different sizes but would also give a more direct indication of what the average issue of a given title would be like in the period sampled. On balance, it was decided that the additional calculation required would not be justified and that the method chosen would produce an equally useful and scarcely different outcome.

(v) The results of this analysis process are subject, as we can see, to several kinds of error or uncertainty. Those which we have been able to cope with best lie beyond the stage of compiling the coding frame and allocating items to categories. Measurement errors may have occurred in some degree, but they are likely to have been small and unsystematic. Cross-checking of figures will have eliminated most. If the measures are accepted, then sampling error can be calculated in such a way that we can estimate the range within which a given percentage can be regarded as a true indication of the figure which would have been arrived at, had the entire set of newspapers for the sample period (the year 1975, in the case of National Dailies) been analysed. Each percentage figure requires its own confidence limit to be calculated, but since this was impracticable, a limited number of such confidence limits for selected percentages and for different newspapers has been calculated. The results are reported in Appendix A2 and give some general idea of the accuracy of percentage estimates. They are generally encouraging in this respect. However, in commenting on tables, or in drawing conclusions, wider margins of error have to be allowed for because of uncertainties of categorisation. Generally, only the largest and most systematic differences have provided the basis for comment. Unreliability of coding, which arises from the intrinsic ambiguity of content, cannot be fully assessed, although Appendix A1 should be helpful in this respect. Finally, the reader is invited to judge the validity of categories by inspecting the coding frames and brief rubrics reproduced in the main body of the report.

## 5. A note on tables

In presenting percentage figures in tables, these have generally, though not invariably, been rounded up or down to the nearest whole number, although based on an exact calculation. The benefits are ease of interpretation and the existence of sampling and coding error justifies the resulting small inaccuracy. Occasionally, there is a misleading impression created, especially when small figures are involved or when a zero is entered for a percentage below $0 \cdot 5 \%$. Where a large amount of space is involved, such a percentage may not be negligible. Rounding of percentages occasionally results in total figures above or below $100 \%$.

# II  Analysis of National Daily Newspapers

## 1. Coding frame for National Dailies

As already indicated, the original list of categories from the 1947 analysis (reproduced as Appendix A3) was taken as the underlying structure of the current research, so that comparisons over time could be made. It is also a framework which has been used in other research and which may help in establishing trends. The differences between the former and the present frameworks involve the following main adaptations and extensions.

(i) The main categories of home (UK) news remain much the same although, within the category of political, social and economic news and crime and police news, we separately identified news relating to industrial relations and the current Northern Ireland crisis, partly because these might be large specific categories, partly because we might wish to make a detailed analysis of content under these headings. The other main change has been to add separate new categories for identifying sex-related news which had been treated as one category for all news and features in 1947. The attention to sex-related news was prompted by an original concern with sensationalism and the number of separate categories only reflects the need to avoid double-classification, since sex-related matters can also fall under other headings.

(ii) The external news categories are similar to the previous ones, although we have replaced Commonwealth news for the previous "Imperial" category, without assuming direct comparability. The two other innovations are to introduce new sub-categories for sex-related external news and to establish a new category for sport news from abroad in view of the volume of such news. We assumed that in 1947 this would have been classified as "Other" foreign or international news.

(iii) Most extensions have been in respect of Features, where a number of new categories and sub-divisions have been introduced. These relate, in particular, to foreign affairs, industrial relations matters, consumer and price matters, sport and personalities. We have also added a category for "Picture Features" where the illustrated (usually photographic) content is more significant than either specific subject matter or text.

(iv) The remaining categories used in 1947 are rather little changed, although advertising content has now been divided into "Classified" and "Display". The previous category for "Parliamentary News" was unclear to us and seems not to have been intended as a category exclusive of home, political, social and economic news. In the present case, we have used such an exclusive category for reports of debates in both houses of parliament and also, where appropriate, classified the figures as "Home political, social and economic news" (even though debate reports may cover foreign affairs). Finally, we have dealt with picture content somewhat differently. This seems previously to have been excluded from the analysis of news and features space and recorded separately. In our view, it was inappropriate to do this for the modern newspaper, and yet necessary for the purposes of comparison. For this reason, our normal space measure includes pictures and we have also made a separate analysis of picture content for all main categories. The comparison tables (2, 3 and 4) for 1947 and

1975 give figures for 1975 which estimate picture content as a separate category. However, elsewhere, picture content is included in the appropriate subject categories. A separate analysis of picture content, by category, is given in Appendix A6. Finally, a category for Sex Features has been used in the present analysis. It differs from the 1947 category in its exclusion of *news* and its primary use for classifying "pin-ups" and equivalent material.

## CODING FRAME FOR NATIONAL DAILIES

### 1.0. HOME NEWS

News relating to events which occurred in the United Kingdom.

#### 1.1. POLITICAL, SOCIAL AND ECONOMIC
Political news; Parliamentary news (excluding records of debates); governmental and administrative news; local government; housing and planning; education; social and health services; employment; production; economic performance; farming; energy-oil, coal, etc; race relations; armed forces news.

##### 1.1L. *Labour/Industrial*
News of strikes and disputes; industrial relations; trade union matters; news of pay settlements and negotiations; Employers' and Professional Associations' affairs when dealing with labour/industrial matters, etc.

##### 1.1U. *Ulster Crisis-Related*
Home affairs news relating primarily to the Ulster troubles (except law and police matters; where Irish Republic is involved, see 2.5U).

#### 1.2. LAW AND POLICE
News of, and reports on, proceedings in all courts of law; legal news (other than appointments); all reports and news where main reference is to police or crime.

##### 1.2L. *Labour/Industrial*
Industrial relations matters involving the police or courts.

##### 1.2U. *Ulster Crisis-Related*
Matters related to the Ulster crisis involving the British and Ulster police and courts.

##### 1.2S. *Sex-Related*
Matters derived from police or court proceedings, where the sexual interest of the case seems predominant.

#### 1.3. ACCIDENTS
Accidents involving death or injury to persons.

#### 1.4. PERSONALITIES
Human interest reports on prominent personalities, eg entertainers; sportsmen (when not involved in practising their particular sport); business and industrial figures; news of Royalty and court; biographical notes on people in the news; news of

functions where the guests were the main focus of interest; promotions and appointments.

1.4S. *Sex-Related*
Where news of personalities has a predominantly sexual reference.

1.5. SPORT
Reports on, and news of, all kinds of sport and games; programmes and fixtures; pools and horse betting news and form; news of well-known personalities (including international fixtures when played in Britain).

1.9. OTHER HOME NEWS
Home news in brief; human interest news not otherwise identifiable; state of roads; weather news not included elsewhere; arts; theatre; film; T.V. and radio news not included elsewhere; accidents not involving injury or loss of life; examination results; religious or Church news when no social or political reference.

1.9S. *Sex-Related*
Other home news, as categorised in 1.9, containing a mainly sexual reference.

2.0. **EXTERNAL NEWS**

2.1. FOREIGN: POLITICAL, SOCIAL AND ECONOMIC
News of, and reports on, events of the same type as are under 1.1, but which occurred in any one foreign country (apart from the Commonwealth).

2.2. OTHER FOREIGN NEWS
All other foreign news similar to that included under 1.2, 1.3, 1.4, 1.9.

2.2S. *Sex-Related*
All other foreign news containing a mainly sexual reference.

2.3. COMMONWEALTH: POLITICAL, SOCIAL AND ECONOMIC
News of, and reports on, events of the type included under 1.1, but occurring in any one country of the present Commonwealth.

2.4. OTHER COMMONWEALTH NEWS
All other Commonwealth news similar to that included under 2.2.

2.5. INTERNATIONAL: POLITICAL, SOCIAL AND ECONOMIC
News of, and reports on, events of the type included under 1.1, which occurred in, or involved, more than one country (including Britain). This includes news of the United Nations and also events

outside territorial limits (sport is separately coded). International events occurring in Britain are coded here (apart from sport).

### 2.5U. *Ulster-Related International News*
Eg relations between Ireland and United Kingdom.

## 2.6. OTHER INTERNATIONAL NEWS
All other international news, similar to that included under 2.2.

### 2.6S. *Sex-Related*
All other international news containing a mainly sexual reference.

## 2.7. INTERNATIONAL SPORT
News of, and reports on, all kinds of sport and games in any one or more foreign countries (international sporting events at home are under 1.5).

## 2.9. MISCELLANEOUS EXTERNAL NEWS
External news in brief; external news not classifiable under 2.1–2.6.

# 3.0. OTHER NEWS

News of events which were neither specifically home or external.

## 3.1. FINANCIAL
Financial and market news and reports from all countries; crop and mining reports affecting market prices; bankruptcy news (plus "company highlights" and brief reports), etc.

## 3.2. SCIENTIFIC AND TECHNICAL
News of scientific and technical events from all countries when such news was not primarily political, social or economic.

## 3.9. MISCELLANEOUS NEWS
Any other news otherwise unclassifiable.

# 4.0. FEATURES

Articles whose primary purpose was to give, not current news, but background material to the news, general information or entertainment. This excludes leading articles (ie editorial comment), fiction and regular information (eg television programme guides—see 5.8).

## 4.1. POLITICAL, SOCIAL AND ECONOMIC
Feature articles relating to topics which are included in category 1.1.

### 4.1L. *Labour/Industrial*
Feature articles relating to topics of the kind included in 1.1L or 1.2L.

## 4.2. FOREIGN/INTERNATIONAL FEATURES
Feature articles on topics of the kind included in categories 2.1, 2.3 and 2.5.

4.31 FINANCIAL COLUMNS
Feature articles as well as regular signed articles, dealing with financial and economic matters and to be found in the financial pages or with at least a distinctive identification (eg City Editor).

4.32. SCIENTIFIC, TECHNICAL, MEDICAL
Feature articles on topics of the kind included in 3.2.

4.33. CONSUMER/PRICES
Feature articles on retail prices and standards (especially evaluative and comparative reports), and to include reports on both goods *and* services, eg insurance.

4.41. POLITICAL COLUMNS
Regular signed features by a particular journalist(s) on matters relating specifically to subjects typically included in 1.1, but which might include topics falling under 2.1, 2.3 or 2.5.

4.42. MIXED COLUMNS
Regular signed features by a particular journalist(s) on matters that may be light and for diversion, but also covering matters of the same type as found in category 4.41, and including satire.

4.43. LIGHT COLUMNS
Regular signed features, as above, which are purely humorous or diverting. Includes gossip columns.

4.44 PERSONALITIES
Feature articles relating to topics such as those included in categories 1.4, but also including reports on foreign personalities, while including features on sportsmen, artists and entertainers only when their sport or art is not the main focus of interest (see 4.5 and 4.6).

4.5. SPORT
Feature articles relating to topics such as those included in categories 1.5 or 2.7.

4.6. ARTS AND ENTERTAINMENT FEATURES
Theatre, film, radio, T.V., art, music and book reviews; plus features on, and interviews with, people and events in the world of books, the arts and entertainment generally. Includes features on art and entertainment matters abroad.

4.61. CHILDREN'S FEATURES
Including children's cartoons.

4.7. WOMEN'S FEATURES
Eg fashion (unless not on a "women's page" and having apparent wider general interest).

4.7S. *Sex-Related*
Where women's features have such an explicitly sexual component as to make this the most significant feature.

## 4.81. OTHER REGULAR FEATURES

Features appearing in a regular place at least weekly, but normally daily. To include, in particular, notices of marriage/social events that were not paid ads., television previews, nature notes, motoring; 25 years ago, etc.

## 4.82. PICTURE FEATURES

Features where picture content accounts for an overwhelming proportion of copy-space and where the picture itself is the main subject of interest (excludes "pin-up" features).

## 4.9. OTHER

Including general human interest not otherwise identifiable, holiday and travel, archaeology, etc.

# 5.0. OTHER EDITORIAL SPACE

## 5.1. LEADING ARTICLES (Editorial Comment)

## 5.2. CORRESPONDENCE

## 5.3. Void

## 5.4. TOPICAL CARTOONS

## 5.5. COMIC AND STRIP CARTOONS

## 5.6. FICTION

## 5.7. PUZZLES, COMPETITIONS AND OFFERS

Crosswords, anagrams, bridge and chess problems; children's competitions; special offers to readers created by the newspaper itself, etc.

## 5.8. OTHER REGULAR INFORMATION

Radio and Television programme guides; weather forecasts; Parliamentary Debate programme; horoscopes; obituaries; wills; premium bond results, etc.

## 5.9. MISCELLANEOUS EDITORIAL SPACE

Index, order forms, advertisement index; publication particulars; subscription and advertising rates; blank spaces (eg empty stop press columns); news of coming attractions in the newspapers.

# 6.0. ADVERTISEMENTS AND OTHER SPACE

Items which were considered to have been paid for by outside firms or individuals, including display and classified advertisements; notices of birth, marriage and deaths; company reports.

## 6.1. CLASSIFIED ADVERTISEMENTS

All advertisements gathered under general subject matter heading.

## 6.2. DISPLAY ADVERTISING

All other advertising content.

## 6.3. HEADINGS AND TITLES

7.0. **PARLIAMENTARY DEBATE REPORTS** (Both Houses)

8.0. **NEWS AND FEATURES OF SEX INTEREST**
Including pin-up photos.

9.0. **PICTURE CONTENT**
Where illustrative of news or features (excluding cartoons and pictures separately coded under 8.0).

14

## 2. National Daily Newspapers, 1947–1975: Comparison Tables

TABLE A1

SIZES OF SIX NATIONAL DAILY NEWSPAPERS 1937, 1947 and 1975

| Title | 1937 Mean number of pages | 1947 Modal number of pages | 1947 Mean number of pages | 1947 Mean printed area per issue (sq. in.) | 1975 Mean number of pages | 1975 Modal number of pages | 1975 Mean printed area per issue (sq. in.) |
|---|---|---|---|---|---|---|---|
| The Times ... ... ... ... | 25·7 | 10 | 9·6 | 3,600 | 26·2 | 24/28 | 8,810 |
| The Daily Telegraph ... ... | 25·0 | 6 | 6·2 | 2,200 | 28·5 | 32 | 9,853 |
| Daily Express ... ... ... | 20·0 | 4 | 4·6 | 1,560 | 17·3 | 18 | 5,270 |
| Daily Mail ... ... ... | 19·3 | 4 | 4·6 | 1,390 | 33·7 | 32 | 4,975 |
| Daily Mirror ... ... ... | 22·5 | 8 | 9·2 | 1,320 | 27·9 | 28 | 3,952 |
| Daily Worker/Morning Star ... ... | 8 | 6 | 6·1 | 1,170 | 6·0 | 6 | 1,442 |

*Notes:*

1. The "printed area" in 1947 was calculated exclusive of margins and titles. In 1975 the calculation also excluded margins, but does include titles and headings. The tendency is thus slightly to exaggerate the size gap. If titles had been excluded in 1975, the reduction in size would have been of the order of 1%. Since measures were not made in square inches in 1975, the figures are estimated.

2. The modal number of pages represent the size of issue which occurred most frequently in the sample; the mean number represents what is generally known as the "average" size of an issue.

3. The six titles comprise those national dailies available for comparison for the two years 1947 and 1975.

4. Figures for 1937 and 1947 are taken in this and all subsequent tables from the Royal Commission on the Press Report, 1947–9, Cmnd 7700.

15

**TABLE A2**

**SIX NATIONAL DAILY NEWSPAPERS, 1947 and 1975:**
**ANALYSIS OF TOTAL PRINT INTO ADVERTISEMENTS AND THREE CATEGORIES OF EDITORIAL SPACE**

| Category | The Times 1947 | 1975 | The Daily Telegraph 1947 | 1975 | Daily Express 1947 | 1975 | Daily Mail 1947 | 1975 | Daily Mirror 1947 | 1975 | Daily Worker Morning Star 1947 | 1975 |
|---|---|---|---|---|---|---|---|---|---|---|---|---|
| | % | % | % | % | % | % | % | % | % | % | % | % |
| **Editorial Space** | | | | | | | | | | | | |
| News ... ... ... ... ... ... | 41 | 39 | 45 | 37 | 50 | 32 | 49 | 30 | 40 | 28 | 45 | 52 |
| Features ... ... ... ... ... | 7 | 16 | 11 | 12 | 16 | 16 | 15 | 24 | 15 | 20 | 23 | 27 |
| Other ... ... ... ... ... | 12 | 10 | 9 | 6 | 13 | 11 | 15 | 12 | 29 | 15 | 13 | 12 |
| Total ... ... ... ... | 60 | 65 | 65 | 55 | 79 | 59 | 79 | 66 | 84 | 63 | 81 | 91 |
| Advertisements ... ... ... | 40 | 35 | 35 | 46 | 21 | 42 | 21 | 35 | 16 | 37 | 19 | 9 |
| TOTAL ... ... ... ... | 100 | 100 | 100 | 101 | 100 | 101 | 100 | 101 | 100 | 100 | 100 | 100 |

*Note:* The percentages, rounded to the nearest whole number, are based on the total printed area of the newspaper. This has been calculated differently for the two years—in 1947 as a measure of area in square inches, in 1975 in terms of standard column centimetres. This should make no significant difference to the comparisons in percentage terms.

16

**TABLE A3**

## SIX NATIONAL DAILY NEWSPAPERS, 1947 and 1975:
## ANALYSIS OF TOTAL NEWS SPACE INTO 16 CATEGORIES

*per cent of news space*

| Category | The Times 1947 % | The Times 1975 % | The Daily Telegraph 1947 % | The Daily Telegraph 1975 % | Daily Express 1947 % | Daily Express 1975 % | Daily Mail 1947 % | Daily Mail 1975 % | Daily Mirror 1947 % | Daily Mirror 1975 % | Morning Star/Daily Worker 1947 % | Morning Star/Daily Worker 1975 % |
|---|---|---|---|---|---|---|---|---|---|---|---|---|
| **Home News:** | | | | | | | | | | | | |
| 1. Political, social and economic | 23 | 21 | 26 | 20 | 23 | 15 | 23 | 18 | 21 | 14 | 34 | 47 |
| 2. Law, police and accidents | 3 | 5 | 8 | 7 | 13 | 12 | 11 | 12 | 23 | 11 | 7 | 4 |
| 3. Personalities, court news, etc. | 7 | 4 | 6 | 4 | 2 | 3 | 4 | 2 | 3 | 3 | — | — |
| 4. Sport | 16 | 14 | 18 | 23 | 32 | 37 | 33 | 34 | 24 | 53 | 31 | 21 |
| 5. Other | 2 | 3 | 6 | 5 | 6 | 8 | 9 | 7 | 15 | 8 | 5 | 3 |
| Total home news | 51 | 47 | 64 | 59 | 76 | 75 | 80 | 73 | 86 | 89 | 77 | 75 |
| **External News:** | | | | | | | | | | | | |
| *Imperial* | | | | | | | | | | | | |
| 6. Political, social and economic | 7 | 1 | 3 | 1 | 2 | — | 2 | — | 2 | — | 3 | — |
| 7. Other | 1 | — | — | — | 2 | — | — | — | 1 | — | — | — |
| Total | 8 | 1 | 3 | 1 | 4 | — | 2 | — | 3 | — | 3 | — |
| *Foreign* | | | | | | | | | | | | |
| 8. Political, social and economic | 5 | 7 | 4 | 6 | 2 | 2 | 2 | 3 | 2 | 2 | 6 | 7 |
| 9. Other | — | 2 | — | 1 | 1 | 3 | 2 | 4 | 3 | 1 | — | 1 |
| Total | 5 | 9 | 4 | 7 | 3 | 5 | 4 | 7 | 5 | 3 | 6 | 8 |

TABLE A3—continued

## SIX NATIONAL DAILY NEWSPAPERS, 1947 and 1975:—continued
### ANALYSIS OF TOTAL NEWS SPACE INTO 16 CATEGORIES—continued

per cent of news space—continued

| Category | The Times | | The Daily Telegraph | | Daily Express | | Daily Mail | | Daily Mirror | | Morning Star/ Daily Worker | |
|---|---|---|---|---|---|---|---|---|---|---|---|---|
| | 1947 % | 1975 % | 1947 % | 1975 % | 1947 % | 1975 % | 1947 % | 1975 % | 1947 % | 1975 % | 1947 % | 1975 % |
| *International* | | | | | | | | | | | | |
| 10. Political, social and economic ... ... | 14 | 9 | 15 | 7 | 8 | 5 | 9 | 4 | 5 | 2 | 11 | 11 |
| 11. Other ... ... ... ... ... | 1 | 4 | 4 | 4 | 4 | 6 | 1 | 4 | 1 | 5 | 2 | 4 |
| Total ... ... ... ... | 15 | 13 | 19 | 11 | 12 | 11 | 10 | 8 | 6 | 7 | 13 | 15 |
| 12. Miscellaneous external news ... ... | — | — | — | — | — | 1 | — | 1 | — | — | — | 1 |
| Total external news ... ... | 28 | 23 | 26 | 19 | 19 | 17 | 16 | 16 | 14 | 10 | 22 | 24 |
| 13. Other news, financial and commercial ... | 19 | 30 | 8 | 21 | 4 | 9 | 4 | 10 | — | 1 | — | — |
| 14. Scientific and technical ... ... ... | 1 | — | — | — | 1 | — | — | — | — | — | — | — |
| 15. Miscellaneous ... ... ... ... | 1 | — | — | — | — | — | — | — | — | 1 | — | — |
| Total other news ... ... ... | 21 | 30 | 8 | 21 | 5 | 9 | 4 | 10 | — | 1 | — | — |
| TOTAL ... ... ... ... | 100 | 100 | 99 | 99 | 100 | 101 | 100 | 99 | 100 | 100 | 99 | 99 |
| 16. All political, social and economic news ... | 49 | 38 | 48 | 34 | 35 | 32 | 36 | 25 | 30 | 18 | 54 | 65 |

*Notes:*

1. For purposes of comparing 1975 with 1947, the figures relating to Commonwealth News have been set against the "Imperial" category employed in 1947.

2. The category of international "other" news for 1975 includes all international sport news. Without this, the figures for some newspapers could be a good deal smaller—see Table A7.

3. For purposes of this comparison, parliamentary debate reports have been included as Home news (political, social and economic), although they will include reports of debates on foreign affairs.

4. To allow comparison with 1947, picture content has been deducted in calculating the figures for news space in 1975. Elsewhere, picture content is included in the news categories. The amount of pictorial content by category is given in Appendix A6.

18

**TABLE A4**

**SIX NATIONAL DAILY NEWSPAPERS, 1947 and 1975:**
**ANALYSIS OF TOTAL FEATURE SPACE INTO SEVEN CATEGORIES**

| Category | The Times | | The Daily Telegraph | | Daily Express | | Daily Mail | | Daily Mirror | | Morning Star/ Daily Worker | |
|---|---|---|---|---|---|---|---|---|---|---|---|---|
| | *1947* % | *1975* % | *1947* % | *1975* % | *1947* % | *1975* % | *1947* % | *1975* % | *1947* % | *1975* % | *1947* % | *1975* % |
| 1. Women's features | — | 2 | 10 | 11 | 4 | 7 | 2 | 6 | 23 | 5 | 8 | 4 |
| 2. Children's features | — | — | 2 | — | 4 | 3 | 3 | — | 11 | 6 | 1 | 4 |
| 3. Theatre, art, etc., criticism | 17 | 20 | 17 | 26 | 12 | 12 | 20 | 13 | 11 | 10 | 12 | 27 |
| 4. Political | — | — | — | — | 1 | — | 2 | 2 | — | 1 | 16 | — |
| 5. Light columns | — | 6 | 24 | 11 | 23 | 13 | 8 | 9 | 5 | 18 | — | — |
| 6. Political, social and economic | 31 | 43 | 20 | 33 | 30 | 23 | 38 | 29 | 14 | 16 | 45 | 49 |
| 7. Other features | 52 | 29 | 27 | 19 | 26 | 42 | 27 | 41 | 36 | 43 | 18 | 16 |
| TOTAL | 100 | 100 | 100 | 100 | 100 | 100 | 100 | 100 | 100 | 99 | 100 | 100 |

*Note:* The figures for 1975 include picture content, which had probably been excluded in 1947. Our own evidence suggests that this makes little difference to overall distributions (Appendix A6).

19

### 3. National Daily Newspapers, 1947–1975: Commentary

(i) The comparison between 1947 and 1975 is limited by two circumstances: one, the unusually small size of 1947 newspapers and the other the disappearance of three titles since 1947 (*News Chronicle, Daily Herald, Daily Graphic*). Our study includes *The Guardian* as a new national title, the *Financial Times* as a more general interest newspaper than it had been and *The Sun* as a newcomer. We can only directly compare six titles and surmise about the effect of other departures and arrivals on the basis of content evidence.

(ii) On the matter of size, Table A1 says all there is to say. Newspapers have all greatly increased in area and page numbers since 1947 and have generally reverted to their 1937 position. The increased page numbers of the *Daily Mail* reflect its changed format. The relative position of each of the six newspapers has remained similar, although *The Daily Telegraph* has now taken the lead as the largest newspaper.

(iii) In terms of the overall allocation of space shown in Table A2 we can see some general decline in the proportion of space allocated to news and some increase in the allocation to features. Only the *Daily Worker/Morning Star* is an exception to this rule. This probably does little more than reflect the greater demand of news on limited newsprint in 1947 and the diversion of additional space since then to alternative, more optional, sorts of content. The actual *amount* of space given to news has, of course, increased in all papers. The proportion of space given to advertising has increased for each paper except *The Times*. The newspapers which have remained most constant since 1947 in terms of this very elementary comparison are *The Times* and *Daily Worker/ Morning Star*, but, when allowance is made for the special circumstances of the earlier year, it seems fair to conclude that there has been rather little general change.

(iv) The comparison of news coverage made in Table A3 also supports this observation. Again *The Times* seems most stable. In all six papers, the relative allocation of space between home and external news is very similar and the customary distinction between smaller circulation "Qualities" and larger circulation "Populars" remains the same in this respect. If we look for exceptions to this general picture of stability, several points suggest themselves. One is the further advance of sport to a position of even greater predominance. The move for the *Daily Mirror* is exceptionally large and only *The Times* and *Morning Star/ Daily Worker* have not shared in this trend. For the *Daily Mirror*, the relative shift seems mainly accounted for by a lower attention to crime and police news. Secondly, we should note the rise of financial news affecting *The Times, The Daily Telegraph*, the *Daily Express* and the *Daily Mail*. Thirdly, there has been an understandable failure of the Commonwealth to retain the attention once given to the Empire although the inclusion of some Commonwealth news in the "international" category in 1975 may exaggerate this trend. Fourthly, there is a general fall in attention given to "political, social and economic" news as a category, although, again, increased space more than compensates.

(v) Because the feature categories used in 1947 are somewhat vague and little differentiated, we can draw few additional conclusions from Table A4. Again, we see that this section of editorial space is still dominated by political, social and economic content and by arts and entertainment material, although the former category seems to have suffered a relative decline in the *Daily Mail* and the *Daily Express* and a rise in *The Times* and *The Daily Telegraph*. This might be interpreted as a sign of an increasing gap between "Qualities" and "Populars"—a point returned to in Appendix A5. Other points to note include the persistence of features designed for women and some decline in relative attention to features for children. The figures show some basic change in feature content of the *Daily Mirror* and a possible diversification of feature content in *The Times*, for which there is other evidence.

(vi) The changes in composition of the whole range of National Dailies stemming from the departures and arrivals mentioned above suggest one general conclusion of interest. The evidence is not tabulated here, but the loss of the *Daily Herald* and *News Chronicle* in particular has involved the loss of papers with a relatively high component of political, social and economic news features and also relatively high circulations. These papers were closer to the "Qualities" in the respects mentioned and closer to the "Populars" in other respects. This again supports the view that the "gap" has widened between two main sorts of newspaper, with the *Daily Mail* and *Daily Express* surviving in the "middle". The addition of *The Guardian* and *Financial Times* to the spectrum of National Dailies and the rise of *The Sun* has tended to accentuate the "polarisation". This judgement is based especially on the use of the criterion of attention to political, social and economic news and features, but other sorts of content are also involved (eg scientific and technical news, business news, external news).

## 4. National Daily Newspapers, 1975: Comparison Tables

TABLE A5

SIZES OF NATIONAL DAILY NEWSPAPERS, 1975

| Title | Mean Number of pages* | Modal Number of pages* | Mean Printed area per issue† st. col. cms. |
|---|---|---|---|
| The Times ... ... ... ... | 26·2 | 24/28 | 10,944 |
| The Guardian ... ... ... | 22·8 | 24 | 9,433 |
| The Daily Telegraph ... ... | 28·5 | 32 | 12,655 |
| Financial Times ... ... ... | 28·6 | 32 | 11,957 |
| Morning Star ... ... ... | 6·0 | 6 | 1,954 |
| Daily Express ... ... ... | 17·3 | 18 | 6,917 |
| Daily Mail ... ... ... ... | 33·7 | 32 | 6,546 |
| Daily Mirror ... ... ... | 27·9 | 28 | 5,367 |
| The Sun ... ... ... ... | 28·0 | 28 | 5,333 |

* The "modal number" and "mean number" are as described in note 2, Table A1

† The printed area is given in the form of a weighted measure of standard column centimetres as described in section I, 4, iii.

The figures for different titles are thus directly comparable in terms of a column width of 5 cm. This adjusted measure is used in all subsequent comparisons for national dailies in 1975.

TABLE A6

NATIONAL DAILY NEWSPAPERS, 1975:
ANALYSIS OF TOTAL SPACE INTO ADVERTISEMENTS AND FOUR CATEGORIES OF EDITORIAL SPACE

| Category | The Times | The Guardian | The Daily Telegraph | Financial Times | Morning Star | Daily Express | Daily Mail | Daily Mirror | The Sun |
|---|---|---|---|---|---|---|---|---|---|
| | % | % | % | % | % | % | % | % | % |
| **Editorial Space:** | | | | | | | | | |
| News ... ... ... | 39·2 | 37·3 | 36·7 | 44·2 | 52·5 | 32·1 | 29·8 | 28·4 | 31·2 |
| Features ... ... | 15·6 | 25·4 | 11·7 | 16·3 | 26·8 | 15·8 | 23·7 | 19·7 | 18·6 |
| Other ... ... | 10·4 | 10·7 | 5·6 | 5·3 | 12·2 | 10·5 | 11·8 | 14·7 | 14·5 |
| Total ... ... | 65·2 | 73·4 | 54·0 | 65·8 | 91·5 | 58·4 | 65·3 | 62·8 | 64·3 |
| Advertisements ... | 34·8 | 26·6 | 46·0 | 34·2 | 8·5 | 41·6 | 34·7 | 37·2 | 35·7 |
| TOTAL ... ... | 100 | 100 | 100 | 100 | 100 | 100 | 100 | 100 | 100 |
| Mean space per issue (adjusted standard col. cms.) ... ... | 10,944 | 9,433 | 12,655 | 11,957 | 1,954 | 6,917 | 6,546 | 5,367 | 5,333 |
| Picture content as % of editorial space ... | 6 | 10 | 10 | 3 | 15 | 15 | 13 | 17 | 17 |

23

**TABLE A7**

**NATIONAL DAILY NEWSPAPERS, 1975:**
**ANALYSIS OF TOTAL NEWS SPACE INTO 21 CATEGORIES**

*per cent of all news space*

| Category | The Times | The Guardian | The Daily Telegraph | Financial Times | Morning Star | Daily Express | Daily Mail | Daily Mirror | The Sun |
|---|---|---|---|---|---|---|---|---|---|
| | % | % | % | % | % | % | % | % | % |
| **Home News** | | | | | | | | | |
| 1. Political, social and economic in general | 11 | 16 | 12 | 7 | 25 | 7 | 9 | 7 | 8 |
| 2. Labour/Industrial relations ... | 4 | 5 | 5 | 5 | 18 | 4 | 6 | 4 | 4 |
| 3. Ulster crisis-related ... | 2 | 3 | 3 | 1 | 3 | 3 | 3 | 3 | 3 |
| 4. Legal and police in general ... | 5 | 5 | 5 | — | 4 | 11 | 10 | 9 | 11 |
| 5. Accidents ... | — | — | — | — | 1 | 1 | 1 | 1 | 1 |
| 6. Personalities, social events ... | 4 | 1 | 4 | 1 | — | 4 | 4 | 5 | 5 |
| 7. Sport ... | 14 | 19 | 23 | 2 | 22 | 33 | 32 | 50 | 45 |
| 8. Other home news ... | 3 | 5 | 5 | 2 | 4 | 9 | 7 | 7 | 9 |
| 9. Sex-related home news ... | — | 1 | — | — | — | 2 | 3 | 4 | 4 |
| 10. Parliamentary debate reports ... | 4 | 2 | 2 | 2 | — | — | — | — | — |
| Total ... ... ... | 47 | 57 | 59 | 20 | 77 | 74 | 75 | 90 | 90 |

**External News**

*Foreign*

| | | | | | | | | | |
|---|---|---|---|---|---|---|---|---|---|
| 11. Political, social and economic... | 7 | 8 | 6 | 5 | 7 | 2 | 3 | 1 | 2 |
| 12. Other | 2 | 2 | 2 | — | 1 | 4 | 4 | 1 | 3 |

*Commonwealth*

| | | | | | | | | | |
|---|---|---|---|---|---|---|---|---|---|
| 13. Political, social and economic | 1 | 1 | 1 | — | — | — | — | — | — |
| 14. Other | — | — | — | — | — | — | — | — | — |

*International*

| | | | | | | | | | |
|---|---|---|---|---|---|---|---|---|---|
| 15. Political, social and economic | 9 | 11 | 7 | 6 | 11 | 5 | 4 | 2 | 2 |
| 16. Other | 1 | 1 | 1 | — | — | 2 | 1 | 1 | 1 |
| 17. Sport | 4 | 3 | 3 | — | 4 | 4 | 4 | 3 | 2 |
| 18. External: sex-related | — | — | — | — | — | — | — | 1 | — |
| 19. External: miscellaneous | — | 1 | — | — | — | 1 | — | — | — |
| Total | 24 | 27 | 20 | 11 | 23 | 18 | 16 | 9 | 10 |

**Other News**

| | | | | | | | | | |
|---|---|---|---|---|---|---|---|---|---|
| 20. Financial, market news | 29 | 16 | 21 | 69 | — | 8 | 9 | 1 | — |
| 21. Scientific and technical news | — | — | — | — | — | — | — | — | — |
| Total | 29 | 16 | 21 | 69 | — | 8 | 9 | 1 | — |
| TOTAL | 100 | 100 | 100 | 100 | 100 | 100 | 100 | 100 | 100 |
| Mean news space per sample issue* | 4,288 | 3,518 | 4,647 | 5,283 | 1,025 | 2,216 | 1,950 | 1,524 | 1,664 |

25

*Note:* In compiling this table some very small categories shown in the coding frame have been collapsed with others or grouped together as follows: the industrial relations category includes legal and police aspects, as does the Ulster crisis-related category. The "sex-related" home news category includes legal and police and personality aspects. The sex-related external news includes "foreign" and "international" aspects. The international aspects of the Ulster crisis are included as political, social and economic news.

* Mean news space is given in adjusted standard col. cms. (see paragraph I, 4 (iii)).

# TABLE A8

## NATIONAL DAILY NEWSPAPERS, 1975:
## ANALYSIS OF FEATURE SPACE INTO 17 CATEGORIES

*per cent of feature space*

| Category | The Times % | The Guardian % | The Daily Telegraph % | Financial Times % | Morning Star % | Daily Express % | Daily Mail % | Daily Mirror % | The Sun % |
|---|---|---|---|---|---|---|---|---|---|
| 1. Home, political, social and economic | 13 | 19 | 8 | 18 | 30 | 11 | 9 | 4 | 3 |
| 2. External, political, social and economic | 10 | 18 | 4 | 13 | 15 | 2 | 7 | 4 | 3 |
| 3. Financial, business | 12 | 6 | 14 | 25 | 1 | 4 | 7 | 1 | — |
| 4. Scientific, technical and medical | 4 | 1 | — | 10 | — | — | — | 1 | 2 |
| 5. Consumer/prices | 3 | 2 | 2 | 2 | — | 2 | 3 | 4 | 3 |
| 6. Political columns | — | 1 | — | — | 1 | — | 2 | 2 | 3 |
| 7. Mixed columns | 1 | 2 | 9 | 2 | — | 14 | 1 | 5 | — |
| 8. Light columns | 3 | 1 | 1 | 1 | — | 13 | 8 | 10 | 1 |
| 9. Personalities | 4 | 5 | 3 | 2 | 8 | 13 | 11 | 10 | 8 |
| 10. Sport | 5 | 5 | 3 | 1 | 27 | 11 | 10 | 11 | 18 |
| 11. Arts, Entertainment | 21 | 21 | 24 | 18 | 4 | 2 | 12 | 8 | 13 |
| 12. Children's features | — | — | — | — | 4 | 8 | — | 5 | 2 |
| 13. Women's features | 3 | 5 | 14 | 2 | 1 | — | 9 | 7 | 5 |
| 14. Other regular features | 6 | 3 | 7 | 4 | 6 | 6 | 6 | 11 | 7 |
| 15. Picture features | 5 | 4 | 8 | — | 5 | 2 | 1 | 6 | 5 |
| 16. Other features | 10 | 8 | 4 | 3 | — | 10 | 13 | 7 | 9 |
| 17. Sex features | — | — | — | — | — | 2 | 1 | 7 | 19 |
| TOTAL … | 100 | 101 | 101 | 101 | 102 | 100 | 100 | 103 | 101 |
| Mean feature space per sample issue (col.cms.) | 1,706 | 2,400 | 1,481 | 1,946 | 524 | 1,095 | 1,554 | 1,056 | 991 |

26

# TABLE A9

## NATIONAL DAILY NEWSPAPERS, 1975:
### ANALYSIS OF OTHER EDITORIAL SPACE INTO NINE CATEGORIES

per cent of other editorial space

| Category | The Times | The Guardian | The Daily Telegraph | Financial Times | Morning Star | Daily Express | Daily Mail | Daily Mirror | The Sun |
|---|---|---|---|---|---|---|---|---|---|
| | % | % | % | % | % | % | % | % | % |
| 1. Editorial comment ... ... ... ... | 12 | 15 | 12 | 13 | 17 | 7 | 9 | 5 | 7 |
| 2. Correspondence ... ... ... ... | 29 | 23 | 19 | 22 | 8 | 6 | 12 | 10 | 17 |
| 3. Topical cartoons ... ... | — | 3 | 5 | 1 | 14 | 9 | 6 | 3 | 8 |
| 4. Comic and strip cartoons ... | — | — | — | — | 2 | 10 | 12 | 25 | 12 |
| 5. Fiction ... ... ... ... ... | 2 | — | — | — | — | 3 | 1 | — | — |
| 6. Puzzles, competitions and offers ... | 6 | 8 | 10 | 9 | 4 | 24 | 15 | 13 | 17 |
| 7. Other regular information ... ... | 24 | 29 | 41 | 23 | 26 | 29 | 30 | 27 | 23 |
| 8. Miscellaneous ... ... ... | 17 | 7 | 7 | 12 | 15 | 6 | 3 | 9 | 11 |
| 9. Headings and titles ... ... ... | 10 | 15 | 6 | 20 | 14 | 7 | 13 | 8 | 5 |
| TOTAL ... ... ... ... ... | 100 | 100 | 100 | 100 | 100 | 101 | 101 | 100 | 100 |
| Mean other space per sample issue (col.cms.) | 1,137 | 1,008 | 702 | 638 | 239 | 726 | 771 | 790 | 776 |

27

# TABLE A10

## NATIONAL DAILY NEWSPAPERS, 1975:
### PROPORTIONS OF TOTAL EDITORIAL SPACE GIVEN TO NEWS AND FEATURES ABOUT:
### (a) INDUSTRIAL RELATIONS;  (b) SEX-RELATED CONTENT;  (c) SPORT

*per cent of editorial space*

| Category | The Times | The Guardian | The Daily Telegraph | Financial Times | Morning Star | Daily Express | Daily Mail | Daily Mirror | The Sun |
|---|---|---|---|---|---|---|---|---|---|
| | % | % | % | % | % | % | % | % | % |
| (a) Industrial relations ... ... ... | 2·6 | 3·2 | 3·0 | 3·4 | 11·9 | 2·7 | 3·4 | 1·9 | 2·1 |
| (b) Sex-related ... ... ... | 0·3 | 0·5 | 0·4 | — | 0·1 | 1·7 | 1·7 | 5·0 | 8·7 |
| (c) Sport ... ... ... | 11·9 | 12·9 | 18·2 | 1·3 | 16·9 | 24·0 | 19·9 | 27·3 | 28·1 |
| Mean editorial space per sample issue (col.cms.) | 7,132 | 6,927 | 6,830 | 7,868 | 1,787 | 4,037 | 4,275 | 3,301 | 3,431 |

# TABLE A11

## NATIONAL DAILY NEWSPAPERS, 1975:
### ANALYSIS OF TOTAL ADVERTISING CONTENT INTO TWO CATEGORIES

*per cent of all advertising*

| Category | The Times | The Guardian | The Daily Telegraph* | Financial Times | Morning Star | Daily Express | Daily Mail | Daily Mirror | The Sun |
|---|---|---|---|---|---|---|---|---|---|
| | % | % | % | % | % | % | % | % | % |
| Classified ... ... ... | 55·1 | 43·6 | 22·6 | 20·2 | 66·0 | 14·0 | 21·5 | 11·4 | 10·3 |
| Display ... ... ... ... | 44·9 | 56·4 | 77·4 | 79·8 | 34·0 | 86·0 | 78·5 | 88·6 | 89·7 |
| TOTAL ... ... ... | 100·0 | 100·0 | 100·0 | 100·0 | 100·0 | 100·0 | 100·0 | 100·0 | 100·0 |
| Mean advertising space per sample issue (col.cms.) ... ... ... ... | 3,811 | 2,515 | 5,825 | 4,089 | 167 | 2,880 | 2,271 | 1,996 | 1,902 |

* In the case of *The Daily Telegraph*, the divergence of the ratio of Classified to Display advertising from other "quality" newspapers is accounted for by the fact that much of its "situation vacant" advertising does not appear under a "classified" heading and has been categorised as "display". Advertisements of a similar kind in *The Guardian*, for instance, appear under a classified heading.

28

## 5. National Daily Newspapers, 1975: Commentary

(i) In terms of printed area, the national newspapers divide into three main groups, corresponding to the division between "Qualities" (*The Times*, *The Guardian*, *The Daily Telegraph*, *Financial Times*), "Middle" newspapers (*Daily Mail* and *Daily Express*) and "Populars" (*Daily Mirror* and *The Sun*). The *Morning Star* is exceptional, because of its small size. The largest single paper is *The Daily Telegraph*, although both *The Times* and *Financial Times* exceed it in volume of editorial space. The average proportion of space given to advertising in the eight main daily newspapers is 36% and the individual titles are spread around this average in no discernible pattern—*The Guardian* lowest at 26%, *The Daily Telegraph* highest at 46%. Five are very close to the mean figure. The most significant aspect of advertising content is the division between "classified" and "display" (see Table A11), with the "Qualities" leading in respect of the former, as they always have. Our own measurement rules account for the apparently low figure for *The Daily Telegraph*, since much "situations vacant" content appeared in a display or semi-display format and outside the normal "classified" columns.

(ii) The news/feature division shows something more of a pattern. In general, the three main "Qualities" have a higher proportion of news than the group of "Middle" or "Popular" papers. On the other hand, the latter do not have markedly higher proportions of feature material. Where advertising takes up a notably high proportion of total space, as with *The Daily Telegraph* and *Daily Express*, it seems associated with lower relative attention to features, rather than news. The allocation of space to pictures follows a predictable pattern, with the *Daily Mirror* and *The Sun* in the lead. It is worth noting, perhaps, that *The Guardian* and *The Daily Telegraph*, at least, are not far behind and that the *Morning Star* is extensively illustrated.

(iii) The comparison in terms of allocation of news space (Table A7) confirms a familiar pattern of differences between types of daily newspaper and also suggests some points of similarity. The pattern which emerges involves the already mentioned division into three main types: "Qualities", "Populars" and two titles in the middle (*Daily Express* and *Daily Mail*). This broadly reflects the facts of circulation (see RCP Interim Report, 1976)*. Here it shows up in respect of several types of content: political, social and economic news generally, external news coverage, financial and business news, police and legal news, sex-related news, reporting of parliamentary debates. We can express the main conclusions summarily in the form of average percentage news composition for three groups of newspapers in the following way:

| Mean % of news space given to: | "Quality" group: The Guardian The Times The Daily Telegraph | "Middle" group: Daily Express Daily Mail | "Popular" group: The Sun Daily Mirror |
|---|---|---|---|
| | % | % | % |
| (a) Home p.s.e. (incl. Labour and Ulster) ... ... | 19 | 16 | 15 |
| (b) External p.s.e. ... ... | 17 | 7 | 4 |
| (c) Sport ... ... ... | 18 | 33 | 47 |
| (d) Sex-related content ... | — | 2 | 4 |
| (e) Parliamentary debates ... | 3 | — | — |
| (f) Finance/business ... | 18 | 9 | — |
| (g) All external ... ... | 24 | 17 | 10 |

* Royal Commission on the Press, Interim Report, 1976, Cmd. 6433 Appendix E.

29

In no case does an individual title deviate from its implied position on the continuum. The *Financial Times* belongs, by these criteria, to the first group and so, on the whole, does the *Morning Star*.

Similarities between newspapers are, at the same time, not insignificant. Firstly, for all main newspapers, sport is the largest single category and, in terms of space, received about equal treatment in all papers. In fact, the newspaper offering most sport news is *The Daily Telegraph*, despite the 50% of news space given to sport by the *Daily Mirror*. The relative attention to international sport is about equal in all newspapers. Secondly, the percentage allocation to "personality" news is about the same for all main titles, although *The Guardian* comes low. In practice, the type of personality news varies a good deal between "Qualities" and others, with the former mainly reporting news of formal social events, appointments, etc., the latter dealing more with entertainment and show business personalities. Thirdly, it is noticeable that in reporting industrial relations and labour matters, the proportions of space are about equal for all newspapers except the *Morning Star* and the same is true for Ulster crisis-related news. This suggests that, for events of great importance or immediate public relevance in the sphere of politics and economics, the "Popular" newspapers do provide quite extensive coverage (see Appendix K). The overall difference mainly reflects a greater commitment, regardless of day-to-day news events, on the part of the "Qualities" to news in the sphere of politics. It would be important not to interpret the basic pattern shown here as evidence that "Popular" newspapers generally observe lower standards in respect of news coverage or have a fundamentally different set of "news values".

(iv) The distribution of space between feature categories (Table A8) shows some additional points of interest despite the continued evidence of the pattern established in news content, described above. In general, we can see a less rigid mould than appears in the latter case. Firstly, the amount of space allocated to features is somewhat different, with the *Daily Mail* exceeding *The Daily Telegraph*. Secondly, the *Daily Mail* also "breaks ranks" with other "non-quality" papers by having a higher proportion (and amount) of foreign features and a higher proportionate allocation to financial and business news than *The Guardian*. Thirdly, although only *The Times* and *Financial Times* give any substantial proportion of space to scientific, technical and medical news, *The Sun* is next in relative terms. Fourthly, the political column seems as well, if not better, established in the "Popular" newspapers, with *The Sun* in the lead. In fact, the regular signed column is in general a more notable characteristic of the "non-quality" press, mainly showing up in the *Daily Express* and the *Daily Mirror*. Fifthly, *The Sun* has a distinctive lead in sex-features, mainly accounted for by its regular "pin-up" on page 3. All the main newspapers give most feature space to the arts and entertainment and all give some space to features for women and content relating to consumer matters and prices. Picture features are also important in most newspapers, although the *Daily Express* and *Daily Mail* seem to lag in this. The overall picture is of a fair amount of diversity, even when broad categories such as these are used. When the specific content of features is looked at, the diversity is much greater since newspapers are less constrained by the day's news and the same set of Fleet Street news values as they are when putting news pages together. The general increase in space given to features is thus likely to have been beneficial from the point of view of diversity and here the distinctive personality of the newspaper may be better established than in the news pages.

(v) The "other" editorial space allocation recorded in Table A9 adds further to this conclusion. There is a good deal of diversity, even if certain items recur in all newspapers: editorials, correspondence columns, topical cartoons, TV and radio information, weather forecasts, etc. In respect of space given to editorials (leading articles) the grouping of newspapers is not that of the "Quality—Middle—Popular" pattern set out above. In terms of actual space, *The Guardian*, *Daily Mail* and *The Times* lead, with *The Daily Telegraph*, *Financial Times* and *Daily Express* as a second group and the *Daily Mirror* and *The Sun* some way behind. Space allocation to correspondence produces a yet different grouping, with *The Times* far ahead, *The Guardian* second, the *Daily Mail*, *The Daily Telegraph*, *Financial Times* and *The Sun* in a third group and the *Daily Express*, *Daily Mirror* and *Morning Star* behind. The general impression from Table A9 is that different newspapers offer different attractions to readers and have their own specialities: *The Times*, *Daily Mail* and *The Guardian* are for letter writers or readers; the *Daily Express*, almost alone, prints fiction; the *Daily Mirror* offers most comic and strip cartoons; the *Daily Express* and *The Sun* provide most puzzles, competitions and offers; *The Daily Telegraph* gives much space to features for women (Table A8). The specific content would reveal further differentiation and special characteristics which are very faintly and indirectly revealed here.

(vi) Even at this level of discussion it is important to record the limitations of the "Quality—Middle—Popular" typification, however inescapable it may be in some respects. The national daily press is undoubtedly patterned and apparently very stable over time in some basic aspects. Even so, the kind of framework used in this description of content is inclined to have some self-fulfilling tendencies in this direction. Despite the framework, there is evidence of diversity and also some sign of alternative groupings to the one which differentiates the "Quality" from the "Popular" press.

## Summary

The main points to emerge from this commentary are:

(*a*) The confirmation of the familiar division into three main types of paper according to criteria of size (also circulation) and several sorts of news space allocation.

(*b*) The fact that in home news coverage all papers seem to share some basic news values, reflected especially in the similarity of relative attention to industrial relations and the Ulster crisis.

(*c*) The similarity of newspapers in terms of basic "components", which include editorials, correspondence columns, attention to sport and "personalities".

(*d*) The greater diversity revealed in the distribution of feature and other editorial space. It is here that different titles tend to reveal their more distinctive *personas* and escape to some extent from the quality-popular dimension. The amount of feature space also produces a different ordering than is revealed by overall newspaper size.

31

# III  Analysis of Sunday Newspapers

**1. Introduction—application of National Daily coding frame to Sunday newspapers**

The basic similarity of content, despite varying emphasis, between the Daily and Sunday newspaper was taken as a justification for applying the same set of categories in the two cases. A case might be made for a greater attention to different sorts of feature content, but in view of the low priority attached to analysing Sunday newspapers (reflected in smaller sample size) this was not acted on. The main problem of application lay in distinguishing between news and features. Because of the longer production time available, Sunday newspapers are not so tied to the immediate reporting of events and the recognition of news is less easy. Incidents and events tend to be treated less urgently and with more background material and comment. A news event during the previous week can turn into a suitable subject for feature treatment by the weekend. The problem had to be solved on an *ad hoc* basis, with an attempt to be consistent in making the general distinction between the two types of content.

## 2. Sunday Newspapers: Comparison Tables

TABLE A12

SUNDAY NEWSPAPERS, 1975:
ANALYSIS OF TOTAL SPACE INTO ADVERTISING AND FOUR CATEGORIES OF EDITORIAL SPACE

per cent of all space

| Category | | | | | | | | The Sunday Times | The Observer | Sunday Telegraph | Sunday Express | Sunday Mirror | Sunday People | News of the World |
|---|---|---|---|---|---|---|---|---|---|---|---|---|---|---|
| | | | | | | | | % | % | % | % | % | % | % |
| News ... | ... | ... | ... | ... | ... | ... | ... | 11 | 14 | 19 | 15 | 21 | 23 | 26 |
| Features ... | ... | ... | ... | ... | ... | ... | ... | 24 | 33 | 28 | 23 | 27 | 21 | 17 |
| Other editorial | ... | ... | ... | ... | ... | ... | ... | 7 | 6 | 6 | 9 | 9 | 12 | 9 |
| Total | ... | ... | ... | ... | ... | ... | ... | 42 | 53 | 53 | 47 | 57 | 56 | 52 |
| Advertising | ... | ... | ... | ... | ... | ... | ... | 58 | 47 | 47 | 53 | 43 | 44 | 48 |
| TOTAL ... | ... | ... | ... | ... | ... | ... | ... | 100 | 100 | 100 | 100 | 100 | 100 | 100 |
| Mean space per sample issue (col.cms.) | | | | | | | ... | 26,047 | 14,934 | 14,591 | 13,437 | 10,155 | 10,943 | 11,590 |
| Picture content as % of *editorial* space | | | | | | | ... | 17 | 12 | 11 | 14 | 22 | 20 | 17 |

33

# TABLE A13

## SUNDAY NEWSPAPERS, 1975:
## ANALYSIS OF TOTAL NEWS SPACE INTO 21 CATEGORIES*

*per cent of all news space*

| Category | The Sunday Times | The Observer | Sunday Telegraph | Sunday Express | Sunday Mirror | Sunday People | News of the World |
|---|---|---|---|---|---|---|---|
| | % | % | % | % | % | % | % |
| **Home News:** | | | | | | | |
| 1. Political, social and economic | 13 | 11 | 13 | 7 | 6 | 2 | 5 |
| 2. Labour/Industrial relations | 2 | 4 | 4 | 4 | — | — | 2 |
| 3. Ulster crisis-related | 3 | 3 | 3 | — | 3 | 3 | 1 |
| 4. Legal and police in general | 3 | 2 | 2 | 6 | 8 | 7 | 11 |
| 5. Accidents | — | 1 | — | — | 2 | — | 2 |
| 6. Personalities, social events | 1 | 1 | 2 | 3 | 1 | 4 | 3 |
| 7. Sport | 24 | 33 | 41 | 50 | 49 | 51 | 47 |
| 8. Other home news | 7 | 3 | 2 | 12 | 17 | 19 | 12 |
| 9. Sex-related home news | — | — | — | — | 2 | 5 | 9 |
| 10. Parliamentary debate reports | — | — | 1 | — | — | — | — |
| Total | 53 | 58 | 68 | 82 | 88 | 91 | 92 |

34

## External News
### Foreign

| | | | | | | | |
|---|---|---|---|---|---|---|---|
| 11. Political, social and economic... | 6 | 9 | 7 | 2 | 1 | 1 | 1 |
| 12. Other | 2 | 2 | 1 | 7 | 6 | 4 | 3 |
| *Commonwealth* | | | | | | | |
| 13. Political, social and economic | — | 2 | 2 | 1 | — | — | — |
| 14. Other | — | — | — | — | — | — | — |
| *International* | | | | | | | |
| 15. Political, social and economic... | 6 | 16 | 6 | 3 | — | — | — |
| 16. Other | 1 | 1 | 1 | 2 | — | — | — |
| 17. Sport | 5 | 4 | 2 | 2 | 1 | 2 | 1 |
| 18. External: sex-related | — | — | — | — | — | 1 | 2 |
| 19. External: miscellaneous | 4 | — | 1 | — | — | — | — |
| Total | 25 | 34 | 20 | 17 | 8 | 8 | 7 |
| **Other News** | | | | | | | |
| 20. Financial/market news | 21 | 7 | 11 | 1 | 2 | — | — |
| 21. Scientific and Technical | 1 | 1 | 1 | — | — | — | — |
| Total | 22 | 8 | 12 | 1 | 2 | — | — |
| TOTAL ... | 100 | 100 | 100 | 100 | 98 | 99 | 99 |
| Mean news space per sample issue (col.cms.) | 2,865 | 2,090 | 2,772 | 2,015 | 2,132 | 2,516 | 3,013 |

* The categories are equivalent to those used in Table A7.

35

# TABLE A14

## SUNDAY NEWSPAPERS, 1975:
## ANALYSIS OF ALL FEATURE SPACE INTO 17 CATEGORIES

per cent of feature space

| Category | The Sunday Times % | The Observer % | Sunday Telegraph % | Sunday Express % | Sunday Mirror % | Sunday People % | News of the World % |
|---|---|---|---|---|---|---|---|
| 1. Home, political, social and economic | 17 | 13 | 15 | 7 | 4 | 3 | 6 |
| 2. External, political, social and economic | 11 | 10 | 6 | — | — | — | 1 |
| 3. Financial/business | 9 | 5 | 13 | 4 | 1 | — | — |
| 4. Scientific, technical, medical | 2 | 4 | 1 | 1 | 2 | 5 | 1 |
| 5. Consumer/prices | 3 | 2 | 3 | — | 1 | 2 | 2 |
| 6. Political columns | — | — | 1 | 2 | 4 | 4 | — |
| 7. Mixed columns | — | — | 2 | 5 | 2 | 4 | — |
| 8. Light columns | 4 | 8 | 5 | 7 | — | — | 4 |
| 9. Personalities | 4 | 8 | 2 | 6 | 16 | 4 | — |
| 10. Sport | 7 | 26 | 5 | 15 | 11 | 11 | 14 |
| 11. Arts, entertainments | 19 | — | 24 | 12 | 11 | 18 | 21 |
| 12. Children's features | — | — | — | — | — | 2 | 8 |
| 13. Women's features | 5 | 8 | 7 | 8 | 4 | 4 | 6 |
| 14. Other regular features | 5 | 9 | 9 | 14 | 8 | 16 | 6 |
| 15. Picture features | 2 | 2 | 2 | 7 | 6 | 2 | 2 |
| 16. Other features | 12 | 5 | 5 | 10 | 10 | 17 | 12 |
| 17. Sex-related features | — | — | — | 1 | 20 | 8 | 17 |
| TOTAL | 100 | 100 | 100 | 99 | 100 | 100 | 100 |
| Mean feature space per sample issue (col.cms.) | 6,333 | 4,473 | 4,135 | 2,861 | 2,216 | 1,858 | 1,619 |

36

**TABLE A15**

SUNDAY NEWSPAPERS, 1975:
ANALYSIS OF OTHER EDITORIAL SPACE INTO NINE CATEGORIES

*per cent of other space*

| Category | The Sunday Times | The Observer | Sunday Telegraph | Sunday Express | Sunday Mirror | Sunday People | News of the World |
|---|---|---|---|---|---|---|---|
| | % | % | % | % | % | % | % |
| Editorial comment | 6 | 16 | 12 | 5 | 9 | 4 | 6 |
| Correspondence | 13 | 23 | 21 | 8 | 21 | 25 | 19 |
| Topical cartoons | 6 | 5 | 8 | 8 | 6 | — | 6 |
| Comic strip cartoons | — | — | — | 19 | 23 | 7 | 5 |
| Fiction/Serialisation | 34 | — | 23 | 23 | — | 2 | — |
| Puzzles, competitions, offers | 9 | 11 | 10 | 12 | 8 | 19 | 32 |
| Other regular information | 11 | 14 | 15 | 14 | 18 | 20 | 20 |
| Miscellaneous | 10 | 12 | 4 | 7 | 9 | 9 | 6 |
| Headlines and titles | 11 | 19 | 7 | 4 | 6 | 14 | 6 |
| TOTAL | 100 | 100 | 100 | 100 | 100 | 100 | 100 |
| Mean "other" space per sample issue (col.cms.) | 1,848 | 790 | 851 | 1,030 | 752 | 1,050 | 796 |

37

TABLE A16

SUNDAY NEWSPAPERS, 1975:
PROPORTIONS OF TOTAL EDITORIAL SPACE GIVEN TO NEWS AND FEATURES ABOUT: (a) SPORT: (b) SEX-RELATED CONTENT

| Category | The Sunday Times | The Observer | Sunday Telegraph | Sunday Express | Sunday Mirror | Sunday People | News of the World |
|---|---|---|---|---|---|---|---|
| | % | % | % | % | % | % | % |
| (a) Sport ... ... ... ... | 12 | 26 | 18 | 23 | 24 | 28 | 31 |
| (b) Sex-related content ... ... | — | — | — | 2 | 10 | 5 | 11 |
| Mean editorial space per issue (col.cms.) ... | 10,939 | 7,165 | 7,719 | 5,516 | 4,716 | 4,907 | 4,812 |

TABLE A17

SUNDAY NEWSPAPERS, 1975:
ANALYSIS OF TOTAL ADVERTISING CONTENT INTO TWO CATEGORIES

| Category | The Sunday Times | The Observer | Sunday Telegraph | Sunday Express | Sunday Mirror | Sunday People | News of the World |
|---|---|---|---|---|---|---|---|
| | % | % | % | % | % | % | % |
| Classified ... ... ... ... ... | 56 | 38 | 25 | 4 | 1 | 5 | 4 |
| Display ... ... ... ... | 44 | 62 | 75 | 96 | 99 | 95 | 96 |
| TOTAL ... ... ... ... ... | 100 | 100 | 100 | 100 | 100 | 100 | 100 |

## 3. Sunday Newspapers: Commentary

(i) Since the sample only included six issues for each title, comments cannot be made with the same certainty as for the national press. It should also be recalled that two Sunday newspapers have magazines which extend their range of content. A brief indication of their content is given in Appendix A11.

(ii) In terms of size, the set of Sunday newspapers is easily led by *The Sunday Times*, which is also exceptional in the amount of advertising it contains. In general, all Sunday newspapers carry more advertising than Dailies, the average of space for seven titles being 49% compared to 35% for the National Dailies. The Sunday newspaper is also different from the daily paper in the ratio of news to feature space. For the former, the allocation of all space to these two broad categories is 18% : 25% compared to a corresponding ratio of 37% to 19% for the daily paper. A difference between "Quality" and "Popular" Sunday shows up, however, in the relatively higher allocation of space by the latter to news. Features as a whole are about equally important for all titles. Picture content is more prominent in the *Sunday Mirror*, *Sunday People* and *News of the World*, but the *amount* of illustration in *The Sunday Times* is greater than in the *Sunday Mirror* and the existence of illustrated weekend magazines also puts *The Sunday Times* and *The Observer* in a class of their own in respect of picture content.

(iii) The pattern of news space allocation in Sunday newspapers is generally similar to that for the dailies when Table A13 is compared with Table A7, although we can see an even larger proportionate attention to sport. In terms of space given to sport, the *News of the World* leads, with *The Sunday Telegraph* in second place. The "Quality-Popular" continuum is predictably prominent, with the *Sunday Express* occupying a middle position in respect of attention to home political, social and economic news and to foreign news generally. Again, where the "Populars" give space to foreign news, it tends not to be categorised as "political, social and economic". The same group of papers is distinguished by its focus on law and police news and to some extent, sex-related news, with the *News of the World* leading in both respects. The figure in Table 16, giving the allocation of space to all forms of sex-related news and features, shows 10% of both the *Sunday Mirror* and *News of the World* editorial space to have fallen in the relevant categories, followed by the *Sunday People* with 6%. It is possibly worth noting that the generally high level of interest in industrial relations exhibited by all National Dailies is not matched in the "Popular" Sunday press. The *Sunday Mirror* and *Sunday People*, for example, showed little interest in this sort of content on the dates sampled.

(iv) Feature content in the Sundays reveals a rather sharper division between "Quality" and "Popular" press than appeared in the Dailies, with the *Sunday Express* again in a middle position. The only matters, in terms of these content comparisons, which seem to bring the two sets of newspapers together are the attention to content for women, that relating to consumer and price matters and picture features. The "Popular" titles are distinctive in the space given to sport, personalities and regular columns of all kinds (including "political" columns). While the percentages are all very small, the attention to scientific or medical features is fairly equal between titles. In interpreting the figures, we should bear in mind the large variation in actual space. The average feature space in *The Sunday Times* exceeds total editorial space in each of the *Sunday Mirror*, *Sunday People* and *News of the World*.

(v) Table A15 adds a few more points about similarities and differences. All the Sunday newspapers carry leading articles and correspondence sections. The latter seem especially important, as do puzzles, competitions and offers. The *Sunday People* and *The Sunday Times* give more space to letters than do any other Sunday paper and in respect of puzzles and offers, the *News of the World* is in the lead. Three papers, *The Sunday Times*, *Sunday Telegraph* and *Sunday Express* are recorded as giving much space to serialised books, the other papers hardly any.

(vi) A general conclusion on the National Sundays as revealed in this small-scale analysis might note the respect in which they complement the Dailies by offering much more background to the news. On the other hand, it might also be recorded that they seem to offer little which is additional to the range of content of the national dailies, apart from a larger component of sex news. They seem, if anything, somewhat less varied as a group, although the gap between "Qualities" and "Populars" is even more pronounced.

(vii) To summarise:

    (*a*) The Sunday newspaper typically contains proportionately more advertising than the National Daily newspaper and its relative allocation of editorial space to news is lower.

    (*b*) There is a division between "Quality" and "Popular" titles and the latter are characterised by some familiar differences in news subject matter as well as by giving proportionately more space to news rather than features. The "gap" between "Popular" and "Quality" is generally more marked than is the case with National Daily newspapers, particularly in respect of attention to political, social and economic news, whether domestic or external. In one sense, the *Sunday Mirror*, *Sunday People*, and *News of the World* represent a further step on the continuum discussed in section II, 5 (iii) above.

    (*c*) In general, Sunday newspapers do complement the Dailies by giving background to news, but otherwise do not seem very evidently to extend the range of content which is available (although note should be taken of the two Sunday magazines).

# IV  Analysis of Provincial Morning Newspapers

## 1. Coding frame for Provincial Morning (and Evening) Newspapers

The coding frame reproduced below is an adapted version of that used for the National Daily Newspapers, and a number of the comments made about that in II, 1, also apply. The intention has been to preserve the broad structure, so that overall comparisons can be made between the two categories of newspaper, but to make a separate record of news relating to the country as a whole (National home news) and that relating specifically to the circulation area of the paper in question. The latter has been analysed in more detail and, in particular, distinctions have been made according to whether such news was "political", "economic", "social" or to do with planning and the environment. Together, these four categories should approximate to the single category of "political, social and economic news" used in the earlier analysis of National Dailies. External news has been treated in much less detail and new categories for feature material relating to the region or locality have been added. Otherwise there has been little change. The same coding frame has been used for the analysis of Provincial evening newspapers. Further comments on the application of this coding frame are given in Appendix A12.

## CODING FRAME FOR SCOTTISH, WELSH AND PROVINCIAL MORNING PAPERS

1.0.  **NATIONAL HOME NEWS**

News relating to events which occurred in the United Kingdom, excluding those occurring in the locality, region or circulation area of the paper being coded.

    1.1.      POLITICAL, SOCIAL OR ECONOMIC

            Political news; Parliamentary news (excluding records of debates); governmental and administrative news; local government; housing and planning; education; social, health and welfare services; employment; production; economic performance; farming; energy matters—oil, coal, etc; race relations; armed forces news.

            1.1L.   *Labour/Industrial*

                News of strikes and disputes; industrial relations; trade union matters; news of pay settlements and negotiations; Employers' and Professional Associations' affairs when dealing with labour/industrial matters, etc.

            1.1U.   *Ulster Crisis-Related*

                Home affairs news related primarily to the Ulster troubles (except law and police matters where Irish Republic is involved).

41

1.2.　LAW AND POLICE
News of, and reports on, proceedings in all courts of law; legal
news (other than appointments); all reports and news where
main reference is to police or crime.

1.2L.　*Labour/Industrial*
Industrial relations matters involving the police or
courts.

1.2U.　*Ulster Crisis-Related*
Matters relating to the Ulster crisis, involving the
British or Ulster police and courts. Major events (eg,
bombings, robberies, trials) which happen to occur in
the locality of the paper being coded should also
appear under this heading.

1.2S.　*Sex-Related*
Matters derived from police or court proceedings,
where the sexual interest of the case seems predominant.

1.5.　SPORT
Reports on, and news of, all kinds of sport and games;
programmes and fixtures; pools and horse betting news and
form; news of well-known personalities (including international
fixtures when played in Britain).

1.9.　OTHER NATIONAL HOME NEWS
Home news in brief; human interest news not otherwise
identifiable; state of roads, weather news not included elsewhere; arts; theatre; film; T.V. and radio news not included
elsewhere; accidents; examination results; religious or Church
news when no social or political reference. This category to
include material coded in national dailies as "accident", or
"personalities".

2.0.　**EXTERNAL NEWS**
Includes news of and reports about events occurring outside the United
Kingdom, without distinction between "foreign", "Commonwealth"
or "international".

2.1.　EXTERNAL: POLITICAL, SOCIAL OR ECONOMIC

2.5.　EXTERNAL: SPORT

2.9.　ALL OTHER EXTERNAL NEWS
Includes external news in brief.

3.0.　**NEWS OF EVENTS NOT SPECIFICALLY HOME, EXTERNAL
OR PROVINCIAL**

3.1.　FINANCIAL
Financial and market news, national, local and external; crop,
livestock and mining reports affecting market prices, bank-
ruptcies. Some items of news about local industry or agriculture will appear under P1.12 below, but, as indicated, a
fair proportion of this category may be local in reference.

3.2.    SCIENTIFIC, TECHNICAL, MEDICAL

3.9.    MISCELLANEOUS
Non-local news otherwise unclassifiable.

## P1.0.  NEWS OF SCOTLAND, WALES AND ENGLISH PROVINCES, REGIONS AND LOCALITIES

### P1.11.  POLITICAL (local government)
Local authority political, administrative and financial matters; minor council business not included under P1.13 or P1.14; conflicts within and with local council; local political party matters, including personalities, elections, appointments; matters to do with local authority social services where procedural, administrative and financial aspects predominate over the substantive references to the services provided. News relating to devolution, Scottish or Welsh nationalist parties.

### P1.12.  ECONOMIC
Industrial and agricultural news relating to locality or region of the paper; local employment matters; developments and closures; production and orders; land and property matters. (Note: Financial and market matters are coded as 3.1, even where local in reference.)

#### P1.12L  *Labour/Industrial Relations*
Strikes, settlements, local trade union matters, whether in industry or agriculture. Industrial safety and health news.

### P1.13.  SOCIAL SERVICES
News of local social services: education, health, housing, welfare; recreation, etc, where substance of report concerns the service and the public rather than local authority political business or finance. Include major voluntary social service efforts. Also matters to do with minorities, race relations, social problems. Local public transport, where issue is social rather than financial. Internal local social administrative matters are included here, eg, local health service boards, etc.

### P1.14.  PLANNING, ENVIRONMENT
Pollution, threats to amenities. Reports of planning enquiries, local protests at development plans. Major road and traffic schemes. Structure plans. Housing, where development has environmental implications.

### P1.2.  LOCAL CRIME, POLICE
News from courts and police, reports of crimes and vandalism, etc; police administrative news. (Political terrorism is coded as national news.)

### P1.3.  ACCIDENTS
Includes natural disasters, missing persons and deaths where the biographical aspect is not newsworthy.

43

P1.4. **PERSONALITIES**
Local people in the news. Social events where guests are the
main news interest. Deaths of local people and obituaries.
Local wills, marriages, engagements, travels, appointments.
National celebrities in the local news.

P1.5. **LOCAL SPORT**

P1.6. **EVENTS AND ACTIVITIES**
Festivals, fund-raising, concerts, drama, competitions, where
events rather than participants are main focus of news. May
include some minor voluntary social welfare activity.

P1.7. **INFORMATION**
Notices of local events, useful information, weather, traffic,
local services, etc.

P1.8. **REGIONAL LANGUAGE**
Items in local language or dialect.

P1.9. **OTHER LOCAL NEWS**
Items in brief; human interest; miscellaneous items; church
or religious matters not covered elsewhere. Military news.

4.0. **NON-LOCAL FEATURES**

    4.1. POLITICAL, SOCIAL OR ECONOMIC

    4.6. ARTS AND ENTERTAINMENT

    4.9. ALL OTHER FEATURES

P4.0. **REGIONAL/LOCAL FEATURES**

    P4.1. POLITICAL, SOCIAL OR ECONOMIC

    P4.2. **LOCAL TOPOGRAPHICAL**
Leisure pursuits; places to visit; diary of local events; nature
notes; archaeology and local history.

    P4.3. **CONSUMER/PRICES**
Matters of local consumer interest relating to shops, services,
housing, etc.

    P4.4. **PERSONALITIES**
Features about local people.

    P4.5. **SPORT**
Local sport features.

    P4.6. ARTS, ENTERTAINMENT, REVIEWS, PREVIEWS

    P4.8. LOCAL PICTURE-FEATURES

    P4.9. OTHER FEATURES

5.0. **OTHER EDITORIAL SPACE**

    5.1. EDITORIAL COMMENT

    5.2. CORRESPONDENCE

5.4.   TOPICAL CARTOONS

5.5.   COMIC AND STRIP CARTOONS

5.6.   FICTION

5.7.   PUZZLES, COMPETITIONS AND OFFERS
Crosswords, anagrams, bridge and chess problems; children's competitions; special offers to readers created by the newspaper itself, etc.

5.8.   OTHER REGULAR INFORMATION
Radio and television programmes; weather forecasts, horoscopes, etc.

5.9.   MISCELLANEOUS EDITORIAL SPACE
Index, order forms, advertisement index; publication particulars; subscription and advertising rates; blank spaces (eg empty stop press columns); news of coming attractions in the newspaper.

6.0.   **ADVERTISEMENTS AND OTHER SPACE**
Items which were considered to have been paid for by outside firms or individuals, including: display and classified advertisements; notices of birth, marriage and death; company reports.

6.1.   CLASSIFIED ADVERTISING
All advertisements gathered under general subject matter heading.

6.2.   DISPLAY ADVERTISING
All other advertising content, including "advertising features".

6.3.   HEADINGS AND TITLES

7.0.   **PARLIAMENTARY DEBATE REPORTS (Both Houses)**

8.0.   **NEWS AND FEATURES OF SEX INTEREST**
Including pin-up photos.

9.0.   **PICTURE CONTENT**
Where illustrative of news or features (excluding cartoons, and pictures separately coded under 8.0.)

## 2. Provincial Morning Newspapers, England and Wales: Comparison Tables

### TABLE A18

#### ENGLISH AND WELSH PROVINCIAL MORNING NEWSPAPERS, 1975

#### ANALYSIS OF TOTAL SPACE INTO ADVERTISING AND FOUR CATEGORIES OF EDITORIAL SPACE

| Category | The Birmingham Post † | Yorkshire Post | Liverpool Daily Post | Morning Telegraph | The Northern Echo | The Journal | Eastern Daily Press | East Anglian Daily Times | Western Mail | Western Daily Press | The Western Morning News | Leamington & District Morning News |
|---|---|---|---|---|---|---|---|---|---|---|---|---|
| | % | % | % | % | % | % | % | % | % | % | % | % |
| **Editorial Space** | | | | | | | | | | | | |
| News... ... ... ... | 39 | 38 | 42 | 47 | 34 | 38 | 30 | 31 | 38 | 47 | 30 | 37 |
| Features ... ... ... | 13 | 14 | 16 | 17 | 12 | 9 | 10 | 9 | 11 | 11 | 8 | 9 |
| Other... ... ... ... | 12 | 13 | 14 | 10 | 9 | 8 | 7 | 13 | 10 | 10 | 6 | 11 |
| Total... ... ... | 64 | 65 | 72 | 74 | 55 | 55 | 47 | 53 | 59 | 68 | 44 | 57 |
| **Advertising** ... ... | 36 | 35 | 28 | 26 | 45 | 45 | 53 | 47 | 41 | 32 | 56 | 43 |
| **TOTAL** ... ... | 100 | 100 | 100 | 100 | 100 | 100 | 100 | 100 | 100 | 100 | 100 | 100 |
| Mean space per sample issue in (col.cms). ... ... | 7,000 | 7,639 | 6,109 | 5,439 | 8,049 | 7,268 | 7,860 | 6,807 | 7,083 | 5,637 | 5,892 | 983 |
| Picture content as % of editorial space... ... ... | 7 | 10 | 11 | 12 | 19 | 10 | 13 | 11 | 11 | 12 | 14 | 16 |
| Mean number of pages per issue ... | 13·8 | 20·3 | 14·2 | 12·3 | 18·3 | 15·5 | 18·8 | 16·7 | 17·0 | 13·0 | 13·5 | 4·7 |

†One issue of The Birmingham Post (Oct. 18) was omitted, in error, from the analysis and consequently the figures for this title relate to eleven issues only.

# ENGLISH AND WELSH PROVINCIAL MORNING NEWSPAPERS, 1975: ANALYSIS OF ALL NEWS SPACE INTO 14 CATEGORIES*

| Category | The Birmingham Post % | Yorkshire Post % | Liverpool Daily Post % | Morning Telegraph % | The Northern Echo % | The Journal % | Eastern Daily Press % | East Anglian Daily Times % | Western Mail % | Western Daily Press % | The Western Morning News % | Leamington & District Morning News % |
|---|---|---|---|---|---|---|---|---|---|---|---|---|
| **National Home News** | | | | | | | | | | | | |
| 1. Political, social and economic | 9 | 8 | 6 | 7 | 5 | 5 | 5 | 5 | 6 | 6 | 6 | 1 |
| 2. Industrial relations | 3 | 3 | 3 | 4 | 2 | 2 | 2 | 3 | 2 | 3 | 2 | — |
| 3. Ulster crisis | — | 2 | 2 | 2 | 2 | 1 | 2 | 2 | 1 | 2 | 1 | — |
| 4. Law and police | 6 | 5 | 5 | 3 | 2 | 4 | 2 | 2 | 3 | 7 | 1 | — |
| 5. Sport | 17 | 16 | 16 | 20 | 19 | 15 | 11 | 10 | 16 | 16 | 13 | — |
| 6. Other | 4 | 5 | 5 | 5 | 4 | 3 | 4 | 3 | 3 | 3 | 2 | 2 |
| 7. Parliamentary debates | 2 | 1 | — | — | 1 | — | — | — | — | — | — | — |
| Total | 43 | 40 | 37 | 41 | 35 | 30 | 26 | 25 | 31 | 37 | 26 | 3 |
| **External News** | | | | | | | | | | | | |
| 8. Political, social and economic | 5 | 8 | 6 | 4 | 3 | 2 | 3 | 3 | 4 | 2 | 3 | — |
| 9. Other | 4 | 4 | 4 | 2 | 3 | 3 | 2 | 1 | 4 | 3 | 2 | — |
| Total | 9 | 12 | 10 | 6 | 6 | 5 | 5 | 4 | 8 | 5 | 5 | — |
| 10. Financial/market news (national, external or local) | 17 | 16 | 14 | 12 | 5 | 7 | 9 | 7 | 9 | 9 | 6 | — |
| **Provincial, Regional and Local** | | | | | | | | | | | | |
| 11. Political, social and economic | 11 | 7 | 11 | 15 | 12 | 17 | 16 | 20 | 22 | 13 | 16 | 29 |
| 12. Crime, police, accidents | 4 | 5 | 7 | 5 | 10 | 12 | 12 | 10 | 7 | 10 | 9 | 35 |
| 13. Sport | 8 | 12 | 12 | 10 | 14 | 16 | 10 | 17 | 13 | 13 | 17 | 6 |
| 14. Other | 10 | 9 | 10 | 11 | 17 | 12 | 22 | 19 | 11 | 13 | 20 | 28 |
| Total | 33 | 33 | 40 | 41 | 53 | 57 | 60 | 66 | 53 | 49 | 62 | 98 |
| TOTAL | 102 | 101 | 101 | 100 | 99 | 99 | 100 | 102 | 101 | 100 | 99 | 101 |
| Mean news space per sample issue (col.cms.) | 2,738 | 2,936 | 2,575 | 2,520 | 2,763 | 2,732 | 2,339 | 2,111 | 2,710 | 2,649 | 1,761 | 366 |

* Very small amounts of "miscellaneous" news, in no case reaching 0·5% for any paper, have been ignored in this table although they are included in the base on which percentages have been calculated.

**TABLE A20**

**ENGLISH AND WELSH PROVINCIAL MORNING NEWSPAPERS, 1975:**

**ANALYSIS OF PROVINCIAL, REGIONAL AND LOCAL NEWS INTO 12 CATEGORIES**

| Category | The Birmingham Post % | Yorkshire Post % | Liverpool Daily Post % | Morning Telegraph % | The Northern Echo % | The Journal % | Eastern Daily Press % | East Anglian Daily Times % | Western Mail % | Western Daily Press % | The Western Morning News % | Leamington & District Morning News % |
|---|---|---|---|---|---|---|---|---|---|---|---|---|
| 1. Political | 4 | 6 | 7 | 10 | 4 | 6 | 7 | 8 | 9 | 8 | 7 | 7 |
| 2. Economic | 15 | 5 | 6 | 7 | 4 | 10 | 5 | 5 | 13 | 6 | 7 | 3 |
| 3. Industrial relations | 5 | 2 | 2 | 7 | 3 | 5 | 1 | 2 | 5 | 2 | 2 | 1 |
| 4. Social services | 5 | 3 | 6 | 5 | 7 | 3 | 5 | 6 | 5 | 6 | 3 | 7 |
| 5. Planning, environment | 5 | 5 | 7 | 7 | 5 | 6 | 9 | 10 | 9 | 6 | 6 | 12 |
| 6. Crime, police | 8 | 14 | 15 | 8 | 13 | 17 | 16 | 12 | 12 | 15 | 13 | 31 |
| 7. Accidents | 4 | 2 | 1 | 5 | 5 | 4 | 4 | 3 | 1 | 6 | 2 | 5 |
| 8. Personalities | 9 | 7 | 9 | 9 | 11 | 10 | 10 | 10 | 6 | 7 | 13 | 11 |
| 9. Sport | 25 | 36 | 31 | 24 | 27 | 28 | 17 | 25 | 25 | 26 | 27 | 6 |
| 10. Events and activities | 1 | 3 | 3 | 4 | 6 | 2 | 10 | 8 | 2 | 10 | 7 | 4 |
| 11. Information | 10 | 4 | 2 | 4 | 3 | 2 | 1 | 1 | 3 | 2 | 2 | 6 |
| 12. Other local news | 10 | 14 | 10 | 11 | 12 | 7 | 16 | 11 | 10 | 7 | 10 | 8 |
| TOTAL | 101 | 101 | 99 | 101 | 100 | 100 | 101 | 101 | 100 | 101 | 99 | 101 |
| Mean local news space per sample issue (col.cms.) | 886 | 985 | 1,030 | 1,040 | 1,486 | 1,555 | 1,408 | 1,387 | 1,427 | 1,301 | 1,103 | 354 |

48

**TABLE A21**

**ENGLISH AND WELSH PROVINCIAL MORNING NEWSPAPERS, 1975: ANALYSIS OF FEATURE SPACE INTO 11 CATEGORIES**

| Category | The Birmingham Post % | Yorkshire Post % | Liverpool Daily Post % | Morning Telegraph % | The Northern Echo % | The Journal % | Eastern Daily Press % | East Anglian Daily Times % | Western Mail % | Western Daily Press % | The Western Morning News % | Leamington & District Morning News % |
|---|---|---|---|---|---|---|---|---|---|---|---|---|
| **Non-Local Features:** | | | | | | | | | | | | |
| 1. Political, social and economic | 11 | 7 | 4 | 3 | 7 | 1 | 1 | 5 | 6 | 3 | 2 | — |
| 2. Arts and entertainment | 23 | 16 | 16 | 11 | 20 | 18 | 10 | 4 | 8 | 15 | 1 | 65 |
| 3. Other | 35 | 36 | 35 | 29 | 18 | 23 | 27 | 20 | 18 | 30 | 24 | 2 |
| Total | 69 | 59 | 55 | 43 | 45 | 42 | 38 | 29 | 32 | 48 | 27 | 67 |
| **Regional or Local Features:** | | | | | | | | | | | | |
| 4. Political, social and economic | 3 | 1 | 8 | 6 | 1 | 11 | 2 | 5 | 3 | 10 | 4 | — |
| 5. Local places, topography | 3 | 7 | 5 | 6 | 4 | — | 9 | 9 | 2 | 1 | 6 | — |
| 6. Consumer, prices | 1 | 1 | 1 | 4 | — | 2 | — | 1 | 3 | — | — | — |
| 7. Personalities | 2 | 1 | 6 | 6 | 5 | 9 | 6 | 5 | 19 | 25 | 16 | — |
| 8. Sport | 3 | 2 | 7 | 13 | 6 | 8 | 7 | 4 | 7 | 1 | 3 | — |
| 9. Arts, reviews, entertainment | 6 | 11 | 4 | 3 | 6 | 9 | 7 | 12 | 13 | 11 | 10 | 21 |
| 10. Local picture features | 2 | 1 | 1 | 10 | 16 | — | 16 | 5 | 4 | 3 | 11 | 11 |
| 11. Other | 10 | 18 | 14 | 8 | 18 | 19 | 15 | 31 | 17 | 2 | 24 | — |
| Total | 30 | 42 | 46 | 56 | 56 | 58 | 62 | 72 | 68 | 53 | 74 | 32 |
| TOTAL | 99 | 101 | 101 | 99 | 101 | 100 | 100 | 101 | 100 | 101 | 101 | 99 |
| Mean feature space per sample issue (col.cms.) | 984 | 1,091 | 988 | 896 | 993 | 674 | 773 | 616 | 745 | 606 | 485 | 88 |

## TABLE A22

### ENGLISH AND WELSH PROVINCIAL MORNING NEWSPAPERS, 1975: ANALYSIS OF OTHER EDITORIAL SPACE INTO NINE CATEGORIES

| Category | The Birmingham Post | Yorkshire Post | Liverpool Daily Post | Morning Telegraph | The Northern Echo | The Journal | Eastern Daily Press | East Anglian Daily Times | Western Mail | Western Daily Press | The Western Morning News | Leamington & District Morning News |
|---|---|---|---|---|---|---|---|---|---|---|---|---|
| 1. Editorial comment | 8 | 9 | 8 | 4 | 9 | 4 | 15 | 9 | 9 | 7 | 20 | — |
| 2. Correspondence | 14 | 7 | 10 | 10 | 12 | 6 | 23 | 10 | 9 | 6 | 18 | 11 |
| 3. Topical cartoons | 1 | 2 | — | 1 | — | — | — | — | — | 3 | — | — |
| 4. Other cartoons | — | 4 | 6 | — | 2 | 7 | 1 | — | 2 | 12 | — | 24 |
| 5. Fiction and serialised books | 3 | — | 8 | — | — | 2 | — | — | 10 | — | — | — |
| 6. Puzzles, offers, competitions | 16 | 17 | 11 | 27 | 17 | 23 | 9 | 14 | 19 | 12 | 11 | — |
| 7. Other regular information | 26 | 23 | 24 | 28 | 23 | 25 | 19 | 18 | 18 | 36 | 29 | 38 |
| 8. Miscellaneous editorial space | 13 | 15 | 20 | 13 | 16 | 22 | 17 | 32 | 9 | 9 | 4 | 10 |
| 9. Headings and titles | 21 | 24 | 13 | 16 | 21 | 11 | 15 | 17 | 24 | 14 | 18 | 18 |
| TOTAL | 102 | 101 | 100 | 99 | 100 | 100 | 99 | 100 | 100 | 99 | 100 | 101 |
| Mean space per sample issue (col.cms.) | 764 | 972 | 809 | 570 | 702 | 587 | 563 | 877 | 682 | 561 | 339 | 113 |

50

TABLE A23

ENGLISH AND WELSH PROVINCIAL MORNING NEWSPAPERS, 1975:
ANALYSIS OF TOTAL ADVERTISING SPACE INTO TWO CATEGORIES

| Category | The Birmingham Post | Yorkshire Post | Liverpool Daily Post | Morning Telegraph | The Northern Echo | The Journal | Eastern Daily Press | East Anglian Daily Times | Western Mail | Western Daily Press | The Western Morning News | Leamington & District Morning News |
|---|---|---|---|---|---|---|---|---|---|---|---|---|
| Classified ... ... ... ... | 66 | 61 | 56 | 76 | 75 | 70 | 51 | 63 | 75 | 70 | 49 | 59 |
| Display... ... ... ... | 34 | 39 | 44 | 24 | 25 | 30 | 49 | 37 | 25 | 30 | 51 | 41 |
| TOTAL ... ... | 100 | 100 | 100 | 100 | 100 | 100 | 100 | 100 | 100 | 100 | 100 | 100 |
| Mean total advertising space per sample issue (col.cms.) ... ... | 2,514 | 2,639 | 1,736 | 1,362 | 3,590 | 3,274 | 4,184 | 3,203 | 2,945 | 1,822 | 3,343 | 416 |

51

## 3. Provincial Morning Newspapers, England and Wales: Commentary

(i) This part of the report is concerned with 12 provincial morning newspaper titles, of which 12 issues each were analysed from the dates in the second half of the year used in the National Daily sample. The papers were as follows, with their place of publication and 1974 or 1975 circulation*.

| Title | Place | Circulation | |
|---|---|---|---|
| The Birmingham Post | Birmingham | 60,550 | (1974) |
| Yorkshire Post | Leeds | 105,366 | (1975) |
| Liverpool Daily Post | Liverpool | 100,933 | (1975) |
| Morning Telegraph | Sheffield | 50,794 | (1974) |
| The Northern Echo | Darlington | 114,386 | (1975) |
| The Journal | Newcastle on Tyne | 98,763 | (1975) |
| Eastern Daily Press | Norwich | 88,895 | (1975) |
| East Anglian Daily Times | Ipswich | 40,362 | (1975) |
| Western Mail | Cardiff | 94,840 | (1974) |
| Western Daily Press | Bristol | 69,785 | (1975) |
| The Western Morning News | Plymouth | 68,910 | (1975) |
| Leamington & District Morning News | Leamington | 9,779 | (1974) |

(ii) According to figures for mean space per issue given in Table A18 we can see a good deal of similarity of size. Apart from the exceptionally small and atypical Leamington paper, the distance between largest (*The Northern Echo*) and smallest (*Morning Telegraph*) can be expressed by a factor of 1·47 and the average size is similar to that of a typical *Daily Mail* or *Daily Express*. The basic pattern of space allocation shown in Table A18 shows several main points. Firstly, advertising content, at an average of 40%, is higher than for the National Dailies (mean of 35%) and there is no sharp internal variation, although the *Morning Telegraph* is low at 26%, and *The Western Morning News* high at 56% of print area. Secondly, the relative allocation of space to news is very close to the figure for National Dailies (both around 37%). Only the papers with high advertising components (*The Western Morning News, Eastern Daily Press*) are noticeably low in relative news content. Thirdly, allocations of space to features is generally rather low (mean of 12%) and only the papers low on advertising attain the National Daily norm of 16-17%. Fourthly, picture content is rather similarly represented in all titles, the average for all 12 being 12% of editorial space, or 8% of total space. This figure is close to the average of the *Daily Express* and *Daily Mail* and in between the National Daily "Qualities" and "Populars". *The Northern Echo* has most illustration, relatively, and *The Birmingham Post* least. The latter newspaper may, however, have been affected by an industrial dispute on one of the days included in the sample.

(iii) Table A19, showing the overall distribution of news space, provides the first evidence for a distinction between types of provincial newspapers which will recur on several matters. Basically, what seems to emerge is a continuum of titles according to the relative prominence accorded to certain kinds of content—in effect the same content which seemed to separate "Quality" from "Popular" newspapers. However, the distinction to be made has a somewhat different basis and significance. If we look at the proportions of external news

---

* British Rate and Data vol. 22, September, 1975

in general and financial news and also at the ratio of "national" to "local" home news, we find *The Birmingham Post*, *Yorkshire Post*, *Liverpool Post* and *Morning Telegraph* to stand somewhat apart from the remaining titles. The latter, apart from the Leamington paper, are rather close on most news indices. It is important not to regard this division as corresponding to that between "Quality" and "Popular" newspapers. It is also important not to overstate it, since it is rather insubstantial, although clear enough when the proportions of "local" news are looked at. The order in which the newspapers have been set in this and other tables was designed deliberately to reflect the point being made. The proportions of total news which is local or regional, as shown in Table A19, may be misleading, since the proportions omit any local business news included in Category 10. This applies especially to papers like *The Birmingham Post* and *Yorkshire Post*, which have high amounts of financial news. If financial news is left out of account, the proportion of news in *The Birmingham Post* which is "local" rises to 40%.

(iv) While various interpretations of the division are possible (more urban vs. more rural; or North and Midlands vs. South) it seems least misleading to regard the difference as one between the more and the less "metropolitan" newspapers. The cities involved are larger, more "centrally" located and are the focus of conurbations. The "missing" city is Manchester whose erstwhile morning paper has been translated to national status.

These remarks have picked out a major structural difference, but in patterns of news the similarities are possibly more striking. For instance, sport gets major attention in all—on average 28% for 11 titles, compared to 29% for eight National Dailies. Secondly, all 11 titles give similar space to national labour news and to Ulster. This agreement was also found in the National Dailies. Thirdly, apart from the greater interest on the part of more "metropolitan" papers, the amount of space given to external news and to financial news is very even and not insubstantial. For instance, the *Western Mail* actually gives more space, on average, to external news, than either *The Sun* or *Daily Mirror* and in "external" space terms the *Yorkshire Post* is ahead of the *Daily Mail* and close to the *Daily Express*. The universal presence of financial and business news supports the view that "non-metropolitan" is a very different classification than "Popular". An attempt was made to assess the extent to which this category of news related to agriculture and four papers emerged as measurably more "agricultural": *The Journal*, the *Yorkshire Post*, the *Eastern Daily Press* and the *Western Daily Press*. It is important to recall that a sizeable, though unknown, proportion of financial news does relate to local firms and businesses.

(v) According to Table A19, the papers are similar in broad attention to the main sorts of local news, although the "non-metropolitan" papers seem to use their additional space by concentrating more on political, social and economic news and on law and police matters. More detailed evidence in Table A20 shows up other points of interest in relation to regional news. We might first bear in mind that the lower attention in proportionate terms by the "metropolitan" papers is also a difference in space terms, since total news space is much the same in the main eleven titles. It is not easy to extract generalizations, but some tendencies are apparent. One is the general predominance of "economic" over "political" news (the average ratio is 7·5%: 6·7% for eleven titles). Another is a tendency for some large industrial city newspapers to report more labour news (Sheffield, Birmingham, Newcastle, Cardiff) and these are the four which lead in economic news. Thirdly, "non-metropolitan" papers seem distinctive in their interest in "events and activities" and for some titles, also "personalities". Perhaps the most striking impression is, nevertheless, one of similarity of basic patterns. Some newspapers, even so, seem to have individual specialities, for instance sport in the *Yorkshire Post*, politics in the *Morning Telegraph* and *Western Mail*, economic news in *The Birmingham Post*.

(vi) Feature space allocation (Table A21) shows the metropolitan papers to be strong in non-local features, especially *The Birmingham Post*. For papers with such content, the single most important component is usually "arts and entertainment", which includes book reviews and theatre and film criticism. The category of "political, social and economic" features does not really differentiate in any systematic way, although *The Birmingham Post* leads. If non-local and local "p.s.e." features are added together, the titles are more or less equal, with only the *Eastern Daily Press* coming very low. What we see is an inverse relation between "p.s.e." content which is non-local and that which is local (the more of the former, the less of the latter, and *vice-versa*). A comparison with Table A8 shows the proportion of such space to be generally lower than it is in the National Daily "Qualities" but higher than in the two National "Populars".

Features on local places and topography are a normal component of most newspapers, but space devoted to matters of specially local prices and consumer affairs is generally very low. Attention to *local* arts and entertainments seems to balance neglect of similar non-local content. Attention to local picture-features varies a good deal from title to title.

(vii) The last table relating to this group of titles (Table A22) indicates the general importance of some basic components of a newspaper: editorials, correspondence sections, competitions and offers. It seems as if editorial space and correspondence are correlated, in that a high allocation to one goes with a high allocation to another. The *Eastern Daily Press* and *Yorkshire Post* give most *space* to editorials and the former leads on correspondence. Topical cartoons are less important than in the national press and three titles had none at all on the dates sampled (*Liverpool Post, The Northern Echo, The Journal*). Strip or comic cartoons are also less common than in National Dailies.

(viii) To summarise:
- (a) The Provincial Morning newspapers examined are noticeably uniform in size, format and basic composition (with one exception). Advertising and news space is higher and feature space lower than in the National Daily papers. The relative homogeneity extends to most aspects of news and feature content profiles.
- (b) There is at least one continuum along which the papers seem to vary and this reflects the degree to which the newspapers concerned are "metropolitan" in character. It shows up particularly in the ratio of local to non-local news or feature content.
- (c) No equivalent to the "Quality-Popular" distinction can be seen. It is striking for instance, that almost all titles give rather similar space to political, social and economic news and the amount of external and financial news is high generally.

54

(d) In the broad category of political, social and economic news, it is the *economic* category which attracts most attention. This is consistent with the attention to financial news. The evidence is not presented, but it seems as if the National Daily Press is likely to give relatively more space to *political* news.

(e) In general, this analysis conveys the impression of a set of substantial newspapers, alternative in their regions to the national daily press, and offering a news and feature coverage which compares well in amount and diversity to the average of the national press.

# 4. Provincial Morning Newspapers, Scotland: Comparison Tables

## TABLE A24A

**SCOTTISH PROVINCIAL MORNING NEWSPAPERS, 1975:**
**ANALYSIS OF TOTAL SPACE INTO ADVERTISING AND FOUR CATEGORIES OF EDITORIAL SPACE**

| Category | The Scotsman | Glasgow Herald | Daily Record | Courier and Advertiser | The Press and Journal |
|---|---|---|---|---|---|
| | % | % | % | % | % |
| **Editorial Space:** | | | | | |
| News ... ... ... ... | 36 | 30 | 33 | 35 | 33 |
| Features ... ... ... | 13 | 13 | 15 | 5 | 9 |
| Other ... ... ... ... | 8 | 8 | 11 | 7 | 6 |
| Total ... ... ... | 57 | 51 | 59 | 47 | 48 |
| **Advertising** ... ... ... | 43 | 49 | 41 | 53 | 52 |
| TOTAL ... ... | 100 | 100 | 100 | 100 | 100 |
| Mean space per sample issue (col.cms.) | 9,261 | 9,264 | 5,817 | 8,746 | 8,404 |
| Pictures as % of editorial space | 9 | 10 | 20 | 11 | 22 |

## TABLE A24B

**SCOTTISH PROVINCIAL MORNING NEWSPAPERS, 1975:**
**ANALYSIS OF ADVERTISING SPACE INTO TWO CATEGORIES**

| Category | The Scotsman | Glasgow Herald | Daily Record | Courier and Advertiser | The Press and Journal |
|---|---|---|---|---|---|
| | % | % | % | % | % |
| Classified ... ... ... | 63 | 66 | 38 | 61 | 65 |
| Display ... ... ... ... | 37 | 34 | 62 | 39 | 35 |
| TOTAL ... ... | 100 | 100 | 100 | 100 | 100 |
| Mean advertising space (col.cms.) | 3,982 | 4,539 | 2,385 | 4,635 | 4,034 |
| Average number of pages per issue ... ... ... ... | 20·7 | 20·6 | 31·3 | 20·3 | 20·3 |

56

**TABLE A25**

SCOTTISH PROVINCIAL MORNING NEWSPAPERS, 1975:
ANALYSIS OF ALL NEWS SPACE INTO 14 CATEGORIES

| Category | The Scotsman | Glasgow Herald | Daily Record | Courier and Advertiser † | The Press and Journal † |
|---|---|---|---|---|---|
| | % | % | % | % | % |
| **National Home News:** | | | | | |
| 1. Political, social and economic | 6 | 5 | 2 | 6 | 3 |
| 2. Industrial relations | 2 | 2 | 2 | 3 | 1 |
| 3. Ulster crisis | 2 | 1 | 2 | 1 | 1 |
| 4. Law, police, accidents | 3 | 1 | 4 | 6 | 1 |
| 5. Sport | 6 | 9 | 27 | 13 | 13 |
| 6. Other | 2 | 1 | 3 | 7 | 2 |
| 7. Parliamentary debates | 2 | 1 | — | — | — |
| Total | 23 | 20 | 40 | 36 | 21 |
| **External News:** | | | | | |
| 8. Political, social and economic | 12 | 9 | 2 | 4 | 2 |
| 9. Other | 4 | 4 | 5 | 3 | 2 |
| Total | 16 | 13 | 7 | 7 | 4 |
| **Other: \*** | | | | | |
| 10. Financial/market (national, external and local) | 25 | 28 | 1 | 11 | 9 |
| **Provincial, regional and local:** | | | | | |
| 11. Political, social and economic | 16 | 15 | 13 | 8 | 18 |
| 12. Crime, police, accident | 4 | 5 | 12 | 6 | 6 |
| 13. Sport | 11 | 13 | 16 | 14 | 13 |
| 14. Other | 5 | 7 | 12 | 18 | 29 |
| Total | 36 | 40 | 53 | 46 | 66 |
| TOTAL | 100 | 101 | 101 | 100 | 100 |
| Mean news space per sample issue (col.cms.) | 3,336 | 2,758 | 1,897 | 3,018 | 2,811 |

\* Very small amounts of "miscellaneous" news, in no case reaching 0·5% for any paper, have been ignored in this table although they are included in the base on which percentages have been calculated.

† Figures for these titles are not directly comparable with others in respect of National and Provincial news for reasons given on p. 61.

**TABLE A26**

## SCOTTISH PROVINCIAL MORNING NEWSPAPERS, 1975:
## ANALYSIS OF PROVINCIAL, REGIONAL, AND LOCAL NEWS INTO 12 CATEGORIES

| Category | The Scotsman | Glasgow Herald | Daily Record | Courier and Advertiser | The Press and Journal |
|---|---|---|---|---|---|
| | % | % | % | % | % |
| 1. Political ... ... ... | 18 | 14 | 11 | 8 | 8 |
| 2. Economic ... ... ... | 9 | 15 | 5 | 4 | 10 |
| 3. Industrial relations ... | 5 | 3 | 4 | 1 | 2 |
| 4. Social services ... ... | 5 | 4 | 3 | 3 | 4 |
| 5. Planning, environment ... | 5 | 2 | 2 | 3 | 4 |
| 6. Crime, police ... ... | 10 | 11 | 19 | 7 | 5 |
| 7. Accidents ... ... ... | 2 | 2 | 4 | 6 | 4 |
| 8. Personalities ... ... | 5 | 5 | 14 | 18 | 23 |
| 9. Sport ... ... ... | 30 | 32 | 31 | 31 | 19 |
| 10. Events and activities ... | 3 | 2 | 1 | 12 | 11 |
| 11. Information ... ... | 3 | 4 | 1 | 2 | 2 |
| 12. Other local news ... ... | 4 | 6 | 6 | 6 | 7 |
| TOTAL ... ... | 99 | 100 | 101 | 101 | 99 |
| Mean space per sample issue ... (col.cms.) | 1,201 | 1,078 | 1,013 | 1,376 | 1,863 |

**TABLE A27**

**SCOTTISH PROVINCIAL MORNING NEWSPAPERS, 1975:**
**ANALYSIS OF FEATURE SPACE INTO 11 CATEGORIES**

| Category | The Scotsman | Glasgow Herald | Daily Record | Courier and Advertiser | The Press and Journal |
|---|---|---|---|---|---|
| | % | % | % | % | % |
| **Non-local features:** | | | | | |
| 1. Political, social and economic | 6 | 6 | 4 | — | 3 |
| 2. Arts and entertainments | 11 | 8 | 17 | 11 | 7 |
| 3. Other | 38 | 39 | 29 | 15 | 23 |
| Total ... | 55 | 53 | 50 | 26 | 33 |
| **Regional or local features:** | | | | | |
| 4. Political, social and economic | 15 | 5 | 4 | 4 | 4 |
| 5. Local places, topography | 5 | 3 | 2 | 3 | 17 |
| 6. Consumer, prices | — | 1 | 3 | — | — |
| 7. Personalities | 2 | 5 | 8 | 20 | 8 |
| 8. Sport | 3 | 2 | 12 | 5 | 5 |
| 9. Arts, reviews, entertainment ... | 12 | 14 | 1 | 3 | 10 |
| 10. Local picture feature ... | 3 | 1 | 2 | 10 | 16 |
| 11. Other | 6 | 16 | 5 | 29 | 7 |
| Total ... | 46 | 47 | 37 | 74 | 67 |
| TOTAL | 101 | 100 | 87* | 100 | 100 |
| Mean feature space per sample issue (col.cms.) | 1,183 | 1,194 | 1,141 | 447 | 719 |

* The balance of feature content in the *Daily Record* (13%) consisted of material classified as "sex-related". No other provincial morning paper had space so classified in the sample.

**TABLE A28**

**SCOTTISH PROVINCIAL MORNING NEWSPAPERS, 1975:**
**ANALYSIS OF OTHER EDITORIAL SPACE INTO NINE CATEGORIES**

| Category | The Scotsman | Glasgow Herald | Daily Record | Courier and Advertiser | The Press and Journal |
|---|---|---|---|---|---|
| | % | % | % | % | % |
| 1. Editorial comment ... | 11 | 10 | 12 | 11 | 6 |
| 2. Correspondence ... ... | 25 | 21 | 10 | 21 | 4 |
| 3. Topical cartoons ... ... | — | — | — | — | — |
| 4. Other cartoons ... ... | — | — | 6 | 9 | 9 |
| 5. Fiction and serialised books | — | — | 4 | 14 | — |
| 6. Puzzles, offers, competition | 11 | 7 | 21 | 5 | 24 |
| 4. Other regular information | 22 | 25 | 27 | 27 | 22 |
| 8. Miscellaneous ... ... | 15 | 7 | 11 | 5 | 19 |
| 9. Headings and titles ... | 16 | 30 | 9 | 9 | 16 |
| TOTAL ... ... | 100 | 100 | 100 | 101 | 100 |
| Mean space per sample issue (col.cms.) ... ... ... | 741 | 806 | 819 | 613 | 491 |

## 5. Provincial Morning Newspapers, Scotland: Commentary

(i) With a sample comparable to that for the English Provincial newspapers, the following Scottish newspapers were examined:

| Title | Place | Circulation |
|---|---|---|
| The Scotsman | Edinburgh | 88,209 (1975) |
| Glasgow Herald | Glasgow | 95,657 (1974) |
| Daily Record | Glasgow | 626,870 (1975) |
| Courier and Advertiser | Dundee | 130,003 (1975) |
| The Press and Journal | Aberdeen | 100,748 (1975) |

In addition, the *Scottish Daily News* was initially included, but its interruption of publication in November, 1975 prevented the conclusion of the study. Some brief conclusions, based on an analysis of six issues are, however, included in this report (Appendix A14).

In discussing the Scottish newspapers, the *Courier and Advertiser* and *The Press and Journal* will have to be treated separately, since a different policy was applied in the allocation of news space between "National" and "Provincial" categories. In the case of these two papers, non-local (ie non-city and immediate region) news, but still relating to Scotland, was classified as "National". For the other three papers, the "National" category only relates to United Kingdom news in general and all Scottish news is "provincial, regional or local". The distinction between the two sets of papers is very evident on other matters. Clearly, the *Courier and Advertiser* and *The Press and Journal* are very much "non-metropolitan".

(ii) Table A24A shows the *Daily Record* to be notably smaller in size than the other two metropolitan papers, but the basic division of space is very similar. The *Daily Record* is, however, much more pictorial, with 20% of its editorial space consisting of pictures, well above the figure for the *Daily Mirror* and *The Sun*. The *Courier and Advertiser* and *The Press and Journal* differ most evidently in the large amount of advertising, a difference which goes with a lower allocation of space to features. The Aberdeen paper is unusually high on picture content—more than a fifth of its editorial space.

The distribution of news in general (Table A25) shows, firstly the clear difference between the *Daily Record* on the one hand and *The Scotsman* and *Glasgow Herald* (which have very similar profiles) on the other. The *Daily Record* gives almost no space to financial news, rather little to external news, more to crime and accident news, more to sport (especially "National") and less to National, political, social and economic news. Again Ulster and industrial relations take the same (rather low) place in all three papers. The distribution of space in *The Scotsman* and *Glasgow Herald* is not unlike that for the two main metropolitan provincial papers (*The Birmingham Post* and *Yorkshire Post*), although there is rather more financial and market news. The *Daily Record* has no parallel in an English provincial newspaper and is closer to the pattern for the *Daily Mirror* or *The Sun*.

The *Courier and Advertiser* and *The Press and Journal* do not appear, on this overall news comparison, very different from the "metropolitan" titles, although external news is low. The other differences are mainly accounted for by the variation in coding policy described above. When this is taken into account, it is evident that there must be very little non-Scottish news in these papers and also a very high concentration on the city and its region. The two titles seem only to differ in the greater focus of the Aberdeen paper on political, social and economic news. The detailed breakdown of local news in Table A26 shows this to be accounted for mainly by a much higher level of economic news coverage. Both papers have high proportions of financial news and in both a fair amount is agricultural or fishing news.

(iv) Table A26 brings out further distinctive features of the "metropolitan" Scottish newspapers as a group. They each have more local political and labour news than the other two and also more local crime and less personality news. The average amount of local news in each case is also lower than in the other pair. The differences in local news coverage are not very great according to this comparison, apart from the *Daily Record*'s lower attention to economic news and greater interest in crime and personalities. The latter paper would also seem less locally oriented, on the criteria of reporting local events and activities and providing local information. Again, it would seem that even in dealing with regional matters the *Daily Record* has some of the characteristic tendencies of the National popular press.

The *Courier and Advertiser* and *The Press and Journal* reflect their identification with town and region by giving much space to local sport, other events and activities, and to personality news. Otherwise the profiles are very similar. The lack of coverage of industrial relations matters is noticable, however, although it matches the relative disinterest of the typical non-metropolitan English provincial newspaper, to which these two titles are very similar.

Table A27 shows up clearly the difference between "metropolitan" and "non-metropolitan" titles, with the former giving more space altogether and much higher proportions of it to non-local subjects or from non-local sources. The *Daily Record* is especially low in its attention to local features and much of what is there is sport or personality news, with little political, social, or economic or local arts and entertainments. *The Scotsman* and *Glasgow Herald* are broadly similar, although the former gives much space to Scottish political, social and economic matters. As the footnote to Table A27 indicates, the *Daily Record* includes a largish component of sex-related features.

(v) Feature content in the other two papers is distinguished mainly by the low quantities of political, social economic content (as in most English provincial morning papers). The absence of features on consumer or price matters is similarly typical of the provincial morning newspaper in general, as is the attention to local personalities. Table A28 shows the *Daily Record* to vary in the expected direction of the popular newspaper towards more puzzles, offers and cartoons. Editorial comment and correspondence columns are quite prominent in all titles, except for *The Press* and *Journal* which gives little space to either.

(vi) The general impression left by this analysis is of some diversity. If a comparison is made with the English press, it seems as if *The Scotsman* and the *Glasgow Herald* are close in content to an English "metropolitan" like the *Yorkshire Post*, the *Daily Record* to an English popular paper, the *Courier and Advertiser* to an English "non-metropolitan" provincial paper, and *The Press and Journal* to an even more "local" paper.

# V  Analysis of Provincial Evening Newspapers

## 1  Provincial Evening Newspapers: Comparison Tables

### TABLE A29

**PROVINCIAL EVENING NEWSPAPERS, 1975:**
**ANALYSIS OF TOTAL PRINT INTO ADVERTISING AND THREE CATEGORIES OF EDITORIAL SPACE**

| Category | Bradford Telegraph & Argus | Cambridge Evening News | Darlington Evening Despatch | Derby Evening Telegraph | Gloucester The Citizen | Leeds Evening Post | Liverpool Echo | Newcastle Evening Chronicle | Reading Evening Post | Worcester Evening News | Wrexham Evening Leader | Glasgow Evening Times |
|---|---|---|---|---|---|---|---|---|---|---|---|---|
| | % | % | % | % | % | % | % | % | % | % | % | % |
| **Editorial Space:** | | | | | | | | | | | | |
| News | 25 | 23 | 37 | 23 | 22 | 20 | 23 | 20 | 24 | 28 | 40 | 19 |
| Features | 12 | 9 | 17 | 12 | 7 | 8 | 9 | 9 | 7 | 10 | 13 | 12 |
| Other editorial space | 8 | 9 | 13 | 8 | 5 | 9 | 10 | 8 | 10 | 7 | 14 | 11 |
| Total | 45 | 41 | 67 | 43 | 34 | 37 | 42 | 37 | 41 | 45 | 67 | 42 |
| **Advertising** | 55 | 59 | 33 | 57 | 66 | 63 | 58 | 63 | 59 | 55 | 33 | 58 |
| TOTAL | 100 | 100 | 100 | 100 | 100 | 100 | 100 | 100 | 100 | 100 | 100 | 100 |
| Mean total space per sample issue (col.cms.) | 9,486 | 7,528 | 4,156 | 7,018 | 6,020 | 9,936 | 8,798 | 9,060 | 7,856 | 6,668 | 5,110 | 7,056 |

# TABLE A30A
## PROVINCIAL EVENING NEWSPAPERS, 1975:
## ANALYSIS OF ADVERTISING SPACE INTO TWO CATEGORIES

| Category | Bradford Telegraph & Argus | Cambridge Evening News | Darlington Evening Despatch | Derby Evening Telegraph | Gloucester The Citizen | Leeds Evening Post | Liverpool Echo | Newcastle Evening Chronicle | Reading Evening Post | Worcester Evening News | Wrexham Evening Leader | Glasgow Evening Times |
|---|---|---|---|---|---|---|---|---|---|---|---|---|
| | % | % | % | % | % | % | % | % | % | % | % | % |
| Classified Advertising... | 62 | 35 | 40 | 57 | 44 | 62 | 66 | 63 | 63 | 45 | 70 | 51 |
| Display Advertising ... | 38 | 65 | 60 | 43 | 56 | 38 | 34 | 37 | 37 | 55 | 30 | 49 |
| TOTAL ... ... | 100 | 100 | 100 | 100 | 100 | 100 | 100 | 100 | 100 | 100 | 100 | 100 |
| Mean advertising space per sample issue (col.cms.) ... | 5,278 | 4,460 | 1,368 | 3,971 | 3,968 | 6,302 | 5,133 | 5,708 | 4,663 | 3,676 | 1,673 | 4,079 |

# TABLE A30B
## PROVINCIAL EVENING NEWSPAPERS, 1975:
## ANALYSIS OF PICTURE CONTENT AS PERCENTAGE OF EDITORIAL SPACE

| Category | Bradford Telegraph & Argus | Cambridge Evening News | Darlington Evening Despatch | Derby Evening Telegraph | Gloucester The Citizen | Leeds Evening Post | Liverpool Echo | Newcastle Evening Chronicle | Reading Evening Post | Worcester Evening News | Wrexham Evening Leader | Glasgow Evening Times |
|---|---|---|---|---|---|---|---|---|---|---|---|---|
| | % | % | % | % | % | % | % | % | % | % | % | % |
| Picture Content ... ... | 17 | 18 | 15 | 19 | 13 | 11 | 15 | 12 | 18 | 17 | 14 | 19 |
| Mean picture space per sample issue (col.cms.) ... ... ... | 697 | 566 | 425 | 572 | 266 | 404 | 531 | 427 | 595 | 502 | 494 | 563 |

TABLE A31
PROVINCIAL EVENING NEWSPAPERS, 1975:
ANALYSIS OF ALL NEWS SPACE INTO 14 CATEGORIES*

| Category | Bradford Telegraph & Argus % | Cambridge Evening News % | Darlington Evening Despatch % | Derby Evening Telegraph % | Gloucester The Citizen % | Leeds Evening Post % | Liverpool Echo % | Newcastle Evening Chronicle % | Reading Evening Post % | Worcester Evening News % | Wrexham Evening Leader % | Glasgow Evening Times % |
|---|---|---|---|---|---|---|---|---|---|---|---|---|
| **National Home News:** | | | | | | | | | | | | |
| 1. Political, social and economic | 2 | 1 | 2 | 1 | — | 1 | 2 | 3 | 1 | 2 | 10 | 10 |
| 2. Industrial relations | 2 | — | 1 | 1 | 2 | — | 1 | 2 | 3 | 1 | 3 | 1 |
| 3. Ulster crisis | 1 | 1 | 1 | 1 | — | 1 | — | 2 | 3 | 1 | 1 | 1 |
| 4. Law and police | 1 | 1 | 1 | 1 | 2 | 1 | 2 | 3 | 2 | — | 7 | 4 |
| 5. Sport | 11 | 17 | 16 | 10 | 9 | 10 | 12 | 12 | 9 | 16 | 15 | 8 |
| 6. Other | 4 | 1 | 3 | 1 | 3 | 2 | 6 | 6 | 6 | 4 | 5 | 7 |
| 7. Parliamentary debates | — | — | — | — | — | — | — | — | — | — | — | — |
| Total | 21 | 20 | 24 | 15 | 17 | 15 | 23 | 28 | 24 | 24 | 41 | 31 |
| **External News:** | | | | | | | | | | | | |
| 8. Political, social and economic | 1 | 2 | 2 | 3 | 3 | 1 | 3 | 3 | 6 | 2 | 4 | 7 |
| 9. Other | 2 | 1 | 3 | 8 | 2 | 3 | 4 | 2 | 5 | 3 | 6 | 3 |
| Total | 3 | 3 | 5 | 11 | 5 | 4 | 7 | 5 | 11 | 5 | 10 | 10 |
| **Other:** | | | | | | | | | | | | |
| 10. Financial/Market news (national, external, local) | 4 | 3 | 2 | 1 | 1 | 3 | 2 | 3 | 2 | 2 | 1 | 6 |
| **Provincial, Regional and Local:** | | | | | | | | | | | | |
| 11. Political, social and economic | 18 | 24 | 15 | 16 | 15 | 18 | 15 | 21 | 18 | 27 | 7 | 10 |
| 12. Crime, police, accident | 11 | 9 | 7 | 16 | 12 | 22 | 13 | 13 | 12 | 7 | 5 | 13 |
| 13. Sport | 16 | 19 | 21 | 21 | 28 | 13 | 21 | 15 | 17 | 17 | 16 | 19 |
| 14. Other | 27 | 21 | 26 | 20 | 22 | 25 | 19 | 15 | 16 | 18 | 20 | 11 |
| Total | 72 | 73 | 69 | 73 | 77 | 78 | 68 | 64 | 63 | 69 | 48 | 53 |
| TOTAL | 100 | 99 | 100 | 100 | 100 | 100 | 100 | 100 | 100 | 100 | 100 | 100 |
| Mean news space per sample issue (col.cms.) | 2,335 | 1,757 | 1,530 | 1,647 | 1,340 | 1,930 | 1,981 | 1,854 | 1,851 | 1,833 | 2,021 | 1,333 |

* Very small amounts of "miscellaneous" news, in no case reaching 0.5% for any paper, have been ignored in this table although they are included in the base on which percentages have been calculated.

65

**TABLE A32**

**PROVINCIAL EVENING NEWSPAPERS, 1975:**
**ANALYSIS OF PROVINCIAL REGIONAL AND LOCAL NEWS INTO 12 CATEGORIES**

| Category | Bradford Telegraph & Argus % | Cambridge Evening News % | Darlington Evening Despatch % | Derby Evening Telegraph % | Gloucester The Citizen % | Leeds Evening Post % | Liverpool Echo % | Newcastle Evening Chronicle % | Reading Evening Post % | Worcester Evening News % | Wrexham Evening Leader % | Glasgow Evening Times % |
|---|---|---|---|---|---|---|---|---|---|---|---|---|
| 1. Political | 7 | 10 | 6 | 6 | 3 | 5 | 10 | 11 | 10 | 14 | 4 | 6 |
| 2. Economic | 5 | 5 | 2 | 3 | 2 | 2 | 1 | 3 | 2 | 6 | 1 | 4 |
| 3. Industrial, labour relations | 1 | 2 | 3 | 4 | 3 | 2 | 4 | 6 | 3 | 2 | 3 | 4 |
| 4. Social services | 6 | 7 | 5 | 5 | 5 | 6 | 4 | 6 | 7 | 5 | 3 | 1 |
| 5. Planning and environment | 5 | 9 | 5 | 4 | 6 | 9 | 3 | 6 | 7 | 11 | 4 | 3 |
| 6. Local crime and police | 14 | 10 | 9 | 17 | 15 | 26 | 14 | 16 | 15 | 9 | 8 | 23 |
| 7. Accidents | 2 | 3 | 2 | 5 | 1 | 3 | 4 | 4 | 3 | 1 | 1 | 2 |
| 8. Personalities | 16 | 11 | 8 | 9 | 7 | 7 | 9 | 8 | 3 | 9 | 10 | 9 |
| 9. Local sport | 23 | 26 | 31 | 29 | 37 | 16 | 32 | 24 | 27 | 25 | 33 | 36 |
| 10. Events and activities | 8 | 6 | 8 | 11 | 14 | 9 | 6 | 4 | 12 | 5 | 6 | 3 |
| 11. Information | 7 | 4 | 13 | 4 | 4 | 3 | 4 | 5 | 5 | 4 | 21 | 5 |
| 12. Other local news | 6 | 7 | 8 | 3 | 3 | 12 | 9 | 7 | 6 | 9 | 6 | 4 |
| TOTAL | 100 | 100 | 100 | 100 | 100 | 100 | 100 | 100 | 100 | 100 | 100 | 100 |
| Mean local news space per sample issue (col.cms.) | 1,704 | 1,282 | 1,058 | 1,198 | 1,038 | 1,502 | 1,336 | 1,182 | 1,178 | 1,260 | 956 | 712 |

# TABLE A33

## PROVINCIAL EVENING NEWSPAPERS, 1975: ANALYSIS OF FEATURE SPACE INTO 11 CATEGORIES

| Category | Bradford Telegraph & Argus % | Cambridge Evening News % | Darlington Evening Despatch % | Derby Evening Telegraph % | Gloucester The Citizen % | Leeds Evening Post % | Liverpool Echo % | Newcastle Evening Chronicle % | Reading Evening Post % | Worcester Evening News % | Wrexham Evening Leader % | Glasgow Evening Times % |
|---|---|---|---|---|---|---|---|---|---|---|---|---|
| **Non-Local Features:** | | | | | | | | | | | | |
| 1. Political, social and economic | 9 | 2 | 13 | 4 | — | 6 | 4 | — | 7 | 5 | 2 | 3 |
| 2. Arts and entertainment | 17 | 11 | 12 | 16 | 13 | 12 | 17 | 17 | 9 | 15 | 13 | 17 |
| 3. All other features | 14 | 34 | 22 | 23 | 23 | 19 | 14 | 46 | 46 | 15 | 39 | 44 |
| Total... | 40 | 47 | 47 | 43 | 36 | 37 | 35 | 63 | 62 | 35 | 54 | 64 |
| **Regional/Local Features:** | | | | | | | | | | | | |
| 4. Political, social and economic | 8 | 2 | 9 | 2 | 7 | 2 | 15 | 1 | — | 13 | 2 | 5 |
| 5. Local topography | 5 | 1 | 1 | 10 | 9 | — | 2 | 4 | 2 | 4 | — | — |
| 6. Consumer/prices | 5 | 3 | 6 | 1 | — | 3 | 9 | 4 | 2 | 4 | — | 1 |
| 7. Personalities | 10 | 4 | 7 | 7 | 6 | 9 | 11 | 4 | 14 | 16 | — | 14 |
| 8. Sport | 7 | 1 | 5 | 3 | 7 | 13 | 3 | 4 | 2 | 4 | 2 | 2 |
| 9. Arts and entertainment | 12 | 10 | 12 | 11 | 1 | 4 | 3 | 2 | 5 | 4 | 6 | 5 |
| 10. Local picture features | 5 | 7 | 4 | 7 | 10 | — | 5 | 4 | 2 | 2 | — | 2 |
| 11. Other features... | 8 | 25 | 9 | 16 | 24 | 32 | 17 | 14 | 11 | 18 | 36 | 7 |
| Total... | 60 | 53 | 53 | 57 | 64 | 63 | 65 | 37 | 38 | 65 | 46 | 36 |
| TOTAL | 100 | 100 | 100 | 100 | 100 | 100 | 100 | 100 | 100 | 100 | 100 | 100 |
| Mean feature space per sample issue... (col.cms.) | 1,116 | 664 | 704 | 854 | 396 | 800 | 798 | 802 | 572 | 700 | 670 | 890 |

# TABLE A34

## PROVINCIAL EVENING NEWSPAPERS, 1975:
## ANALYSIS OF OTHER EDITORIAL SPACE INTO NINE CATEGORIES

| Category | Bradford Telegraph & Argus % | Cambridge Evening News % | Darlington Evening Despatch % | Derby Evening Telegraph % | Gloucester The Citizen % | Leeds Evening Post % | Liverpool Echo % | Newcastle Evening Chronicle % | Reading Evening Post % | Worcester Evening News % | Wrexham Evening Leader % | Glasgow Evening Times % |
|---|---|---|---|---|---|---|---|---|---|---|---|---|
| 1. Editorial comment | 5 | 6 | 5 | — | — | 1 | 7 | 1 | 1 | 5 | 3 | 4 |
| 2. Letters | 15 | 14 | 12 | 15 | 11 | 17 | 9 | 16 | 9 | 11 | 4 | 13 |
| 3. Topical cartoons | — | — | — | — | — | — | — | — | — | — | — | — |
| 4. Comic cartoons | 11 | 3 | 7 | 9 | 4 | 6 | 3 | 4 | 3 | 5 | 14 | 18 |
| 5. Fiction | — | 1 | — | 3 | 3 | — | — | — | — | — | — | — |
| 6. Puzzles, competitions and offers | 17 | 11 | 22 | 19 | 10 | 30 | 26 | 24 | 33 | 10 | 10 | 19 |
| 7. Other regular information | 22 | 25 | 27 | 25 | 34 | 21 | 18 | 31 | 24 | 33 | 23 | 18 |
| 8. Miscellaneous editorial space | 19 | 32 | 15 | 16 | 12 | 15 | 24 | 17 | 23 | 19 | 22 | 15 |
| 9. Headings and titles | 11 | 8 | 12 | 13 | 26 | 10 | 13 | 7 | 7 | 17 | 24 | 13 |
| TOTAL | 100 | 100 | 100 | 100 | 100 | 100 | 100 | 100 | 100 | 100 | 100 | 100 |
| Mean other editorial space per sample issue (col.cms) | 756 | 644 | 556 | 554 | 356 | 904 | 886 | 727 | 770 | 460 | 746 | 752 |

## 2. Provincial Evening Newspapers: Commentary

(i) Twelve titles out of approximately 82 provincial evening newspapers were chosen on grounds discussed in section I, 3 (iv). They do not form a representative sample and the issues studied relate only to one complete week, that of 3 to 7 November 1975. Consequently, the findings can only be taken as broadly indicative of evening newspaper content and as a basis for comparison between particular titles. However, some well-known city newspapers have been included and the papers are drawn from a range of different locations and include papers of widely varying circulation size and different forms of ownership. The actual titles and circulation sizes were as follows:

| Title | Circulation | Ownership |
|---|---|---|
| Bradford *Telegraph and Argus* | 115,217 (1975) | Westminster |
| *Cambridge Evening News* | 50,189 (1974) | Independent |
| Darlington *Evening Despatch* | 18,473 (1975) | Westminster |
| *Derby Evening Telegraph* | 93,658 (1975) | Associated Newspapers |
| Gloucester *The Citizen* | 40,869 (1974) | Associated Newspapers |
| Leeds *Evening Post* | 201,131 (1975) | Yorkshire Newspapers Limited |
| *Liverpool Echo* | 311,705 (1975) | Liverpool Post & Echo Limited |
| Newcastle *Evening Chronicle* | 98,703 (1974) | Thomson |
| Reading *Evening Post* | 49,690 (1974) | Thomson |
| Worcester *Evening News* | 37,748 (1974) | News International |
| Wrexham *Evening Leader* | 12,684 (1974) | N. Wales Newspapers |
| Glasgow *Evening Times* | 235,775 (1974) | SUITS |

A grouping either according to circulation size, or to location, suggests itself. In the former case we have three titles above 200,000, three between 90,000 and 200,000, four around 40,000 and two with notably small circulation. If the papers are divided according to location, we might distinguish five papers from large industrial cities, four from country towns and three others (Darlington, Wrexham, Reading). In the event, as we will see, neither basis for classification seems to show up in the pattern of content. Nor does common ownership appear to be related to similarities of content as revealed in these tables. The analysis which follows results from the application of the same coding frame as for the Provincial Morning Newspapers, which is reproduced above in IV, 1 and discussed in Appendix A12.

(ii) The overall structure of the newspapers is shown in Tables A29, A30A and A30B. Advertising (at 55% of space) plays a large part, much more so than in provincial morning or national daily newspapers. The two titles with low advertising ratios are the two with lowest circulations. Most advertising is classified (mean proportion 59%) but there is some variation. In terms of overall editorial space, the papers are not dissimilar, although the big city papers are generally somewhat larger. The ratio of news to features is also similar as between titles, comparable also to the Provincial Mornings, with a ratio of about $2\frac{1}{2}$ to 1. The proportion of editorial space given to pictures is higher than any of the groups of papers looked at so far in this report, with an average figure of 15·5%, compared to 11·5% for provincial mornings.

(iii) The distribution and amount of news (Table A31) again suggests a general similarity with the morning provincial paper. However, there is a noticeably higher allocation of space to local rather than national news. Here the average proportion of all news space for the 12 titles (and they do not vary greatly) given to national home news is 23%, while for 11 of the English provincial morning titles, the comparable figure was 34%. It is worth noting that external news is not unduly neglected, although some papers give more than others, with the Derby, Reading, Wrexham and Glasgow papers rating at the level of the "metropolitan" provincial morning newspapers. Since the papers all date from the same week, the differences cannot easily be accounted for except in terms of varying newspaper policy. All newspapers carry some financial news but the amounts are very small and are, on average, well below the figures for the provincial morning papers.

Much of the relatively small amount of national news goes to sport—a majority, in fact, in all but four of the papers looked at. Correlatively, national, political social and economic news is often negligible in amount and a high proportion of what is there is about industrial relations. There are two notable exceptions—the Wrexham *Evening Leader* and Glasgow *Evening Times* which each give 10% of news to national home political, social and economic content. The allocation of local news to different categories is rather similar between papers and follows the basic pattern set by the Provincial Mornings (Table A20). More detailed evidence on this can be seen from Table A32.

(iv) Reporting of local events, personalities and crime and police news is a noticeable feature of all titles and can be regarded as a characteristic aspect of a more locally minded newspaper. The allocation of space between the sub-categories of political, social and economic news is similar in overall structure and amount to the provincial morning newspapers (Table A20). There seems to be a good deal of variation between titles in the amount of space given to political news, the leading papers in this respect being from Worcester, Newcastle, Liverpool, Reading and Cambridge. Since coverage may vary according to local political happenings in one week, we cannot conclude much more from these figures about newspaper policy and the same applies to the variable allocation of space to planning and environmental matters.

(v) The remaining content of evening newspapers is dealt with in Tables A33 and A34. The proportion of feature space given to political, social and economic matters as a whole is at least as high on average as in the provincial morning papers and again a few titles seem to "score" especially high—those from Darlington (22%), Liverpool (19%), Bradford (17%) and Worcester (18%). The titles from Wrexham, Newcastle and Cambridge, on the other hand, only have figures of 4%, 1% and 4% respectively. Taking regional features on their own, some newspapers seem to give special attention to this sort of content: especially the *Liverpool Echo* and the Worcester *Evening News*. Content given to local consumer and price matters seems to have a reasonable place in most newspapers, with only two of the 12 titles omitting it in the sampled week. The most striking conclusion to be drawn from Table A34 is the very low allocation of space to editorial comment: five titles give 1% or less space to this, and the average allocation in space terms is very small indeed. The contrast with provincial morning newspapers is sharp. Correspondence, however, is given extensive space in the Evening Newspapers. Finally, we can note the importance of cartoons, puzzles, offers, etc. Together, the two categories account for an average 27% of this part of newspaper space.

(vi) A summary of points to emerge from this brief look at Evening News-papers as a category, as represented by this sample, might include the following:

(a) Advertising takes up a very high proportion of space in most news-papers and the balance between classified and other advertising is related to circulation size—the larger the circulation, the more classified (a reverse of the National Daily pattern).

(b) In overall structure, the papers looked at are rather similar to each other and to the Provincial Morning papers. This is particularly true of the balance between news and features.

(c) Picture content is generally high.

(d) There is a low proportion of national news in most papers and sport predominates. External news is relatively well represented.

(e) Two or three titles stand out as more diverse and less locally oriented in news coverage: eg, Wrexham *Evening Leader*, Glasgow *Evening Times*, Reading *Evening Post*.

(f) Attention to consumer and price matters generally quite high.

(g) About half the titles looked at give little or no space to formal editorialising.

(h) Neither size nor ownership seems systematically related to "performance" according to these content criteria.

# VI  Analysis of Local Weekly Newspapers

## 1. Coding frame for local weekly newspapers

The categories employed for analysing the local weekly newspapers were chosen on the basis of a preliminary analysis of a set of the newspapers to be studied. The resulting coding frame reflects the main different sorts of subject matter and of format of such newspapers, while allowing an overall comparison of space distribution with other kinds of paper. Some new categories have been devised for this study. For example local *political* content has been separated out from local council business which contains no such reference, on the assumption that there is a qualitative difference between these two sorts of coverage and that the former may indicate a more active reporting policy. The allocation of space to news concerning local M.P.s has also been measured. Coverage of local social services and social welfare has also been examined in more detail, with an attempt to distinguish between voluntary and statutory social services and to pick out "social problems", where this is the focus of reporting. Such content may be an indication of the "watchdog" activity of a local newspaper, although, of course, it may only reflect a preference for "negative" news.

Otherwise, the categories are largely self-explanatory and follow the pattern already established in other analyses presented in this report. Some new categories have been added to reflect the particular circumstances of the local weekly paper, for instance the large attention to activities and events by local groups or the common tendency for a weekly newspaper to collect miscellaneous news items from outlying villages and to present them in a single format. The classification of local features follows the pattern of the provincial morning newspaper analysis and here the consumer/price category might be looked at as an indication of the way a paper performs a service to its readers. The "advertising feature" is quite commonly found in weekly newspapers and this has been separately coded and measured. There are cases where, in presenting results, distinctions built into the coding frame have not been reflected in compiling tables for the sake of clarity of presentation. However, the commentary on the analysis incorporates any points which might usefully be made on such matters, even if the evidence is not presented.

## CODING FRAME FOR LOCAL WEEKLIES

### 1.0.  LOCAL NEWS
(All local *and* regional news.)

1.1.    POLITICAL
Matters concerning local politics and local government, where the main focus is on parties, politicians, elections, party organisation, inter-party relations, political appeals to public and vice versa.

72

1.1N.   *National politics locally*, including news and views of
local M.P.s, their doings in parliament, etc. In Wales
and Scotland news to do with devolution, nationalism
will be included.

(NOTE: These two categories will include items which might otherwise
have been included elsewhere—eg appointments, personality items,
reports of events, crimes by M.P.s, etc. If in doubt between political and
other coding, give precedence to the political.)

1.11.   ADMINISTRATIVE AND FINANCIAL
Council and local authority business not included elsewhere,
where procedural, administrative and financial aspects predominate over the substantive references to particular services,
etc. Also to include financial and administrative matters to do
with major public services such as water, power, transport.

1.12.   ECONOMIC
Industrial and agricultural news relating to locality or region of
paper; local employment matters; new developments and
closures; production and orders; land and property matters.
Includes local market and price news.

1.12L.  *Industrial/Labour Relations*
Disputes, settlements, local trade union matters, whether
in industry or agriculture. Industrial safety and health
matters.

1.13.   SOCIAL SERVICES
News of local social services where the substance of a report
concerns the service provided and the public, rather than
administrative, political, business or financial aspects. Includes:
matters to do with race and community relations; social welfare
and social work; local public transport where issue is social, not
financial; the major social services of health, housing, education,
recreation. Internal local social administrative matters go here,
eg, local health service boards, public consumer associations.
Also news concerning nationalised industries and public utilities
where service to public is involved.

1.13V.  *Voluntary social service activity* including events, fund-
raising, meetings. This category is mainly confined to
organisations concerned with social welfare (health,
children, old people, destitute, disabled, etc). Some of
this activity will be carried out by organisations and clubs
which are not solely welfare organisations, eg, Rotary
Clubs, Lions, Churches, etc.

73

1.13P.  *Local Social Problems*
News relating to social problems (normally concerning social services), where focus is on the exposure or evidence of *need*, rather than on the service actually being provided. Examples might include reports of juvenile delinquency in particular areas, old people alone, poorly equipped hospitals, itinerants, etc.

1.14.  PLANNING, ENVIRONMENT AND TRAFFIC
Reports on planning enquiries, development requests and plans, local protests. Road and traffic schemes and problems. Structure plans and town and country planning generally. Housing where development has environmental implications. Pollution, threats to (or improvement of) local amenities. Loss of shopping or other commercial facilities (eg, cinemas).

1.2.  CRIME AND POLICE
News from courts and police, reports of crimes, vandalism, etc; police administrative news. (Political terrorism news coded as 2.0.)

1.3.  ACCIDENTS
News of all accidents, missing persons, fires and damage, natural disasters, missing persons, sudden deaths (where biographical aspect is not prominent) and injuries. Includes accidents to animals.

1.4.  PERSONALITIES
Local people in the news. Social events where guests provide main news interest. News of deaths, marriages, engagements, travel, appointments, exam results, prizes and awards. National celebrities in the local news.

1.5.  LOCAL SPORT

1.6.  EVENTS AND ACTIVITIES
News of, and reports from, local events where the event rather than participants provides main focus of news; this includes meetings and activities of local clubs and societies, festivals, concerts, drama, fairs and sales, church services, competitions, dances, fund-raising, community council and association meetings.

(NOTE: This category excludes those events coded elsewhere either under "political", "sport", "voluntary social service", "local news in brief" or "around the district" column.)

1.7.  INFORMATION
Notices of local events and other specific local information, like tide times, road closures, church services, etc.

1.8.  REGIONAL LANGUAGE
Items in local language (Welsh) or dialect.

1.91.   AROUND THE DISTRICT COLUMN
Small items of news collected together under the heading of particular localities or under a single heading.

1.92.   OTHER LOCAL NEWS
Items in brief; human interest; miscellaneous items; religious news not covered elsewhere; military news.

## 2.0. NATIONAL OR EXTERNAL NEWS
News from or about the U.K. generally or the rest of the world which has no particular references to the local area.

## 3.0. NON-LOCAL FEATURES
All features with no specific local reference.

## 4.0. LOCAL FEATURES

4.1.   POLITICAL, SOCIAL OR ECONOMIC
Features dealing with the subjects mainly covered under categories 1.1, 1.1N, 1.11, 1.12, 1.12L, 1.13, 1.13V, 1.13P, 1.14, 1.3.

4.1F.   *Local Farming Features*

4.2.   LOCAL TOPOGRAPHICAL AND LEISURE
Features about places to visit, things to do, local life and amenities, environment and things of interest. Include nature notes, local history and archaeology, extracts from the paper in the past (eg, 25 years ago). Features about local weather also.

4.3.   CONSUMER/PRICES
Advice to shoppers and other matters of consumer interest relating to shops, services, housing, etc. (excludes advertising features).

4.4.   PERSONALITIES AND ASSOCIATIONS
Features about local people, including local gossip or "social life" columns. Also includes features on local clubs and associations.

4.5.   SPORT
Local sport features.

4.6.   ARTS, ENTERTAINMENTS, REVIEWS
Books, theatre, music, etc.

4.71.   WOMEN'S FEATURES
Includes cooking, dressmaking, housewifery, fashion.

4.72.   CHILDREN'S FEATURES

4.8.   LOCAL PICTURE FEATURES

4.9.   OTHER FEATURES
Including mixed features.

## 5.0. OTHER EDITORIAL SPACE

### 5.1. EDITORIAL COMMENT

### 5.2. LETTERS

### 5.3. HEADINGS AND TITLES

### 5.5. CARTOONS

### 5.6. FICTION AND SERIALISED BOOKS

### 5.7. PUZZLES, COMPETITIONS AND OFFERS

### 5.8. OTHER REGULAR INFORMATION
Radio and T.V. programmes; weather forecasts; horoscopes, etc.

### 5.9. MISCELLANEOUS EDITORIAL SPACE
Index, order forms, advertisement index; publication particulars; subscription and advertising rates; blank spaces; news of coming attractions in the paper.

## 6.0. ADVERTISEMENTS AND OTHER SPACE
Items which were considered to have been paid for by outside firms or individuals.

### 6.1. CLASSIFIED ADVERTISING
All advertisements gathered under general subject matter headings.

### 6.2. DISPLAY ADVERTISING
All other advertising content.

6.2F. *Advertising Features*

## 8.0. NEWS AND FEATURES OF SEX INTEREST
Includes pin-up photos.

## 9.0. PICTURE CONTENT

## 2. Local Weekly Newspapers: Comparison Tables

TABLE A35   ANALYSIS OF TOTAL SPACE OF 28 LOCAL WEEKLY NEWSPAPERS INTO FIVE CATEGORIES

|  | GROUP A Merseyside | | | GROUP B Strathclyde | | | |
|---|---|---|---|---|---|---|---|
| Category | Southport Visiter | Maghull Times | Maghull and Aintree Advertiser | Clydebank Press | Govan Press | East Kilbride News | Kilmarnock Standard |
|  | % | % | % | % | % | % | % |
| 1. News | 19 | 28 | 27 | 30 | 50 | 23 | 15 |
| 2. Features | 7 | 6 | 6 | 4 | 7 | 5 | 8 |
| 3. Other editorial | 7 | 6 | 6 | 5 | 10 | 7 | 5 |
| 4. Advertising | 67 | 60 | 62 | 61 | 33 | 65 | 72 |
| TOTAL | 100 | 100 | 100 | 100 | 100 | 100 | 100 |
| 5. Pictures* | 23 | 25 | 25 | 17 | 14 | 23 | 25 |
| Mean space per issue (col.cms) | 18,596 | 13,068 | 10,886 | 3,837 | 1,771 | 6,836 | 10,102 |

|  | GROUP C Bradford/Leeds | | | GROUP D Hereford/Worcs. | | | |
|---|---|---|---|---|---|---|---|
| Category | Keighley News | Bingley Guardian | Leeds South Advertiser | Hereford Times | Ross Gazette | Ross-on-Wye Advertiser | Berrow's Worcester Journal |
|  | % | % | % | % | % | % | % |
| 1. News | 25 | 33 | 41 | 28 | 33 | 37 | 25 |
| 2. Features | 2 | 3 | 6 | 7 | 2 | 19 | 7 |
| 3. Other editorial | 5 | 4 | 11 | 5 | 3 | 5 | 5 |
| 4. Advertising | 68 | 60 | 42 | 60 | 62 | 39 | 63 |
| TOTAL | 100 | 100 | 100 | 100 | 100 | 100 | 100 |
| 5. Pictures* | 8 | 13 | 24 | 13 | 9 | 28 | 19 |
| Mean space per issue (col.cms) | 12,613 | 12,613 | 2,610 | 13,305 | 4,128 | 2,527 | 9,374 |

* Percentages of picture content have been calculated as a proportion of *editorial* space in these and subsequent local weekly tables.

TABLE A35—*continued*  ANALYSIS OF TOTAL SPACE OF 28 LOCAL WEEKLY NEWSPAPERS INTO FIVE CATEGORIES—*continued*

| Category | GROUP E Chester/North Wales | | | | | GROUP F Cambs. | |
|---|---|---|---|---|---|---|---|
| | Deeside and District Advertiser | Chester Chronicle (Clwyd) | Wrexham Leader | Rhyl Journal and Advertiser | Flintshire Leader | Cambridge Independent Press | Newmarket Weekly News |
| | % | % | % | % | % | % | % |
| 1. News | 29 | 21 | 23 | 28 | 28 | 34 | 34 |
| 2. Features | 8 | 9 | 4 | 3 | 8 | 14 | 14 |
| 3. Other editorial | 5 | 7 | 5 | 5 | 6 | 3 | 3 |
| 4. Advertising | 58 | 63 | 68 | 64 | 58 | 49 | 49 |
| TOTAL | 100 | 100 | 100 | 100 | 100 | 100 | 100 |
| 5. Pictures | 16 | 31 | 15 | 23 | 21 | 28 | 26 |
| Mean space per issue (col.cms) | 5,335 | 23,166 | 13,825 | 10,700 | 9,000 | 8,853 | 8,853 |

| Category | GROUP G North-East | | | | GROUP H Other | | |
|---|---|---|---|---|---|---|---|
| | Darlington and Stockton Times | Aycliffe Chronicle | Stanley News | Gateshead Post | Gloucester Journal | Reading Chronicle | Derbyshire Advertiser |
| | % | % | % | % | % | % | % |
| 1. News | 21 | 23 | 21 | 28 | 40 | 27 | 48 |
| 2. Features | 7 | 4 | 3 | 3 | 21 | 8 | 13 |
| 3. Other editorial | 5 | 11 | 11 | 5 | 9 | 6 | 3 |
| 4. Advertising | 67 | 62 | 65 | 64 | 30 | 59 | 36 |
| TOTAL | 100 | 100 | 100 | 100 | 100 | 100 | 100 |
| 5. Pictures | 14 | 19 | 15 | 21 | 50 | 22 | 10 |
| Mean space per issue (col.cms) | 13,367 | 12,533 | 13,103 | 8,456 | 4,032 | 18,924 | 5,674 |

**TABLE A36**

**ANALYSIS OF NEWS CONTENT OF 28 LOCAL WEEKLIES INTO 12 CATEGORIES**

| Category | GROUP A Merseyside | | | GROUP B Strathclyde | | | |
|---|---|---|---|---|---|---|---|
| | Southport Visiter | Maghull Times | Maghull and Aintree Advertiser | Clydebank Press | Govan Press | East Kilbride News | Kilmarnock Standard |
| | % | % | % | % | % | % | % |
| **Political, social and economic** | | | | | | | |
| 1. Local and national politics | 4 | 1 | 3 | 1 | 3 | 4 | 1 |
| 2. Administrative and financial | 3 | 4 | 5 | 6 | 4 | 4 | 6 |
| 3. Economic, industrial | 1 | 1 | 2 | 5 | 3 | 10 | 5 |
| 4. All social services | 3 | 9 | 9 | 8 | 10 | 15 | 12 |
| 5. Environment, planning | 5 | 7 | 5 | 4 | 7 | 4 | 4 |
| Total p.s.e. | 16 | 22 | 24 | 24 | 27 | 37 | 28 |
| **Other:** | | | | | | | |
| 6. Crime, police, accidents | 4 | 6 | 2 | 9 | 3 | 5 | 5 |
| 7. Sport | 32 | 26 | 26 | 26 | 25 | 20 | 24 |
| 8. Personalities | 13 | 16 | 17 | 20 | 12 | 14 | 24 |
| 9. Events, activities and information | 22 | 27 | 29 | 17 | 23 | 14 | 17 |
| 10. District news | 11 | — | — | — | 9 | 9 | — |
| 11. Other local | 2 | 3 | 3 | 4 | 2 | — | 1 |
| 12. National or external news | — | — | — | — | — | 1 | 1 |
| TOTAL | 100 | 100 | 101 | 100 | 101 | 100 | 100 |
| Mean news space per sample issue (col.cms) | 3,533 | 3,659 | 2,939 | 1,151 | 885 | 1,572 | 1,515 |

*Note:* Apart from category 12 and national politics in 1, all news is local.

79

# TABLE A36—continued

## ANALYSIS OF NEWS CONTENT OF 28 LOCAL WEEKLIES INTO 12 CATEGORIES

| Category | GROUP C Bradford/Leeds | | | GROUP D Hereford/Worcs. | | | |
|---|---|---|---|---|---|---|---|
| | Keighley News | Bingley Guardian | Leeds South Advertiser | Hereford Times | Ross Gazette | Ross-on-Wye Advertiser | Berrow's Worcester Journal |
| | % | % | % | % | % | % | % |
| **Political, social and economic** | | | | | | | |
| 1. Local and national politics ... | 3 | 3 | — | 4 | 4 | 10 | 4 |
| 2. Administrative and financial ... | 2 | 1 | 1 | 9 | 8 | 11 | 12 |
| 3. Economic, industrial ... | 3 | 1 | — | 10 | 2 | 7 | 6 |
| 4. All social services ... | 7 | 8 | 9 | 5 | 8 | 4 | 6 |
| 5. Environment, planning | 9 | 10 | 5 | 10 | 8 | 10 | 5 |
| Total p.s.e. ... ... ... | 24 | 23 | 14 | 38 | 30 | 42 | 33 |
| **Other:** | | | | | | | |
| 6. Crime, police, accidents ... | 10 | 5 | 13 | 4 | 11 | 3 | 4 |
| 7. Sport ... ... ... | 21 | 26 | 37 | 17 | 24 | 22 | 22 |
| 8. Personalities ... ... | 12 | 10 | 2 | 13 | 8 | 11 | 11 |
| 9. Events, activities and information | 18 | 19 | 28 | 20 | 23 | 18 | 19 |
| 10. District news ... ... | 13 | 11 | 1 | 4 | — | — | 7 |
| 11. Other local ... ... | 2 | 5 | 4 | 3 | 2 | 4 | 5 |
| 12. National or external news ... | — | — | 1 | — | 2 | — | — |
| TOTAL ... ... ... | 100 | 99 | 100 | 99 | 100 | 100 | 101 |
| Mean news space per sample issue (col.cms.) ... ... ... | 3,153 | 4,162 | 1,070 | 3,800 | 1,362 | 935 | 2,343 |

80

**TABLE A36**—*continued*

**ANALYSIS OF NEWS CONTENT OF 28 LOCAL WEEKLIES INTO 12 CATEGORIES**

| Category | GROUP E *Chester/North Wales* | | | | | GROUP F *Cambs.* | |
|---|---|---|---|---|---|---|---|
| | Deeside and District Advertiser | Chester Chronicle (Clwyd) | Wrexham Leader | Rhyl Journal and Advertiser | Flintshire Leader | Cambridge Independent Press | Newmarket Weekly News |
| | % | % | % | % | % | % | % |
| **Political, social and economic** | | | | | | | |
| 1. Local and national politics | 7 | 2 | 1 | 1 | 2 | 3 | 2 |
| 2. Administrative and financial | 7 | 5 | 4 | 5 | 4 | 8 | 8 |
| 3. Economic, industrial | 7 | 3 | 2 | 6 | 6 | 5 | 7 |
| 4. All social services | 9 | 7 | 3 | 5 | 8 | 4 | 4 |
| 5. Environment, planning | 6 | 5 | 10 | 5 | 7 | 10 | 10 |
| Total p.s.e. | 36 | 22 | 20 | 22 | 27 | 30 | 31 |
| **Other:** | | | | | | | |
| 6. Crime, police, accidents | 10 | 6 | 14 | 8 | 7 | 12 | 11 |
| 7. Sport | 20 | 25 | 17 | 25 | 23 | 13 | 13 |
| 8. Personalities | 13 | 10 | 12 | 15 | 12 | 10 | 9 |
| 9. Events, activities and information | 19 | 22 | 21 | 22 | 13 | 12 | 11 |
| 10. District news | — | 13 | 11 | 7 | 14 | 22 | 22 |
| 11. Other local | 1 | 3 | 4 | 2 | 3 | 2 | 3 |
| 12. National or external news | 1 | 1 | 1 | — | — | — | — |
| TOTAL | 100 | 102 | 100 | 101 | 99 | 101 | 100 |
| Mean news space per sample issue (col.cms.) | 1,547 | 4,864 | 3,179 | 2,996 | 2,520 | 3,010 | 3,010 |

81

# TABLE A36—continued

## ANALYSIS OF NEWS CONTENT OF 28 LOCAL WEEKLIES INTO 12 CATEGORIES

| Category | GROUP G North-East | | | | GROUP H Other | | |
|---|---|---|---|---|---|---|---|
| | Darlington and Stockton Times | Aycliffe Chronicle | Stanley News | Gateshead Post | Gloucester Journal | Reading Chronicle | Derbyshire Advertiser |
| | % | % | % | % | % | % | % |
| **Political, social and economic:** | | | | | | | |
| 1. Local and national politics | 1 | 1 | 1 | 3 | — | 2 | 4 |
| 2. Administrative and financial | 6 | 4 | 3 | 3 | — | 4 | 2 |
| 3. Economic, industrial | 14 | 5 | 4 | — | — | 4 | 11 |
| 4. All social services | 4 | 7 | 10 | 9 | 5 | 8 | 4 |
| 5. Environment, planning | 7 | 4 | 2 | 5 | — | 8 | 6 |
| Total ... ... ... | 32 | 21 | 20 | 20 | 5 | 26 | 27 |
| **Other:** | | | | | | | |
| 6. Crime, police, accidents | 7 | 1 | 6 | 21 | — | 16 | 7 |
| 7. Sport ... ... | 8 | 29 | 30 | 21 | 12 | 32 | 29 |
| 8. Personalities ... ... | 11 | 10 | 17 | 14 | 27 | 11 | 4 |
| 9. Events, activities and information ... ... | 24 | 28 | 25 | 19 | 54 | 11 | 13 |
| 10. District news ... ... | 15 | 10 | 1 | — | — | 2 | 17 |
| 11. Other local ... ... | 3 | 2 | 2 | 4 | 1 | 1 | 1 |
| 12. National or external news ... | — | — | — | — | — | 2 | 1 |
| TOTAL ... ... ... | 100 | 101 | 101 | 99 | 99 | 101 | 99 |
| Mean news space per sample issue (col.cms.) ... ... ... | 2,807 | 2,882 | 2,751 | 2,367 | 1,612 | 5,109 | 2,723 |

82

TABLE A37

ANALYSIS OF FEATURE SPACE OF 28 LOCAL WEEKLY NEWSPAPERS INTO TEN CATEGORIES

| Category | GROUP A Merseyside | | | GROUP B Strathclyde | | | |
|---|---|---|---|---|---|---|---|
| | Southport Visiter | Maghull Times | Maghull and Aintree Advertiser | Clydebank Press | Govan Press | East Kilbride News | Kilmarnock Standard |
| | % | % | % | % | % | % | % |
| 1. Non-local features ... | 27 | 20 | 12 | 13 | 14 | 28 | 33 |
| 2. Political, social and economic ... | 11 | — | 3 | 20 | — | 16 | — |
| 3. Local places and leisure ... | 11 | — | 35 | 14 | 7 | — | 15 |
| 4. Consumer/prices ... | — | — | — | — | — | — | 7 |
| 5. Personalities ... | 8 | 30 | 14 | — | — | 19 | 1 |
| 6. Sport ... | 2 | 17 | 13 | — | — | 8 | 2 |
| 7. Arts, entertainment ... | 18 | 4 | 3 | 41 | 38 | 5 | — |
| 8. Women and children ... | 17 | 26 | — | 11 | 30 | 6 | 24 |
| 9. Picture features ... | 4 | — | 2 | — | 11 | 5 | 9 |
| 10. Other features ... | 2 | 3 | 18 | 1 | — | 13 | 8 |
| TOTAL ... | 100 | 100 | 100 | 100 | 100 | 100 | 99 |
| Mean feature space per sample issue (col.cms.) ... | 1,367 | 829 | 609 | 141 | 129 | 344 | 808 |

TABLE A37—*continued*

ANALYSIS OF FEATURE SPACE OF 28 LOCAL WEEKLY NEWSPAPERS INTO TEN CATEGORIES

| Category | GROUP C Bradford/Leeds | | | GROUP D Hereford/Worcs. | | | |
|---|---|---|---|---|---|---|---|
| | Keighley News | Bingley Guardian | Leeds South Advertiser | Hereford Times | Ross Gazette | Ross-on-Wye Advertiser | Berrow's Worcester Journal |
| | % | % | % | % | % | % | % |
| 1. Non-local features ... | — | — | 17 | 11 | — | 12 | 7 |
| 2. Political, social and economic ... | — | — | — | 33 | — | 33 | 6 |
| 3. Local places and leisure ... | 11 | 38 | — | 18 | 25 | 27 | 28 |
| 4. Consumer/prices ... | — | — | — | 2 | — | 10 | — |
| 5. Personalities ... | 11 | 7 | 43 | 22 | 3 | 10 | 25 |
| 6. Sport ... | 11 | 9 | — | 4 | — | — | — |
| 7. Arts, entertainment ... | 15 | 7 | 26 | 7 | 13 | 3 | 8 |
| 8. Women and children ... | 44 | 35 | 1 | — | — | — | 13 |
| 9. Picture features ... | 4 | 4 | 13 | 3 | — | — | — |
| 10. Other features ... | 2 | — | — | — | 59 | 4 | 13 |
| TOTAL ... | 100 | 100 | 100 | 100 | 100 | 99 | 100 |
| Mean feature space per sample issue (col.cms.) ... | 289 | 361 | 148 | 919 | 98 | 476 | 668 |

TABLE A37—continued

ANALYSIS OF FEATURE SPACE OF 28 LOCAL WEEKLY NEWSPAPERS INTO TEN CATEGORIES

| Category | GROUP E Chester/North Wales | | | | | GROUP F Cambridgeshire | |
|---|---|---|---|---|---|---|---|
| | Deeside and District Advertiser | Chester Chronicle (Clwyd) | Wrexham Leader | Rhyl Journal and Advertiser | Flintshire Leader | Cambridge Independent Press | Newmarket Weekly News |
| | % | % | % | % | % | % | % |
| 1. Non-local features ... ... | 24 | 9 | 33 | 6 | 12 | 6 | 6 |
| 2. Political, social and economic ... | 10 | — | 4 | 16 | — | 17 | 17 |
| 3. Local places and leisure ... | 7 | 3 | 17 | — | — | 6 | 6 |
| 4. Consumer/prices ... ... | 1 | — | — | — | — | — | — |
| 5. Personalities ... ... ... | 28 | 21 | 30 | 60 | 35 | 2 | 2 |
| 6. Sport ... ... ... ... | — | 8 | — | — | 4 | 1 | 1 |
| 7. Arts, entertainment ... ... | — | 6 | 1 | 18 | 10 | — | — |
| 8. Women and children ... ... | 30 | 27 | 10 | — | 8 | 16 | 16 |
| 9. Picture features ... ... | — | 23 | — | — | 18 | 39 | 39 |
| 10. Other features ... ... | — | 2 | 5 | — | 13 | 13 | 13 |
| TOTAL ... ... ... | 100 | 99 | 100 | 100 | 100 | 100 | 100 |
| Mean feature space per sample issue (col.cms.) ... ... ... | 434 | 2,070 | 602 | 289 | 744 | 1,273 | 1,273 |

TABLE A37—*continued*

ANALYSIS OF FEATURE SPACE OF 28 LOCAL WEEKLY NEWSPAPERS INTO TEN CATEGORIES

| Category | GROUP G North-East | | | | GROUP H Other | | |
|---|---|---|---|---|---|---|---|
| | Darlington and Stockton Times | Aycliffe Chronicle | Stanley News | Gateshead Post | Gloucester Journal | Reading Chronicle | Derbyshire Advertiser |
| | % | % | % | % | % | % | % |
| 1. Non-local features ... ... | 2 | 17 | 21 | — | 20 | 16 | 11 |
| 2. Political, social and economic ... | 7 | 20 | 11 | — | 22 | 14 | 6 |
| 3. Local places and leisure ... | 15 | 3 | 3 | 6 | 14 | 4 | 7 |
| 4. Consumer/prices ... ... | — | — | — | 7 | — | 3 | — |
| 5. Personalities ... ... | 12 | 36 | 40 | 16 | 6 | 5 | 17 |
| 6. Sport ... ... ... | — | — | — | 3 | 1 | 5 | 12 |
| 7. Arts, entertainment ... | 6 | 18 | 12 | — | 8 | 11 | 30 |
| 8. Women and children ... | 11 | 4 | 10 | 27 | 7 | 21 | 1 |
| 9. Picture features ... ... | 17 | 2 | 3 | 20 | 13 | 4 | 7 |
| 10. Other features ... ... | 30 | — | — | 21 | 9 | 17 | 8 |
| TOTAL ... ... ... | 100 | 100 | 100 | 100 | 100 | 100 | 99 |
| Mean feature space per sample issue (col.cms.) ... ... ... | 919 | 446 | 401 | 227 | 847 | 1,474 | 758 |

**TABLE A38**

**ANALYSIS OF OTHER EDITORIAL SPACE OF 28 LOCAL WEEKLY NEWSPAPERS INTO EIGHT CATEGORIES**

| Category | GROUP A Merseyside | | | GROUP B Strathclyde | | | |
|---|---|---|---|---|---|---|---|
| | Southport Visiter | Maghull Times | Maghull and Aintree Advertiser | Clydebank Press | Govan Press | East Kilbride News | Kilmarnock Standard |
| | % | % | % | % | % | % | % |
| 1. Editorial comment | 2 | 6 | 3 | 14 | — | — | — |
| 2. Correspondence | 18 | — | 19 | 24 | 16 | 20 | 29 |
| 3. Headings and titles | 31 | 34 | 36 | 20 | 25 | 24 | 23 |
| 4. Cartoons | — | 1 | — | — | — | 4 | — |
| 5. Fiction and serialised books | — | — | — | — | — | — | 7 |
| 6. Puzzles, competitions and offers | 20 | 26 | 7 | 2 | 13 | 31 | 4 |
| 7. Other regular information | 9 | — | 6 | 15 | 28 | 18 | — |
| 8. Miscellaneous editorial space | 20 | 33 | 29 | 25 | 18 | 3 | 37 |
| TOTAL | 100 | 100 | 100 | 100 | 100 | 100 | 100 |
| Mean other editorial space (col.cms.) | 1,353 | 734 | 632 | 191 | 159 | 486 | 453 |

# TABLE A38—continued

## ANALYSIS OF OTHER EDITORIAL SPACE OF 28 LOCAL WEEKLY NEWSPAPERS INTO EIGHT CATEGORIES

| Category | GROUP C Bradford/Leeds | | | GROUP D Hereford/Worcs. | | | |
|---|---|---|---|---|---|---|---|
| | Keighley News | Bingley Guardian | Leeds South Advertiser | Hereford Times | Ross Gazette | Ross-on-Wye Advertiser | Berrow's Worcester Journal |
| | % | % | % | % | % | % | % |
| 1. Editorial comment ... ... ... | 9 | 8 | — | 8 | — | 4 | 5 |
| 2. Correspondence ... ... ... | 26 | 14 | 6 | 37 | 60 | 10 | 20 |
| 3. Heading and titles ... ... | 31 | 35 | 18 | 21 | 38 | 46 | 33 |
| 4. Cartoons ... ... ... ... | — | — | — | — | — | — | — |
| 5. Fiction and serialised books ... | — | — | — | — | — | — | — |
| 6. Puzzles, competitions and offers ... | 5 | 5 | 14 | — | — | — | 26 |
| 7. Other regular information ... | 8 | 9 | 42 | — | — | — | — |
| 8. Miscellaneous editorial space ... | 21 | 29 | 20 | 34 | 2 | 40 | 16 |
| TOTAL ... ... ... | 100 | 100 | 100 | 100 | 100 | 100 | 100 |
| Mean other editorial space (col.cms.) | 568 | 528 | 282 | 606 | 110 | 137 | 436 |

TABLE A38—*continued*

## ANALYSIS OF OTHER EDITORIAL SPACE OF 28 LOCAL WEEKLY NEWSPAPERS INTO EIGHT CATEGORIES

| Category | GROUP E Chester/North Wales | | | | | GROUP F Cambridgeshire | |
| --- | --- | --- | --- | --- | --- | --- | --- |
| | Deeside and District Advertiser | Chester Chronicle (Clwyd) | Wrexham Leader | Rhyl Journal and Advertiser | Flintshire Leader | Cambridge Independent Press | Newmarket Weekly News |
| | % | % | % | % | % | % | % |
| 1. Editorial comment... | — | 4 | 4 | 5 | 5 | — | — |
| 2. Correspondence | 12 | 7 | 13 | 24 | 2 | 5 | 5 |
| 3. Headings and titles | 53 | 37 | 33 | 30 | 42 | 21 | 21 |
| 4. Cartoons | — | — | — | — | — | — | — |
| 5. Fiction and serialised books | — | — | — | — | — | — | — |
| 6. Puzzles, competitions and offers... | 10 | 33 | — | 27 | — | 28 | 28 |
| 7. Other regular information | 8 | 9 | — | — | — | 22 | 22 |
| 8. Miscellaneous editorial space | 17 | 10 | 50 | 13 | 51 | 24 | 24 |
| TOTAL | 100 | 100 | 100 | 99 | 100 | 100 | 100 |
| Mean other editorial space (col.cms.) | 260 | 1,633 | 639 | 560 | 493 | 229 | 229 |

TABLE A38—*continued*

ANALYSIS OF OTHER EDITORIAL SPACE OF 28 LOCAL WEEKLY NEWSPAPERS INTO EIGHT CATEGORIES

| Category | GROUP G North-East | | | | GROUP H Other | | |
|---|---|---|---|---|---|---|---|
| | Darlington and Stockton Times | Aycliffe Chronicle | Stanley News | Gateshead Post | Gloucester Journal | Reading Chronicle | Derbyshire Advertiser |
| | % | % | % | % | % | % | % |
| 1. Editorial comment... | 4 | — | — | — | — | 3 | — |
| 2. Correspondence | 10 | — | 3 | 11 | — | 16 | 6 |
| 3. Headings and titles | 28 | 16 | 16 | 26 | 42 | 24 | 74 |
| 4. Cartoons | — | — | — | — | — | — | — |
| 5. Fiction and serialised books | — | — | — | — | — | — | — |
| 6. Puzzles, competitions and offers... | 54 | 47 | 46 | 7 | 20 | 21 | 12 |
| 7. Other regular information | — | 5 | 5 | 25 | 6 | 5 | 7 |
| 8. Miscellaneous editorial space | 4 | 31 | 30 | 31 | 32 | 31 | 1 |
| TOTAL | 100 | 99 | 100 | 100 | 100 | 100 | 100 |
| Mean other editorial space (col.cms.) | 718 | 1,387 | 1,461 | 394 | 357 | 1,146 | 155 |

# TABLE A39

## ANALYSIS OF ADVERTISING CONTENT OF 28 LOCAL WEEKLY NEWSPAPERS INTO THREE CATEGORIES

| Category | GROUP A — Merseyside | | | GROUP B — Strathclyde | | | |
|---|---|---|---|---|---|---|---|
| | Southport Visiter | Maghull Times | Maghull and Aintree Advertiser | Clydebank Press | Govan Press | East Kilbride News | Kilmarnock Standard |
| | % | % | % | % | % | % | % |
| 1. Classified ... ... ... | 57 | 53 | 71 | 35 | 11 | 37 | 52 |
| 2. Display ... ... ... | 40 | 44 | 27 | 65 | 89 | 63 | 48 |
| 3. Advertising feature... ... | 3 | 3 | 2 | — | — | — | — |
| TOTAL ... ... ... | 100 | 100 | 100 | 100 | 100 | 100 | 100 |

| Category | GROUP C — Bradford/Leeds | | | GROUP D — Hereford/Worcs. | | | |
|---|---|---|---|---|---|---|---|
| | Keighley News | Bingley Guardian | Leeds South Advertiser | Hereford Times | Ross Gazette | Ross-on-Wye Advertiser | Berrow's Worcester Journal |
| | % | % | % | % | % | % | % |
| 1. Classified ... ... ... | 48 | 38 | 25 | 48 | 39 | 59 | 44 |
| 2. Display ... ... ... | 50 | 60 | 75 | 52 | 61 | 39 | 54 |
| 3. Advertising feature ... ... | 2 | 2 | — | — | — | 2 | 2 |
| TOTAL ... ... ... | 100 | 100 | 100 | 100 | 100 | 100 | 100 |

**TABLE A39**—*continued*

## ANALYSIS OF ADVERTISING CONTENT OF 28 LOCAL WEEKLY NEWSPAPERS INTO THREE CATEGORIES

| | GROUP E | | | | | GROUP F | |
| | *Chester/North Wales* | | | | | *Cambridgeshire* | |
| Category | Deeside and District Advertiser | Chester Chronicle (Clwyd) | Wrexham Leader | Rhyl Journal and Advertiser | Flintshire Leader | Cambridge Independent Press | Newmarket Weekly News |
|---|---|---|---|---|---|---|---|
| | % | % | % | % | % | % | % |
| 1. Classified ... ... ... | 56 | 65 | 56 | 33 | 35 | 22 | 22 |
| 2. Display ... ... ... | 43 | 35 | 41 | 66 | 63 | 77 | 77 |
| 3. Advertising feature ... | 1 | — | 3 | 1 | 2 | 1 | 1 |
| TOTAL ... ... ... | 100 | 100 | 100 | 100 | 100 | 100 | 100 |

| | GROUP G | | | | | GROUP H | |
| | *North-East* | | | | | *Other* | |
| Category | Darlington and Stockton Times | Aycliffe Chronicle | Stanley News | Gateshead Post | Gloucester Journal | Reading Chronicle | Derbyshire Advertiser |
|---|---|---|---|---|---|---|---|
| | % | % | % | % | % | % | % |
| 1. Classified ... ... ... | 63 | 64 | 61 | 27 | 15 | 48 | 50 |
| 2. Display ... ... ... | 36 | 35 | 38 | 69 | 81 | 50 | 44 |
| 3. Advertising feature ... | 1 | 1 | 1 | 4 | 4 | 2 | 6 |
| TOTAL ... ... ... | 100 | 100 | 100 | 100 | 100 | 100 | 100 |

## 3. Local Weekly Newspapers: Commentary

(i) The scope of the discussion of material presented in the preceding tables needs some introduction. It will be recalled that the selection of 28 titles was guided by the choice of regions used as sampling points in the sample survey of local "influentials", as was the selection of evening newspaper titles. The purpose was to concentrate the study of local newspapers in a number of places where reader attitudes were also being investigated. It is not possible in this report to make any comparison between content and reader attitudes but the tables have been presented in some detail so that such comparisons can subsequently be made. While the sample of 28 titles cannot be regarded as a random representative sample of all such newspapers, the group does contain newspapers varying quite widely in size, circulation, format, pattern of ownership and control and geographical location. Consequently, the aim of the commentary which follows is to attempt a brief, and inevitably incomplete, assessment of the local weekly press, taking account of some of these factors. This will be done, firstly, by taking each local group and making any appropriate comparisons and judgements and, secondly, by drawing some general conclusions about key features of the weekly press and about its diversity, standards and functions. Any generalisation will be subject to a high degree of qualification, because the sample is not statistically representative and because the number of issues of each title studied is small (only three copies of each for the weeks ending 1, 8 and 15 November 1975).

### (ii) Group A: *Merseyside*

Of the three titles involved, two, the *Southport Visiter* and *Maghull Times* belong to the Liverpool Daily Post and Echo Limited, while the *Maghull and Aintree Advertiser* is a competitor belonging to the Ormskirk Advertising Group of United Newspapers. These three are all fair-sized papers with large amounts of news and feature space and a good deal of diversity within them. There is little in the tables presented to show an influence on content from the joint ownership and control of the *Southport Visiter* and *Maghull Times*. A more detailed look at the issues sampled confirms this. In general, neither of the Maghull titles is any more like the Southport paper than the other. The only differentiating feature of the Post and Echo affiliates seems to be the high amount of non-local features and of features for women and children and space given to "puzzles, competitions and offers".

One aspect of the local press which the analysis has seemed to reveal is the presence of similarities across papers in each of the locality groups examined— a similarity independent of size or form of ownership. It is as if local norms for the local press were informally established and conformed to. In the case of these three papers, it is the general similarity of content profiles which is striking, rather than any unusual deviation from the average.

### (iii) Group B: *Strathclyde*

Of the four titles, two, *Clydebank Press* and *Govan Press* belong to John Cosser, while two, *East Kilbride News* and *Kilmarnock Standard* belong to the large chain, SUITS. There is some point, therefore, in comparing the two pairs of titles, differing in size and ownership. In terms of news content, the four titles exhibit an overall similarity of profile, having a relatively high coverage of political, social and economic matters, with particular reference to news of the social services. The four papers are also very similar in appearance and format. There are, however, certain broad differences between pairs, apart from the higher allocation of space to advertising by the two SUITS papers and their greater size. The latter are also more likely to give more space to "non-local features" and less to local arts and entertainments. They are also disinclined to give space to editorials—none recorded on the dates sampled. The overall impression is of four similar, but internally diverse newspapers, relatively active in dealing with local issues. The main differences seem accountable in terms of size, the *Govan Press* being most handicapped in this respect so that, for example, its coverage of political, social and economic matters is, in absolute terms, scanty.

## (iv) Group C: *Bradford and Leeds*

One of the three titles, the *Leeds South Advertiser* is small, carrying little advertising and lacking the diversity of the normal local weekly newspaper. Its coverage of local political, social and economic news is proportionately and absolutely low and especially weak in respect of politics. On the other hand, it gives feature space to these matters. Its news coverage of local personalities is unusually low and this may reflect a lack of clear local identification with a particular community.

The Keighley and Bingley titles, both belonging to Westminster Press, are interesting in being two editions of essentially the same paper. This near-identicality shows up in all the tables and in their having the same average size. As a local paper, we can characterise either as: (*a*) rather low on coverage of political, social and economic news and features, with a predeliction for covering the social services and voluntary social services in particular; (*b*) very high on coverage of staple local matters included under the headings of "personalities" and "events and activities"; (*c*) giving a high attention to features for women and children and those about local places and leisure. We also find a not unusual combination of attention to editorialising and correspondence columns. The separate identity of the editions is established by having different front page news, different editorial columns and letter sections and a different coverage of miscellaneous news from outlying villages and districts.

## (v) Group D: *Hereford/Worcs*

This represents perhaps the most interesting group of titles in the set of weekly papers sampled. Three belong to News International (*Hereford Times*, *Ross-on-Wye Advertiser* and *Berrow's Worcester Journal*), while the *Ross Gazette* is a long established independent paper (Ross Gazette Limited) with which the *Ross-on-Wye Advertiser* may compete. The interest of the group stems mainly from the generally very high attention of these papers, especially the three first mentioned, to political, social and economic matters. They set a high standard for diversity and weight of news and feature coverage, again supporting an impression that a local norm of both appearance and content seems to operate.

The *Ross Gazette*, as the independent newspaper and the most distinctive of the four, can be mentioned first. It has much less feature space and a more restricted range of types of content than the other four. Its format is more traditional, reflected in its lower proportion of picture content. At 9% of editorial space, this contrasts sharply with the 27% of its competitor, the *Ross-on-Wye Advertiser*. Having said this, it should also be noted that its coverage of political, social and economic news is above average for the set of weekly papers as a whole.

The *Ross-on-Wye Advertiser* is very different in appearance and in certain characteristics of content. Its political, social and economic content is the highest of the whole set of 28, at 42%, and more than half of this is about politics or local administration. The feature content is also extensive and diverse, with a third devoted to political, social and economic matters and an unusual 10% to consumer/price matters. No other paper gave as much space relatively or absolutely to this. The paper also includes correspondence and editorial sections. The overall impression from this analysis is of a small but lively paper.

The *Hereford Times* and the *Berrow's Worcester Journal* are similar in appearance and in content profiles, though without any apparent overlap in specific content. They are sizeable, diverse, newspapers, with much space given to political, social and economic news and features. Editorial and correspondence sections are large and the *Hereford Times* gives more space to letters than any other titles sampled. Economic news coverage in both papers is mainly reflective of agricultural interests.

## (vi) Group E: *Chester/North Wales*

The district is represented by a Thomson paper (the Clwyd edition of the Chester Chronicle), a paper from the Liverpool Post and Echo group (the *Deeside and District Advertiser*), and three papers belonging to North Wales Newspapers Limited and produced on the same plant: *Wrexham Leader, Rhyl Journal and Advertiser, Flintshire Leader*. The latter might be thought to compete with the *Deeside and District Advertiser*.

The three titles from North Wales Newspapers are rather similar in size, appearance and content profile. They all give about the same attention to political, social and economic news but seem to have avoided political content as such. All give a lot of space to local personalities and events and activities. Outside the news sections, there is more variability, with each title seeming to establish a different style.

The *Deeside and District Advertiser*, apart from being the smallest of the five, is most distinctive in appearance and content profile, with a very high attention to political, social and economic news and features coupled with a big allocation of feature space for women and children. The *Chester Chronicle* differs again in appearance as well as being very large. It is extensively illustrated, with 30% of editorial space as pictures. It is low proportionately in space for political, social and economic news, but much space is involved. It gives very large amounts of space to features for women and children and to puzzles, competitions and offers. Three of the titles give a little space to Welsh language content.

## (vii) Group F: *Cambridgeshire*

The two titles involved here are two editions of the same paper, with a different front page and slight changes to the sports page. On the days sampled, 18 out of 20 pages were the same in both papers and even the letters were the same. The papers belong to Cambridge Newspapers Limited (Iliffe).

95

In content, the papers show up strongly in coverage of political, social and economic matters and have rather below average sports coverage. Feature content is extensive and diverse. The lack of space for editorial and correspondence may be related to the need to serve a rather wide area.

### (viii) Group G: *North East*

The group comprises two titles with very similar content which belong to the Durham Advertiser series of Westminster Press (*Aycliffe Chronicle* and *Stanley News*), one independent paper, the *Gateshead Post*, and another Westminster title, the *Darlington and Stockton Times*, associated with the *Darlington Evening Despatch*. If the four can be thought of as sharing a set of common local characteristics, this seems to lie in the low attention to political, social and economic news and the high orientation to puzzles, competitions and offers.

The *Gateshead Post* is unremarkable in the basic outline of its news and features. It gives a lot of space to crime news and its feature content is noticeable for its attention to consumer/price matters. The *Darlington and Stockton Times* is large, with much classified advertising (its front page is given to this) and it concentrates its more "serious" coverage on economic matters. The two Westminster Press papers share a certain amount of content in identical form, although this is much less noticeable than with the other similar cases looked at (Bingley/Keighley and Cambridge/Newmarket). The similarity in this case is much more a matter of format and type of content. These are very local papers, concentrating on news of local people, events and sport. On the other hand, the feature content tends to be less parochial. There is no editorial comment and little readers' correspondence.

### (ix) Group H: *Other*

The final three weekly titles are from varied localities: Gloucester, Reading, Derbyshire. The papers belong, respectively, to Associated NS, Berkshire Associated News (a private company) and Burton Daily Mail.

The *Gloucester Journal* is small and low on advertising. Its content is oriented to feature material and its news coverage overwhelmingly concerned with local events, activities and personalities, to the virtual exclusion of all political or economic matters.

The *Reading Chronicle*, by contrast, is a large and varied paper, with a noticeably "non-political" outlook and the second largest amount of feature space of all the titles looked at. Editorial comment and correspondence columns are also present.

The *Derbyshire Advertiser* is rather small and apart from a high attention to economic news and arts and entertainment features, unremarkable in its general profile.

(x) The "weekly newspaper", as it emerges from this set of case studies, is not easy to characterise either as a single entity or as a range of alternative types. There is a great deal of diversity and the alternative versions which have been looked at are much more like different ways of combining a certain stock of basic components than examples of distinct types. Nevertheless, there are certain staple ingredients and some possibility of ordering different papers according to different criteria. The most notable common element in the local weekly newspaper, in contrast with other sorts of paper examined, is the attention to the doings of local people and to local events. Outside advertising, this seems to be the one indispensible component, if we include sport news as part of this service to the local community. Beyond this, all other main types of content seem to be dispensible or almost so: editorials, letters from readers, particular types of feature, political news. Even so, we should also note that some sort of political, social and economic news coverage is also a staple feature of the weekly newspaper, even if in rather small quantities. The importance of such content, symbolically at least, is suggested by the fact that the main front page stories in the papers looked at were very frequently related to local council matters and especially to environmental or planning subjects. The importance of the political, social and economic component in the weekly newspaper is also underlined by the fact that it comprises, on average, 26% of all news space in the 28 papers sampled, while the same figure for local news in the 12 evening papers studied was 25% and for the English Provincial Morning papers, 29%. However, the total *amount* of local news space is a good deal higher in the average weekly newspaper than in the other two types of paper. One conclusion to be drawn from these remarks is that the most important aspects of the local newspaper, which all the titles studied seem to confirm, are, firstly, the contribution to local political and social awareness and, secondly, the contribution to local identification and attachment. Optional elements include the use of the newspaper to provide background information about politics and social issues, to entertain, to form or express opinions. It is clearly possible for weekly newspapers to do much more than fulfil basic, non-controversial and inexpensive functions. The titles examined provide examples of newspapers which do extremely well, quantitatively, in a number of different respects as well as some which, by comparison, are not very adequate.

(xi) It is difficult, with limited "extra-newspaper" evidence and small samples and without a qualitative study in depth, to assess the contribution of different factors to the variability of weekly newspapers. On the face of it, however, it would *not* seem as if type of ownership is a very useful discriminator. There is no reason, on evidence presented, for concluding that the titles owned by large chains or other newspaper groups are less adequate than those under more individualistic forms of ownership, whether the criteria be taken as internal diversity of content, or expression of editorial views, or the quantity of attention to matters of local controversy. There might even be some basis in the evidence presented, since some of the seemingly "best" newspapers belong to chains or groups, for the reverse conclusion. On the other hand, size of newspaper is an important and complicating factor and the sample is too small than to allow more than a "non-proven" verdict. Whatever the ownership pattern involved, it is evident that the practice of duplication under different titles can mean a reduction in diversity and we have examined three cases of varying degrees of content overlap between titles—the Cambridge/Newmarket case representing the most extreme of the three. If multiple ownership increases this practice, then it will tend to undermine some of the key features of the local weekly press.

(xii) In summary, this discussion has suggested the following:
    (a) The local weekly press is important in what it has to offer to a locality, not least in the quantity of political, social and economic news it can provide.

(*b*) There is considerable variability in the extent to which different local papers offer services to the local community—both in respect of quantity of news and comment and of background information. The analysis suggests the existence of certain "optional" components in the local press—areas where a given title may be strong but others weak. The more "options" are taken up, the more varied is the newspaper. The options seem to include: high attention to political, social and economic news, in general, with a variant of concentration on the social welfare component; much feature space to puzzles, competitions or offers and to features for women and children; extensive use of illustrations; attention to editorial comment and letters from readers (the two are correlated); much space to local personalities and events; use of non-local news and features.

(*c*) Varying press "performance" does not seem related to structural factors (eg circulation, types of locality, ownership pattern), although these have not been closely examined. This in turn suggests that editorial or proprietorial initiative may be the most critical factor.

(*d*) The number of separate titles conceals duplication of content and this may go to lengths where it reduces diversity and tends to emasculate the press, since the newspaper trying to serve a more disparate area may also be blander and less specific.

(*e*) The results, as presented in tabular form, given an impression of similarity of content between different titles in the same area, as if a local norm or standard was informally operating. This impression may only be reflective of the fact that several titles looked at share ownership and/or production and editorial facilities, but the similarity seems to apply across titles in the same area, despite varying ownership patterns.

# Part B

**Industrial Relations Content in National Daily Newspapers, 1975: Sample survey of 1,492 items.**

# Main Tables

# I Background, Aims and Methods

## 1. Introduction

The coverage of industrial relations and labour matters is, in quantitative terms, an important component of political, social and economic news in the daily press. According to the general analysis of newspaper content (Part A of this report) the proportion of all news space allocated to such content in 1975 ranged from 4% to 6% in eight main national morning newspapers. From the present study, we know that almost a quarter of main lead stories on the days sampled were devoted to these topics. News of industrial relations and trade union matters is also politically important because of the relationship between Government and trade unions and the general political significance of anything affecting economic activity. It is also a politically sensitive area of news reporting and provides a test of the impartiality and diversity of a press which is not generally owned or controlled by those sympathetic to trade union aims. While this study is not concerned to make a specific assessment of impartiality, it was undertaken so that fuller information would be available about the amount and kind of press coverage in the national daily press and about the editorial standards which can be imputed. Underlying the choice of matters for investigation and the analysis itself is the assumption that a full, accurate and balanced reporting of industrial relations and trade union matters is a desirable component in any national newspaper and important for a political democracy.

What follows is a *description*, largely in numerical terms, of the industrial relations contents of 24 days' issues of the National Daily Press in 1975. The method of the sample survey has been applied to newspaper content, in that a small part of the total amount of news coverage has been chosen on a near-random basis, with a view to generalising about the total amount. In addition, as with a sample survey, a limited number of "questions" are asked about each newspaper item in a systematic way, in order to produce a standardised set of results and to reduce variations in the way the content of items is recorded. The fact that the results are *descriptive* has to be emphasised, since a statistical survey of this kind cannot in itself explain why things appear in a certain way nor give an assessment of quality. The commentary and analysis which accompany the presentation of numerical results are, nevertheless, intended to offer some interpretation of the findings. It should also be noted that the scope of the study is limited to what is contained in newspaper reports and does not extend to the question of readership or to a discussion of the events which form the subject of reports. With one exception, no evidence is drawn on which is not available in the newspapers themselves.

## 2. Aims of the research

The particular aims of this study can be expressed as a series of questions about newspaper content which were formulated before the coding scheme was prepared:

(i) What are the main topics of industrial relations coverage and how much space and prominence is allocated to each?

(ii) How do different newspapers compare in their attention to different topics?

102

(iii) What is the distribution of allocation of industrial relations content as between different branches of industry?

(iv) In dealing with industrial disputes, what causes are reported and how do newspapers compare in the reporting of these and other details?

(v) How much attention is given to different kinds of participants in industrial relations events?

(vi) What are the main sub-themes of reporting of industrial relations? For instance, what degree and kind of attention is given to such matters as the effects of industrial action on the public, the relations between unions and Government, the occurrence of conflict or violence?

(vii) What, if any, is the relationship between the topics of news coverage and the themes which may imply some evaluation or editorial attitude?

(viii) What evidence is there of differences between newspapers in the attention given to topics and themes which might reflect unfavourably on any of the participants in the events reported?

(ix) How does the pattern of attention to different sectors of industry compare with the distribution of the work force?

## 3. Selection of content for analysis

The definition of content for study involved some problems, although, for the most part, the category of news involved is easily recognisable on common-sense grounds and made fairly clear in the practice of newspapers themselves. Basically, an item was eligible for inclusion if it concerned a trade union or any matter of industrial relations. The problem of definition arose, however, where the subject of the news report was primarily political or economic, with only tangential reference to trade unions and then in their capacity as political entities or economic forces and not in their role as representing the interests of employees in the context of employment. Thus, some political events in which the unions were referred to, but took no principal part, were not included and economic news affecting employment where the trade unions were not mentioned was generally excluded. Broadly speaking, an item of a political kind would only be included where some form of industrial action might be involved or threatened. Thus, statements or actions by union leaders or unions with no direct bearing on labour relations would not qualify. Nevertheless, as will be seen, a good deal of the industrial relations news examined has a large overlap with general political and economic matters and the topics under which it was categorised acknowledge this fact. It may be that 1975 was exceptional in the degree to which political and labour news were inter-connected. It is quite possible that some inconsistency has occurred and that some items have been looked at and others omitted which an alternative reading would treat differently. However, experience with the main survey of newspaper content led to the conclusion that this particular category of content could be reliably identified.

## 4. Sampling procedure

The items for analysis were chosen by taking the sample of 24 days used in the general content analysis of national daily newspapers and studying relevant

103

items contained in newspapers selected. The method of choosing the sample is described in some detail in the report of that study (above, pp.2–3). In brief, it involved a random choice of days in 1975, after ensuring that the quarters of the year and, in those quarters, the different week-days, would be correctly represented. In the newspaper issues chosen, the next step was to identify the separate items and to treat each as a "case" for detailed study. A "case" or item would consist of the report of a single event. Thus, an item forming a separate case in our study might stand on its own under a separate heading in a newspaper, or it might be placed in a subsidiary position with other items under a general heading.

This sampling procedure has certain disadvantages (mainly self-evident, but requiring comment) which might affect the way in which results are interpreted. One drawback is that a day's news is taken in isolation from what preceded and might follow. The "story" is almost always incomplete, since many industrial relations stories continue over several days. Our procedure abstracted one bit of a longer story and, consequently, will have failed to capture important aspects of story development. Secondly, by taking the same day for each newspaper, we limit the number of different events to be analysed. Much of the time we are looking at the same story several times over. Where results of all titles are aggregated, as they are for some purposes, the duplication has to be borne in mind. The scale of duplication may be appreciated from the fact that the 1,492 different items coded and analysed comprise only about 670 different events or stories. It is for this reason, as much as for any wish to compare newspapers, that so many of the results in this report are given separately for each newspaper title.

The procedure was adopted, however, for two main reasons. One is the wish to produce results which relate to the more general content analysis which has been reported. Another is the wish to compare newspapers. Since the comparison between newspapers was a primary objective of the study, the alternatives (for instance, different samples of item for different newspapers) were less attractive. It should perhaps be added that reasons of economy and practicality also weighed against some of the more elaborate alternatives.

## 5. Design and methods

The basic approach and method of analysis used in this study have been developed in previous research and the subject of industrial relations coverage in particular has been looked at recently in a not dissimilar way in at least two other research projects. One of these was conducted in the Department of Sociology at the University of Glasgow, and was particularly concerned with television coverage of industrial news.* Another was located at the Centre for Mass Communication Research at the University of Leicester.** We are particularly grateful to Professor John Eldridge and his colleagues of Glasgow University and Paul Hartmann of Leicester University for help and advice in the preparation of the present research and, in particular, for making available their own coding schedules and indicating some of their unpublished results. Another piece of research influential in the design of our coding schedule was the report of an investigation into press content dealing with race, carried out

---

* Published as *Bad News* by Routledge and Kegan Paul, 1976.
** Paul Hartmann "Industrial relations in the news media", *Industrial Relations Journal*, Winter 1975/6

by Paul Hartmann and Charles Husband for UNESCO (*Race as News*, The Unesco Press, Paris, 1974). In particular, this study establishes the utility of a coding scheme with two or three levels of classification, distinguishing between topic or broad subject matter, more specific sub-topics and other themes which might be referred to in the treatment of topics.

Central to this form of content analysis, as to the sample survey, is the preparation in advance of a coding schedule which can be applied systematically to all the cases under study. This involves some prior knowledge of the material and a pilot investigation to test the applicability of the measuring instrument. In the preparation of the coding schedule the main aim is to anticipate the full range of data likely to be encountered and to prepare categories which will account for all observations made in the actual study. This is not always easy to achieve, but in the present instance, it has seemed feasible to prepare an adequate coding scheme on the basis of prior expectation, pilot investigation and expert advice. The range of material was already broadly familiar, since all the items examined had already been scanned and identified as industrial relations content in the general analysis of same sample of newspapers. A weakness of the method is that such a coding frame is selective and omits categories which are not expected to occur. As a result, we cannot say much about what is *left out* of newspaper content.

The analysis was carried out by applying standard SPSS programmes, after a punched card had been prepared for each item recording the data indicated in Appendix B2.

## 6. The analysis of themes in industrial relations news

The coding schedule is reproduced as Appendix B1 and some comments and explanations are given in Appendix B2. Some more extended discussion is needed of the attempt to record themes or "news angles".

The basic assumption underlying the attempt to identify themes in the content examined was that news stories, in addition to providing factual accounts of specific events, also often contain references to ideas, criteria of judgement or longer-term concerns which affect the interpretation of the news event. Thus, in any given period, there will be some continuing matters of public interest which help to shape news values, and particular events may be noticed because of these concerns or may be related to them. The themes themselves do not normally provide the main substance of a news story although in some circumstances they might do. Consequently, the distinction from "topic" or "sub-topic" which has been formally observed in the coding scheme is not an absolute one. The "theme" may well expand in importance to form the main substance of a news report but more usually, the conventions of factual, "objective" reporting ensure that a news report will be confined to the events and an expansion of the theme will be reserved for the leader column or for feature treatment.

The underlying idea and the method for making practical use of it may be better understood by listing the main themes which were anticipated and which formed the basis for the final section of the coding frame. These were:

(1) The *relative* size of a claim or settlement (eg whether large or excessive).
(2) The presence or absence of discord in relations between unions, government and employers.

(3) The general effects of industrial action.

(4) The failings of unions or employers.

(5) The implications for Government pay policy.

(6) Conflict or violence.

(7) Sex angles.

(8) Public sympathy or its absence.

(9) Support by workers for industrial action (or absence of support).

A number of miscellaneous themes were also anticipated, for instance, the "strike-proneness" of a firm or industry, the subsidising of strikes by social security payments, the occurrence of "good news" in industrial relations. It can be seen that, while themes have a factual basis and could be the subject of a news story, the theme is generally a broader and more permanent part of the background to news reporting. The theme, as conceived here, also differs from the "topic" of a news story in not providing an exclusive category for a given news item. An item may draw on several themes or none at all, the latter especially in the case of the shortest and most factual items.

The purpose in including this dimension of analysis was, firstly, to extend the descriptive possibility of the study so as to include some indication of the principles of selection and interpretation without which news would be a mere random collection of facts. The criteria which give news events their significance are not always made explicit but nor are they very obscure and it has seemed useful to try and record them where possible. A second reason for trying to extend the basic description of news items derives from the observation that a reference to these themes may involve some judgement or selective interpretation. In a newspaper report a decision has to be made whether or not, for instance, to stress the large size of a pay claim, or the level of government disagreement with unions, or the unpopularity of a strike. Normally, the reference to one of these themes is not made by injecting a value judgement or personal opinion, but by reporting a verifiable event or statement indicating the point in question. It should thus be emphasised that, in recording the incidence of themes, it is not assumed that these are the editorial views of the newspapers. The practice by which themes and the underlying ideas get incorporated into news reports need be no less objective and factually based than in the direct reporting of hard news events. For the most part, the themes themselves are simply aspects of the frame of reference shared by trade unionists, employers, newspaper readers and newspaper writers.

It is easier to describe this aspect of content than to record it in a reliable way. The method of content analysis, as it is used in this study, is based on the requirement that account should only be taken of what is present as a matter of surface meaning. It is not easy to uphold this rule in respect of themes. However, a method has been developed and applied which conforms to the rules for objective analysis, although it has a somewhat mechanistic character and it is not very sensitive to the context or to nuances of meaning. In brief, what has been done is, firstly, to turn the broad themes into a number of fairly specific points of the kind that might occur in news reports (the relevant section of the coding frame on pp. 324-329 shows what is involved), taking care to allow for the occurrence of "counter-themes" (eg *accord* as well as *discord*, or public sympathy as well as lack of it). Secondly, the instructions for coding asked that a record be made of the occurrence of a given theme only where a clear and specific reference could be found to any of the points listed in the coding scheme. While it was not a requirement that the exact words in the coding schedule should appear in the news report, there had to be a minimum of ambiguity about the correspondence between a point in the coding frame and a phrase in the news report. The result has probably been a general under-recording of themes. The fact that only 1,180 references to themes were coded in 1,492 news items suggests as much and it is clearly preferable to err on the conservative side.

Finally, it should be stressed that the results of this analysis need to be treated with great caution. The method is barely adequate to the task and has been chosen more for its objectivity than its sensitivity. In particular, the counting of "references" to points which reflect a wider theme gives no direct indication of the importance or salience of the theme in a given news report. A complete item about the effects of a strike might have equal weight with a single sentence in another item. The larger the sample, however, the less this objection holds since frequency of occurrence will in the long run be related to space and the material is reported in the belief that it does give an indication of the relative importance of different themes in 1975.

## 7. Coding procedure

The coding was carried out by two coding assistants, under the supervision of the principal investigators, who had earlier carried out a pilot study with part of the data. An analysis sheet (Appendix B3) was prepared on which, for each case, a summary record was made of the information called for by the coding schedule. The coders worked systematically through the sample of newspapers, conferring where necessary on disputed points and sharing the different titles between them, so as to maximise the consistency of application of the pre-coded categories. It will be recalled that the newspapers studied had already been coded and industrial relations content identified and measured. However, it was quite often necessary to sub-divide and re-measure content which had been treated as a single item for purposes of the earlier investigation.

## 8. The assessment of bias or impartiality

It has been noted that this study was not primarily an attempt to measure bias in news reporting. That task would require a much larger and specially designed survey and analysis. However, since the question of fairness is obviously central to many people's concern with this topic, it cannot be avoided. There are several alternative forms in which "bias" may show itself (taking bias to mean a tendency to favour one side or direction against another): one is by explicit argument and compilation of evidence favouring one view; another is by a tendentious use of facts and comment, without any explicit statement of preference; another is by the use of language which colours an otherwise factual report and conveys an implicit but clear value judgement; another is by the omission of points on one "side", in an otherwise straight news report. These, and other forms of "bias", would require some intention or awareness on the part of the writer or editor. For the most part, they are not open to investigation by the methods of this study.

There is a further kind of "bias" or effect which is believed to occur more often and which results from the way in which news is selected and shaped for the daily newspaper, rather than from any intentional departure from standards of objective reporting. In brief, it is often said that newspapers concentrate too much on negative aspects of the world, on conflict and disagreement rather than on constructive matters or "good" news generally. There are a number of arguments in support of this view: news does favour the unexpected and bad news is more unexpected than good news; readers are generally interested in conflict and violence catches attention; the function of the press to warn readers of problems requires some attention to potential trouble; newspaper reports have to select and they will tend to omit what is least likely to be read by readers, and so on. In the present case, it is sometimes argued that the unintended *effect* of these reporting tendencies is to give union activity and perhaps the "employee side" a negative image. For instance, the constructive side of union activity is not reported because uninteresting, industrial action is presented as if necessarily bad, the causes of action are given less attention than the harmful consequences to the public, etc.

*Hence the Advent of the illustrated war- guide being so big.*

To assess these complaints would take much detailed work, but the present survey clearly has some relevance to these matters. It can, for instance, help to show how far industrial relations is dominated by "negative" news. It can give an indication of the extent to which causes of disputes are not reported. It can show how frequently "negative" themes occurred and in respect of what topics. It can show whether particular newspapers were more or less inclined to provide negative news, especially under the exigencies of a lower overall space allocation to industrial relations news. It is possible to see whether the allocation of reporting effort fairly represents the overall distribution of industrial activity. These and other points are taken up in the course of the report and some assessment is made at the end. Generally, however, the intention is to make the evidence available so that the reader can make his or her own assessment.

# II  Description of the results

This section of the report is designed to give a preliminary indication of the amount and kind of data which the study produced. Firstly, the total number of cases, or separate items for analysis, which the study produced was 1,492. Of these, 1,414 were *news* items, 32 were feature articles and 46 were editorials. While editorials have been separately looked at, for most purposes of analysis the total of 1,492 cases has been used as the source of evidence, without distinction according to type. The distribution of each type between the nine national daily newspapers is shown in Table B1.

TABLE B1

INDUSTRIAL RELATIONS ITEMS IN NATIONAL DAILY NEWSPAPERS,
24 ISSUES IN 1975: FREQUENCY OF EACH TYPE

| Type | The Times | The Guardian | The Daily Telegraph | Financial Times | Morning Star | Daily Express | Daily Mail | Daily Mirror | The Sun |
|---|---|---|---|---|---|---|---|---|---|
| News items... | 205 | 162 | 189 | 293 | 230 | 92 | 81 | 72 | 90 |
| Features ... | 4 | 7 | — | 4 | 6 | 1 | 7 | 2 | 1 |
| Editorials ... | 2 | 3 | 7 | 3 | 12 | 6 | 5 | 1 | 7 |
| Total ... | 211 | 172 | 196 | 300 | 248 | 99 | 93 | 75 | 98 |

There are large differences between newspapers in the quantity of items which were included, with the *Financial Times* well ahead, followed by the *Morning Star* and *The Times*. The *Daily Mirror*, with 75 items, has only a quarter the number contained in the *Financial Times*. The variation is greater than that which showed up between titles in the general content analysis of newspapers. According to Table A10, the *Morning Star* led with 11·9% of *editorial* space devoted to the subject, while the remaining percentages lie between the 3·4% attained by the *Financial Times* and *Dail Mail* and the 1·9% in the *Daily Mirror*. However, the differences in space terms are very close to the pattern shown above, as Table B2 shows.

TABLE B2

INDUSTRIAL RELATIONS CONTENT IN NATIONAL DAILY NEWSPAPERS:
AVERAGE AMOUNT OF SPACE PER ISSUE ALLOCATED,
IN ADJUSTED STANDARD col. cms*.

| The Times | The Guardian | The Daily Telegraph | Financial Times | Morning Star | Daily Express | Daily Mail | Daily Mirror | The Sun |
|---|---|---|---|---|---|---|---|---|
| 183 | 219 | 205 | 265 | 198 | 109 | 145 | 66 | 72 |

*Extrapolated from Table A10, above, p. 28.

The *Financial Times* also allocated four times as much space, on average, to industrial relations as did the *Daily Mirror*. This is in line with the finding of the general content analysis (Appendix A10), that the average size of each item of industrial relations news does not vary greatly between newspapers. There was some day-to-day variation in the number of items recorded on each of the 24 sample days, with a maximum of 86 and a minimum of 40. This seems mainly to reflect chance fluctuations in the availability of news, although there is a general decline in the number of cases as the year progresses. Thus, the first quarter yielded 444, the second 341, the third 348 and the fourth, 309. No doubt, this does reflect the changing pattern of events in 1975 and the imposition of the £6 pay policy in August. Further comment is offered below in Section III, 3. It is notable that the *Financial Times* is alone in not reflecting this trend since it has the same number of items in each quarter. Presumably this reflects its consistently wide coverage for a specialist readership. It may also be less subject to the competitive pressure on space of topical news values than are other newspapers.

The main measure of space used in this study was the index of item size described in Appendix B2, iii. The relative size of items in each newspaper is shown in Table B3, in summary form.

TABLE B3

INDUSTRIAL RELATIONS ITEMS IN NATIONAL DAILY NEWSPAPERS:
PERCENTAGE DISTRIBUTION ACCORDING TO SIZE (n=1,492)

| Item size in s. col. cms.* | The Times | The Guardian | The Daily Telegraph | Financial Times | Morning Star | Daily Express | Daily Mail | Daily Mirror | The Sun |
|---|---|---|---|---|---|---|---|---|---|
| | % | % | % | % | % | % | % | % | % |
| 0–10 ... | 35 | 22 | 34 | 31 | 48 | 32 | 15 | 39 | 37 |
| 11–20 ... | 25 | 13 | 15 | 25 | 24 | 23 | 29 | 29 | 22 |
| 21–60 ... | 34 | 54 | 43 | 41 | 19 | 28 | 36 | 19 | 27 |
| 61+... ... | 6 | 11 | 8 | 3 | 9 | 16 | 20 | 13 | 14 |
| Total ... | 100 | 100 | 100 | 100 | 100 | 99 | 100 | 100 | 100 |
| No. of items | 211 | 172 | 196 | 300 | 248 | 99 | 93 | 75 | 98 |

* In allocating items to these categories, no allowance was made for varying column widths between papers. The figures are thus not strictly comparable and overestimate the space in *The Sun* and *Daily Mirror*.

The main difference between papers lies in the tendency for the "Popular" papers to have a high *proportion* of big items, despite the smaller numbers involved. It is for this reason that popular papers manage to have an average size per item similar to that of the larger papers. In practice, of course, the results reflect the fact that a similar number of industrial relations stories get prominent treatment in all newspapers, because basically the same news values are being applied. This point is confirmed when papers are compared according to relative prominence (as distinct from size). The *number* of industrial relations stories receiving front page lead treatment does not vary greatly between papers. The *Morning Star*, gave first place to industrial or labour relations on ten out of 24 days, *The Sun* only did so on three days, while all the others ranged between four and eight, the latter being the figure for the *Daily Mail*.

110

The measure of prominence used took account of overall size and of placing—whether front page or not. The most informative single index of prominence is probably the percentage of stories which appeared as large items on a front page. According to this criterion, and taking the minimum size as 21 col. cms., the different titles were assessed as follows:

TABLE B4

**INDUSTRIAL RELATIONS ITEMS IN NATIONAL DAILY NEWSPAPERS: PERCENTAGE OF TOTAL WHICH WERE LARGE FRONT PAGE ITEMS (n=1,492)**

| The Times | The Guardian | The Daily Telegraph | Financial Times | Morning Star | Daily Express | Daily Mail | Daily Mirror | The Sun |
|---|---|---|---|---|---|---|---|---|
| % 7·1 | % 11·6 | % 13·7 | % 6·0 | % 9·7 | % 9·1 | % 13·9 | % 6·7 | % 5·1 |

The all-paper average was 9·2%. By comparison with this, *The Daily Telegraph* and *Daily Mail* give exceptional prominence to industrial relations news and the *Daily Mirror* and *The Sun* rather little. However, the tabloid format of the latter two gives them much less chance of rating high on this particular measure. A comparison in terms of the proportion of stories accorded main lead treatment gives a different result. The overall proportion of stories which did appear in the front page lead position was 3·5%. All titles, apart from the *Financial Times* (at 1·3%), the *Daily Mail* (at 8·6%), and the *Daily Mirror* (at 5·3%) were very close to this figure. The results of an analysis according to prominence should remind us that absolute frequency of occurrence, as shown in table B1, is only part of the picture. Certain newspapers, especially the *Daily Mail*, make up in prominence for what is lacking in quantity, since on the 24 days sampled, a third of its front page lead stories were devoted to some aspects of industrial relations. The rather high degree of prominence overall should also be remembered, since 23% of all main lead stories looked at were concerned with this subject matter.

# III Main topics

## 1. Introduction

Each item examined was classified, where possible, according to one of 11 main topics and the remainder of cases allocated to a residual category. In the event, the latter has been little used. The purpose of the classification was to identify the principal subject matter of a report, normally by reference to the main news event. As the examination of detailed cases of industrial relations reporting shows, such news can often be quite complex, with more than one theme and set of actions involved. Nevertheless, it is normal for there to be a central focus for a news report and it did not prove too difficult to find a main topic for an item. Coding was also facilitated by our practice of separating out the distinct items of news which are sometimes brought together in reports under the same headline. In addition, as the instructions in the coding frame (Appendix B1) show, it was permitted to record a *second* main topic where this was unavoidable. In practice, this facility was little used, and only 4% of the total cases were "double-coded". The figures in Table B4 and B5 are based on the total number of topics recorded (1,557) rather than the total number of cases (1,492), but in subsequent analyses, where cross-tabulation is involved, the double coding has been eliminated. In 90% of such cases, the "dispute" category was one of those involved and this has been taken as the dominant code. In the remaining six cases an arbitrary decision has been taken to use whichever of two topic classifications has the highest overall frequency and to ignore the second code. The misrepresentation involved is minimal.

## 2. The main subject matter of industrial relations reports

As Table B5 shows, there is a good deal of variation in the frequency of occurrence of different topics, with a small number accounting for the bulk of all items. More than half of all items can be classified as either about disputes and stoppages or about actions and statements by unions and the TUC, while

TABLE B5

MAIN TOPICS OF INDUSTRIAL RELATIONS ITEMS, IN ORDER OF
FREQUENCY (n=1,557)

|     |                                                                                          | %   |
| --- | ---------------------------------------------------------------------------------------- | --- |
| 1.  | Disputes, stoppages and industrial action generally...                                   | 36  |
| 2.  | Actions or statements by TUC, particular unions, professional associations or union leaders ... | 18  |
| 3.  | Negotiations between unions and employers over pay                                       | 11  |
| 4.  | Union elections, other internal union matters and inter-union relations ...              | 10  |
| 5.  | Industrial, commercial or technical developments affecting unions and members            | 8   |
| 6.  | Actions or statements by Government, Ministers, political parties or politicians          | 6   |
| 7.  | Actions or statements by employers or their organisations                                | 4   |
| 8.  | Legal action ...                                                                          | 2   |
| 9.  | Worker control, participation, profit-sharing, work-ins, etc.                            | 2   |
| 10. | General economic context to industrial relations ...                                     | 2   |
| 11. | Other (including actions or statements from both sides of industry jointly)              | 1   |
|     |                                                                                          | 100 |

**TABLE B6**

**SUB-TOPICS OF INDUSTRIAL RELATIONS ITEMS: PERCENTAGE DISTRIBUTION WITHIN EACH MAIN TOPIC CATEGORY (WHOLE SAMPLE)**

| | % |
|---|---|
| (a) Disputes (n = 557) | |
| 1. Strikes | 61 |
| 2. Unspecified action | 13 |
| 3. Work to rule/overtime ban | 8 |
| 4. Picketing | 7 |
| 5. Token stoppage | 4 |
| 6. Blacking/lockout | 2 |
| 7. Other | 5 |
| | 100% |
| (b) Pay negotiations (n = 172) | |
| 1. Settlement | 32 |
| 2. In progress | 55 |
| 3. Future | 13 |
| | 100% |
| (c) Government actions (n = 91) | |
| 1. Directed at: TUC or workers in general | 46 |
| 2. : particular union or workers | 30 |
| 3. : employers | 10 |
| 4. Other | 14 |
| | 100% |
| (d) Union/TUC action (n = 273) | |
| 1. Directed at Government | 66 |
| 2. Directed at employers | 16 |
| 3. Other | 18 |
| | 100% |
| (e) Inter- and intra-union affairs (n = 163) | |
| 1. Union elections | 12 |
| 2. Other internal union matters | 57 |
| 3. Inter-union relations | 26 |
| 4. Other | 5 |
| | 100% |
| (f) Industrial and commercial developments (n = 119) | |
| 1. Developments beneficial | 9 |
| 2. Developments harmful | 89 |
| 3. Other | 2 |
| | 100% |
| (g) Legal action (n = 41) | |
| 1. Against employer | 34 |
| 2. Against union | 10 |
| 3. Against workers | 54 |
| 4. Other | 2 |
| | 100% |
| (h) Employer actions (n = 62) | |
| 1. Directed at Government | 45 |
| 2. Directed at unions/workers | 47 |
| 3. Other | 8 |
| | 100% |

the top six topics between them cover almost 90% of all cases. While the categories are broad and include quite diverse items of news, the figures in Table B5 tend to confirm the view that industrial relations reporting was concentrated very heavily on a limited number of subjects, with a particular focus on strikes, stoppages and industrial action. Further information about the coverage of industrial disputes is given in sections 6 and 7 below.

The coding scheme allowed us to make some finer distinctions of subject matter within categories and the results are shown in Table B6. Several points stand out amongst these results. Firstly, there is the dominant position of strikes amongst disputes, accounting for 61% of all dispute stories. Secondly, there is a lower emphasis on reporting the *settlement* of pay negotiations. Assuming that as many pay negotiations reach a conclusion as are initiated, there could be some under-reporting of outcomes. Thirdly, it is clear that, where Government initiatives were reported, they were overwhelmingly directed at unions or workers and initiatives from unions and the TUC were directed back at Government rather than at employers. Fourthly, reports of union elections did not play much part in the news examined. Fifthly, changes in economic and industrial circumstances, as reported, generally had negative connotations for workers, no doubt reflecting the economic difficulties of 1975. Finally, we find employers as much involved with Government, in this reporting, as with unions.

## 3. Changes over the year in industrial relations subject matter

A seasonal variation in the overall frequency of industrial relations reporting was described in section II p. 110. In addition to this overall change, there was a change in the nature of topics covered which helps to account for what happened. Basically, the content analysed is indeed reflecting the events of the year, with its build-up to the £6 pay limit in July and a subsequent dearth of strike action in support of claims. Table B7 gives the details of changes over the four quarters of the year for the most important topics. It should be remembered that the sample provided only six days' newspapers for each quarter and these were not necessarily evenly spread over the four three-month periods.

Most significant is the steady decline in the incidence of "strikes" as a news topic, with 40% of such stories falling in the first quarter and 12% in the last. The topic of "pay negotiations" has an almost identical trajectory. Coinciding with these changes is a marked decrease in reports of Government action and statements on industrial relations matters from the first to the second-half of the year. More detailed analysis of sub-topics (not tabulated here) showed there also to have been some change in the *direction* of Government actions after the pay policy implementation. In the fourth quarter employers, rather than unions, predominated in news reports as the main recipients of such initiatives.

Table B7 also gives some indication of what took the place of the declining topics in the second half of the year, although the general falling off in amount of news should be remembered. In the third quarter, reports of Union/TUC actions tended to concentrate, as did news of union affairs. Otherwise, news of disputes other than strikes and of industrial developments helped to fill the gap. The greater attention to trade union affairs in part reflects the activity generated by the pay policy and also the union conference season. There was not, for instance, any increase in the reporting of union elections in the latter half of the year. While strikes and other disputes together still occur frequently in the third and fourth quarter, the pattern shown in Table B7 provides support for the view that news reporting does respond to events with some sensitivity.*

TABLE B7

MAIN TOPICS OF INDUSTRIAL RELATIONS CONTENT: PERCENTAGE DISTRIBUTION IN FOUR QUARTERS OF 1975†

| Topic | First Quarter | Second Quarter | Third Quarter | Fourth Quarter | Total |
|---|---|---|---|---|---|
| | % | % | % | % | % |
| 1. Strikes ... ... ... ... ... | 40 | 33 | 15 | 12 | = 100 |
| 2. Other disputes ... ... ... | 34 | 16 | 24 | 26 | = 100 |
| 3. Union/TUC actions ... ... ... | 13 | 27 | 36 | 24 | = 100 |
| 4. Pay negotiations ... ... ... | 41 | 33 | 15 | 11 | = 100 |
| 5. Inter- and intra-union affairs ... | 19 | 24 | 33 | 24 | = 100 |
| 6. Industrial and commercial developments ... ... ... ... | 39 | 14 | 19 | 28 | = 100 |
| 7. Government actions ... ... | 34 | 29 | 24 | 13 | = 100 |
| All topics ... ... ... ... ... | 31 | 26 | 24 | 19 | = 100 |

* The topics omitted from this table only accounted for 10% of all topic codings. In addition, the disputes category has been divided into "strikes" and "other disputes".

## 4. Differences between newspapers in subject matter

It is apparent from Table B8 that newspapers differed from each other rather little in their relative attention to the main topics. The overall similarity is illustrated by the fact that in only two instances do the six most important topics for each title vary from the six most important for the sample as a whole. The four "Quality" papers were closest to the overall average, although they, of course, contributed most to the composition of that average. While disputes comprise, in all papers, the single most important topic, they figure more noticeably in the four "Popular" newspapers. However, a more detailed analysis of the internal composition of the "dispute" category shows that, in fact, "Popular" papers generally gave a lower proportionate attention to strikes than did "Quality" papers. The percentages of *dispute* items which were about strikes appear for each title as follows:

| The Times | The Guardian | The Daily Telegraph | Financial Times | Morning Star | Daily Express | Daily Mail | Daily Mirror | The Sun |
|---|---|---|---|---|---|---|---|---|
| % | % | % | % | % | % | % | % | % |
| 67 | 62 | 69 | 63 | 58 | 48 | 53 | 48 | 48 |

† Statistics for "prominent stoppages" in 1975 show the proportion of all starting dates to be distributed against the four quarters of the year as follows: 1st, 27%; 2nd, 43%; 3rd, 19%; 4th, 11%. Source: DOE Gazette, May 1976, Table 4.

Other broad variations between papers shown by Table B8 include the greater attention by "Quality" papers to "actions or statements by unions and the TUC", while "Popular" newspapers generally paid more attention to "pay negotiations". A similar tendency affected the topics, respectively, of "industrial and commercial developments", and of "actions and statements by Government". No obvious explanations for these general differences between "Popular" and "Quality" newspapers suggests itself, although the overall difference in amount of coverage between the groups of newspapers is bound to have consequences, given the agreement on basic news values. The "Popular" papers are constrained to cover the same stories as the "Qualities" and the latter are more free to pick up items of a less insistent kind. Apparently, these tended to include news of developments affecting employment and initiatives stemming from

**TABLE B8**

**MAIN TOPICS OF INDUSTRIAL RELATIONS ITEMS:**
**PERCENTAGE DISTRIBUTION IN NATIONAL DAILY NEWSPAPERS, 1975**

| Topic | The Times | The Guardian | The Daily Telegraph | Financial Times | Morning Star | Daily Express | Daily Mail | Daily Mirror | The Sun | All newspapers |
|---|---|---|---|---|---|---|---|---|---|---|
| | % | % | % | % | % | % | % | % | % | % |
| 1. Disputes, stoppages and industrial action generally | 36 | 32 | 35 | 32 | 39 | 38 | 36 | 42 | 39 | 36 |
| 2. Actions or statements by TUC, particular unions, prof. assocs. or union leaders ... ... ... | 20 | 16 | 17 | 16 | 30 | 13 | 9 | 10 | 9 | 18 |
| 3. Negotiations between unions and employers over pay ... ... ... | 9 | 12 | 10 | 15 | 6 | 16 | 11 | 13 | 12 | 11 |
| 4. Union elections, other internal union matters and inter-union relations | 11 | 12 | 9 | 12 | 9 | 10 | 11 | 8 | 14 | 10 |
| 5. Industrial, commercial or technical developments affecting union members | 8 | 8 | 12 | 9 | 5 | 3 | 6 | 6 | 7 | 8 |
| 6. Actions or statements by Government, ministers, political parties or politicians ... ... ... | 6 | 5 | 4 | 4 | 3 | 9 | 11 | 11 | 7 | 6 |
| 7. Actions or statements by employers or their organisations ... ... ... | 5 | 4 | 6 | 4 | 2 | 4 | 3 | 6 | 3 | 4 |
| 8. Legal action ... ... | 2 | 2 | 3 | 2 | 3 | 2 | 5 | 3 | 2 | 2 |
| 9. Worker control, participation, profit-sharing, work-ins, etc. ... ... ... | 2 | 3 | 2 | 3 | — | 2 | 4 | 1 | 4 | 2 |
| 10. General economic context to industrial relations ... | 1 | 4 | 1 | 2 | 2 | 3 | 4 | — | 2 | 2 |
| 11. Other (including actions or statements from both sides of industry jointly) | — | 1 | 1 | 1 | 1 | — | — | — | 1 | 1 |
| Total % ... ... | 100 | 99 | 100 | 100 | 100 | 100 | 100 | 100 | 100 | 100 |
| Total frequency* ... | 219 | 186 | 203 | 310 | 254 | 104 | 102 | 79 | 100 | 1,557 |

* The total frequency differs from the sample total because of double coding of 65 items. See section I p.112 above.

unions or the TUC. Apart from these, relatively minor, general differences between the main sorts of newspaper, Table B8 shows few instances of distinctive reporting policies on the part of individual newspapers. The *Morning Star* gives most attention to trade union matters (topics 2 and 4), which the *Daily Mirror* and *Daily Mail* report least. *The Sun* gave proportionately most space to topic 4—intra- and inter-union matters—and least to topic 2—actions or statements by unions or the TUC. The differential attention by *The Guardian* to the general economic context should also be noted.

A number of main topics were further sub-divided according to sub-topics and the overall results have been shown in Table B6. A detailed comparison between newspapers confirmed the finding that on sub-topic categories newspapers were also in agreement.

## 5. Relative prominence of the main topics of industrial relations news

A measure of prominence has been described in Section II and there is some purpose in comparing the degree of occurrence of topics with the prominence they received in newspapers. Table B9 shows the relative prominence accorded to the seven most frequent topics and indicates some dissociation between frequency and prominence. In particular, items dealing with actions by the Government were the most likely to be given extensive front page placing, although such items ranked only sixth in overall frequency of occurrence (see Table B5). These items are also the most likely to have provided the subject for editorial comment and for feature article treatment. The attention accorded to "Union or TUC actions" was similar. A second group of topics—including "strikes", "other disputes" and "pay negotiations"—was characterised by rather frequent front page coverage and also by very frequent occurrence as small news items.

TABLE B9

**SEVEN MAIN TOPICS OF INDUSTRIAL RELATIONS CONTENT: PERCENTAGE DISTRIBUTION ACCORDING TO A FIVE-POINT SCALE OF PROMINENCE**

| Main Topic | Degree of prominence | | | | | |
|---|---|---|---|---|---|---|
| | Large front page news | Features | Editorials | News items 21+ cms | News items Under 21 cms | |
| Government actions ... | 18 | 4 | 5 | 35 | 38 | = 100% |
| Union/TUC actions ... | 11 | 2 | 4 | 36 | 47 | = 100% |
| Strikes ... ... ... | 10 | 2 | 1 | 21 | 66 | = 100% |
| Other disputes ... ... | 9 | — | 2 | 30 | 59 | = 100% |
| Pay negotiations ... ... | 11 | — | 1 | 26 | 62 | = 100% |
| Industrial and commercial developments ... ... | 7 | 1 | 2 | 30 | 60 | = 100% |
| Inter- and intra-union affairs ... ... ... | 6 | 3 | 1 | 40 | 50 | = 100% |

## 6. Industrial relations content dealing with strikes

Items dealing with strikes on their own comprise the single most frequent topic of industrial relations content in the sample studied. The number of such items was 342, or 22%, of all topics coded. Newspapers were also remarkably similar in the proportion of items devoted to strikes as the following percentage figures for each title show:

| | | | | | | | | |
|---|---|---|---|---|---|---|---|---|
| *The Times* | ... | ... | ... 24% | *Daily Express*... | ... | ... | 20% |
| *The Guardian* | ... | ... | ... 20% | *Daily Mail* | ... | ... | ... 21% |
| *The Daily Telegraph* | ... | ... 25% | *Daily Mirror* ... | ... | ... | 24% |
| *Financial Times* | ... | ... | 20% | *The Sun* | ... | ... | ... 22% |
| *Morning Star* | ... | ... | ... 23% | | | | |

Our analysis of strike reports (and of all dispute items) allowed us to identify several aspects of each case, including: the timing—whether past, current or future; the status—whether official or unofficial; whether or not a reference to the settlement of a dispute was included; the cause or causes of the dispute, where this information was given. In addition, as with all items, the branch of industry involved was recorded.

The main result of our analysis is to show that news of strike action takes a characteristic pattern in terms of several of these variables. There is a typical, or "modal", strike story, in the sense that the most common strike report is about a current dispute, the status of which is not given but where a cause is given, usually relating to pay. Thus 63% of strikes were current, 75% had no indication of status, 88% did not involve news of a settlement and in only 11% of cases was no cause mentioned. The typical profile of strike stories is indicated in Figure I.

Where a timing other than the present was involved it can be seen from Figure I that a past reference was almost as common as a future one. For the whole set of cases, an "unofficial" status was attributed in only 12% of cases. The relatively low proportion of strike settlements reported (12% of all strike stories) does suggest some tendency to regard a settlement of a strike as less newsworthy than a threat of one in the future, although these data on their own cannot prove this.

As has been shown, it was unusual to find a news item about a strike without some cause being attributed and, despite the freedom given to coders to record multiple causes where appropriate, in only ten cases was more than one cause noted. By far the most important cause of all strikes recorded was pay (at 52% of cases), with manning and demarcation matters a poor second (17%). The overall figures for causes of strikes are as shown in the last column of Table B10. The apparent tendency to assign a single cause to strikes, and that generally to be pay, may be an artefact of a coding procedure which itself tends to simplify more complex matters, but may also be the consequence of a style of reporting which tries to be specific and tends to simplify issues. The evidence of case studies reported separately lends some support to this view. While it is plausible that strike action or its threat does ultimately relate to pay negotiations in most cases, there are presumably often other reasons why normal channels of settlement have failed or factors which complicate the issue.

118

## FIGURE I: TYPICAL PROFILE OF ITEMS DEALING WITH STRIKES (ACTUAL FREQUENCIES FOR ALL NEWSPAPERS)

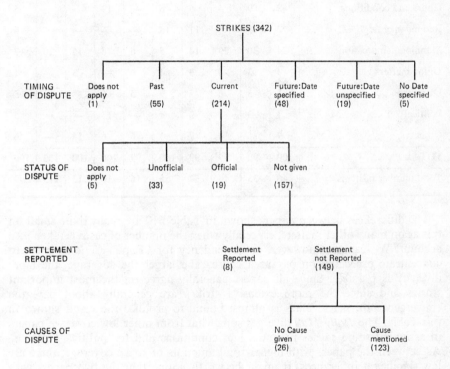

In all, 36% of all strikes stories followed the pattern indicated in Figure I and a further 43% differed in only one respect—that is by a difference of time reference, or reporting a settlement, or giving the status of the dispute.

**TABLE B10**

**REPORTED CAUSES OF STRIKES: PERCENTAGE DISTRIBUTION, NATIONAL DAILY NEWSPAPERS, 1975**

| Causes | The Times | The Guardian | The Daily Telegraph | Financial Times | Morning Star | Daily Express | Daily Mail | Daily Mirror | The Sun | ALL |
|---|---|---|---|---|---|---|---|---|---|---|
| | % | % | % | % | % | % | % | % | % | % |
| Pay ... ... ... ... | 50 | 42 | 44 | 53 | 47 | 75 | 50 | 62 | 67 | 52 |
| Hours and conditions ... | 2 | 9 | 4 | 5 | 6 | — | 19 | — | — | 5 |
| Redundancy ... ... ... | 2 | 3 | 4 | 11 | 18 | — | — | — | — | 6 |
| Manning/demarcation ... | 24 | 30 | 29 | 14 | 5 | 6 | 6 | 15 | 20 | 17 |
| Union matters ... ... | 4 | 3 | 4 | 3 | 4 | 6 | — | 8 | — | 4 |
| Dismissal ... ... ... | 2 | 3 | 6 | 3 | 9 | 6 | 6 | — | 13 | 5 |
| Political ... ... ... | 7 | 3 | 4 | 3 | 7 | — | 13 | — | — | 5 |
| Other ... ... ... ... | 9 | 6 | 4 | 7 | 4 | 6 | 6 | 15 | — | 6 |
| TOTAL ... ... ... | 100 | 99 | 99 | 99 | 100 | 99 | 100 | 100 | 100 | 100 |
| Total number of items ... | 46 | 33 | 48 | 57 | 55 | 16 | 16 | 13 | 15 | 299 |

The differences between papers shown in Table B10 are really quite small on this as on many other matters, especially when the number of cases is taken into account. We can see, however, some tendency for "Popular" newspapers to concentrate especially on pay as a cause. The larger the coverage, the more diversity is possible. Since all papers generally agree on the most important stories and since the more extensive strikes are generally about pay, the convergence on news values is almost bound to produce the result shown in this Table. The *Daily Mail* diverges somewhat from other low coverage papers in assigning some causes to hours and conditions and to "political" matters. As between the papers with higher total amounts of strike coverage, there are few significant differences. It might be worth noting that the two papers with most strike stories—the *Financial Times* and the *Morning Star*—are both more likely to have recorded redundancy as a cause of strikes.

## 7. Industrial relations content: "other disputes"

While strikes predominate in reports of disputes as the single most common form of industrial action, other disputes were not unimportant, accounting for 14% of all items. The main types of dispute and their frequency of occurrence are shown in the following table.

The largest single category includes disputes or industrial action of an unspecified kind. The size of this category may be due to the fact that a fair number of stories involved a reference to an ongoing dispute which the interested reader might be expected to know about. Thus, it would be mistaken to conclude that a large proportion of disputes are not given a specific description. A large

# TABLE B11

OTHER DISPUTES BESIDES STRIKES: ACTUAL FREQUENCY OF OCCURRENCE IN EACH NEWSPAPER AND OVERALL PERCENTAGE DISTRIBUTION

| Type | The Times | The Guardian | The Daily Telegraph | Financial Times | Morning Star | Daily Express | Daily Mail | Daily Mirror | The Sun | ALL |
|---|---|---|---|---|---|---|---|---|---|---|
| | N | N | N | N | N | N | N | N | N | % |
| Work-to-rule/overtime ban... | 5 | 7 | 3 | 6 | 3 | 5 | 6 | 2 | 6 | 20 |
| Blacking/lockout ... ... | — | — | 1 | 2 | 4 | — | 1 | 1 | 1 | 5 |
| Picketing/lobbying/demonstrations ... ... ... | 5 | 3 | 4 | 5 | 11 | 4 | 2 | 2 | 6 | 20 |
| Token stoppage ... ... | 1 | 2 | 2 | 4 | 3 | 3 | 2 | 2 | 1 | 9 |
| Unspecified ... ... ... | 9 | 7 | 9 | 16 | 13 | 5 | 3 | 6 | 3 | 33 |
| Other ... ... ... ... | 6 | 4 | 2 | 4 | 7 | 2 | 1 | 1 | 2 | 13 |
| TOTAL% ... ... ... | | | | | | | | | | 100 |
| Total number of items: ... | 26 | 23 | 21 | 37 | 41 | 19 | 15 | 14 | 19 | 215 |

number of these unspecified dispute cases may, of course, involve strikes. Where information is available, it seems that "work to rule or overtime bans" and "picketing, lobbying or demonstrations" share first place. Individual newspapers diverge little from the general pattern. The newspapers with highest coverage tend to have more "unspecified" dispute cases, probably because they carry more continuing reports of ongoing disputes and assume reader awareness of particulars. In *proportionate* terms, the *Daily Mail* gives particular attention to cases of working to rule and overtime bans. The *Morning Star* notices picketing and lobbying more and so, marginally, does *The Sun* newspaper. The figures provide a reminder of a point made earlier that, in absolute terms the newspapers do not differer so greatly in the number of "other dispute" stories, leaving aside the *Financial Times* and *Morning Star*. This is because of the relatively greater attention to such dispute stories, by comparison with strike stories, in the "Popular" papers (see above p. 115).

The causes attributed to disputes other than strikes take a somewhat different pattern. For the largest category—unspecified disputes—the distribution is similar, with 63% of causes connected with pay. Much the same applies to working to rule and overtime bans (73% with a pay cause). However, "Picketing or lobbying" and token stoppages are much less linked with pay as a cause— in the former case only 5% and the latter, 41%. Instead, a varied range of causes is referred to. The full details are in Table B12.

When different newspapers are compared according to the frequency of reference to the various causes of disputes, taking strikes and other disputes together, the pattern apparent in Table B10 tends to be confirmed and in some respects accentuated. Pay is the most important of all causes and the percentage

121

attribution ranges from 39% in the *Morning Star* to 58% in *The Sun*, with an average of all titles at 48%. The *Daily Mail* stands out more sharply as the paper most likely to mention political causes of disputes and 17% of its references to causes are so classified. It is also the paper most likely to mention hours and conditions—also 17% of its cause references.

**TABLE B12**

**CAUSES ASSOCIATED WITH DISPUTES OTHER THAN STRIKES**

| Cause | Type of industrial action | | | | | |
|---|---|---|---|---|---|---|
| | Work-to-rule/ Overtime ban | Blacking/ Lockout | Picketing/ Lobbying | Token Stoppage | Unspecified | Other |
| | % | % | % | % | % | % |
| Pay ... ... ... | 73 | 60 | 5 | 41 | 63 | 21 |
| Hours/conditions ... | 9 | — | — | 5 | 5 | 14 |
| Redundancy ... ... | 7 | 10 | 22 | 9 | 7 | 25 |
| Manning/demarcation | 9 | 10 | 20 | 5 | 4 | 11 |
| Union matters ... | 2 | 20 | 5 | — | — | — |
| Dismissal ... ... | — | — | 5 | 18 | 8 | 14 |
| Political ... ... | — | — | 22 | 9 | 13 | — |
| Other ... ... ... | — | — | 22 | 14 | — | 14 |
| TOTAL% ... ... | 100 | 100 | 101 | 101 | 100 | 99 |
| Total number ... | 43 | 10 | 42 | 21 | 71 | 29 |

# IV Themes

## 1. Introduction

The idea of a theme as distinct from a topic or sub-topic was discussed in some detail in I, 7. In brief, themes have been thought of as the underlying public concerns which at a given time provide either the criteria for selecting events as newsworthy or the frame of reference for interpreting events and assessing their significance.

The *topics* of reporting provide a set of mutually exclusive categories for classifying reports of events. *Themes*, on the other hand, do not normally classify whole items but simply appear in the content in the form of a reference to a particular aspect of an event. They may perhaps be thought of as "news angles", since they give perspective and context to reports. The analysis reported here is based on a selected number of themes which were pre-selected according to their anticipated relevance to the events of 1975. Obviously, other definitions of relevant themes might have produced somewhat different results. It should also be recalled that any number of different theme references could be recorded for a given item although, in the event, on average less than one theme per item was coded. The main purposes behind the theme analysis were to pick up some of the more incidental aspects of news content, which the classification by topic does not capture, to be able to compare newspapers in terms of "preferred" themes; to be able to "profile" different topics in terms of the themes which characterised them in general; to add a somewhat more qualitative dimension to the analysis without loss of objectivity in the method of recording and without departing from the quantitative approach which is some security against investigator bias. Finally, it should be pointed out again that to record a reference to a theme which implies a value judgement is not to record a view of the newspaper or writer. Generally, in news reports at least, the reference will derive from some source, to which an attribution is made (this is fairly clear from the case-study material contained in Part C). It is a weakness of the method that no distinction can be made according to source. For instance, references to support for the pay policy might come from a union leader, a Government Minister, an employer or the newspaper itself.

## 2. Frequency of theme references

It is clear from Table B13 below that the different themes appeared very unevenly in news reports, with a great majority of references concentrating on a small number out of the 38 which were available. Themes are listed according to the wording in the coding frame (see Appendix B1) and in order of overall frequency. Three general subjects dominate the list of themes: discord in union/ Government relations; the harmful consequences of industrial actions; and internal union conflict. The latter is connected with the first mentioned, since much conflict related to disagreement between "militant" and "moderate" elements in unions over the size of pay claims or over the recourse to industrial action, in the light of the social contract. It is noticeable that the points which head the list are all "negative" in their implications in that they refer to conflict, or failure, or harmful effects of industrial action. The second point to note is the relative scarcity of theme references, bearing in mind that 1,492 items were coded and, in all, only 1,180 theme references were recorded. There are two

## TABLE B13

**THEMES IN THE REPORTING OF INDUSTRIAL RELATIONS: OVERALL FREQUENCY, ALL NINE NATIONAL DAILY NEWSPAPERS***

| | Theme | No. of references |
|---|---|---|
| 1. | Union or TUC *discord* in relations with Government (46) | 173 |
| 2. | Loss of output or money by firm or industry as effect (50) | 91 |
| 3. | Conflict within union, especially left vs right (59) | 78 |
| 4. | Inconvenience or danger to public as effect (48) | 73 |
| 5. | Weakness or failure of Government pay policy (58) | 58 |
| 6. | Loss of work by non-disputants as effect (51) | 57 |
| 7. | Success of, or support for, Government pay policy (58) | 50 |
| 8. | Worker participation, profit-sharing (70) | 47 |
| 9. | Alleged political motivation, left-wing militancy (57) | 43 |
| 10. | Solidarity between workers in dispute (68) | 43 |
| 11. | Inter-union disputes or TUC vs union (61) | 42 |
| 12. | Employer *discord* in relations with Government (47) | 41 |
| 13. | Unreasonable behaviour by employers (53) | 38 |
| 14. | Anti-union activity by employers (55) | 36 |
| 15. | Pay claim or award large or excessive (45) | 29 |
| 16. | Union or TUC *accord* in relations with Government (46) | 28 |
| 17. | Closed shop references (74) | 26 |
| 18. | Damage or threat to economy, as effect (49) | 25 |
| 19. | Financial danger to firm or industry, as effect (53) | 20 |
| 20. | Criticism of unions, unreasonable, "wildcat" strikes (56) | 18 |
| 21. | Blacklegs, "lump", non-union labour (72) | 18 |
| 22. | Intimidation or violence by strikers, pickets (60) | 16 |
| 23. | Women's work, equal pay (63) | 16 |
| 24. | Lack of solidarity of workers (68) | 15 |
| 25. | Good news in industrial relations (75) | 14 |
| 26. | Pay claim or settlement in line with policy (45) | 14 |
| 27. | Pay claim or settlement low or inadequate (45) | 13 |
| 28. | The class struggle (62) | 12 |
| 29. | Sex aspects generally (64) | 11 |
| 30. | Strike—proneness (73) | 11 |
| 31. | Public ignorance or misunderstanding (71) | 7 |
| 32. | Public sympathy or support for disputants (66) | 4 |
| 33. | Dispute unnecessary or absurd (65) | 4 |
| 34. | Welfare costs, "fiddles" and subsidies (69) | 3 |
| 35. | Lack of public sympathy (66) | 2 |
| 36. | Employer *accord* in relation with Government (47) | 2 |
| 37. | Resentment at, or criticism of, employer privileges (54) | 1 |
| 38. | Objections to strike by families of strikers (67) | 1 |
| | | **1,180** |

* The numbers in the brackets after each item refer to the numbers in the left-hand column of the coding frame in Appendix B1.

explanations for this. One relates to the strict application of the rule that only clear and specific references should be coded. This has almost certainly led to under-recording and, as a result, these data have to be regarded as minimum figures. As a further consequence, they can only be regarded as giving a *relative* picture of the incidence of themes. A second explanation relates to the character of most news reporting, which is generally of a "factual" kind. Since many of the themes do imply value judgements their appearance in news reports is, for that reason, less likely. The evidence from detailed case studies (Part C of this report) supports this interpretation.

This incidence of theme references works out as an overall average of 0·8 per item. However, we know from a separate count that 654 items (44% of the total) had no theme recorded. The average number of themes per item for the remainder of the sample was 1·4. In general, as one would expect, the longer the item the more themes recorded and very small factual reports (under 10 col. cms) carried no indications of a theme. Not surprisingly, in view of what has been said about the evaluative character of some themes, editorials have a disproportionately large number of themes (see Section VII below).

## 3. Themes in relation to main topics

One purpose of the attempt to record themes in the way described was to help further characterise the content under the separate topic headings. The question to be answered is: what themes are associated with a particular topic?

**TABLE B14**
**SEVEN MAIN TOPICS AND THREE MOST ASSOCIATED THEMES**
(The percentage figures show what proportion of the items under each topic heading carried the listed theme)

| Main Topic | Most frequent theme | % | Second most frequent theme | % | Third most frequent theme | % |
|---|---|---|---|---|---|---|
| Strikes (n = 342) | Loss of output to firm or industry | 19·5 | Loss of work by non-disputants | 15·5 | Inconvenience or danger to the public | 11·5 |
| Union or TUC actions or statements (n = 269) | Discord in relations between unions and Government | 36·5 | Accord in relations between unions and Government | 6·0 | Weakness or failure of pay policy | 5·0 |
| Disputes, other than strikes (n = 215) | Inconvenience or danger to the public | 13·0 | Discord in relations between unions and Government | 10·5 | Obstinacy or unreasonable behaviour by employers | 9·5 |
| Pay negotiations (n = 164) | Success of, or conformity with, Government pay policy | 7·5 | Pay claim large or excessive | 7·0 | Pay claim small or inadequate | 6·0 |
| Union elections and other internal matters (n = 140) | Conflict within union especially left versus right | 22·0 | Disputes between unions | 8·5 | Alleged political motivation | 4·0 |
| Industrial developments (n = 109) | Employer-Government relations | 7·5 | Discord in relations between unions and Government | 6·5 | — | — |
| Actions or statements by Government (n = 83) | Weakness or failure of pay policy | 14·5 | Success of pay policy | 12·0 | Discord in relations between unions and Government | 9·5 |

In this case it was thought necessary to look only at the seven topics which accounted for most of the items and at the more frequently occurring themes in each case. The analysis carried out was to count the number of different themes which were recorded for items under each main topic category. The results are given in Table B14, with the number of themes expressed as a percentage of the total of items for each topic.

Table B14 confirms common-sense expectations and helps to clarify the context in which the theme references occurred. It also suggests that some topics are generally more likely than others to have an associated theme. For instance, news of pay negotiations and industrial developments are least likely to do so. This may be interpreted as reflecting their more barely factual character. In so far as the occurrence of themes does, albeit indirectly, reflect the intrusion of judgement and interpretation, their presence or absence may indicate something of editorial policy in this respect. If this is so, news reports seem more prone to give *some* interpretation to strike stories and union initiatives.

Four main points emerge from the table. Firstly, news of strikes was particularly likely to be accompanied by some reference to the undesirable effects of strikes—20% of such stories referred to loss of output, 16% to loss of work by others, 12% to inconvenience to the public. (The cumulative percentage of strike items with at least one of those references cannot be obtained by adding the percentages since the references might have occurred jointly). Secondly, in more than a third of the cases, news of union or TUC initiatives was associated with a reference to disagreement with the Government. For the most part, given the events of 1975, we can assume the disagreement to relate to pay policy. Thirdly, where news of pay negotiations is involved, there are marginally more references to the success of Government pay policy than to its failure. This might seem an exception to the "negative" tendency of reporting otherwise apparent. Fourthly, news of internal union matters, in over a fifth of cases, carried a reference to conflict within the union, especially conflict between "militants" and "moderates".

These results and Table B14 tell only part of the story of the way in which subjects are characterised by themes. In particular, we can take note of a marked lack of association between a topic and a theme—in the sense that some topics carry a disproportionately low number of references to a theme which might logically have been associated. The fuller evidence from which Table B14 is drawn shows, for example, that in only seven out of 342 cases did the topic of strikes carry a reference to union/Government discord, although there were 173 such references. By contrast, other sorts of disputes (see Table B14) did carry such a reference in over 10% of cases. There are two possible explanations for this. One is that strikes are less "political" than other sorts of dispute. Another is that reporting does tend to keep politics out of strictly industrial conflicts.

Some other points to emerge from data not presented in Table B14 are: references to worker solidarity are concentrated in strike or dispute stories; references to worker control or participation occur in several contexts, but 18 out of 43 are associated with strikes or other disputes; references to conflict within unions are linked with strike stories—more than a quarter of the 78 references occur in that context; of 43 references to political motivation, 17 were linked to news of strikes or disputes.

126

TABLE B15

FOURTEEN MOST FREQUENTLY OCCURRING THEMES: PERCENTAGE DISTRIBUTION

| Main Themes | The Times | The Guardian | The Daily Telegraph | Financial Times | Morning Star | Daily Express | Daily Mail | Daily Mirror | The Sun | All newspapers |
|---|---|---|---|---|---|---|---|---|---|---|
| | % | % | % | % | % | % | % | % | % | % |
| Union/TUC discord with Government | 14 | 12 | 16 | 19 | 43 | 22 | 24 | 25 | 10 | 20 |
| Loss of output due to dispute | 16 | 9 | 12 | 14 | 6 | 4 | 1 | 17 | 6 | 11 |
| Conflict within union | 10 | 9 | 11 | 10 | 7 | 7 | 10 | 5 | 6 | 9 |
| Inconvenience or danger to public | 9 | 10 | 11 | 7 | — | 9 | 15 | 9 | 10 | 8 |
| Weakness of Government pay policy | 4 | 7 | 5 | 10 | 5 | 5 | 7 | 8 | 10 | 7 |
| Loss of work by non-disputants | 11 | 6 | 4 | 7 | 10 | 2 | 3 | 5 | 8 | 7 |
| Success of pay policy | 5 | 6 | 8 | 7 | 1 | 8 | 3 | 7 | 10 | 6 |
| Worker participation/profit sharing | 7 | 6 | 4 | 7 | 7 | 4 | 1 | 5 | 6 | 5 |
| Alleged political motivation | 5 | 2 | 9 | 3 | 1 | 9 | 7 | 4 | 12 | 5 |
| Solidarity between workers | 2 | 4 | 3 | 1 | 17 | 4 | 7 | 7 | 6 | 5 |
| Inter-union disputes | 4 | 8 | 4 | 7 | 2 | 9 | 4 | 4 | — | 5 |
| Unreasonable behaviour by employers | 5 | 8 | 6 | 2 | — | 6 | 7 | 2 | 6 | 4 |
| Employer/Government discord | 7 | 10 | 4 | 5 | 2 | 4 | 3 | 3 | — | 5 |
| Pay claim or award excessive | — | 4 | 4 | 3 | — | 9 | 9 | — | 8 | 3 |
| Total per cent | 99 | 101 | 101 | 102 | 101 | 102 | 101 | 101 | 100 | 100 |
| Total number | 135 | 114 | 114 | 167 | 92 | 55 | 74 | 59 | 49 | 860 |

## 4. Inter-relationships between themes

It was intended, in planning the examination of themes, to see whether or not certain themes tended to occur together to any unusual degree in the reporting of particular items. Underlying this aim was the wish to see whether or not a pattern or structure of interpretation might be inferred as lying beneath the objective reporting of facts. The more different themes cluster together in their occurrence, the more likely this would have seemed to be the case. For instance, one might have found a tendency for various points critical of unions or workers to cluster together, beyond the level of chance association. In the event, there was very little evidence of inter-relationship between themes. In part this only reflects the paucity of references and the fact that relatively few items had more than one theme coded. In part, it probably also indicates a generally non-tendentious character of news reporting.

## 5. Comparisons between newspapers

In Table B15 figures are given showing the frequency of coding of the most common themes in different newspapers. The full set of data from which this table is derived is contained in Appendix B4.

The first impression is of a good deal of consistency between newspapers. The four most frequent themes are much the same in each newspaper. Even so, this leaves a good deal of scope for variation. A closer inspection shows that only *The Daily Telegraph* and *The Guardian* conform in their top four to the overall four most frequently mentioned themes. The *Morning Star* is most divergent, with the reference to union/Government discord being the only one theme of its first four to conform to the overall distribution. The most salient points of the comparison can be given on a paper-by-paper basis.

*The Times* differs from the overall mean in its high level of mentions of loss of work by non-disputants and its relatively high mention of loss of output due to disputes.

*The Guardian* is very close to the overall mean, deviating only in the higher proportion of references to "unreasonable behaviour" on the part of employers.

*The Daily Telegraph* is also near to the average, apart from a greater tendency to mention political motivation and militancy.

The *Financial Times* is differentially more inclined to mention loss of output and disinclined to mention worker solidarity and militancy.

The *Morning Star* concentrates on union/Government conflict and worker solidarity. On several points, it remains close to the norm—for instance in references to inter-union conflict, loss of work by non-disputants, weakness of Government pay policy.

The *Daily Express* differs from the norm in its lower attention to the industrial effects of disputes and its greater number of references to political motivation or militancy, to inter-union disputes and to excessive pay claims or awards.

The *Daily Mail* has rather similar characteristics, although the number of references it makes to public inconvenience from strikes is especially high, at 15%, compared to 9% overall.

The *Daily Mirror* is exceptionally inclined to refer to loss of output as a result of industrial action and above average in mentions of union/Government conflict.

*The Sun* has a distinctive profile, with references to political motivation appearing most often, followed by those to public inconvenience, pay policy generally and to union/Government conflict. Its attention to the latter is, of all newspapers, proportionately the lowest.

It is not easy to discern in all this any clear pattern of difference between groups of newspapers, although *The Guardian* and *The Daily Telegraph* and the *Daily Express* and *Daily Mail*, respectively, pair off as rather similar to each other. For example, the more "Popular" titles do not systematically differ from the "Qualities" although some themes are disproportionately concentrated in one group rather than another. Thus, *The Times, The Guardian, The Daily Telegraph* and *Financial Times* account for 60% of all themes, but for 77% of references to loss of output, 70% of those refer to intra-union conflict and 72% of those to inter-union disputes.

One of the reasons for looking at these themes was the wish to provide some evidence on the question of newspaper bias—especially the possibility of unfavourable impressions being unintentionally made on the reader because of the application of certain news angles. What can be concluded from the evidence contained in Table B15 and the fuller data in Appendix B3? Firstly, it should again be said that the reporting of a theme does not necessarily implicate the newspaper itself in any judgement or interpretation. Secondly, the absence of contextual evidence makes it impossible to equate a count of references with an assessment of newspaper direction or bias. One thing that can be done with the data in their present form is to show whether or not certain themes which might reflect more "negatively" on unions or workers showed up to a greater or lesser extent in different newspapers. For instance, four themes refer to harmful effects of industrial action (nos, 2, 4, 6, and 18 in Appendix B4 p. 332); another refers to left-wing militancy or political motivation (no 9); another relates to criticism of the unreasonable behaviour of unions (no 20); another relates to intimidation or violence by strikers (no 22). If these seven themes are taken together and regarded as indicating the level of unfavourability of presentation of unions, the following result is achieved when the total of references to the seven is expressed as a percentage of all references coded in each newspaper:

| The Times | The Guardian | The Daily Telegraph | Financial Times | Morning Star | Daily Express | Daily Mail | Daily Mirror | The Sun | All newspapers |
|---|---|---|---|---|---|---|---|---|---|
| % 31 | % 26 | % 32 | % 26 | % 12 | % 20 | % 32 | % 32 | % 28 | % 25 |

Apart from the *Morning Star* and the *Daily Express*, all the results fall within the range of 26% to 32%, which tends to confirm the view that the papers differ rather little from each in the news angles and frames of reference they employ and in the degree of partiality. It should be remembered that these results relate not to news alone, but also to editorials where directly evaluative comments are more likely to be found. If editorials are left out of the calculation, the figures for news and features on their own are somewhat changed. The main differences would be that *The Daily Telegraph* and *Daily Mail* percentage figures would both fall to 30%.

129

# V   Branches of industry reported

1. For each item, where appropriate, the actual industry or firm involved was recorded and also classified according to one of 27 main branches of industry, as set out in the standard industrial classification (1968) of the Department of Employment. The details of the scheme are given in Appendix B5. In a number of cases, no industry could be coded, often because the story involved general trade union matters or Government relations with industry. In addition to listing the distribution of reports according to industry, we have looked at relationships with some other aspects of the data, and made comparisons between papers and between our findings and other relevant statistics.

## 2. Number of items in each industry group

The data presented in col. I of Table B16 show a strong tendency for reports to concentrate in a small number of branches of industry. Thus, three in particular—transport and communication (18%), vehicles (15%) and professional and scientific services (11%)—account between them for 44% of all items. Since 21% of items involve no specific industry reference, the remaining 35% of items are distributed amongst a large number of industries. Of these, 7% go to printing and publishing, 5% to public administration and 4% to mining and quarrying. It is not surprising, consequently, to find that several branches of industry hardly receive any reporting and the various branches of engineering are notably absent. It should be remembered that some of the branches of industry, as tabulated, are quite diverse. For instance, the most represented group, "transport and communication", involves rail and bus services, docks, ports, air services and post and telecommunications. "Vehicles" includes locomotive and aerospace equipment as well as motor cars. "Professional and scientific services" includes education and medicine, and so on. Even so, the picture is one of high concentration on a small number of areas of employment. This may be an artefact of the year sampled, or it may reflect other tendencies in news reporting and other factors not apparent from these data. Further comment is made in 6 below, where the comparative figures given in Table B16 are discussed.

## 3. Prominence accorded to different branches of industry

Reports relating to each industry group were looked at in terms of relative prominence according to the "scale of prominence" which has already been described. The main result was to show that relative frequency of mention was strongly correlated with degree of prominence—the more frequently mentioned an industry group, the more prominent the presentation. Thus, stories involving no industry were most prominent, accounting for 36% of all front page lead stories while the top three industry groups (transport, vehicles, professional services) accounted for a further 52% of lead items. If anything, the concentration of attention apparent in relative frequency is accentuated by positioning and also length. Some figures in Table B18 help to illustrate this point.

**TABLE B16**

**DISTRIBUTION OF THE FOLLOWING AGAINST THE STANDARD INDUSTRIAL CLASSIFICATION OF MAIN BRANCHES OF INDUSTRY**

I     Percentage of all industrial relations reports (n=1,492).
II    Percentage of all items with strikes as main topic (n=342).
III   Percentage of all stoppages in 1975*.
IV   Percentage of aggregate working days lost in 1975*.
V    Percentage of working population*.

| Branches of industry | I | II | III | IV | V |
|---|---|---|---|---|---|
| | % | % | % | % | % |
| 0 No industry coded ... ... ... | 21 | 6 | NA | NA | NA |
| 1 Agriculture, forestry and fishing ... | 1 | — | — | — | 2 |
| 2 Mining and quarrying ... ... ... | 4 | 1 | 10 | 1 | 2 |
| 3 Food, drink and tobacco ... ... | 1 | 1 | 4 | 3 | 3 |
| 4 Coal and petroleum products... ... | — | — | — | 1 | — |
| 5 Chemicals and allied industries ... | 1 | 1 | 2 | 3 | 2 |
| 6 Metal manufacture ... ... ... | 2 | 2 | 7 | 6 | 2 |
| 7 Mechanical engineering ... ... | — | 1 | 15 | 12 | 4 |
| 8 Instrument engineering ... ... | — | — | 1 | — | 1 |
| 9 Electrical engineering ... ... ... | 2 | 2 | 7 | 16 | 4 |
| 10 Shipbuilding and marine engineering... | 1 | 2 | 3 | 8 | 1 |
| 11 Vehicles ... ... ... ... ... | 15 | 29 | 9 | 19 | 3 |
| 12 Metal goods not elsewhere specified ... | — | 1 | 6 | 3 | 3 |
| 13 Textiles ... ... ... ... ... | 2 | — | 3 | 4 | 3 |
| 14 Leather, leather goods and fur ... | — | — | — | — | — |
| 15 Clothing and footwear ... ... | 1 | 1 | 2 | 2 | 2 |
| 16 Bricks, pottery, glass, cement, etc ... | — | — | 2 | 1 | 1 |
| 17 Timber, furniture, etc ... ... ... | — | — | 1 | 2 | 1 |
| 18 Paper, printing and publishing ... | 7 | 5 | 2 | 2 | 3 |
| 19 Other manufacturing industries ... | — | — | 2 | 2 | 2 |
| 20 Construction ... ... ... ... | 2 | 1 | 9 | 4 | 6 |
| 21 Gas, electricity and water ... ... | 2 | 3 | 1 | — | 2 |
| 22 Transport and communication ... | 18 | 29 | 8 | 7 | 7 |
| 23 Distributive trades ... ... ... | — | — | 2 | 1 | 12 |
| 24 Insurance and banking, etc ... ... | 1 | — | — | — | — |
| 25 Professional and scientific services ... | 11 | 9 | 1 | — | 20 |
| 26 Miscellaneous services ... ... ... | 3 | 2 | 2 | 1 | 9 |
| 27 Public administration and defence ... | 5 | 5 | 3 | 2 | 7 |
| TOTAL ... ... | 100% | 101% | 102% | 100% | 102% |

*Note:* Due to rounding, a nil entry in the table signifies any value between 0 and 0·5%.

\* Data extrapolated from DOE Gazette, May, 1976.

In certain cases, there is evidence that industry groups which were generally little reported did get prominent treatment where news of them did appear. This would show up, for instance, in the ratio of prominent and long to less prominent and short items relating to the industry groups involved. However, the general pattern for "under-reported" industry groups is for short items to far outweigh long items. Exceptions occur in the case of mining (group 2), metal manufacture (group 6), ship and marine engineering (group 10) and gas, electricity and water (group 21). For instance, of the 53 items dealing with mining, 13% occur on the front page and of non-front page items, 32% are over 20 col.cms. and 26% under 11 col.cms. The pattern for metal manufacture (33 items) is very similar. An industry with the "less prominent" pattern would be textiles (24 items), where no items were on the front page, 25% were over 20 col.cms. and 50% were ten or less.

**TABLE B17**

**DEGREE OF PROMINENCE ACCORDED TO MAIN INDUSTRY GROUPS**

| Degree of Prominence | No industry | Transport, Commu- nication | Vehicles | Professional and Scientific | All other | Total |
|---|---|---|---|---|---|---|
| | % | % | % | % | % | % |
| Percentage of front page lead items to industry n = 50 ... | 36 | 26 | 16 | 10 | 12 | 100 |
| Percentage of other large front page items n = 81 ... | 22 | 23 | 15 | 12 | 28 | 100 |
| Percentage of feature articles n = 30 ... | 53 | 3 | 13 | 3 | 28 | 100 |
| Items under 10 col. cm. n = 501 ... | 13 | 20 | 18 | 8 | 41 | 100 |

## 4. Comparisons between newspapers in reporting of industry groups

Detailed figures for the distribution of items according to industry groups for each of the nine national daily newspapers showed there to be few deviations from the overall pattern recorded in Table B16. The "no industry" category and the same three industry groups account for the large majority of all items in all newspapers. The only exceptions worthy of notice might be: the lower interest in the *Daily Express* in the "no industry" items (only 15% of items) and the higher than average attention to transport (25%); the relative inattention of the *Daily Mail* and *Daily Express* to "vehicles", with the *Daily Mail* also attending more to transport (23%). Otherwise, there is some small evidence of specialist attention to some employment areas: the *Morning Star* alone accounts for 48% of the 27 items dealing with the construction industry, and 36% of those on electrical engineering; the *Financial Times* accounts for a high proportion of reports in several "minority" industries (eg insurance and banking). Finally, there is a marked concentration of reports on the paper, printing and publishing industry in the *The Daily Telegraph*, *The Guardian* and *The Times*.

## 5. Relationship between main topics and industry groups

Some further light in the nature of reporting of different branches of industry can be shed by looking at the different topics of news associated with particular industries. For this purpose, we have considered only the seven main topics of reports which between them accounted for 90% of all cases and we have also paid attention only to the most frequently occurring industry groups. The evidence on which this discussion is based is set out in Table B18.

The table helps first to clarify the character of the items where no industry was coded—these were the cases where unions and Government were involved in matters unrelated to a specific industry. Secondly, we can see that the overall distribution of reports against industry groups does not closely fit the distribution for particular topics, although the general pattern is still evident, once allowance is made for the effect of the "no industry" category. For strike reports, the

**TABLE B18**

**MAIN TOPIC CATEGORIES: PERCENTAGE DISTRIBUTION OF ITEMS ACCORDING TO BRANCH OF INDUSTRY**

| Industry group | Main topic | | | | | | |
|---|---|---|---|---|---|---|---|
| | Strikes | Other disputes | Union/TUC actions | Pay negotiations | Union affairs | Industrial developments | Government actions |
| | % | % | % | % | % | % | % |
| No industry ... ... ... ... | 4 | 4 | 45 | 6 | 34 | 3 | 46 |
| Transport and communications ... ... | 29 | 20 | 18 | 26 | 4 | 6 | 8 |
| Vehicles ... ... ... ... | 29 | 8 | 6 | 9 | 2 | 36 | 10 |
| Professional and scientific ... ... | 9 | 28 | 11 | 13 | 10 | 1 | 2 |
| Paper, printing and publishing... ... | 5 | 16 | 3 | 4 | 11 | 6 | 7 |
| Public administration ... ... ... | 5 | 3 | 4 | 15 | 2 | 1 | 2 |
| Mining and quarrying ... ... ... | 1 | 1 | 3 | 7 | 9 | 2 | 12 |
| Metal manufacturing ... ... ... | 2 | 2 | 2 | 2 | — | 11 | 2 |
| Electrical engineering ... ... ... | 2 | 3 | — | — | 1 | 8 | 2 |
| Other industry groups ... ... ... | 14 | 15 | 8 | 18 | 27 | 26 | 5 |
| TOTAL ... ... ... | 100 | 100 | 100 | 100 | 100 | 100 | 96 |
| Total number of items with main topic heading ... | 342 | 215 | 269 | 164 | 140 | 109 | 83 |

133

three "top" industry groups still lead, but there are some divergences on most other topics. For "other disputes", paper and printing replaces vehicles as an important category. For "pay negotiations", public administration replaces vehicles. Under the heading of "industrial development", metal manufacturing and electrical engineering now precede transport and communications, probably because of bad news about closures and redundancy.

From a different perspective, the data on which Table B18 was based tell us which topics were most likely to have occurred in reports about particular industries. Taking only the larger industry groups with some concentration on particular topics, the following points can be made: mining is most associated with "union affairs" and "pay negotiations"; metal manufacturing goes with "industrial developments", as does electrical engineering; 50% of reports in the "vehicles" category are about strikes; printing and publishing and also professional and scientific services go strongly with "other disputes"; 39% of reports on transport and communication are about strikes; public administration is associated with pay negotiations as a topic of reporting.

## 6. Comparison between the representation of industry groups in industrial relations stories and evidence from other industrial statistics

The pattern of reporting recorded in column I of Table B16 appears an unusual one, in its concentration on a few industry groups. An original purpose in recording data about industry groups in the content analysis was to examine possible deviations from other versions of events in the field of industrial relations. In particular, we would like to find explanations, where our descriptive data allow, of characteristic patterns of content. At first sight, the high incidence of reports in three or four main fields of employment seems unusual. A comparison between this distribution and the distribution of the working population (column V of Table B16) amongst industry groups confirms this impression. There is little relationship between the two sets of figures, since the working population is fairly evenly distributed between the industry groups. The five industries which capture, between them, 71% of all content items where an industry was specified, only account for 40% of the working population. Many important groups of workers go largely unreported in the context of industrial relations.

Another possible point of comparison, given the strong focus of reporting on strikes and disputes, is between statistics relating to stoppages during the year 1975 and our own sample evidence of attention to strikes in different industries. Two main external indices were available—one of days lost through stoppages and the other of actual stoppages initiated in different industry groups. Columns III and IV of Table B16 provide the relevant data. It is apparent, again, that neither index accords very closely with our sample record of the distribution of strike stories by industry. On the other hand, it is true that in both sets of figures, the vehicles industry group ranks highest (or jointly so). However, several notably "strike-prone" industry groups (in 1975), expecially in engineering, have not figured in our sample of newspaper items as associated with strikes and vice versa. Of the five industry groups which account for 5% or more of strike stories, only two are amongst the six groups which accounted for 6% or more of aggregate working days lost. It does not seem, at least, as if actual incidence of stoppages plays, in general, a strong part in determining whether or not an industry group should figure in column II of Table B16.

However, the evidence already discussed shows that strikes and disputes do, in any case, provide only a subsidiary topic for a number of industry groups and it would be mistaken to concentrate only on stoppages as a possible explanatory factor. The topic of strikes is concentrated very much (58% of all cases) in the industry groups of "vehicles" and "transport and communications". As we can see, the "vehicles" industry group does in fact figure very prominently in the table of working days lost in 1975 and transport and communication ranks fifth. We also know from other evidence in DOE statistics that the *recently past* record of the transport and communications group for work stoppages had been one of industrial trouble. Taken together, this lends some support to the view that reports are not altogether divergent from the "reality", although it also suggests that a complex explanation would be required to account for all the features of the pattern of reporting.

From the evidence available from this content study, no conclusive answer can be arrived at. However, we can comment briefly on the character of those industry groups which were prominent in the overall distribution of reports of all kinds. Whether or not the strike topic was the most common in each case, they are all characterised by some degree of divergence in the extent of "strike" reporting from the actual 1975 strike record, as a comparison between columns II and IV shows. Thus, when were fer to the most prominent industry groups, we are also referring to industry groups where "strike proneness" has been indirectly reported. Principally involved are: vehicles; transport and communications; professional and scientific services; public administration; and gas, electricity and water. Apart from the first mentioned, all have in common a main location in the public sector. More generally, all are important politically for one of four main reasons. Either the Government or local government is involved in management (as in public administration); or the Government is employer or paymaster; or Government intervention is involved for financial reasons (as with the Motor industry); or Government incomes policy may be critically tested in these groups. One quite strong general impression to have emerged from this study as a whole and the related case studies, is of the closeness of political and industrial relations reporting. This shows up in the character of the most important topics and themes. It helps to explain why so much prominence is given in newspapers to what otherwise might seem relatively dry matters, lacking in much drama or human interest. The findings may bear the stamp of the particular year in which the survey was conducted, but it seems likely that political factors do normally play an important part in determining the focus of topics on different industries and the amount of attention paid.

The complexity of the forces which determine content has been emphasised. It would be simple-minded to judge the validity of the version of industrial relations apparent in this sample against one criterion, or to explain it by one factor. It is very likely that other factors help to account for the pattern of concentration which has been described. For instance, the importance of some industries in the groups singled out to the rest of the national or local economy is one such factor. Another is the likely public interest in industries which most

135

closely affect daily life, especially transport and communication. It would be easier to account for press interest, industry by industry, than for the pattern as a whole. Our conclusion that political factors play an important part does not exclude other explanations, but it helps to account for what might otherwise appear to be anomalies.

# VI    Participants reported

## 1. Introduction

The analysis procedure involved recording, for each item, the names of participants according to whether they were directly quoted, reported from or simply mentioned. Subsequently, participants were categorised according to the pre-coded scheme of classification which can be consulted in the coding frame (Appendix B1) or in Table B19 below. The intention has been to collect information about *main* participants and this has not generally been difficult. However, in some stories large numbers of minor participants were mentioned (for instance in conference reports), though not often quoted or reported. No exact rule could be established about the omission of minor participants and this has led to some uncertainty, although there is no reason to expect this to have had any systematically distorting effect on results.

## 2. Comparison between newspapers in reporting of participants

Table B19 shows, firstly, the overall distribution of participants against the main categories, without distinguishing according to the kind of reference made. The most obvious conclusion is that references to participants were concentrated amongst Government or trade union representatives, of one kind or another. The three categories of trade union participant between them account for 41 % of all references, with Government accounting for 24 %. There is a notable absence of representation of the political opposition, and the management "side" is also relatively under-represented.

Again, agreement between newspapers (which closely reflect, in numbers of participants referred to, the overall number of items) is very marked. All give about the same proportionate attention to Government, TUC and local or national trade union officials. The deviations from the overall average are confined to a small number of points: the *Morning Star* was least inclined to refer to management sources, and more inclined to refer to a worker or member of the public (unfortunately not separately coded); the *Daily Mail* was least inclined to refer to a trade union official (21 % compared to an overall 32 %) but high in attention to management sources; *The Sun* was highest and the *Financial Times* lowest in relative frequency of references to workers or members of the public.

## 3. Comparisons according to type of reporting

The distinction according to whether a person was mentioned, reported or quoted is an important one and the following tables (B20, B21 and B22) show the distribution of participants in terms of each. There was, overall, a greater number of mentions than either quotations or direct reports: for every 100 participants mentioned there were 73 quoted and 55 reported. This ratio varied somewhat from newspaper to newspaper but generally held good. In every case, the "mentioned" classification was largest and in all but one instance (the *Financial Times*), the "quoted" classification came second. There are, nevertheless, some divergences from the average which may reflect differences of reporting policy. The *Daily Express* and *Daily Mail* are much more likely to quote than to report, while the *Morning Star*, *The Times* and *The Guardian* lean in the other direction. The figures are as follows:

TABLE B19

PARTICIPANTS (MENTIONED, REPORTED OR QUOTED) IN INDUSTRIAL RELATIONS ITEMS: OVERALL PERCENTAGE DISTRIBUTION AGAINST MAIN CATEGORIES FOR EACH NEWSPAPER

| Type of Participant | The Times | The Guardian | The Daily Telegraph | Financial Times | Morning Star | Daily Express | Daily Mail | Daily Mirror | The Sun | All newspapers |
|---|---|---|---|---|---|---|---|---|---|---|
| Government ministers MP, Official | %21 | %24 | %20 | %24 | %25 | %28 | %26 | %27 | %24 | %24 |
| Opposition MP, etc. ... | 3 | 1 | 1 | 1 | — | 1 | 2 | 1 | 1 | 1 |
| TUC leader or spokesman ... | 4 | 4 | 2 | 7 | 4 | 5 | 4 | 6 | 5 | 5 |
| CBI leader or spokesman ... | 1 | — | — | 1 | — | — | — | 2 | 1 | 1 |
| Expert ... ... ... ... | 3 | 4 | 2 | 2 | 2 | 1 | 2 | 1 | 1 | 2 |
| Management, employer ... ... | 17 | 13 | 16 | 15 | 5 | 9 | 17 | 14 | 11 | 13 |
| TU Official... ... ... ... | 31 | 37 | 34 | 37 | 34 | 32 | 21 | 26 | 24 | 32 |
| Shop steward, convenor ... ... | 5 | 3 | 5 | 3 | 5 | 6 | 4 | 5 | 1 | 4 |
| Worker or member of public ... | 15 | 14 | 20 | 10 | 25 | 18 | 24 | 18 | 32 | 18 |
| TOTAL ... ... ... ... | 100 | 100 | 100 | 100 | 100 | 100 | 100 | 100 | 100 | 100 |
| Total number of references ... | 417 | 446 | 415 | 485 | 482 | 211 | 243 | 125 | 172 | 2,996 |

TABLE B20
PARTICIPANTS IN INDUSTRIAL RELATIONS CONTENT: RATIO OF FREQUENCY OF MENTIONS, TO REPORTS, TO QUOTES

| Type of Mention | The Times | The Guardian | The Daily Telegraph | Financial Times | Morning Star | Daily Express | Daily Mail | Daily Mirror | The Sun | All newspapers |
|---|---|---|---|---|---|---|---|---|---|---|
| Mentioned = ... ... ... | 100 | 100 | 100 | 100 | 100 | 100 | 100 | 100 | 100 | 100 |
| Reported = ... ... ... | 60 | 58 | 65 | 72 | 54 | 37 | 29 | 48 | 38 | 55 |
| Quoted = ... ... ... | 82 | 72 | 96 | 50 | 56 | 92 | 82 | 92 | 66 | 73 |

138

Different categories of participant tended to receive somewhat different kinds of reporting as the data in Tables B21 and B22 show. Firstly, we can compare the percentage distribution of all these mentioned, reported or quoted against the main categories of participant (Table B21). Secondly, we can see the degree to which each category of participant was either mentioned, reported or quoted (Table B22).

TABLE B21

PERCENTAGE DISTRIBUTION OF THOSE "MENTIONED", "REPORTED" OR "QUOTED" AGAINST CATEGORY OF PARTICIPANT

| Type of Participant | Mentioned | Reported | Quoted |
|---|---|---|---|
| Government Minister MP, etc. ...      ...      ... | %<br>40 | %<br>13 | %<br>9 |
| Opposition MP, etc.      ...      ...      ...      ... | 1 | 2 | 2 |
| TUC Leader/spokesman ...      ...      ...      ... | 3 | 6 | 5 |
| CBI Leader/spokesman ...      ...      ...      ... | — | 1 | 1 |
| Expert      ...      ...      ...      ...      ...      ... | 3 | 3 | 1 |
| Management/employer      ...      ...      ...      ... | 9 | 18 | 14 |
| TU Official ...      ...      ...      ...      ...      ... | 16 | 42 | 47 |
| Shop steward, convenor ...      ...      ...      ... | 2 | 5 | 7 |
| Worker or member of public      ...      ...      ... | 26 | 10 | 14 |
| TOTAL      ...      ... | 100 | 100 | 100 |
| Total frequencies ...      ...      ...      ...      ... | 1,315 | 726 | 955 |

It seems from this evidence, that "mentioned only" participants concentrate amongst Government representatives, while participants who are reported or quoted are much more likely to be trade union officials. The overall distribution shown in Table B19 should be modified if we are interested in the more "active" forms of participation in an industrial relations event. The following table puts the same data in a somewhat different light. The percentages should be read across the rows.

From this we can see that: Government figures rarely appear as quoted, or even reported, sources of statements; CBI leaders and shop stewards are more likely than not to appear as sources of quoted remarks. The table confirms the relative absence of quoted comments from management or employers. It would seem as if reporters of industrial relations events are "closer" to local trade union officials than to Government or employers.

Detailed figures were available comparing newspapers within the three main groupings of type of report, rather than in the undifferentiated way followed in Table B19. When the comparison is made, some of the tendencies which

139

show up in that table are accentuated, but the basic pattern (and its similarity across titles) is undisturbed, once allowance is made for the differences in reporting policy between newspapers which have just been discussed.

TABLE B22

**PERCENTAGE DISTRIBUTION OF CATEGORIES OF PARTICIPANT AGAINST MAIN TYPES OF REPORTING**

| Type of Participant | Mentioned | Reported | Quoted | Total |
|---|---|---|---|---|
| | % | % | % | % |
| Government Minister MP, etc. ... ... | 75 | 13 | 12 | 100 |
| Opposition MP, etc. ... ... ... ... | 28 | 31 | 41 | 100 |
| TUC Leader/spokesman ... ... ... | 29 | 33 | 38 | 100 |
| CBI Leader/spokesman ... ... ... | 19 | 25 | 56 | 100 |
| Expert ... ... ... ... ... ... | 50 | 32 | 18 | 100 |
| Management/employer ... ... ... | 31 | 34 | 35 | 100 |
| TU Official ... ... ... ... ... | 22 | 32 | 46 | 100 |
| Shop steward, convenor ... ... ... | 18 | 31 | 51 | 100 |
| Worker or member of public ... ... | 62 | 14 | 24 | 100 |

## 4. Frequency of mention of named participants

As well as categorising individuals mentioned in reports, names were recorded wherever these were given. In analysing the results, attention was paid particularly to names mentioned in the context of a quotation or a direct report of a speech, comment or statement. As we have seen (Table B20), more participants figured as "mentioned only" rather than as "reported" or "quoted", although, taken together, the latter categories outweigh the former. However, a report or quotation usually indicates a much more specific and probably more active involvement in an event and consequently it is more useful to record such data. Table B23 shows the main participants by name and the frequency with which they appeared in news reports in each newspaper. Two points should be borne in mind: firstly, the fact that in any given news report only one reference to a name will have been counted; secondly, the data are based on *name* references only and not "titles". Thus, where Mr Murray is referred to as "TUC leader" or Mr Benn as "Industry Secretary" this would not have been counted. Under-representation of absolute frequencies will have resulted, by other criteria, but the *order* of frequency will not have been much affected.

The results of this analysis show that on this, as on so many other matters, the newspapers are largely agreed. On the whole, no newspaper appears to have its own separate set of named sources and, in most cases, to appear as a quoted or reported "participant" is to appear as a source of information or comment. The list of names clearly reflects the incidence of particular disputes on the days sampled and an alternative set of sample days would probably have yielded a somewhat different set of names and frequency distribution. The full list of participants named at least once in a story contained 58 names in all.

140

# TABLE B23

FREQUENCY OF OCCURRENCE OF NAMED PARTICIPANTS AS REPORTED OR QUOTED IN INDUSTRIAL RELATIONS CONTENT (AT LEAST 10 REFERENCES)

| Participants | The Times | The Guardian | The Daily Telegraph | Financial Times | Morning Star | Daily Express | Daily Mail | Daily Mirror | The Sun | All newspapers |
|---|---|---|---|---|---|---|---|---|---|---|
| Mr Jack Jones | 6 | 12 | 4 | 12 | 7 | 7 | 4 | 5 | 5 | 62 |
| Mr S. Weighell | 5 | 7 | 7 | 6 | 5 | 5 | 4 | 2 | 3 | 44 |
| Mr Len Murray | 7 | 6 | 3 | 8 | 5 | 2 | 2 | 3 | 4 | 40 |
| Mr Ray Buckton | 4 | 4 | 7 | 5 | 4 | 4 | 4 | 2 | 2 | 36 |
| Mr Foot | 4 | 6 | 6 | 6 | 4 | 4 | 3 | 1 | 1 | 35 |
| Mr Wilson | 3 | 3 | 0 | 1 | 1 | 2 | 2 | 2 | 5 | 20 |
| Mr Hugh Scanlon | 3 | 4 | 2 | 3 | 2 | 0 | 1 | 0 | 2 | 19 |
| Mr Clive Jenkins | 5 | 5 | 0 | 4 | 3 | 1 | 2 | 1 | 0 | 19 |
| Mr Benn | 2 | 2 | 2 | 2 | 1 | 0 | 1 | 0 | 1 | 13 |
| Mr Frank Chapple | 3 | 3 | 0 | 3 | 2 | 0 | 2 | 1 | 1 | 13 |
| Mr Sirs | 2 | 1 | 2 | 5 | 1 | 0 | 0 | 1 | 1 | 13 |
| Mr Poore (NVT) | 2 | 0 | 0 | 2 | 0 | 1 | 1 | 1 | 1 | 12 |
| Mrs Castle | 3 | 2 | 1 | 3 | 1 | 0 | 1 | 0 | 0 | 11 |
| Mr Wade | 2 | 0 | 2 | 2 | 1 | 1 | 1 | 0 | 1 | 11 |
| Mr David Basnett | 1 | 0 | 0 | 4 | 1 | 1 | 1 | 0 | 1 | 10 |
| Mr Bowman | 1 | 1 | 1 | 1 | 1 | 2 | 2 | 1 | 1 | 10 |
| Mr Larry Smith | 2 | 0 | 1 | 2 | 1 | 2 | 2 | 0 | 1 | 10 |
| Mr Bob Morriss | 0 | 1 | 1 | 2 | 2 | 1 | 0 | 1 | 2 | 10 |
| Mr Bob Wright | 1 | 2 | 1 | 2 | 2 | 1 | 0 | 1 | 0 | 10 |

# VII   Editorial content in newspapers sampled

1. It is clear from case studies (Part C of this report) that editorial comment in the press often does contain strongly worded expressions of opinion about industrial relations matters. In that context, newspapers are free to interpret and comment in ways which are inappropriate in news columns. While the number of cases of editorials picked up by this sample is, inevitably, low (46), it is worth looking separately at the results of the analysis for this category of item. It will be recalled that, in most of the foregoing analyses, editorials have been included as part of the general sample of 1,492 items. It should also be borne in mind that the frequency of 46 represents 21% of all individual issues of newspapers sampled, which means that, on average, every newspaper had at least one leader item each week on an industrial relations matter. This is fairly prominent treatment and matches the prominence given to this subject matter in terms of front page lead stories (24% of all).

## 2. Main topics of industrial relations content in editorials

The distribution of cases between the 12 main topics for editorials was quite different from that for all industrial relations items, as Table B25 shows. The topics which are news-worthy but less suitable for editorial treatment include, especially, "disputes" and "pay negotiations". In editorials they still account for 24% of all cases, but this contrasts with the figure of 47% for all items.

TABLE B24

MAIN TOPICS OF EDITORIAL COMMENT COMPARED TO ALL ITEMS

| Topic | Editorials (N=46) | All Items (N=1,492) |
|---|---|---|
| | % | % |
| Disputes ... ... ... ... ... ... ... | 20 | 36 |
| Pay negotiations ... ... ... ... ... ... | 4 | 11 |
| Government actions ... ... ... ... ... ... | 13 | 6 |
| Union/TUC actions ... ... ... ... ... ... | 26 | 18 |
| Inter- and Intra-Union affairs ... ... ... ... | 4 | 10 |
| Employer actions ... ... ... ... ... ... | 4 | 4 |
| Industrial and commercial developments ... ... ... | 4 | 8 |
| General economic context ... ... ... ... ... | 13 | 2 |
| Workers participation ... ... ... ... ... ... | 2 | 2 |
| Legal action ... ... ... ... ... ... ... | 2 | 2 |
| Other ... ... ... ... ... ... ... | 7 | 1 |
| TOTAL ... ... | 99% | 100% |

The place of these items was largely taken by the topics of "government actions" and "union/TUC actions". Perhaps it is unsurprising that the more strictly factual matters (as represented by dispute reports) should not carry proportionate editorial comment, but the pattern is consistent with our view that political aspects of industrial relations reports are particularly important. The relative importance of "general economic context" as a topic of industrial relations editorials is also to have been expected.

## 3. Themes in editorials

It is in the nature of themes as defined for this study that they are more likely to be found in editorials than in other sorts of content. This proved to be so, in that the average number of themes per editorial was 1·3 compared to 0·8 for a news or feature item. In section IV, 5 the proportion of all themes accounted for by the seven items most likely to reflect unfavourably on unions was calculated at 25% for the sample as a whole. The corresponding proportion of themes in editorials was 32%. The single most frequent theme referred to was conflict in relations between unions and Government which accounted for a further 20% of the 61 themes recorded in editorials.

## 4. Industry groups in editorials

The representation of different industries in editorials was also very close to the pattern for the whole sample of items. Those industries likely to get most frequent and prominent news coverage also predominated in editorials. In 20 cases, no industry was involved, and where one was directly mentioned transport and communications accounted for ten references and professional and scientific services for seven.

## 5. Comparisons between newspapers

The 46 editorials were distributed unevenly between titles and in a way which does not reflect the overall distribution of space or numbers of items devoted to industrial relations content. The actual frequency of editorials per newspaper in the 24 days sampled was as follows:

| | | | | |
|---|---|---|---|---|
| The Times | : 2 | | Daily Express | : 6 |
| The Guardian | : 3 | | Daily Mail | : 5 |
| The Daily Telegraph | : 7 | | Daily Mirror | : 1 |
| Financial Times | : 3 | | The Sun | : 7 |
| Morning Star | : 12 | | | |

The Times, Financial Times, The Guardian and Daily Mirror are notably low on editorialising in relation to their space allocation to the general subject of industrial relations and other papers rather high, apart from The Daily Telegraph. The Morning Star had most editorials and the most distinctive pattern of content in its editorials, insofar as the small sample allows us to say. One half of its editorials were devoted to just one topic (Union or TUC actions and statements). It differed markedly in the incidence of themes and the way in which these were used. For instance, references to union discord with the Government and to the class struggle were frequent. Otherwise, distinctive aspects of newspaper editorials cannot be established on the basis of this very small sample. However, 18 of the 46 editorials happen to have been described as part of the set of case studies in Part C of this report and some further qualitative data on editorial content can be found there.

# VIII   Summary and Conclusions

(The numbers in brackets refer to the relevant sections of the report)

## 1. Attention paid to industrial relations content

Industrial relations content was found to be unevenly distributed between the main national daily newspapers, with the *Financial Times* and *Morning Star* having most items. However, those papers with relatively low coverage in terms of numbers of items tended to compensate by giving more space and prominence to such content. As a result, we might conclude that no national newspaper departs very sharply from what is a generally high level of attention to news of this kind. Prominence in terms of front page and headline treatment is paralleled by a generally high incidence of editorialising in the leader column. The high level of attention to industrial relations content may reflect the important events of 1975, involving Government, employers and unions in the Social Contract and the later anti-inflation policy. The decline in industrial relations coverage in the latter part of the year, as reflected in the sample, seems to confirm this view (III, 3).

## 2. Topics of coverage

The content analysed was concentrated heavily on a small number of general topics (II, 2). The single dominant topic was that of disputes (at 36% of all items). Within that broad category, the topic of strikes alone was still the single most frequently occurring topic (22% of all items). Following disputes, actions or statements by unions or the TUC and then pay negotiations accounted, respectively, for a further 18% and 11% of all topics. Few differences were found between newspapers in the order of importance of topics, suggesting that these newspapers share much the same news values (III, 4). This similarity between newspapers shows up also in the agreement on assigning causes to strikes (III,6). As the case studies (Part C of this report) confirm, different newspapers are essentially reporting the same main stories on each day in much the same way. There seems a general tendency for the *settlement* of strikes and pay negotiations to be unreported (III, 6). Finally, it is noticeable that the degree of prominence given to different topics does not closely match the order of frequency (III, 5). In particular, we find the subject of actions and statements by Government in relation to unions to advance to first place, while "strikes" as a topic declines in importance.

## 3. Coverage of different branches of industry

A small number of industry groups receive a very high proportion of all attention—in particular, transport and communications, vehicles, and professional and scientific services (V, 2). This concentration of attention was common to all newspapers, with only slight deviations (V, 4). In this case, prominence of treatment was strongly correlated with frequency of occurrence (V, 3). A more diverse pattern of attention emerged when the topics of coverage were considered in relation to the main industry groups—that is to say that industries which were "neglected" overall might figure more prominently on particular topics, while some industry groups were prominent overall because of one topic only. For instance, news of strikes and of negative economic developments were largely responsible for the high prominence given to "vehicles" as an industry group (V, 5). The pattern of attention as a whole was not found to relate closely to the distribution of the labour force between industry groups or the incidence of stoppages in 1975 (V, 6). Amongst factors thought to account for this divergence, particular emphasis was placed on the political significance of certain public sector industries in the context of Government relations with unions and the TUC. Several pieces of evidence seemed to support this view, although our data cannot on their own explain what is evidently a complex phenomenon. If political circumstances are taken into account and if the political character of much industrial relations reporting is accepted, the seeming divergence of reporting from the statistical "reality" can be largely accounted for.

## 4. Themes in industrial relations content

The attempt to identify and quantify certain themes "cutting across" topics which might indicate something of the interpretive frameworks in news reporting produced rather modest results. The number of references to themes was relatively low, which in itself suggests that news items are normally "factual" and orientated to precise topics, and lacking any explicit framework of interpretation (IV, 2). When themes were looked at in relation to topics (IV, 3) there was some evidence of exceptions to this in three cases: there was a tendency for items categorised under the topic of "actions or statements by unions or the TUC" to be accompanied by a reference to discord in relations with Government; secondly, strike stories tended to carry some reference to possible damaging effects (although a majority did not); thirdly, reports of intra- and inter-union affairs quite often (22% of cases) carried a reference to internal conflict, usually "left vs right" or "militants" vs "moderates" (Table B14). These points lend some support for the view that there are recurring "news angles" in reporting industrial relations, although in the sample surveyed it did not seem as if news was strongly "shaped" by these news angles. The case studies (Part C of this report) provide more evidence in the matter.

Newspapers were found not to differ greatly in the incidence of references to themes, although newspapers tended to show certain distinctive, if minor, deviations from the overall average (IV, 5). The *Morning Star* was most distinctive in this respect, with *The Sun* also different. A comparison between newspapers in terms of frequency of occurrence of themes which might reflect unfavourably on unions showed variations within a narrow range, apart from the *Morning Star* and the *Daily Express*.

## 5. Participants in industrial relations news

The main participants in the industrial relations coverage sampled were trade unionists themselves, in one capacity or another (VI, 2). They are followed in order of frequency by Government Ministers, MPs or officials, although not generally as directly quoted or reported sources. Nevertheless, the findings do point to the relative "invisibility" or silence of management and employers. Amongst trade unionists, two or three prominent names dominate the field and there is an apparent lack of diversity in references to political sources (VI, 4). Again, different newspapers follow almost exactly the same pattern in the relative prominence accorded to different sorts of participant and to particular people.

## 6. Bias and Impartiality

An approach to the question of bias and impartiality was discussed in Section I, 9. In brief, the issue raised there concerned the possibility that news reporting might, whether intentionally or not, reflect unfavourably on one of the parties to industrial relations activity or misrepresent the true state of affairs. No clear adjudication is possible, since independent criteria of acceptable performance have not been formulated or applied and the method used in this survey was not appropriate to giving a direct answer to the question. Nevertheless, the survey of content has produced a number of points which are relevant to the question and contribute to a partial assessment. Firstly, it is the case that "negative" events are more likely to "make news" than "positive" or neutral events. Industrial disputes, clashes between Government and unions and internal union disagreements provide the main examples. Secondly, in the present sample, the distribution of content according to the industry does not closely match the pattern recorded in some comparable official statistics (distribution of the labour force and incidence of days lost and stoppages recorded). Thirdly, the evidence about themes and "news angles" does indicate some tendency to associate union activity with developments inimical to the public interest (economic problems, difficulties for government policy). Fourthly, there is an apparent under reporting of the part played by management or employers. These points provide some support for the view that, whatever the cause, the tendency of reporting of industrial relations news may be either to reflect unfavourably on unions and workers, or to give a partial (hence biased) view of the "reality". At the same time there are also points in the evidence which indicate an attempt on the part of the press to avoid partiality and to reflect faithfully the daily events which are believed to be most significant and relevant for the general public. Firstly, we can note the general similarity in patterns of attention between newspapers which represent, in their editorial attitudes, some degree of diversity. Secondly, despite a tendency for conflict themes to be more frequently invoked than others, themes which imply the most direct criticisms or dislike of union activity are generally avoided. "Criticism of unions for unreasonable, 'wildcat' strikes" is an example of a little-recorded theme. In addition, it has seemed, from the rather low incidence of themes actually recorded, as if news reports generally avoid the use of interpretive frameworks and are confined to factual matters. Thirdly, despite the evidence of divergence of the pattern of industrial news from other statistical patterns, there were some points of correspondence with other indices of "real activity"—for instance in respect of the *relative* position of some industry groups and the changing incidence of strikes over the course of the year. It was also open to argument that the apparent "bias" in reflecting "reality" could reasonably be accounted for by external economic and political factors. Fourthly, the view that reports of disputes and strikes are often unaccompanied by an indication of their cause was not supported, although it was the case that the *settlement* of strikes seemed to be under-reported. Fifthly, the evidence about "participants" might also be adduced to show that reporters do normally go to union sources for their information.

In the light of these points it should probably be concluded that the evidence from this survey is ambiguous and could be used to support a case for or against press "bias", if the problem is expressed in these terms. Account should also be taken of the fact that, however one interprets the evidence in terms of intention or probable effect, the national daily newspapers are very similar in their selection and treatment of news. As a result, the "point of balance" which the reader might infer on matters of controversy is located rather similarly in most newspapers and further, for reasons which have already been suggested (especially because of normal "news values" and conceptions of public interest and political relevance), this point does not lie equally between the two "sides" of industry. More often than not its location tends to be to the disadvantage of unions. At the same time, it should be remembered that, in the period sampled, the news reported often involved the Government as a party to industrial relations activity and to negotiations with unions, and a simple union-management division was far from common.

7. The coding scheme on which this survey was based incorporated certain expectations about what would be found in newspapers about trade unions and industrial relations and is itself, consequently, "biased". Its categories may tell us little about what is *omitted* by newspapers. Even so, the fact that most content could be accommodated by the limited range of categories chosen does allow us to conclude that the National Daily press offers a highly selective version of industrial relations activity and must fail to reflect much of the work that unions and management engage in on a day to day basis and which forms the context of the relatively few "news-worthy" events.

It is relevant, however, to make a comparison with the treatment accorded to other kinds of news. The studies of social welfare and foreign news described elsewhere in this report provide an opportunity for doing so. Briefly, one would have to conclude that these subject areas are not treated with any greater respect for the recording of "normal" activity. They too are treated very selectively, according to similar criteria of what is "news-worthy". In the case of social policy news, it was clear that large areas of the social services receive little routine coverage and that attention to health and education is very uneven. It might even be concluded that the sheer volume of coverage of industrial relations and union matters helps to ensure a more diverse and complete coverage than is received by other subjects of comparable importance. Any attempt to find causes of, and remedies for, failings in the coverage of trade union matters should take account of the parallel tendencies in other content areas.

In discussing the findings, the fact of similarity between newspapers has been emphasised on several occasions. While this is the dominant impression, it should also be recorded that there are important differences of character and quality which the method is not very sensitive to. The two papers with the largest coverage, the *Morning Star* and *Financial Times* are, in general, the most inclined to show patterns of coverage which diverge from the average, and one might expect a more detailed qualitative assessment to provide more evidence of individual newspaper variations.

# Part C

**Industrial Relations Content in National Daily Newspapers, 1975:**
**Eight Case Studies**

# Main Tables

# I  Introduction

## 1. Aims

This report deals with several aspects of the coverage of industrial relations, as revealed by a comparative study in some detail of the way in which eight stories were presented in the national daily press on eight different days in 1975. The intention is to supplement the evidence produced by the statistical analysis of 1,492 newspaper items (Part B of this Report) and the stories studied here in greater depth are included in that sample of items. In particular, this analysis attempts to reach some more qualitative conclusions about the practices and standards of reporting, with reference to completeness of coverage, balance and impartiality, editorialising and the separation of fact from comment. As far as possible, quantitative evidence is used to support judgements, but some interpretation of the evidence is inevitable and the conclusions must be regarded as tentative.

## 2. Content chosen for study

The stories chosen for analysis include most, but not all, of those which were most prominent in national newspapers on the days sampled for the main study of all newspaper content (Part A above). Eight days were involved out of the sample of 24 days. No strict criteria for selection were applied, except that the stories concerned should be the lead story in at least one of the nine newspapers, and be dealt with in all newspapers. The only exception to the latter rule arises for the 6 March, where other criteria of prominence were present, but *The Sun* carried no report. The analysis was carried out on the newspapers used in the general analysis of newspaper content. No control was possible over the actual *editions* chosen for analysis and consequently the presence or absence of a report, or of points in a report, cannot be taken as evidence of omission from a given title. It should also be emphasised that the selection is not entirely random and no claim to representativeness can be made. On the other hand, no attempt has been made to choose stories according to any principle other than prominence, and the subject matter of news items is reasonably diverse.

The stories examined are not necessarily single news items, although often they are. Rather, they may be composite treatments of a "news issue", sometimes dealt with by different journalists in the same paper under separate headings, sometimes brought together in a single item format. Often, the content relates to quite different events, which are mutually related, as where a political event and an industrial action connect closely. The result is "messy" from the point of view of the analysis and classification of content, but reflects an aspect of the reality of the way in which the press provides an account of news events. While the facts about separate treatment are recorded in each case, the main analysis disregards the boundaries between "items" and takes as its material any news or feature content dealing with the issue in a given newspaper. In practice, only *news* content has been analysed systematically and reduced to tabular form, while feature material and editorial comment is dealt with by brief description. It follows from these procedures that the "stories" do not normally correspond with single items in the statistical analysis but may relate to several items. It is possible that some relevant content has been omitted by accident, although efforts have been made to be comprehensive.

151

## 3. Methods

The methods of analysis need little advance explanation and can be understood from the main substance of the report. The main principle observed has been to deal only with content as printed and to make no recourse to information not contained in the newspaper reports themselves. Thus, for any given story, the universe of what is known or knowable is established by what is in the nine national morning newspapers themselves. There are two main procedures involved in this study. One is to establish the component "facts" or main points of any story taken as a whole and to compile a checklist which can be used both to summarise story content and to compare newspapers in terms of what they have included or omitted. A second procedure is to search for words or phrases in headlines and news text which might indicate an attitude on the part of the writer or of the newspaper or which gives "colour" to the story and consequently might affect its interpretation by a reader. The validity of this procedure can be judged by its results in the report which follows. There are precedents, and the method has been used with some success by other analysts of content (eg Evans, 1965)*. Beyond, this several subsidiary and simple tools of analysis have been used where it seems appropriate, for instance distinguishing between "factual" elements in a story and "non-factual" according to whether a statement is attributed or can be verified; or comparing the precise details (facts and figures) in a story given by different newspapers as some guide to relative accuracy.

The compilation of the checklist of story elements or main points is the key operation and it entails some possibility of misrepresentation, partly because the continuity of a newspaper account is missing and partly because the wording of a point in the table cannot reflect all variations of phrasing. Occasionally, too, a newspaper has to be checked as giving the point as worded, when the reference is either incomplete or somewhat different in meaning. These limitations are inherent to methods of this kind, if economy of representation is to be achieved. The impression that newspaper stories are made up of discrete and discontinuous items of information is not, however, so misleading, given the way such news items are written. At least, that is the impression derived from this particular reading and it is connected with the strong efforts which newspapers seem to make to keep stories factual and concise. The method has at least two obvious weaknesses. Firstly, the results reflect the reading and judgements of only one person. Secondly, there is no source independent of the press itself against which to assess completeness, accuracy or other matters.

## 4. The assessment of bias and impartiality

In the report of the survey of industrial relations content (Part B of this Report) some brief comments were made on the nature of bias and its assessment (Section I, 9). Four main ways in which a newspaper item might incorporate some tendency to favour one "side" over another were suggested there: firstly, by explicit argument and advocacy; secondly, by the tendentious use of facts and comment with no explicit advocacy; thirdly, by the use of language which colours an otherwise factual and balanced report and conveys a value judgement implicitly; fourthly, by the simple omission of points which might favour one side, with a resulting imbalance in one direction. The techniques of incorporating a point of view in writing are of course more numerous and more subtle than this

---

* Harold Evans, *The Suez Crisis: a study in press performance*. M.A. thesis, Durham, 1965.

classification suggests. Quite certainly they are far more advanced than the techniques for detecting, let alone proving, a case of "bias" in an objective way. There are two added complications in that "balance" and "fairness" or their opposites are relative, depending on the assessor's own standpoint and values; and, secondly, "bias" does not have to be conscious, but may be a matter of unintended or presumed effects.

In these circumstances, only very limited conclusions are likely to emerge and, as far as possible, the method has been designed so that the reader has the material for deciding whether or not to accept the assessment. For the most part, three tests have been applied. Two are quite straightforward, involving, firstly, a judgement about evaluative "colour" in words and phrases and, secondly, a search for any tendentious comment in news reports. The third approach is more complex and is designed to deal particularly with the case where an objective and verifiable fact (event or statement) may, however unintentionally, reflect unfavourably on a participant or side. In the present instance, the unions or workers may feature as a "side" *vis á vis* employers or Government. Quite often, however, there is a triangular relationship, involving all three principal parties. The cumulation of "facts" on one "side" without a balance of facts on the other side may be interpreted as a situation of bias. While the compilation of checklist of factual points provides the basis for the third method of analysis, a further step is required if points are to be classified as "unfavourable" or "favourable" in their implication. This can only be done on a hypothetical basis, with the results depending entirely on whether one accepts the stated assumptions. An attempt has been made to classify some points as tending to be "for" or "against" one party to a dispute—generally the unions or Government. For instance, if it is supposed that strikes are undesirable then some point relating to union, or worker attempts to call a strike might be classified as "unfavourable" to unions and union moves to avert or stop strike action might be classified as "favourable" (in their likely effect or interpretation). The assumptions made in each case are made clear and points chosen accordingly. A principal weakness of the method is that all newspapers do not share the same values (nor do all readers). As a case in point, the *Morning Star* does not oppose strikes in principle and in the period it generally supported union resistance to Government pay policy. It is the most clearly divergent case and for that reason omitted from those parts of the report where this method is applied. The approach is very plainly exploratory and the results quite tentative. The reader is free to diverge from the value judgements and resist any conclusions based on a simple counting of items "for" and "against".

Ultimately, the assessment of "bias" is a matter of personal judgement and depends on where one places the "middle" position and on the conventions one accepts about what is fair or proper. There are no absolute standards and the intention has been to shed some light on actual practice rather than to measure performance against an ideal. Finally, the reader is reminded that cases were not chosen on any basis related to the possible occurrence of "bias" but were intended to reflect normal or average performance in the period studied.

## 5. Summary

Each case study entails the following main procedures and methods. Firstly, the space and degree of headlining is measured for each news report. Secondly, the headlines are reproduced for the set of nine national dailies. Thirdly, a check-list of "main points" is established covering the whole range of points made in all newspapers and including "non-factual" points (eg interpretation, speculation, judgements) where these are clear and specific enough to warrant listing. Fourthly, the newspaper reports are compared, with the help of this checklist, in order to: assess the amount of agreement between titles; see where agreement in news reporting is most pronounced; assess the relative completeness of each news report; look for evidence of diversity and measure variability. Fifthly, where possible, a brief assessment of relative accuracy is made on one point in the story, by comparing facts in different reports. Sixthly, editorial views are summarised, where there is leader comment. Finally, an effort is made to assess the direction or "bias" of a story: by noting "non-factual" statements which imply an evaluation; by looking at the balance of facts "for" or "against" a party or participant in the story; by reporting any "colour" in the use of words or phrases which might also imply some editorial attitude.

# Industrial Relations Content Case Studies

## II  CASE 1: British Leyland troubles, Tuesday, 7 January 1975

### 1. Introduction

The story as a whole has two main parts: firstly, the report of a meeting the previous day between the Secretary for Industry, Mr. A. W. Benn and leaders of the Confederation of Shipbuilding and Engineering Union to discuss the future of British Leyland; secondly, the hopes of ending the strike by engine tuners at the BL Cowley plant which caused loss of production and lay-offs since the weekend. While the two are separate and unrelated events they are both relevant to the company's future. An additional connection was established by reports of criticisms, made by Harold Wilson at the weekend, of unnecessary strikes in the motor industry, with particular reference to British Leyland.

### 2. Space and prominence

The story is the main lead story in *The Times* and parts of it occur on the front pages of *The Guardian*, *Financial Times*, *Morning Star* and *The Daily Telegraph*. The *Daily Mail*, *Daily Mirror* and *The Sun* give it less prominence. The amount of space is given in Table C1.

TABLE C1

NEWS SPACE ALLOCATED TO BRITISH LEYLAND STORY, 7 JAN. 1975

| Title | Total space (col cms) | Headlines as % of space | Presentation |
|---|---|---|---|
| The Times ... ... | 63 | 21% | 3 connected items |
| The Guardian ... ... | 87 | 22% | 2 separate items |
| The Daily Telegraph ... | 66 | 14% | 1 item |
| Financial Times ... ... | 39 | 24% | 1 item |
| Morning Star ... ... | 46 | 26% | 2 separate items |
| Daily Express ... ... | 20 | — | 2 connected items |
| Daily Mail ... ... | 9 | — | items in brief |
| Daily Mirror ... ... | 87 | 51% | 2 connected items |
| The Sun ... ... ... | 20 | 33% | 2 connected items |

Space and headline treatment are similar as between titles, except that the *Daily Mirror* gives relatively large headline treatment (although on pp. 4–5) and the *Daily Mail* and *Daily Express* barely notice the story. Both the *Daily Express* and *The Sun* give precedence to a separate story of short-time working at Chrysler Ryton works. The *Daily Mail* cedes to the story of a bid for Aston Martin.

### 3. Headlines

Table C2 gives the text of the main headlines and sub-headings. A main headline is in capitals, a sub-head in lower case. Continuation headings are not recorded. The figures (1), (2), etc. refer to separate item headings.

155

**TABLE C2**

**HEADLINES RELATING TO BRITISH LEYLAND, 7 JAN. 1975**

| | |
|---|---|
| *The Times* ... ... | MR. BENN INVITES UNIONS HELP IN ENDING TROUBLE AT LEYLAND |
| | Hope of agreement at Cowley today |
| *The Guardian* ... ... | (1) LEYLAND UNIONS WANT PEACE |
| | (2) UNION HUSTLE TO END COWLEY STRIKE |
| *The Daily Telegraph* ... | UNIONS UNIMPRESSED BY LEYLAND CRISIS |
| *Financial Times* ... ... | BL STRIKERS EXPECTED BACK TODAY |
| *Morning Star* ... ... | (1) WHAT IS WRONG WITH LEYLAND? UNIONS MEET |
| | (2) 250 COWLEY STRIKERS TO MEET TODAY |
| *Daily Express* ... ... | — |
| *Daily Mail* ... ... | — |
| *Daily Mirror* ... ... | LEYLAND IS BACK IN TUNE |
| | Unions support Benn rescue plan |
| *The Sun* ... ... ... | Leyland back to work call |

The main point to note in these headlines, apart from the general difference in amount of attention between "Quality" and "Popular" newspapers, is the divergence of *The Daily Telegraph* from other papers in suggesting a lack of accord between unions and Government. This interpretation of events is reflected in the editorial comment but is not strongly supported in the news report. The *Morning Star* picks out for headlining a future event which is not mentioned elsewhere.

## 4. Completeness and diversity in news reports

Table C3, compiled from the nine newspapers in the way described earlier (p. 152), lists all the main points or separate items of information and comment relating to the British Leyland issue. The points vary in importance, complexity and in the space actually given to them in different newspapers. The judgement of what is a main point is a fine one, but in practice few separate items of information have been omitted and those only where they occurred in only one newspaper report, or where they might be considered as subsumed under another item which is listed.

**TABLE C3**

## CHECKLIST OF MAIN POINTS
## BRITISH LEYLAND TROUBLES, 7th JAN. 1975

| Category | The Times | The Guardian | The Daily Telegraph | Financial Times | Morning Star | Daily Express | Daily Mail | Daily Mirror | The Sun |
|---|---|---|---|---|---|---|---|---|---|
| **I. Benn discussions with BL Union Leaders** | | | | | | | | | |
| 1. Benn has meeting with BL Union Leaders (CSEU) | × | × | × | × | × | × | × | × | × |
| 2. Mention of points on which union advice was sought | × | | | × | × | × | × | | |
| 3. Four points or issues specified | × | | | × | × | | | | × |
| 4. Financial aid to BL of £50m mentioned as being discussed | | × | | | | | | | × |
| 5. Meeting was cordial (says Wright of AUEW) | | × | | | | | | | |
| 6. Unions next to meet Sir Don Ryder | × | × | × | × | × | × | | | × |
| 7. Meeting did not discuss attack on strikes by PM at weekend | | × | × | | × | | | | |
| 8. Meeting was arranged a month ago | | | × | | | | | | |
| 9. Decided at meeting that union leaders would meet again to discuss BL problem | × | × | × | × | × | × | | | |
| 10. R. Sanderson (of electricians and plumbers) proposed a year strike moratorium | × | × | × | × | × | × | | | × |
| 11. Meeting did not accept this proposal | × | | × | × | × | | | | |
| 12. Bob Wright (AUEW) recognised need to avoid unnecessary industrial conflict | | | × | × | × | × | | | |
| 13. Wright also defended union right to strike if necessary | | | | | | | | | |
| 14. Union leaders attributed problems to recession, not strikes | | | | × | × | | | × | |
| 15. Benn makes commitment to worker participation | | | | | × | | | | |
| 16. Bob Wright approves of more industrial democracy | | | | | | | | × | |
| 17. British Leyland to remain British | | | | | | | | | |
| **II. Cowley Stoppage** | | | | | | | | | |
| 18. Hopes raised of end to Cowley stoppage | × | × | × | × | × | × | × | × | × |
| 19. Meeting tomorrow to decide about return to work | × | × | × | | × | × | | × | × |
| 20. Shop stewards will recommend return to work | | × | × | | | | | × | × |
| 21. Strike is of 250 engine-turners | × | × | × | × | × | × | × | × | × |
| 22. Cause of strike is skill classification (regrading) | | × | × | | × | × | | × | × |
| 23. 12,000 have been laid off by stoppage | × | × | × | × | × | | | × | × |
| 24. Management anticipated return by recalling day shift | × | × | × | × | × | | | × | |

157

## CHECK LIST OF MAIN POINTS—*continued*
### BRITISH LEYLAND TROUBLES, 7th JAN. 1975—*continued*

| Category | The Times | The Guardian | The Daily Telegraph | Financial Times | Morning Star | Daily Express | Daily Mail | Daily Mirror | The Sun |
|---|---|---|---|---|---|---|---|---|---|
| **II.  Cowley Stoppage**—*continued* | | | | | | | | | |
| 25. Local union influenced by PM's weekend speech ... | | x | x | | | | | x | x |
| 26. Loss of production £1¼m (or would soon be £8m) ... | | x | x | | | | | x | |
| 27. Cowley workers impatient at engine-tuners' strike ... | | | x | | | x | | | |
| 28. Engine-tuner regrading opposed by Company and other Union ... | | | | | | | | | |
| 29. PM alluded to this strike as unnecessary at weekend ... | | | | | x | | | x | |
| 30. National meeting scheduled tomorrow on regrading issue ... | | | | | x | | | | |
| 31. Tuners action will be renewed unless company relents ... | | | | | x | | | | |
| 32. Strike has local official support ... | | | | | x | | | x | |
| 33. Advance of restructuring talks enabled action to end strike. ... | | | | | | | | x | |
| **III.  Other British Leyland matters** | | | | | | | | | |
| 34. Labour MP (Raymond Carter) tells shop stewards at Longbridge of danger to survival of Company ... | x | | | | | | | | |
| 35. MP also blames management for industrial conflict ... | x | | | | | | | | |
| 36. MP also blames workers who undermine union ... | x | | x | | | | | | |
| 37. Mr. Lowry of BL speaks on TV of disruptive elements ... | | | x | | | | | | |
| 38. Lowry says problem is retaining market share ... | | | x | | | | | | |
| 39. Lowry mentions risk in receiving Government money ... | | | | | | | | | |
| **IV.  Other** | | | | | | | | | |
| 40. All-party committee of MPs to consider motor industry problems ... | | | | | | | | | |
| 41. TUC economic committee to discuss motor industry problems ... | | x | | | | | x | x | x |
| 42. Reports also refer to or give details about Chrysler lay-offs ... | x | x | x | x | x | x | x | x | x |
| 43. PM in touch with Jack Jones over weekend remarks ... | | | | x | | | | | |
| Total number of points  ...  ... | 17 | 18 | 23 | 15 | 22 | 13 | 6 | 17 | 12 |

(*a*) Between them the nine newspapers produced 43 main points, of which only three were common to all newspapers, with an average number of points per newspaper of 16. The "highest scoring" titles were the *Morning Star* and *The Daily Telegraph*, with 22 and 23, or just over 50% of the "maximum".

The points which were picked up by all or most papers may be regarded as the key elements of the story and this provides an alternative criterion of completeness or adequacy of coverage. The following 11 points were all covered by at least six of the nine newspapers in their news reports:

that Benn had met BL union leaders                                        (1)
that one union leader proposed a one year strike moratorium              (10)
that the union leaders are due to meet Don Ryder                          (6)
that Wright of AUEW acknowledged need for industrial peace               (12)
that an end to the Cowley stoppage was expected                          (18)
that strike is of 250 engine tuners                                      (21)
that the cause of the strike is skill classification                     (22)
that 12,000 workers have been laid off because of the stoppage           (23)
that a meeting will be held to decide on return to work                  (19)
that management have recalled the day-shift in anticipation              (24)
that lay-offs are occurring at Chrysler                                  (42)

The main emphasis of these points is on government-union agreement and the peace hopes at Cowley, thus closely mirroring the expectation raised by headlines. Since these 11 points out of 43 account between them for 84 out of 143 references, it seems that newspapers are generally agreed on what are the most important facts. By this criterion, four newspapers report all the main facts (*The Times, The Guardian, Morning Star, The Daily Telegraph*). The *Financial Times* and the *Daily Express* report nine, *The Sun* and *Daily Mirror* eight each and the *Daily Mail* only four. While this scoring broadly reflects space allocation to the story, it also suggests that even short reports (as in *The Sun* and *Daily Express*) tend to pick up the most important points.

(*b*) At the other extreme, we can see a number of points reported by only one or two newspapers. Altogether there are 19 points reported by one newspaper only. These are:

that the Benn-union talks were cordial (*The Guardian*)                   (5)
that £50m aid for BL was under discussion (*The Sun*)                     (4)
that union leaders would meet again (*Morning Star*)                      (9)
that the Benn-union meeting was arranged a month ago
(*The Daily Telegraph*)                                                   (8)
that recession, not strikes was cause of problem (*The Daily Telegraph*)  (14)
that AUEW man approves of industrial democracy (*Morning Star*)           (16)
that BL to remain British pledge (*Daily Mirror*)                         (17)
that regrading opposed by Company and Union (*The Daily Telegraph*)       (28)
that the Cowley strike was the object of PM's weekend remarks
(*Morning Star*)                                                          (29)
that tuners are ready to renew action unless company relents
(*Morning Star*)                                                          (31)
that restructuring talks were advanced to help solve strike
(*Daily Mirror*)                                                          (33)

Report of Labour MPs speech to Longbridge workers (*The Times*) (34, 35, 36)
Report of Pat Lowry TV interview (*The Daily Telegraph*) (37, 38, 39)
TUC economic committee to discuss problems (*Financial Times*) (41)
PM contacts at weekend with Jack Jones (*Financial Times*) (43)

On the whole these "singleton" points reflect either a slightly different angle to the story as a whole, with different sources of information (as with the *Morning Star*) or the inclusion of matters not considered relevant by other newspapers, as with the report of the Carter speech and the Lowry TV interview. The low incidence of such divergent items is more striking than their content.

(*c*) The general impression left by Table C3 is that newspapers were largely agreed on the most significant aspects of the story and differed in the *extent*, not *kind* of coverage. There were some signs of diversity, however. For instance, newspapers differed according to their emphasis in one or other of the main components of the story—the Benn talks or the Cowley settlement. Overall, most attention was directed to the latter and the low coverage papers (*Daily Mirror*, *The Sun*, and *Daily Express*) tended to neglect the former. Apart from this, although some significance may attach to the specific content of points picked out by individual newspapers (for instance the reference by the *Daily Express* and *The Daily Telegraph* to shop-floor impatience at the tuners' strike) there is little sign of systematic differentiation between titles.

One aspect of diversity not revealed by the tabulation of main points is the extent to which the reports made a specific interpretative connection between the Benn-union meeting, the PM's speech and the Cowley dispute ending. The connection was generally made by *The Guardian*, the *Financial Times*, *The Sun* and the *Daily Mirror*, but not by the other papers.

## 5. Accuracy

In so far as the reports indicate (by consensus) the "agreed facts" of events reported, we may look for some evidence of inaccuracy. In practice, this particular story offers little scope for applying such a check. There are few precise details in the story, although some figures are mentioned and attributions of statements are made to named individuals. Where the number of engine-tuners on strike is mentioned it is put at 250. The number of other workers affected by the strike is similarly consistently put at 12,000, although there are two versions of the number who have been recalled. The more precise figure given by the *Financial Times* is of 6,000 day-shift workers in the first instance rather than the full 12,000 indicated by some reports (eg *The Guardian*). The amount of lost production is put at £1½m by *The Daily Telegraph* and £2m by the *Daily Mirror*. These differences are obviously not any indication of serious inaccuracy. All attributions of remarks seem consistent between newspapers.

## 6. Attitude of newspaper as revealed in editorial comment

Three newspapers offer leader comment on the issue: *Daily Express*, *The Daily Telegraph* and the *Financial Times*. The *Daily Express* cites British Leyland as a case of a company being "ensnared" into the "nationalisation net" by inflation, without reference to the precise news issue. *The Daily Telegraph* under the heading "Mr Wilson's Hard Road" says that unions have "made a major contribution to the plight of British Leyland". Secondly, **Mr** Benn's ideas about worker participation are seen as not "relevant": Thirdly, advancing public money is rejected as a solution. The *Financial Times'* comment is mainly on the problem of disputes over differentials and recommends greater union activity in resolving such disputes internally. It also attributes a large share of responsibility for trouble at BL to management, referring to "serious management deficiencies". The heading "A precondition for survival" refers to a "joint effort by management and union".

### 7. Editorial attitude or "colour" in news reports

There are three main ways in which editorial attitude in news reports (headlines apart) may be revealed. One consists of evaluative or interpretive comments of a tendentious kind, another of verifiable "facts" damaging to one participant or group, a third of words and phrases which give "colour" to a report and in doing so may lead to a particular judgement on the part of the reader and reflect newspaper attitude.

(*a*) There are remarkably few unverifiable or interpretative comments in **any of** the newspapers. None of the 43 points in Table C3 has a "non-factual" character in the sense that it cannot be checked or does not come from a specified source. Unsupported statements or opinions were eligible for inclusion in the list, but no clear example could be found.

(*b*) An attempt to assess attitude or tendency as revealed by the reporting of facts "unfavourable" to one side can be made if we classify some of the points in table C3 according to their implications for the "image" of trade unions. This can be done only if, as suggested in the Introduction, we make some hypothetical value judgements about what is desirable or undesirable. In this case, we might assume industrial conflict to be undesirable and co-operation with management and Government to be desirable. On this basis, the following points seem to reflect unfavourably on unions:

(11)  Rejection of proposed strike moratorium;
(13)  Right to strike defended;
(14)  Unions blame recession, not strikes;
(23)  12,000 laid off by stoppage;
(26)  Cost of lost production;
(29)  PM said strike unneccessary;
(37)  Disruptive elements blamed;

The more favourable points include:

(10)  Proposal for a strike moratorium;
(12)  Need to end conflict recognised by union;
(20)  Return to work recommended;
(33)  End to strike assisted.

The relative frequency of the two groups of items was as follows (excluding the *Morning Star* for reasons given on p. 153)

161

**TABLE C4**

**RATIO OF "LESS FAVOURABLE" TO "MORE FAVOURABLE" POINTS**

| | | | | | | | | |
|---|---|---|---|---|---|---|---|---|
| *The Times* | ... | ... | ... | 2:2 | *Daily Express* | ... | ... | 1:3 |
| *The Guardian* | ... | ... | ... | 3:3 | *Daily Mail* | ... | ... | 0:0 |
| *The Daily Telegraph* | ... | ... | 6:3 | *Daily Mirror* | ... | ... | 2:2 |
| *Financial Times* | ... | ... | 3:2 | *The Sun* | ... | ... | 1:2 |

*The Daily Telegraph* emerges on this measure as the paper with a ratio most weighted "against" the unions and this is at least consistent with its headline indicating union non-ccoperation. Even so, the weight of evidence is not sufficient to support a conclusion of "bias", witting or otherwise, in the selection of facts by any newspaper.

(*c*) "Colour" is notably absent from accounts of this story. No clear example of colour in writing could be found in any news report.

# III CASE 2: Rail Pay Claim, Saturday, 15 February 1975

## 1. Introduction

The main focus of the story is on the details of pay claims lodged by the NUR and ASLEF. Subsidiary but related stories concern references to the miners' pay settlement, the claims expected from power workers and other unions and reports of a speech by Mr Foot at Ebbw Vale, in which he commented on the miners' settlement and its implications. All are connected by their common implications for the Social Contract. In this account, all are treated together as a composite issue, for purposes of space measurement and recording main points. A further subsidiary matter reported in some papers is the continuing dispute between the rail signalmen, NUR and BR. This is not covered in detail by this study.

## 2. Space and prominence

The issue is a main lead story in *The Daily Telegraph*, and *Daily Mirror* and on the front page of the *Daily Mail* and *The Times*. Parts of the story (the Foot speech) are also reported on page one of *The Guardian*, *Daily Express* and *Morning Star*. Only the *Daily Mail* and *Daily Mirror* treat the issue as a single story. The amount of space is given in Table C5.

TABLE C5

NEWS SPACE ALLOCATED TO RAIL PAY CLAIM STORY, 15 FEB. 1975

| Title | Total Space (co. cms) | Headline as % of space | Presentation |
|---|---|---|---|
| The Times | 70 | 12% | 2 separate items |
| The Guardian | 69 | 21% | 2 separate items |
| The Daily Telegraph | 163 | 16% | 3 connected items |
| Financial Times | 110 | 15% | 2 separate items |
| Morning Star | 43 | 33% | 2 separate items |
| Daily Express | 76 | 38% | 2 separate items |
| Daily Mail | 23 | 20% | 1 item |
| Daily Mirror | 80 | 43% | 1 item |
| The Sun | 64 | 26% | 2 connected items |

Where space is divided between the rail pay story and the Foot speech report, the division is generally even. The unusually large *Daily Telegraph* allocation partly reflects its treatment of wider political aspects which were left out or dealt with quite separately in other papers.

163

## 3. Headlines

Table C6 gives the text of main headlines and sub-headings.

**TABLE C6**

**HEADLINES RELATING TO RAIL PAY CLAIM, 15 FEB. 1975**

| | |
|---|---|
| *The Times:* ... ... | (1) UNION CLAIMS PAY RISES OF UP TO £9 A WEEK FOR 250,000 RAIL WORKERS |
| | (2) CONTRACT STILL BEST SHIELD  SAYS MR FOOT |
| *The Guardian* ... ... | RAIL UNIONS BACK PIT-TYPE CONTRACT |
| *The Daily Telegraph* ... | (1) RAILWAYMEN WANT "SAME AS MINERS"<br>Pay leads prices as Foot backs contract |
| | (2) AT LEAST 28% SAY UNION |
| | (3) FOOT'S "SPECIAL CASE" |
| *Financial Times* ... ... | (1) RAILMEN CITE PIT OFFER IN UP TO 35% CLAIM |
| | (2) FOOT DEFENDS MINERS 30% —<br>"SOCIAL CONTRACT STAYS" |
| *Morning Star* ... ... | (1) MINERS PAY DEAL GETS BACKING FROM FOOT |
| | (2) RAIL WORKERS SEEKING 25%  PAY  INCREASES |
| *Daily Express* ... ... | (1) REJOICE FOR THE MINERS SAYS FOOT |
| | (2) RAILMEN SPEED TO CATCH UP MINERS |
| *Daily Mail* ... ... | NOW BIG PAY SCRAMBLE IS ON |
| *Daily Mirror* ... ... | OFF THE PAY RAILS |
| *The Sun* ... ... ... | (1) PITS DEAL WAS FAIR SAYS FOOT |
| | (2) "GIVE US THE SAME RISES" |

These headlines call for little comment. *The Times* provides the most information in a self-explanatory heading. The *Daily Mirror* provides least and, as in Case 1, its heading seems more eye-catching than informative. None of the headlines seems directly to involve any evaluation or judgement, although the first *Daily Express* headline strikes an ironic note and the *Daily Mail* headline has a pejorative connotation (pay "scramble").

## 4. Completeness and diversity in news reports

The main points of the story are listed in Table C3 and the same general comments as for Case 1 (p. 156) apply here. Because of the wide-ranging character of this news issue, there is more chance of points being dealt with by newspapers elsewhere in the paper.

TABLE C7

## CHECKLIST OF MAIN POINTS
### RAIL PAY CLAIM, 15 FEB. 1975

| Main points | The Times | The Guardian | The Daily Telegraph | Financial Times | Morning Star | Daily Express | Daily Mail | Daily Mirror | The Sun |
|---|---|---|---|---|---|---|---|---|---|
| **I. Main points** | | | | | | | | | |
| 1. Miners' settlement leads to other claims | x | x | x | x | | x | x | x | x |
| 2. Rail unions ask for big increase | x | x | x | x | | x | x | x | x |
| **II. Details of rail pay claim** | | | | | | | | | |
| 3. Railmen seeking 28% plus (or 34% or 24% or 35% or 25%) | x | x | x | x | x | x | x | x | x |
| 4. Buckton, for ASLEF, would seek 25%–33% (or 30% or 35%) | x | x | x | | x | x | x | | |
| 5. Railmen want £9 p.w. on basic rate | | | x | | x | x | | | x |
| 6. Current rail pay details | | x | | | | | | | |
| 7. Differentials within rail pay to be preserved (Buckton) | | | | | | | | | |
| 8. Claim to include sick pay, holidays and productivity deal | | | | | | | | | |
| 9. Increases asked for are above Social Contract | | | | x | | | | | |
| **III. Arguments in Support of Claim** | | | | | | | | | |
| 10. Maintain relativities with miners (not parity) | x | x | | x | | | | | |
| 11. Comparison with miners important, but timing accidental | x | x | | x | | | | | |
| 12. Comparison with other industries besides mining would indicate 24% plus | x | | | | | | | | |
| 13. Need to maintain position achieved by previous year's settlements | | | x | | | | | | |
| 14. Rail work interdependent with mining (eg moving coal) | | x | | | x | x | | | x |
| 15. Main comparison with surface mine-workers | | x | | | | x | | | |
| **IV. Comment by S. Weighell of NUR on Contract and miners' settlement** | | | | | | | | | |
| 16. Railmen want same interpretation of Contract as miners ("no less favourable") | x | x | x | x | x | x | x | x | x |
| 17. Weighell waiting to hear Government & TUC comment on miners' deal | | x | x | | | x | x | x | |
| 18. Weighell respectful of Social Contract (or Buckton ditto) | | | x | | | x | | | |
| 19. Weighell says his job is not to save Britain, but help railmen | | | | | | x | | x | x |
| **V. Report of Foot's speech at Ebbw Vale** | | | | | | | | | |
| 20. Foot warns other unions not to expect what miners got | x | x | x | x | x | x | x | x | x |
| 21. Foot says miners rise deserved and/or overdue | x | x | x | x | x | x | x | x | x |
| 22. Foot says miners award is above what was needed to compensate for cost of living | x | x | x | x | x | x | x | | x |
| 23. Foot says Contract still alive—special factors in miners' case | x | x | x | x | x | x | | | x |
| 24. Foot says Contract still best shield vs inflation | x | | x | x | | x | | | x |
| 25. Miners case was partly a restructuring operation (says Foot) | | x | | | | | | | |
| **VI. Context of prices, cost of living** | | | | | | | | | |
| 26. Price inflation now reached rate of 20% (25.9%) | x* | x* | x | x* | x* | x* | x | x* | |
| 27. RPI for Jan. up 2.6% (food 3.4%) | x* | x* | x | x* | x* | x* | x | x* | |
| 28. Wage increases well ahead of prices | x* | x* | x | x | | | | x* | |

**TABLE C7**—*continued*

## CHECKLIST OF MAIN POINTS—*continued*
### RAIL PAY CLAIM, 15 FEB. 1975—*continued*

| Main points | The Times | The Guardian | The Daily Telegraph | Financial Times | Morning Star | Daily Express | Daily Mail | Daily Mirror | The Sun |
|---|---|---|---|---|---|---|---|---|---|
| **VII. Miner's pay settlement references** | | | | | | | | | |
| 29. Amount of miner's settlement mentioned (eg 30 or 35%) or size commented on | × | ×* | × | | | × | × | | |
| 30. Some miners dissatisfied with pay deal | × | | × | | | | | | |
| 31. Miners likely to accept | | | × | | | | | | |
| 32. Pithead ballot to be held | | | | × | | | | | |
| 33. New claim from miners expected in July | | | × | | | | | | |
| 34. NCB to face demands from clerical workers | | | | | | | | | |
| **VIII. Other current or expected pay claims** | | | | | | | | | |
| 35. Influence of miners' deal on power workers | × | × | × | | | × | | × | × |
| 36. Chapple wants parity with mine surface workers (£41 minimum) | × | × | | | | | | | × |
| 37. Chapple says work of power men similar to pit surface men | | | | | | × | | × | × |
| 38. Bank workers want to match miners' settlements | | × | × | ×* | | | | | |
| 39. Teachers, engineers similarly | | × | × | | | | | | |
| 40. Systematic details of other claims and deals | | | | | | | | | × |
| **IX. Employer response and timing** | | | | | | | | | |
| 41. BRB will reply in two weeks | × | | | | | | | | |
| 42. New pay settlement not due till May | × | | | | | | | | |
| 43. No reply from BRB | | | × | × | × | | | | |
| 44. Disagreement with BRB over inclusion of threshold payments in deal | × | × | | × | × | | | | |
| 45. BR to agree to closed shops as part of deal | | | | × | × | | | | |
| **X. Economic Consequences of Claim** | | | | | | | | | |
| 46. Robert Carr on danger to Britain | × | ×* | × | | | × | × | × | |
| 47. Healey warns of risk of unemployment through wage rises | × | | × | | | × | × | × | |
| 48. Contract threatened or dead | | | | | | | | | |
| **XI. Other points** | | | | | | | | | |
| 49. NUR wants to control rebel signalmen (pay restructuring & union) | × | × | × | × | | | | | |
| 50. NUM leaders to address NUR executive | | | × | × | | | | | |
| 51. Carr warns of militants | | | | | | × | | × | |
| 52. Buckton confident there will be no strike | | × | | | | | | | |
| **Total number of points** | 26 | 29 | 28 | 22 | 13 | 25 | 14 | 17 | 15 |

*Point made in separate news items.

166

(*a*) Between them, the nine newspapers produced at least 52 separate main points, none of which were common to all papers, although six were in eight out of nine papers. The average number of points per paper was 21. The "highest scoring" title was *The Guardian* with 29 points, while *The Times*, *The Daily Telegraph* and *Daily Express* had at least 25 each. The *Morning Star* had fewest points.

(*b*) The 15 points picked up by at least six of the nine titles consisted of the basic facts of the rail pay claim and the comparison with miners (2, 3, 4, 16, 17) the main statements made by Mr Foot (20, 21, 22, 23, 24), the price index rise (26, 27), the influence of the miners' pay deal (1, 35) and the resulting threat to the Social Contract (48). These 15 points out of 52 account for 106 out of 189 total references (57%), again suggesting a high level of agreement on the main points of the story. If these 15 points are taken as providing a criterion for assessing completeness of coverage, the different papers rank as follows:

| 15/15 | 14/15 | 13/15 | 12/15 | 11/15 | 9/15 | 7/15 |
|-------|-------|-------|-------|-------|------|------|
| The Guardian | The Daily Telegraph Daily Express | The Times | Daily Mail | Daily Mirror Financial Times | The Sun | Morning Star |

It is evident that even short reports, as in the case of the *Daily Mail*, can pick up a high proportion of the main points of the story. It appears from Table C7 that the part of the whole story most completely covered by the newspapers as a whole is the report of the Foot speech. An average of 4·5 points out of six was scored for each newspaper on this subject. Apart from this, other areas fully covered were the basic facts of the pay claims, Sidney Weighell's reference to the miners' settlement, the context of rising prices and the political and economic consequences of this and similar pay settlements.

(*c*) At the other extreme, fourteen of the points listed were referred to in only one newspaper. Of this number, all but one are either minor details or points on the fringe of the main story. The exception is comment in the *Financial Times* to the effect that the rail pay increases are above the Social Contract limits. Other papers hinted at this, but were not specific.

(*d*) Given what has already been said, there is little scope for finding much diversity of treatment, except as a consequence of having more space. The papers with larger coverage tended to use this to give more attention to the arguments in support of the rail claim (eg *The Guardian* and *The Times*) or to details of other impending claims and the connection with the miners' pay settlement (*The Guardian* and *The Daily Telegraph*). *The Sun* is also noticeably more attentive to other claims and settlements. The *Financial Times* and *Morning Star* are strongest on the details of employer response and future timing. The same two papers, along with *The Sun*, both avoid discussion of the political and economic consequences of the claim which most other papers deal with.

## 5. Accuracy

Without reference to information not contained in these reports we can make only tentative references about accuracy on details. There are at least five factual matters on which information is given by most newspapers. These are: the number of rail workers involved; the percentage size of the NUR claim; the percentage size of the ASLEF claim; the present minimum rail wage; the size of the pay award to the miners. The following results emerge from a comparison between papers.

**COMPARISONS ON REPORTING OF FACTS**

| Fact | The Times | The Guar-dian | The Daily Tele. | Fin. Times | M. Star | Daily Expr. | Daily Mail | Daily Mirror | The Sun |
|---|---|---|---|---|---|---|---|---|---|
| (a) Percentage NUR pay claim | — | 25–33% | 28% | up to 35% | over 25% | 28% | at least 34% | — | at least 28% |
| (b) Percentage ASLEF pay claim | 25–30% | 25–33% | 25–33% | — | 25–33% | up to 33% | up to 33% | — | — |
| (c) Current minimum wage | £25.65 | £30.05 | £25.65 | | £25.65 | £25.65 | — | — | £25.65 |
| (d) Percentage miners' award | 20% or 35% | over 30% | up to 35½% | 30% | — | over 30% | over 30% | 30% | 28% |
| (e) Number of rail workers | 250,000 | — | 280,000 | 200,000 | — | — | — | 270,000 | — |

The variations in figures for claims and wages can almost all be accounted for by differences in application to *different* groups of workers or in the inclusion of thresholds or not. The varying estimate of numbers of workers is likely to reflect the division of the whole group into three unions. No clear instance of inaccuracy can be established. The *Daily Mirror* gives least precise detail about the rail claim.

## 6. Editorials

Only the *Financial Times* included editorial comment bearing on this issue. It quoted Mr Healey's remark about the danger of national bankruptcy, and stated two disadvantages of the miners' settlement, which "plainly breached the Social Contract": the likely effect on rail and electricity pay claims and the risk that 30% has now been established as the "going rate" because it is in the public sector.

## 7. Editorial attitude or "colour" in news reports

(a) A very small number of the points made in reports might be regarded as implying an attitude or judgement on the part of the newspaper or writer and as lacking attribution to some source. One example might be the *Financial Times'* conclusion that the rail claims breach the Social Contract and the widespread conclusion that the Social Contract is threatened or defunct.

(b) If we attempt to categorise points as listed in Table C7 as more "unfavourable" or more "favourable" to the rail union position, we might place the following in the former group:

( 9)  Increases asked are above Social Contract;
(19)  Job not to save Britain, but help railmen;
(28)  Wage increases ahead of prices;
(46)  Carr on danger to Britain;
(47)  Healey on unemployment risk;

(48) Contract threatened;
(51) Carr warns of militants.

Amongst more supportive points would be:

(12) Comparison with other industries indicates 24% +;
(14) Railwork interdependent with mining;
(18) Union leaders respectful of contract;
(52) Buckton confident of no strike.

This classification is based on the hypothetical assumption that moderation of claims and respect for the Social Contract is good and the reverse bad. The frequencies for the two groups of items (based on Table C7) for the main national newspapers are as follows:

TABLE C9

RATIO OF POINTS "LESS FAVOURABLE" TO "MORE FAVOURABLE" TO UNION POSITION

| The Times ... ... ... 2:1 | Daily Express ... ... 4:2 |
|---|---|
| The Guardian ... ... ... 3:3 | Daily Mail ... ... ... 2:0 |
| The Daily Telegraph ... ... 4:1 | Daily Mirror ... ... ... 5:0 |
| Financial Times ... ... 1:0 | The Sun ... ... ... 0:1 |

The Guardian emerges as most inclined to balance the more favourable with the more critical points, but the assumptions made and the character of the story ensures an "anti-union" ratio overall and these results on their own tell us little about "bias".

(c) There is some "colour" in reports which is not revealed in the table and the following instances can be cited. The Daily Mirror shows the clearest tendency to label the rail pay claim as excessive. It speaks of a "demand" for "massive" pay rises, a "pay-rise band wagon", a "scramble" for increases. It calls Foot's warning to other unions a "grim" one. In part, this reflects a general tendency to the dramatic, which is consistent with the headline ("Off the Pay Rails") and shows up in the reference to price rises as a "huge leap". The Sun also uses the word "scramble" and calls the miners' deal "mammoth", but is otherwise neutral. The Daily Mail also uses the word "scramble" and calls the miners' settlement "huge" and "massive". The railmen are said to be looking for increases "way over" 28%. The Daily Express is neutral on the rail claim, but critical of Mr Foot for only "mildly wagging his finger" at the other unions and calls his claim that the miners' settlement is within the Social Contract "astonishing". No "colour" can be identified in reports in The Times, The Daily Telegraph, The Guardian, Financial Times and Morning Star. Colour is thus largely confined to the "Popular" dailies and to the issue of size of pay claim or settlement.

169

# IV CASE 3: Mr Foot, Mr Jones and the dockers, Thursday, 6 March 1975

## 1. Introduction

This story has three different aspects, with a common basis in reference to the dock workers' dispute and brought together in varying degrees by different newspapers. One part of the story concerned Mr Foot's address to the national executive of the TWGU, another a dock meeting addressed by Mr Jones, a third part concerning an ACAS inquiry into the dock dispute. All events occurred on the same day. All are treated as part of a single issue for the purposes of space-measurement and tabulation of main points.

## 2. Space and prominence

Parts of the story are on the front page of *The Guardian*, *Daily Express*, *Morning Star*, *Daily Mail* and *The Daily Telegraph*, but in no case is it the main lead story. There is no report in *The Sun* of any aspect of the story, in the edition examined. The amount of space is shown in Table C10. Only in *The Times* is the issue covered in a single item, although some aspects are dealt with in a leading article.

TABLE C10

NEWS SPACE ALLOCATED TO FOOT, JONES AND DOCKERS, 6 MARCH 1975

| Title | Total space (col. cms.) | Headline as % of space | Presentation |
|---|---|---|---|
| The Times ... ... | 30 | 12% | 1 item |
| The Guardian ... ... | 90 | 21% | 2 separate items |
| The Daily Telegraph ... | 51 | 14% | 2 separate items |
| Financial Times ... | 94 | 15% | 2 connected items |
| Morning Star ... ... | 10 | — | item |
| Daily Express ... ... | 34 | 34% | 2 separate items |
| Daily Mail ... ... | 80 | 40% | 3 separate items |
| Daily Mirror ... ... | 34 | 21% | 2 separate items |

The papers generally gave equal prominence to the two main aspects of the story.

## 3. Headlines

Table C11 gives the text of the main headlines and sub-headings.

TABLE C11

HEADLINES RELATING TO FOOT, JONES AND DOCKERS, 6 MARCH 1975

| | |
|---|---|
| The Times ... ... | MR FOOT URGES TRANSPORT UNIONS TO BACK CONTRACT |
| The Guardian ... ... | (1) JONES PLEA HOWLED DOWN |
| | (2) FOOT STAYS SANE IN DEFENCE OF CONTRACT |
| The Daily Telegraph ... | (1) JONES JEERED BY DOCKERS |
| | (2) SUPPORT FOR DOCKERS GROWS |
| | (3) "KEEP TO CONTRACT" WARNING BY FOOT |

170

| | |
|---|---|
| *Financial Times* ... ... | (1) NO STATUTORY PAY POLICY |
| | (2) FOOT URGES TGWU TO HELP GET PORT OF LONDON MOVING |
| *Morning Star* ... ... | No headline |
| *Daily Express:* ... ... | (1) DOCKERS JEER JONES |
| | (2) FOOT'S NEW DIG AT "WELSH" REG |
| *Daily Mail* ... ... | (1) "GANGSTERS" INVADE JACK JONES DOCK TALKS |
| | (2) NOW FOOT AND JONES COME OUT SHOOTING |
| *Daily Mirror* ... ... | (1) DOCKERS IN "JUDAS JONES" ROW |
| | (2) FOOT WARNS ON JOBS |

Five of the newspapers draw attention to the row between Jack Jones and some dockers. The two which do not, *The Times* and *Financial Times* provide the most generally informative headlines. There is "colour," especially in the references to conflict, but no clear tendency or evaluation can be imputed.

## 4. Completeness and diversity in news reports

(*a*) Between them, news reports in the eight newspapers produced 39 main points, of which only one was common to the eight. The average number of points per newspaper was 15. *The Guardian* was highest, with 23, the *Morning Star* notably low, with five.

There were nine points which at least five of the eight papers all reported and which may be taken as reflecting press judgement on the key points of the story. These accounted for 60 out of 122 references in all, and consisted of:

the appeal by Foot to the TGWU to maintain the Social Contract (1)
the warning by Foot of dangers of ignoring wage restraint (2)
the rejection of statutory pay control (3)
the appeal by Jones for a return to work (17)
the rejection of this appeal (18)
the stormy character of Jones' reception by dockers (19)
the cause of the dock dispute (30)
the fact of support elsewhere for the London dockers (39)
the accusation that Jones was a traitor (22)

If reporting of these nine points is taken as a criterion of completeness, the different newspapers can be scored as follows:

| 8/9 | 9/9 | 8/9 | 7/9 | 2/9 | 7/9 | 8/9 | 8/9 |
|---|---|---|---|---|---|---|---|
| The Times | The Guardian | The Daily Telegraph | Financial Times | Morning Star | Daily Express | Daily Mail | Daily Mirror |

The scoring again suggests that relatively short reports manage to pick up main story points.

TABLE C12

## CHECKLIST OF MAIN POINTS, FOOT, JONES AND THE DOCKERS
### 6 MARCH 1975

| Main points | The Times | The Guardian | The Daily Telegraph | Financial Times | Morning Star | Daily Express | Daily Mail | Daily Mirror |
|---|---|---|---|---|---|---|---|---|
| I. Foot at TGWU Executive Meeting | | | | | | | | |
| 1. Foot appeals to TGWU to maintain Social Contract wage guidelines ... | × | × | × | × | × | × | × | × |
| 2. Foot warns that alternative to wage restraint is unemployment and inflation ... | × | × | × | × | × | | × | × |
| 3. Foot ruled out statutory wage control ... | × | × | | × | × | × | | × |
| 4. Jack Jones pledged to take the message to the work people (or to help) ... | × | | | × | | | | |
| 5. Foot says many firms put in genuine difficulties through pay claims ... | | × | | × | | | | |
| 6. Foot says too early to judge success of Contract ... | | × | | × | | × | | |
| 7. Foot called for speedy return to work at docks ... | × | × | | × | × | | | |
| 8. Dock trouble said to make economic troubles worse ... | × | × | | × | × | | | |
| 9. Foot says Government is committed to extend dock labour scheme ... | | × | | × | | | | |
| 10. Foot emphasises Social Contract is about more than wages ... | | × | | × | | | | |
| 11. Moderate Labour position in Foot speech applauded ... | × | | | × | × | × | × | |
| 12. Quiet reception for Foot speech ... | | | | | | × | | |
| 13. Jack Jones praises Foot as heart and soul of labour movement ... | × | | | × | | × | × | |
| 14. Jones voices some suspicion about other Ministers (Prentice) ... | | | × | | | × | × | |
| 15. Decision to admit press and TV unusual ... | | | | | | | | |
| 16. Near-criticism of Prentice for attack on unions ... | | | × | | | × | × | × |

172

## II.  Meeting at docks

| | 14 | 15 | 11 | 5 | 21 | 20 | 23 | 13 |
|---|---|---|---|---|---|---|---|---|
| 17. Jones tries to persuade dockers to call off strike | × | × | × | | × | × | × | × |
| 18. Call for return rejected | × | × | × | | × | × | × | × |
| 19. Meeting a stormy one, shouts, jeers, etc. | × | × | × | | | | × | × |
| 20. Dockers waiting for proposals on extension of registered dock work to other ports and depots | | | | | | | | × |
| 21. Jones promised statement soon by Government | × | × | | | | | | |
| 22. Jones accused of being a "traitor", as he drove away | × | × | × | | | × | × | |
| 23. Reference to mass lobby of TGWU headquarters later in day | | | | | × | × | × | × |
| 24. Jones later blamed hooligans (non-union) for trouble | × | | | | | | | |
| 25. No formal statement to press after meeting | × | × | | | | | | |
| 26. Jones promised no loss of jobs | × | × | | | | | | |

## III.  Dock Workers' Dispute

| | 14 | 15 | 11 | 5 | 21 | 20 | 23 | 13 |
|---|---|---|---|---|---|---|---|---|
| 27. London dock strike now in second week (port at standstill) | | × | | | × | × | × | |
| 28. Increasing backlog of shipping and/or cost of strike | | × | | | | × | × | |
| 29. Strike followed a month-long blacking campaign | | | | | | × | × | |
| 30. Dispute is over use of non-registered dockers in container depots | | | | | × | × | × | × |
| 31. Inquiry held yesterday by ACAS | | | | | × | × | × | |
| 32. Cronin, for dockers, complained of firms breaking spirit of agreement | | × | | | × | × | × | |
| 33. Firms said to operate outside docks to avoid employing dockers | | | | | × | × | × | |
| 34. Firms named said employing dockers was uneconomic | | | | | | × | × | |
| 35. Strike is over dispute between dockers and lorry drivers | × | × | × | | | | | × |
| 36. Dock labour scheme has so far cost £22m | | | | | | × | × | |
| 37. Dockers objected to presence of press | | | | | | | × | |
| 38. Mass meeting again on Monday | × | × | | | | × | × | |
| 39. Support elsewhere for strike (blacking) | × | | | | | | | × |
| Total number of points | 14 | 15 | 11 | 5 | 21 | 20 | 23 | 13 |

(b) Twelve of the points listed (5, 8, 11, 12, 15, 20, 23, 26, 29, 35, 36, 37) were referred to in only one newspaper report. Of these, most are details or peripheral to the main story. Three of the points seem of more substance: the comment by Mr Foot on difficulties of firms faced by big pay demands (5, *The Daily Telegraph*); the promise by Jones to preserve all London docks jobs (26, *Daily Mirror*); and the unusual decision to admit press and TV to the TGWU executive meeting (15, *Financial Times*). The comments on the reception given to Mr Foot (points 11 and 12) seem inconsistent.

The papers thus largely agree in reporting what Mr Foot said to the TGWU and the way in which the dockers received Jack Jones' appeal to return to normal work. In the main, they also explain the cause of the docks dispute, although the explanation is fairly thin outside the "Quality" papers, which reported details of the ACAS inquiry hearing. The apparent absence of this material in *The Times* reports is due to its being given as part of a leading article.

(c) The extent of diversity is this limited, apart from the following: The *Daily Mail* and *Daily Mirror* report comments by Jack Jones about the dock meeting which are not picked up by other papers; some papers are more inclined than others to make a point of the internal Labour party quarrel between Mr Prentice and Mr Foot (*Daily Mail, Daily Express, The Daily Telegraph*). Otherwise, the main differences, which have already been mentioned, lie in the greater tendency for the "Qualities" to give more details of the dock dispute and more attention to Mr Foot's speech.

5. There are no inconsistencies between reports which suggest inaccuracy of substance in any one report. The number of dockers involved at the dockside meeting is variously put at 100, 200, 300, but it is unclear whether or not this refers to those inside the hall only and the press was excluded from the meeting.

### 6. Attitude expressed in editorial comment

Only *The Times* carries editorial comment on the issue, devoted mainly to analysing the causes of the dispute at the docks. It concludes that traditional dock labour is uneconomic and that it is "perverse" to attempt to prop up a system based on restrictive practices and not always popular with other workers. Mr Foot is criticised for leaning in the direction of pleasing the dockers.

### 7. Editorial attitude or "colour" in news reports

(a) There is virtually nothing of a tendentious kind in any unsupported or unattributed remarks in any newspaper. None of the main points found in the papers had a clearly non-factual character, although *The Times*' comment that applause was given to Mr Foot's presentation of the moderate Labour position on wages and unions possibly involves some selective interpretation.

(b) A clear division into points "favourable" or "unfavourable" to unions or workers is not possible in this case, since there is a division between the official union position represented by Jack Jones and the unofficial position of the dockers. There are several points which reflect official TGWU co-operation with Government policy in the interests of general welfare and several points which reflect unfavourably on the unofficial action and attitude of striking dockers. Amongst the former could be included points 4, 11 and 17 and, amongst the latter, points 8, 18, 19, 22, 27 and 28. If these are taken as giving a basis for calculating a ratio, the different newspapers rate as follows.

**TABLE C13**

**RATIO OF POINTS "FOR" OFFICIAL AND "AGAINST" UNOFFICIAL ACTION**

| | | | | | | | | |
|---|---|---|---|---|---|---|---|---|
| *The Times* | ... | ... | ... | 3:2 | *Daily Express* | ... | ... | 1:3 |
| *The Guardian* | ... | ... | ... | 1:4 | *Daily Mail* ... | ... | ... | 1:5 |
| *Daily Telegraph* | ... | ... | ... | 1:5 | *Daily Mirror* ... | ... | ... | 2:3 |
| *The Financial Times* | | ... | ... | 1:4 | | | | |

This is too tenuous a basis for making any comparison between newspapers, but it is apparent that most papers were inclined in general to report items reflecting poorly on the attitude of the dockers.

(*c*) "Colour" is mainly to be found in reference to the reception given to Jack Jones by the Dockers. Most papers reported a stormy reception, as the headlines indicate. The *Daily Mail* gives perhaps the most detail about this, including the fact that Jones was spat at. Little or no other evidence of "colour" could be cited.

175

# V   CASE 4: Union reaction to the Budget, Thursday, 17 April 1975

## 1. Introduction

The story involved is a complex one and extends over into the more strictly political area. Papers thus vary according to the context in which union response was dealt with. However, basically there were three main events: the Scottish TUC meeting in Aberdeen, after which Jack Jones gave his personal response; the Healey-PLP meeting and coming TUC-Labour Party Liaison meeting; the specific reaction of ASLEF on the implication for their pay claim. In addition, there was some news of employer response to union reaction and of price and wage rate increases. In selecting the content for treatment in this case study, a somewhat arbitrary line has had to be drawn between content directly concerned with union response to the Budget and other material. Where necessary, points made elsewhere in the papers have been noted, but it should be borne in mind that there is other relevant content, especially in the "Quality" papers.

## 2. Prominence and space allocation

The main story of union response was a main lead story in all national dailies except the *Daily Mail*, *The Sun*, and *Financial Times*. *The Times*, *The Daily Telegraph*, *Financial Times* and *The Sun* carried editorials. The space allocation was as follows in Table C14.

TABLE C14

NEWS SPACE ALLOCATION TO UNION REACTION TO BUDGET, 17 APRIL 1975

| Title | Space (col.cms.) | Headline as % of space | Presentation |
|---|---|---|---|
| *The Times* ... ... | 130 | 25% | 1 item |
| *The Guardian* ... ... | 94 | 33% | 2 separate items |
| *The Daily Telegraph* ... | 113 | 28% | 2 separate items |
| *Financial Times* ... ... | 45 | 25% | 1 item |
| *Morning Star* ... ... | 90 | 55% | 1 item |
| *Daily Express* ... ... | 132 | 49% | 1 item |
| *Daily Mail* ... ... | 58 | 20% | 1 item |
| *Daily Mirror* ... ... | 138 | 46% | 1 item |
| *The Sun* ... ... ... | 66 | 41% | 2 separate items |

There is a notable tendency here for very prominent headlines, reflecting the page one lead treatment and also for newspapers to bring points together to make a single item. On the one hand, this reflects the disparate nature of the content which goes to make up the story, such that it would be difficult to make separate stories of much interest out of the component parts (although several of the "Quality" titles do so). But, on the other hand, it may be interpreted as an attempt to convey the importance of what might otherwise seem an insubstantial event (the comments by Jack Jones). While there is clearly a basis for reporting a strong and clear union reaction, the news events to embody this information are lacking. In general, the story is a good example of industrial relation matters acquiring significance because of their direct political implications.

## 3. Headlines

TABLE C15

**HEADLINES TO STORY OF UNION REACTION TO BUDGET, 17 APRIL 1975**

| | |
|---|---|
| *The Times* ... ... ... | ANGRY UNIONS SAY BUDGET MEASURES FREE THEM FROM THE SOCIAL CONTRACT<br>Car and rail claims to be increased |
| *The Guardian* ... ... | (1) UNIONS GETTING HOT UNDER THE HEALEY COLLAR<br>(2) SCOTS SAY HEALEY HAS BROKEN FAITH |
| *The Daily Telegraph* ... | (1) UNIONS SCORN BUDGET PLEA<br>Jack Jones, Buckton and McGahey warn Healey<br>(2) PAY SETS INFLATION RECORD |
| *Financial Times* ... ... | SCOTTISH TUC SPEARHEAD UNIONS' ATTACK ON BUDGET |
| *Morning Star* ... ... | SCOTS TUC "FIGHT THIS BUDGET" PLEDGE |
| *Daily Express* ... ... | THAT'S RUINED THE CONTRACT |
| *Daily Mail* ... ... | BOSSES' SOS TO TUC: LET'S TALK ON WAGES |
| *Daily Mirror* ... ... | BACKLASH FROM THE UNIONS<br>Railmen fight against Budget |
| *The Sun* ... ... ... | (1) NOW JONES GIVES JOLT TO CONTRACT<br>(2) NOW UNION BLACKLASH ON BUDGET |

Again, *The Times* provides a very specific and long headline. Generally, the tone and content of other headlines is very similar although the *Daily Mail* gives prominence to a CBI statement which is generally treated in a subsidiary way by other papers.

## 4. Completeness and diversity in news reports

(*a*) In all, 39 points are listed in Table 16, with an average number of points per title of 18. *The Times* and *The Guardian* score highest with 25 and 24 respectively the *Morning Star* lowest with nine.

(*b*) No single point is reported by all nine newspapers, mainly because of the different patterns of report in the *Daily Mail* and *Morning Star*.

Seven different points are picked up by eight of nine papers. The 11 points which at least six of the nine papers reported cover: the threat to, or end of, Government-union co-operation; the newly critical attitude of Jack Jones to the Contract; the overwhelming vote at the Scottish TUC condemning the Budget; the rise in wage rates and prices; the stepped-up rail pay claim as an example of union response; the criticism of Mr. Healey for increasing unemployment. If these 11 points (Nos. 1, 2, 4, 5, 10, 11, 16, 17, 24, 31, 32) are taken as the

177

**TABLE C16**

## CHECKLIST OF MAIN POINTS
## UNION REACTION TO BUDGET, 17 APRIL 1975

| Main points | The Times | The Guardian | The Daily Telegraph | Financial Times | Morning Star | Daily Express | Daily Mail | Daily Mirror | The Sun |
|---|---|---|---|---|---|---|---|---|---|
| **I. Union–Government relations in light of Budget** | | | | | | | | | |
| 1. Budget threatens to end union-Government co-operation | × | × | × | × | × | × | | × | × |
| 2. TUC-Labour party liaison meeting on Monday... | × | × | × | × | × | × | | × | × |
| 3. Monday's meeting likely to be difficult | | × | × | | | × | × | × | |
| 4. Jack Jones doubtful about future of Contract | × | × | × | × | | × | × | × | × |
| 5. Jack Jones believes Government should change its line | × | × | × | | | × | × | × | × |
| 6. Jones earlier supported the Contract | | × | × | | | × | | × | |
| 7. Jones criticises failure to deal with pensions and food subsidies | | | | × | | | | | |
| 8. Jones not threatening to end TUC wage restraint | × | | | × | | | × | | × |
| 9. TUC chiefs will reconsider contract at monthly meeting | | | | × | | | | | |
| **II. Scottish TUC proceedings** | | | | | | | | | |
| 10. Resolution passed condemning budget at Scots TUC | × | × | × | × | × | × | | × | × |
| 11. Few votes against (3 or 5) | × | × | × | × | × | | | × | × |
| 12. Detailed report of Scots TUC debate | × | × | | × | × | | | | |
| 13. Jones did not speak at Scots TUC debate (nor Basnett, Jenkins, Fisher) | × | × | × | × | | | | | |
| 14. McGahey calls Budget "vicious" or attacks it generally | | | | × | × | | | | |
| 15. Today's speech at Aberdeen by Foot awaited | | × | | | | | | | |
| **III. ASLEF and other unions' reactions** | | | | | | | | | |
| 16. Buckton warns his claim likely to be accepted | × | × | × | × | | × | × | × | × |
| 17. Present rail claim likely to rise by 2¾% | × | × | × | × | | × | × | × | × |
| 18. Buckton demands 11% more on top of 30% | | | × | | | | | × | |
| 19. ASLEF has already rejected 20% offer | × | | | | | | | | |
| 20. ASLEF due to meet rail board tomorrow | × | | × | | | × | | | |
| 21. ASLEF wants to retain relativities with miners... | × | | × | | | × | | | |
| 22. Fisher of NUPE says wage demands will go up... | | × | | | | × | × | | × |

| | | | | | | | | | |
|---|---|---|---|---|---|---|---|---|---|
| 23. Car workers say higher wage claims inevitable ... ... ... ... ... ... ... | x | x* | | | | | | | |
| 24. Healey criticised for failure to stop unemployment ... ... ... ... ... ... | x | x* | | x | x* | x | | x | |
| 25. Unions likely to seek compensation outside Contract ... ... ... ... ... ... | x | | x | x | | | | | x |
| 26. Healey warns unions that wage compensation self-defeating ... ... ... ... ... | x* | x | | x | | | | | |
| **IV. Employer/CBI response** | | | | | | | | | |
| 27. CBI doubts value of Social Contract ... ... ... ... ... ... ... ... | | | | x* | | | x | | |
| 28. CBI chief warns of unemployment ... ... ... ... ... ... ... ... | x* | | | | | x | | x | |
| 29. CBI describes wage rate increases as "frightening", etc. ... ... ... ... ... | | | x* | | | | x | x | |
| 30. Employers offer to talk to TUC (or new initiative) ... ... ... ... ... ... | x* | | | x* | | | x | x | |
| **V. Context of pay and price figures** | | | | | | | | | |
| 31. DEP says wages have risen 32% (or £38 to £52, or earnings 29%) ... ... ... ... | x | x* | x | x | | x | x | x | x |
| 32. Prices have risen 20% ... ... ... ... ... ... ... ... ... | x* | x* | | x | | x | x | | x |
| 33. Cost of budget increase will be 3% (or 2.75%) ... ... ... ... ... ... | x | x* | x | x | | x | | | |
| **VI. Political aspects** | | | | | | | | | |
| 34. Foot and others have tried to avoid clash ... ... ... ... ... ... ... | | x | | | | | | | |
| 35. Tribune MPs likely to be split on Monday ... ... ... ... ... ... ... | | | | x | | | | | |
| 36. Healey counters left wing PLP attack ... ... ... ... ... ... ... ... | | x | x | x | | x | | | |
| 37. Labour MPs say Contract broken by Government (or critical) ... ... ... ... | x | x | | | x* | | x | x* | |
| 38. Healey attacks Scargill, McGahey, Clive Jenkins ... ... ... ... ... ... | | | | x | | | | | |
| 39. Right wing MPs support Healey ... ... ... ... ... ... ... ... ... | | x* | x* | | x* | | | | |
| Total number of points ... ... | 25 | 24 | 21 | 23 | 9 | 18 | 13 | 18 | 13 |

* Points made in separate reports.

criterion of full reporting of main elements in the story, the newspapers rank as follows:

| 11/11 | 10/11 | 9/11 | 6/11 | 5/11 |
|---|---|---|---|---|
| The Times | Daily Express | The Daily Telegraph | Daily Mail | Morning Star |
| The Guardian | Daily Mirror | Financial Times | | |
| | The Sun | | | |

This largely reflects space allocation and the total number of points scored, but again it is clear that relatively short reports as in the *Daily Mirror* and *The Sun*, do not necessarily have to omit what are, by consensus, the more important elements of the story as a whole.

There are no large variations in completeness of coverage between different parts of the story as a whole. The general question of union-Government relations was represented by nine points and, of these, five were reported on average by each paper despite major omissions by the *Daily Mail* and *Morning Star*. An average of three out of five points relating to the proceedings in Aberdeen were reported. On the more specific union reactions, five out of 11 was the average score. The most fully covered section related to pay and price rise figures, with an average of two/three points per title. The CBI response and the political (Labour Party) aspects of the issue were least fully covered, especially by the "Popular" dailies.

(c) Of the points picked up in only one or two papers, the most interesting one is perhaps item 9 which records the view of the *Financial Times* that Jack Jones was not threatening to end the Social Contract. The interest lies in the fact that it conflicts with the tenor of most reports which generally associated the relatively guarded comments made by Jack Jones with explicit attacks on the Social Contract made by other unions' leaders. Item 18, that ASLEF wanted 11% on top of 30%, is putting the pay claim more strongly than any other report (*The Daily Telegraph* and *Daily Mirror*).

(d) Divergences between papers are few, apart from those which arise as a result of incompleteness. The most distinctive reports are those mentioned, in the *Morning Star* and *Daily Mail*. The former concentrates almost exclusively on points which reflect criticism of the Government, omitting points which support an opposing viewing and omitting any reference to Jack Jones. The *Daily Mail* picks up two or three points in each sub-topic area, but concentrates on the CBI story, which *The Sun* and *The Guardian* omit altogether.

5. In the nature of the story, there are no crucial facts and figures which might, if presented inaccurately, affect the interpretation of the story. Perhaps the most important basic element to check for accuracy consists of the remarks attributed to Jack Jones which provided the main substantiation for the story of hostile reaction to the budget, aside from the Scottish TUC proceedings themselves. Only the *Morning Star* omitted to mention or quote the comments and, of the other papers, only the *Financial Times* did not offer a verbatim quotation.

The following separate remarks were quoted:

(a) "The TUC will be considering the whole situation"

(b) "What we have to do is see what can be done to change the line of the Government in certain directions" (*c*) "The TUC will have to consider the whole thing and will be meeting representatives of the Government next Monday"

(*d*) "We must do things to show that the Government has not lost its sense of social purpose"

(*e*) "Certainly I am not enthusiastic about the Budget"

(*f*) "We must now consider how we can still pursue the original aims of the Social Contract"

These quotation are taken from *The Daily Telegraph*, which was the only paper to report all six points as quotations.

*The Times* reproduced as quotation points (*b*), (*c*), and (*d*) and reported the substance of point (*f*) from a P.A. report. The three points quoted are word-for-word identical with *The Daily Telegraph* version.

*The Guardian* quoted only point (*f*) and reported points (*b*) and (*c*), closely following the text quoted elsewhere. It omitted references to lack of enthusiasm for the Budget and loss of social purpose.

The *Financial Times* reported only point (*f*).

The *Daily Express* quoted points (*d*) and (*f*), using the same words as in *The Daily Telegraph*, apart from substituting "objectives" for "aims".

The *Daily Mail* quoted points (*b*), (*d*) and (*f*), also using the word "objectives".

The *Daily Mirror* quoted point (*f*) as in *The Daily Telegraph*, but presented points (*b*) and (*d*) as a single statement with slight changes of wording.

*The Sun* reported that "Jack Jones had warned that Mr Healey's Budget had put the Social Contract in danger" and that he suggested that "unions would have to rethink their attitude towards the Social Contract". Only point (*b*) is quoted as in *The Daily Telegraph*. The reported views of Jack Jones use expressions which are not found in quotations elsewhere.

In general, this detailed look at quotations and reported statements suggest a high level of agreement on the text of Jack Jones' remarks and unless all are wrong, there seems to have been accurate and careful reporting on this particular point.

## 6. Attitudes of newspapers as revealed in editorial comment

Five newspapers comment editorially on this issue.

*The Daily Telegraph*, under the heading "Healey versus Unions" sees the success of Budget policy as depending on large trade unions and foreign money lenders. The rise in wages is seen as due mainly to "unrestrained trade union monopoly power". The wage rise is far in excess of an "elastic Social Contract". Government is correct to reject statutory incomes policy. Government should not intervene in the private sector and let public sector finance itself. Higher unemployment will reduce union power and also wage increases.

*The Times*, under the heading "The Best Chancellor We Have", supports Healey's attempt to convey the "wage sanity" message to the unions. Rise of a third in wages is "responsible for most serious economic crisis". Mr Healey referred to as one of the "responsible members" of Government. Mr Healey may be right in rejecting statutory control. Budget said to "err on side of inadequacy". The "left wing" is criticised for having no policy, only a "few slogans and too much power". Their attitude and policies would bring us to disaster. We should support Mr Healey until we can get a "better champion of responsible Government".

The *Financial Times* ("Failure of a Contract") also cites wage increase rates as alarming, but warns against misleading character of basic wage index. Even so, Contract guidelines "have not been strictly observed". Perhaps we should now forget about the Social Contract. Need to apply a ceiling to wage bill in public sector to give same check to wages as unemployment does in private sector.

*The Sun* ("Suicide Leapfrog"), quotes Scanlon and McGahey in opposition to Budget, calls Len Murray a "mock-moderate" and regrets Jack Jones' withdrawal of support for Contract. Government have stuck to their side of the Social Contract in the Budget. Now Government must give up exhortation and find a tough pay and prices policy backed by the law. "Budget-busting pay leapfrog now being openly encouraged by union leaders is both selfish and suicidal".

All these four editorials are clear in their criticism of union reaction to the Government and, in varying degrees, supportive of the Government (*The Sun* and *The Times* more so than the *The Daily Telegraph* or *Financial Times*). The *Morning Star* takes an alternative line, describing the budget as "economic lunacy", likely to cause unemployment and cut living standards. Budget denunciation at Scottish TUC called "absolutely correct": "The fight for higher pay is crucial for working-class advance". The *Daily Express* has no editorial comment, but it has a major cartoon by Cummings beside its Opinion column, showing Murray, Scanlon, Gormley, Buckton and Mikardo as devils being exorcised by Healey and the caption "Writing my Ten Commandments was easy, but I need a miracle to exorcise the devils from the TUC and the Left!".

### 7. Editorial attitude or "colour" in news reports

(*a*) Interpretative points are, as usual, hard to find, although in a sense the main point of the whole story (1) is an interpretation, however well supported. Otherwise the *Financial Times* comment that Jack Jones is not threatening to end wage restraint might indicate a more cautious attitude than other newspapers show.

(*b*) The story as a whole is about Government-union relations and, as the editorial comments show, it is possible to come down on the union "side" or on the Government "side". Some of the points listed in Table C16 do lend themselves to classification according to whether they favour the Government or union view of the merits of the budget. The points (from Table C16) which might be regarded as either favouring the "Government" side or implying criticism of union reaction are:

(13)   Abstention by Jones and other "moderates" at TUC debate criticising the Budget

(18)   ASLEF demand for $30\% + 11\%$

(25)   Unions to seek compensation outside Contract

(26), (28), (29)   Danger of unemployment through wage increases

(31)   News of $32\%$ wage rate increases

(39)   Support for Government from some labour MPs

(36), (38)   Healey counters left-wing attacks

182

Items more likely to support union case are:

( 7)   Government neglect on pensions and food subsidies
(24)   Budget threat to employment
(32)   Price rise of 20%
(33)   Cost of Budget increase 3%
(37)   Labour MP says Contract broken by government.

With this possible ratio of 10:5 "pro-Government" or "pro-union" as a standard, the count for each paper appears as in Table C17.

TABLE C17
RATIO OF POINTS "PRO-GOVERNMENT" TO "PRO-UNION"

| The Times | ... | ... | ... | 5:5 | Daily Express | ... | ... | 3:3 |
|---|---|---|---|---|---|---|---|---|
| The Guardian | ... | ... | ... | 5:4 | Daily Mail | ... | ... | 2:2 |
| Daily Telegraph | ... | ... | 6:2 | | Daily Mirror | ... | ... | 4:3 |
| Financial Times | ... | ... | 6:4 | | The Sun | ... | ... | 2:2 |

The general balance of reporting, strongly affected by the different overall frequency of each item, is not far from the 10:5 standard. On average, there is a 40% use of "pro-Government" points and a 60% use of "pro-union" points.

(c) Such evidence as there is of colour relates either to the degree of conflict with the Government which the union response implies, or the degree of alarm appropriate to the consequences for wage claims, etc. The themes have already been indicated in headlines and this comment relates only to news text and, in particular, to the main item on union reaction. Most newspapers show some evidence of the use of dramatic expressions or unattributed words and phrases which involve interpretation. The Times says the Social Contract "suffered severe blows". The Financial Times spoke of a "major clash" developing between union leaders and Government and described the former as "angry and startled". An "outspoken" session is expected at the next Government-TUC meeting. Throughout, there is a strong, though documented, emphasis on discord over the Budget: The Guardian speaks of an impending end to the honeymoon; Jack Jones is referred to as "ominously" making his remarks; the Daily Express referred to "severe pressure from militants" on Jack Jones. His words are described as a "warning that things have changed overnight". He is described as the "only wall between the country and a tidal wave of pay demands". The Daily Telegraph refers to a "storm of trade union protests". The Daily Mail has little colour, except to sub-headline the word "frightening", taken from CBI comments.

The Daily Mirror refers to "hammer blows" struck at the Social Contract, to an "angry backlash" and to the fact that wages had "soared".

The Sun refers to a "four-pronged attack" launched by the unions.

These are the main indications of "colour". There is, evidently a good deal of agreement on what points should receive this emphatic treatment and perhaps it does not go beyond what was warranted by some trade unionist comment (eg at Scots TUC meeting).

183

# VI  CASE 5: Chrysler profit-sharing offer, Friday, 9 May 1976

## 1. Introduction

This story has three main strands connected by their common relationship to Chrysler's difficulties and the interest of the Government in the company's future. The central story is the offer by Chrysler of a participation and profit-sharing scheme. Secondly, there is the news of Chrysler seeking a loan from Finance For Industry. Thirdly, there is the unofficial strike threatened by men at the Stoke, Coventry engine works, in support of a pay claim.

## 2. Space and prominence

The story is the main lead story in *The Times*, *The Guardian* and *Daily Express* and on the front page of *The Daily Telegraph*, *Daily Mail* and *Financial Times*. It is treated as a single item in all papers. The details of space allocation are give in Table C18.

**TABLE C18**
**NEWS SPACE ALLOCATED TO CHRYSLER PROFIT-SHARING OFFER, 9 MAY 1975**

| Title | Space (col.cms.) | Headline as % of space | Presentation |
|---|---|---|---|
| The Times ... ... | 63 | 36% | 1 item |
| The Guardian ... | 94 | 28% | 1 item |
| The Daily Telegraph ... | 53 | 11% | 1 item |
| Financial Times ... ... | 79 | 27% | 1 item |
| Morning Star ... ... | 13 | 23% | 1 item |
| Daily Express ... ... | 144 | 57% | 1 item |
| Daily Mail ... ... | 25 | 36% | 1 item |
| Daily Mirror ... ... | 43 | 48% | 1 item |
| The Sun ... ... ... | 41 | 53% | 1 item |

The *Daily Express* gives most space and prominence and is the only paper to devote an editorial. The *Morning Star* is little interested and the other "Populars" give rather little space.

## 3. Headlines

The text of headlines is as follows:

**TABLE C19**
**HEADLINES RELATING TO THE CHRYSLER PROFIT-SHARING OFFER, 9 MAY 1975**

| | |
|---|---|
| The Times... ... ... | CHRYSLER SEEKS £35m LOAN AND OFFERS DEAL TO WORKERS<br>Company hopes pact can avert strike |
| The Guardian ... ... | CHRYSLER OFFERS SHARES DEAL TO RESTIVE UNIONS |
| The Daily Telegraph ... | CHRYSLER PROFIT-SHARE PLAN TO STOP STRIKE |
| Morning Star ... ... | "STUNT" FAILS TO DISSUADE CAR WORKERS |
| Financial Times ... | CHRYSLER PEACE BID WITH PROFIT-SHARING PLAN FOR WORKERS |
| Daily Express ... ... | DONT BEAT US, JOIN US! |
| Daily Mail ... ... | CHRYSLER OFFERS WORKERS SHARE TO WIN PEACE |
| Daily Mirror ... ... | CHRYSLER: IT'S SHARES FOR ALL |
| The Sun ... ... ... | "TAKE A SHARE" OFFER BY CHRYSLER |

At least six of the nine papers connect the share offer with the threatened strike. Only *The Times* refers to the loan request. The *Daily Express*, *Daily Mirror* and *The Sun* gives least information in their headlines. While their headlines are more colloquial, they do not imply an editorial attitude or involve "colour". Both these are found in the *Morning Star* where the plan is called a "stunt", quoting from Brian Sedgemoor, M.P.

## 4. Completeness and diversity in news reports

(*a*) News reports produce altogether 51 separate main points which are listed in Table C20. Three points are common to all nine reports and the average number of points per newspaper is 18 (35%).

There are eight points which at least six out of nine newspapers included and these may be taken as the key elements of the story. They account for 63 out of 167 references (38%) and cover: the fact of a meeting between Lander and unions (1); details of the offer (2, 3, 4); the aim of averting a strike (10); the probability that the strike will go on (29); the involvement of 4,000 engine workers at Coventry in the strike (40); the unique nature of the plan (19).

Since the story is a complex one and references have been dispersed more widely than in most of the other cases examined, a more discriminating criterion for assessing completeness, on a comparative basis, might be to take points reported by five out of nine papers as the standard. There were 11 such points and the newspapers scored as follows for completeness:

| 11/11 | 10/11 | 9/11 | 7/11 | 6/11 | 5/11 |
|---|---|---|---|---|---|
| Financial Times | The Times | Daily Mail | Daily Mirror | The Sun | Morning Star |
| | The Guardian | | | | |
| | The Daily Telegraph | | | | |
| | Daily Express | | | | |

(*b*) Of the 51 main points, 14 were in only one news report. The isolated points are mainly matters of detail which would have been available to all papers but were left out. A few, however, are of more significance. These include: (26, *The Times*) which interprets the profit-sharing offer as an attempt to meet Government conditions for investment; (30, *The Daily Telegraph*) which reports worker opposition to Wild's negative comments; (37, *The Guardian*) explaining the significance of an FFI loan; (42, *Daily Mail*) on the possible closure of the firm due to the strike; (23, *The Sun*) which gives a more "moderate" version of Wild's reaction. Several of the 14 points involve some interpretation and are not strictly "factual" for this reason. This applies to 21, 26, 28, 30, 37, 43, of which three were in *The Guardian*.

(*c*) The different parts of the whole story were treated with varying degrees of completeness. The Chrysler offer received the most complete coverage, with an average "score" overall of 9·2 points out of 18. The other sections of the story were each treated with about equal completeness (around 30% of points covered).

(*d*) Table C20 tells us a little about diversity as between titles, although the variation between papers mainly reflects completeness, with shorter reports

185

**TABLE C20**

## CHECKLIST OF MAIN POINTS

### CHRYSLER PROFIT-SHARING OFFER, 9 MAY 1975

| Main points | The Times | The Guardian | The Daily Telegraph | Financial Times | Morning Star | Daily Express | Daily Mail | Daily Mirror | The Sun |
|---|:--:|:--:|:--:|:--:|:--:|:--:|:--:|:--:|:--:|
| I. Chrysler offer details | | | | | | | | | |
| 1. Meeting last night between Don Lander and senior shop stewards | × | × | × | × | × | × | × | × | × |
| 2. Chrysler offered 27,000 workers share in profits (without share in losses) | × | × | × | × | × | × | × | × | × |
| 3. Chrysler offers participation to workers | × | × | × | × | | × | × | × | × |
| 4. Offer of representation on key decision making committees | | | | | | × | × | × | × |
| 5. Offer of seats on board | | | | | | × | | × | |
| 6. Books to be opened to workers | | | | | | × | | | |
| 7. Text of offer seen in advance by Benn | × | × | × | × | | | | | |
| 8. Plan already discussed in Detroit/USA | × | × | × | × | × | × | × | × | |
| 9. Plan brought forward (to help avert strike) | | | × | | | | | | |
| 10. Aim is to avert strike action at Stoke, Coventry | × | × | | × | | × | × | × | × |
| 11. Offer would not affect pay negotiations | × | | × | × | | | | | |
| 12. D. Lander on "bold new programme" for changed times, etc. | × | | | | | | | | |
| 13. Unions given two-week deadline to work out agreement | × | × | × | × | | × | × | | |
| 14. Meanwhile work should continue | | | | × | | × | | | |
| 15. Offer includes plan for new vehicle range | × | | × | × | | × | | | |
| 16. Offer conditional on improved labour relations | | | | × | | × | | | |
| 17. Offer would not affect pay negotiations | | | | | | | | | |
| 18. Plan will be discussed with Government | | | | | | | | | |
| 19. Plan is in advance of any other (unprecedented, revolutionary) | | × | | | | × | × | × | × |

186

## II. Reaction to plan

| | | | | | | | | | |
|---|:-:|:-:|:-:|:-:|:-:|:-:|:-:|:-:|:-:|
| 20. Unions taken by surprise | x | x | x |  |  | x |  | x |  |
| 21. Labour MPs taken by surprise | x |  | x |  |  |  |  |  |  |
| 22. Ray Wild (AUEW) calls ideas "radical" |  | x | x | x |  | x | x | x | x |
| 23. Ray Wild cautious—need to consider |  |  | x | x |  |  | x |  |  |
| 24. Offer welcomed by union (or official) | x | x | x | x | x |  | x | x |  |
| 25. Chater (or officials) thinks moves to avert strike needed | x |  |  |  |  |  |  |  |  |
| 26. Move interpreted as response to Benn conditions for investment | x |  |  |  |  |  |  |  |  |
| 27. B. Sedgemoor, MP, calls offer a "stunt" |  |  |  |  | x |  |  |  |  |
| 28. Ripples will be felt elsewhere (eg B.L.) |  |  |  |  | x |  |  |  |  |
| 29. Wild (or leaders) says offer will not stop strike, needs a cash offer | x | x | x | x | x | x | x | x | x |
| 30. Wild possibly to be opposed by many strikers |  |  |  |  |  |  |  |  |  |

## III. Financial Aspects

| | | | | | | | | | |
|---|:-:|:-:|:-:|:-:|:-:|:-:|:-:|:-:|:-:|
| 31. Chrysler has asked for £35m loan from FFI | x | x | x | x |  | x | x | x |  |
| 32. Approach made some days ago (or weeks) | x |  |  |  |  |  |  |  |  |
| 33. Reason for loan is to solve cash flow problem | x | x | x | x |  |  |  | x |  |
| 34. Main reason for loan to finance export deal to Iran | x | x | x | x |  |  |  | x | x |
| 35. Details of Iran deal |  |  | x | x |  |  |  | x |  |
| 36. Chrysler had loss of £17m in 2nd half 1974 | x | x | x | x |  |  |  |  |  |
| 37. Loan from FFI implies some commercial weakness | x | x |  | x | x | x |  |  |  |
| 38. Chrysler also believed looking for Government investment/aid | x | x |  | x |  |  |  |  |  |
| 39. Iran deal vital to future of company |  |  |  |  |  |  |  |  |  |

## IV. Planned Strike details

| | | | | | | | | | |
|---|:-:|:-:|:-:|:-:|:-:|:-:|:-:|:-:|:-:|
| 40. 4,000 workers will be involved at Coventry engine factory | x | x | x | x | x | x | x | x |  |
| 41. Strike is for £15 p.w. in July (or 30%) | x | x | x | x |  | x | x |  |  |
| 42. Immediate demand is for £5 p.w. |  |  |  |  |  |  | x |  |  |
| 43. Strikers admit action could close company |  |  |  |  |  |  | x |  |  |
| 44. Shop stewards fear offer is stalling |  |  |  |  |  |  |  |  |  |
| 45. Next meeting not due until Wednesday | x | x |  |  |  |  | x |  |  |
| 46. Similar claim being tabled in Scotland |  |  |  |  |  |  |  |  |  |
| 47. Strike described as "suicide strike" |  |  | x | x |  | x | x |  | x |
| 48. Strike is unofficial |  |  |  |  |  |  |  |  |  |

## V. Context

| | | | | | | | | | |
|---|:-:|:-:|:-:|:-:|:-:|:-:|:-:|:-:|:-:|
| 49. Chrysler have had conflict with unions | x | x | x | x |  | x | x | x |  |
| 50. Workers' fears about failure of Company to develop Chrysler UK vis à vis Europe |  |  |  |  |  |  |  |  |  |
| 51. Benn has been critical of Chrysler |  |  | x | x |  |  |  |  |  |
| **Total number of points** | **23** | **23** | **25** | **26** | **7** | **22** | **17** | **15** | **9** |

*Points made in separate reports.

187

concentrating on the points generally agreed as most important. We can, however, note: the much greater attention to the financial aspects in *The Times*, *The Daily Telegraph*, *Daily Mirror* and *Financial Times*; similarly, the attention of *The Guardian* and *The Daily Telegraph* to the *reception* of the plan; thirdly, the specific response of Frank Chater in saying that the offer should lead to new moves to end the dispute was noted only by *The Times*, *The Daily Telegraph*, *Daily Express* and *Daily Mail* and the omission may indicate a different evaluation of the situation. Other evidence of diversity in substance is not very noticeable.

## 5. Accuracy

The scope for a comparative assessment of accuracy is limited. The main figures given relate to the number of employees at Chrysler, the number of men due to strike, the wage claim involved, the size of the loan requests by Chrysler, the size of last year's losses by the firm. While ways of putting the wage claim vary, there is no significant variation in the figures given on other points mentioned.

## 6. Editorial Comments

Only the *Daily Express* made an editorial comment on this issue, under the heading "The herald of prosperity". The main point is to urge that uneconomic industries should not be maintained by public funds. In the course of the argument, the editorial refers to "extravagant wage demands" bringing Chrysler into jeopardy, to "militants relying on nationalisation", to overmanning and blame attaching to management. It concludes that factories should not be kept going "just for the sake of it". While the news report itself is not generally tendentious it does seem to have a relationship to this editorial line in the choice of some points, particularly the fact that Chrysler is believed to be looking for Government aid, that Mr Benn had seen the plan in advance, that workers have fears about the failure of Chrysler to develop its UK operation. It also picks up a reference to the dispute as a "suicide strike".

## 7. Editorial attitude or "colour" in news reports

(a) Several of the points listed in Table C20 are of an unverifiable kind and hence not strictly factual. Amongst these, a few imply some attitude or judgement. One is the reference to the strike as a "suicide strike" (47); another to the fact that strikers admit it could close the factory (43). The papers involved are *The Daily Telegraph*, *Daily Express* and *Daily Mail*. Another point, made only by *The Daily Telegraph*, is the possibility that many strikers may disagree with Ray Wild in his reported views that the strike should go ahead (29). Thirdly, there is the indication that the Chrysler offer is of an unprecedented or revolutionary character (19). While this is supported by Chrysler's own statement, it is not easy to verify and implies some favourability. Only *The Times*, *The Daily Telegraph* and *Morning Star* avoid the point.

(b) In previous case studies, an attempt was made to categorise the main points of the story according to whether or not they reflect unfavourably on unions or another party to the event. Here, there is little scope for such an analysis, since most points relate only to a management offer and related contextual matters. In general, the presentation suggests goodwill towards the Chrysler offer rather than any criticism of unions and virtually all newspapers (apart from the *Morning Star*) join in mentioning the advantageous aspects of the offer. The main union response (by Wild) is reported as negative (29) and all but *The Sun* are involved. Apart from this, we can note the report that Frank Chater wants the strike to be reconsidered (point 25), which reflects favourably on both the union and on the management offer.

(c) There is little or no "colour" in the news reports, apart from the three references to the strike as a "suicide" strike (Table C20, point 47) and a few phrases emphasising the dramatic and critical nature of the events—for instance *The Sun* reference to a "crisis-torn" car giant; the *Daily Mirror* reference to a "last ditch bid" to prevent a strike; the *Daily Express* report that the offer "astonished" the car industry. Certainly, there is little "colour" for a story which was on the front page of six newspapers.

# VII CASE 6: NUR Strike Decision, Tuesday, 3 June 1975

## 1. Introduction

The story is a straightforward account of the results of the NUR executive meeting at which a majority voted for a national stoppage in support of a pay claim in excess of an offer made by an arbitration tribunal. The likely effects and political context of the event form the remainder of the story.

## 2. Space and prominence

The story is on the front page of all newspapers and in all but *The Sun* is the main lead story. The allocation of space and relative headlining is as follows:

**TABLE C21**
**NEWS SPACE ALLOCATED TO NUR STRIKE DECISION, 3 JUNE 1975**

| Title | Space (col.cms.) | Headlines as % of space | Presentation |
|---|---|---|---|
| The Times ... ... | 68 | 41% | 1 item |
| The Guardian ... ... | 81 | 40% | 1 item |
| The Daily Telegraph ... | 94 | 26% | 1 item |
| Financial Times ... ... | 70 | 43% | 1 item |
| Morning Star ... ... | 75 | 71% | 1 item |
| Daily Express ... ... | 108 | 70% | 1 item |
| Daily Mail ... ... | 93 | 64% | 1 item |
| Daily Mirror ... ... | 75 | 71% | 1 item |
| The Sun ... ... | 36 | 33% | 1 item |

For almost all papers these figures show an unusually high ratio of headline to printed text. This partly reflects the number of lead stories involved, partly the unusual and important nature of the event reported and partly the limited amount of substance that can be said about something which has still to occur and which will have had extensive coverage as a possibility over the previous weeks.

## 3. Headlines

**TABLE C22**
**HEADLINES RELATING TO NUR STRIKE DECISION, 3 JUNE 1975**

| | |
|---|---|
| The Times ... ... | RAIL UNION LEADERS CALL FOR NATIONAL STRIKE TO BEGIN ON 23 JUNE<br>NUR decision by 21 votes to 3 |
| The Guardian ... ... | ALL-OUT STRIKE AS RAILMEN INSIST ON 30 p.c. |
| The Daily Telegraph ... | NUR ORDER NATIONWIDE RAIL STRIKE<br>21-day deadline for pay talks |
| Financial Times ... ... | NATIONAL RAIL STRIKE CALLED FOR 23 JUNE |
| Morning Star ... ... | RAILWAYMEN GIVE STRIKE NOTICE<br>21-3 vote for national stoppage on 23 June |
| Daily Express ... ... | MIDSUMMER MISERY!<br>Railmen decide: Its an all-out strike |
| Daily Mail ... ... | ALL-OUT MIDSUMMER RAIL STRIKE<br>"Pay or trains stop on 23 June" |
| Daily Mirror ... ... | END OF THE LINE |
| The Sun ... ... ... | ALL-OUT RAIL STRIKE<br>3-week fight for peace |

Most headlines are factual and generally informative, if the sub-heading is taken into account. The *Daily Express* headline implies dislike, if not disapproval, the *Daily Mirror* headline is obscure in the absence of other information.

## 4. Completeness and diversity in news reports

(*a*) For each newspaper, the average number of points covered was 19 out of 49 listed. The papers are much closer together in extent of cover of this story than they have been in other cases. This is consistent with the similarity of space allocation shown in Table C21.

There is also an unusually high degree of concentration on a small number of main points. The 12 points covered by at least six of the nine news reports accounted for 53% of all references. If these 12 points are taken as representing the basic facts of the story, the newspapers can be scored as follows:

| 12/12 | 11/12 | 10/12 | 9/12 | 8/12 |
|---|---|---|---|---|
| *The Daily Telegraph* | *Financial Times* | *The Guardian* | *The Times* | *Morning Star* |
| | *Daily Express* | *Daily Mail* | | |
| | *Daily Mirror* | *The Sun* | | |

(*b*) The different sections of Table C23 help to establish some similarities and divergences between newspapers. The most fully reported are sections I and III—the facts of the decision and details of claim and offer. The basic points are common to almost all newspapers and the variations relate to points of detail or matters of judgement. Only *The Daily Telegraph* and, to a lesser extent, *The Guardian*, give full information about the new pay claim and the "Qualities" are generally more informative on the offer and the cost of the claim. On the strike decision itself, it is *The Times*, *The Guardian* and *The Daily Telegraph* who are most inclined to view the executive decisions as a victory for militants over moderates, although the more moderate position of Weighell is widely recorded. The consequences and next steps in the dispute attract more interest from the *Daily Express*, *Daily Mail* and *The Sun* than from other newspapers. The political aspects of the story are more evident in the *The Times*, *Daily Mirror* and *The Sun* than elsewhere and are notably absent in *The Daily Telegraph* and *The Guardian*, given the length of these reports. In general, the reports reflect a high degree of concentration on the same sources. The *Morning Star* is the only paper to say what actions NUR will take to prepare for the strike (Table C23, point 38).

## 5. Accuracy

The main matter on which accuracy is important and can be checked related to the pay claim itself. Unfortunately, the amount of information on this point is not very full. The various versions of the claim are less inconsistent than incomplete. The figure of 30% is included in all reports, but what this really means is only apparent from *The Guardian*, *The Daily Telegraph*, and *Financial Times*. It is obviously a complicated matter and not an easy one to convey to the general reader.

## 6. Attitude expressed in editorial comment

The *Financial Times* has a lengthy editorial comment ("There is no more money") which notes that the Social Contract has already been "smashed beyond repair", but without the cost of a strike. It locates the problem as one of

# TABLE C23

## CHECKLIST OF MAIN POINTS
## NUR STRIKE DECISION, 3 JUNE 1975

| Main points | The Times | The Guardian | The Daily Telegraph | Financial Times | Morning Star | Daily Express | Daily Mail | Daily Mirror | The Sun |
|---|---|---|---|---|---|---|---|---|---|
| **I. Strike decision details** | | | | | | | | | |
| 1. NUR call strike for 23 June | × | × | × | × | × | × | × | × | × |
| 2. First total strike by NUR since 1926 | × | × | × | × | × | × | × | × | × |
| 3. Vote for strike action was 21–3 | × | × | × | × | | × | × | × | × |
| 4. Three-week interval to allow intervention (says Weighell) | × | | × | × | | × | × | × | |
| 5. Gen. Sec. of NUR, Weighell, favoured more negotiation (moderacy) | × | × | × | × | × | × | | × | |
| 6. Weighell now loyal to decision of executive | × | | | × | | | | × | |
| 7. Resolution for further talks received three votes | × | | | | | | | | |
| 8. Weighell cannot now start further talks; up to BR | | | | | | × | | | |
| 9. Weighell disappointed | | | | | | | | | |
| 10. Decision was a surprise | × | | | | | | | | |
| 11. No ballot of members needed | × | | × | | × | | | | |
| 12. Left-wing wanted earlier strike | | | | | | | | | |
| 13. NUR branches wanted negotiation | | | | | | | | | |
| 14. Claim represents militant line | | | | × | | | | | |
| **II. Effects of strike** | | | | | | | | | |
| 15. Effects will be complete—no trains without NUR | × | × | × | × | × | × | × | × | × |
| 16. Industry and power stations will be affected | | × | × | × | × | × | | × | × |
| 17. Damage to £ and more inflation (economic damage) | | | × | × | | × | | × | |
| 18. Effect on holidays, car ferries | | × | | | | | | | |
| 19. Effect on office workers felt first | | | | | | × | × | | |
| 20. Fare increases inevitable | | | | | | × | | | |

192

## III. Main facts of offer and claims

| | 17 | 18 | 17 | 21 | 13 | 20 | 22 | 20 | 24 |
|---|---|---|---|---|---|---|---|---|---|
| 21. NUR rejects 27·5% arbitration offer | × | × | × | × | × | × | × | × | × |
| 22. ASLEF accepts 27·5% offer | × | × | × | × | × | × | × | × | × |
| 23. TSSA accepts 27·5% offer | × | × | × | × | × | × | × | × | × |
| 24. NUR claim is for 30–35% | × | × | × | × | × | × | × | × | × |
| 25. Claims will cost £25m more than offer of £75m | | | | | | | | | × |
| 26. NUR wants £34.65 for lowest paid | × | × | × | × | | × | × | × | × |
| 27. Claim figures in detail | | | | | | | | | × |
| 28. Buckton of ASLEF says offer fair in circumstances | | | | | × | | | | |
| 29. Weighell wants same as other public sector awards | | | | | | × | × | | |
| 30. Tribunal said to have conceded comparability under Social Contract | | | | × | | | | | |
| 31. Offer only gave £2.65 to lowest paid | | | | | | | | × | |
| 32. Offer would have eroded NUR differentials | | | | | | | | | |
| 33. ASLEF would want any increase gained by NUR | | | | | | | | | |
| 34. Offer would have meant 30% on earnings | | | | | | | | | |
| 35. Offer is generous | | | | | | | | | |

## IV. Next steps

| | 17 | 18 | 17 | 21 | 13 | 20 | 22 | 20 | 24 |
|---|---|---|---|---|---|---|---|---|---|
| 36. Hopes for a settlement raised | | | | | | | | | |
| 37. Cabinet to prepare for state of emergency | | | | | | | | | |
| 38. NUR executive to set up co-ordinating committee | | | | | | | | | |
| 39. Support to be sought from other unions | | | | | | | | | |
| 40. BR expected to call talks | | | | | | | | | |
| 41. BR has to make first move | | | | | | | | | |
| 42. Government will have to act | | | | | | | | | |

## V. Context of pay policy: relations with Government and TUC

| | 17 | 18 | 17 | 21 | 13 | 20 | 22 | 20 | 24 |
|---|---|---|---|---|---|---|---|---|---|
| 43. Claim challenges or breaks Social Contract | × | × | × | × | | × | × | × | × |
| 44. NUR is challenging the Government or country | | × | | | | | × | | × |
| 45. NUR rejects TUC line as pay restraint | × | × | × | × | × | | | | × |
| 46. Murray (or TUC) will press for settlement | | | | | | | | | × |
| 47. Weighell admits to "political motivation" of some executive members | | | | | | | × | | × |
| 48. Labour party will press for settlement | × | | × | × | × | | | | × |
| 49. Weighell is member of Labour national executive | × | × | × | × | × | | | | × |
| **Total number of points** | **17** | **18** | **17** | **21** | **13** | **20** | **22** | **20** | **24** |

193

pay differentials but also finds the NUR "intransigent" in believing that financial constraints should not apply to the rail wage settlement. The principle of no Government subsidy to inflationary wage increases should apply especially to the public sector.

The *Morning Star* editorial supports the rail claim, finding the offer unrealistic in not anticipating future inflation. As a result: "for the workers, it would mean accepting the burdens of the crisis, cushioning the bosses' profits at the expense of the working class".

The *Daily Mail* ("This strike threat must not succeed") says the Rail Board and Government "must stand and fight", even at the cost of a strike. The alternative is to hurtle "towards the worst economic crisis in our history". There is reference to larger increases which "some other workers in the public sector have grabbed".

## 7. Editorial attitude or "colour" in news reports

(a) There is some evidence in news reports of an editorial slant, generally one of disapproval at the NUR decision. Compared to other reports looked at in this series of case studies, the degree to which editorial attitude shows through is unusual. Perhaps it stems from the awareness of a split in the union, the knowledge that other unions had accepted and that the general secretary of the union had himself been disinclined to opt for strike action. Editorial attitude shows up mainly in the words and phrases which "colour" the reports of factual matters, but there is also some evidence of interpretation and expression of unsupported opinion. In particular, section V of table C23 includes several points referring to conflict with the Contract and Government which may be justified but are not strictly factual and also imply criticism.

(b) If we look for an indication of attitude in terms of the reporting of "favourable" or "unfavourable" facts, we can list a number of points in Table C23 as telling more against the NUR and others which are more supportive (either by reporting moderate tendencies or supporting the actual claim). The former category might include:

(11)  The lack of any ballot of members;
(13)  The apparent conflict with rank and file wishes;
(14)  The association with militancy;
(15) to (20)  The effects of the strike;
(25)  Extra cost of the claim;
(28)  Buckton's view that the offer is fair;
(34)  Value of offer put at 30%;
(35)  Generosity of offer;
(43) to (48)  On the challenge to Social Contract, Government, Labour Party and TUC and the "political motivation" of members of NUR executive.

Amongst more "favourable" points, might be listed:

( 4)  Time allowed for intervention;
( 5)  Moderate position of General Secretary Weighell;
( 9)  Weighell disappointment at decision;
(29) and (30)  Equal treatment with public sector under contract;
(31)  Low amount for lowest paid;
(32)  Erosion of differentials by offer.

194

Table C24 shows the frequency of inclusion of the two sets of points in the main national daily newspapers.

**TABLE C24**

**RATIO OF POINTS "UNFAVOURABLE" TO "FAVOURABLE"**

| | | | | | | | | |
|---|---|---|---|---|---|---|---|---|
| The Times | ... | ... | ... | 8:3 | Daily Express | ... | ... | 7:4 |
| The Guardian | ... | ... | ... | 4:3 | Daily Mail | ... | ... | 4:2 |
| The Daily Telegraph | ... | ... | 6:5 | Daily Mirror | ... | ... | 5:1 |
| Financial Times | ... | ... | 6:4 | The Sun | ... | ... | ... | 6:2 |

(c) An examination of words and phrases used in news reports reveals a somewhat different and much clearer picture. This is most conveniently shown by taking each paper in turn, as follows:

*The Times*—The "wage demand" is ascribed to "militants" and there is a reference to the "unrepentant rejection of the TUC line" on demand for comparability.

*The Guardian*—The moderate/militant framework is used, but otherwise there is no evidence of attitude or the use of "colour".

*The Daily Telegraph*—Apart from the ascription of the claims to "militants", the report is factual in content and tone.

*Financial Times*—The views expressed in the editorial (6 above) may perhaps be reflected in the description of the claim as "the most blatant challenge to the Social Contract", and in the stress on damaging effects of the strike.

*Daily Express*—The opening paragraph refers to "midwinter bleakness" and to the NUR demanding its "full lion's share" of the Contract. The claim is a "direct challenge" to the Government and the NUR is said to be "threatening the country for the sake of a claim that has already had a jumbo offer".

*Daily Mail*—Report stresses "chaos" for holiday makers, and conflict with Government, which must now decide "whether to fight to a finish with the railwaymen, or to surrender again to Contract busters in the public sector". The NUR is also said to have "tossed out" the 27·5% offer and "demanded" more.

*Daily Mirror*—Apart from referring to a "shock" decision there is no evidence of editorial attitude or colour.

*The Sun*—Despite the high "score" on points "unfavourable" to the NUR, this report is without "colour" and is both level and optimistic in tone.

# VIII CASE 7: Norton-Villiers Liquidation Decision, Saturday, 2 August 1975

## 1. Introduction

The story centres on the announcement by the chairman of Norton-Villiers Triumph, Mr Dennis Poore, that an application will be made to put its subsidiary, Norton-Villiers Limited, into liquidation. The rest of the story concerns the causes and consequences of the action, the reaction of workers involved, the involvement of the Industry Secretary, Mr Benn, and the connections with the Meriden co-operative. It is a fairly complicated story, with several possible levels of analysis and with rather little in the way of actual events to report.

## 2. Space and prominence

Only the *Daily Mail* and *The Daily Telegraph* treat the story as the main lead, although it is placed beside a related editorial in *The Sun* and on page one of the *Financial Times*, *The Guardian* and *Morning Star*. The amount of space and type of presentation are as follows:

TABLE C25
NEWS SPACE ALLOCATED TO NORTON-VILLIERS LIQUIDATION DECISION, 2 AUGUST 1975

| Title | Space (col.cms.) | Headline as % of space | Presentation |
|---|---|---|---|
| The Times ... ... | 73 | 10% | 1 item |
| The Guardian ... ... | 76 | 21% | 2 separate items |
| The Daily Telegraph ... | 150* | 16% | 3 separate items |
| Financial Times ... | 75 | 13% | 1 item |
| Morning Star ... ... | 53 | 28% | 1 item |
| Daily Express ... ... | 36 | 30% | 1 item |
| Daily Mail ... ... | 117 | 48% | 1 item |
| Daily Mirror ... ... | 54 | 40% | 1 item |
| The Sun ... ... ... | 43 | 22% | 1 item |

*Includes city comment.

## 3. Headlines

The text of headlines is as follows:

TABLE C26
HEADLINES RELATING TO NORTON-VILLIERS LIQUIDATION, 2 AUGUST 1975

| | |
|---|---|
| The Times ... ... | NORTON TO CLOSE PLANT AND LOSE 2,000 MEN<br>Angry NVT men threaten Meriden style sit-in |
| The Guardian ... ... | (1) NVT PLANS SALVATION AT COST OF 2,000 JOBS<br><br>(2) NVT MEN THREATEN SIT-IN AS ANGER AGAINST BENN GROWS<br>Benn's letter: "Fully committed to the future" |
| The Daily Telegraph ... | (1) NVT FACTORY GOING INTO LIQUIDATION<br>"We're ready to run it" say pickets<br><br>(2) NVT HAS THE FAITH BUT NO BACKING<br><br>(3) STEWARDS RELEASE BENN LETTERS |
| Financial Times ... ... | NORTON PLANT MOVED TOWARDS LIQUIDATION |
| Morning Star ... ... | MPs, STEWARDS FIGHT TO SAVE AN INDUSTRY |

**TABLE C26**—*continued*

| | |
|---|---|
| *Daily Express* ... ... | WE'LL FIGHT TO THE END SAY ANGRY NORTON MEN |
| *Daily Mail* ... ... | SIT-IN THREAT TO NORTONS <br> Pickets guard the gates of motor-cycle plant |
| *Daily Mirror* ... ... | (1) NORTON'S ANGRY BLOCKADE <br> Pickets out at crisis factory <br><br> (2) BOSS BACKS THE UNIONS |
| *The Sun* ... ... ... | 2,200 NORTON JOBS TO GO IN CRASH |

The headlines are generally fairly informative. The main variation is between those which stress the main news event, or the statement about impending liquidation, or those which emphasise the angry reaction. Generally, the *Daily Express*, *Daily Mail*, and *Daily Mirror* take the latter approach and the *Daily Mail*'s large headline is particularly inclined to stress the factory occupation.

### 4. Completeness and diversity of news reports

(*a*) The average number of points reproduced in each paper, out of the 62 listed in Table C27, is 21. Of the 62, two were common to all papers.

The key element of the story, according to the criterion of consensus between newspapers (reported in at least six of nine), account for ten points and for 73 references in all (39%). The main points deal with the main fact and cause of the liquidation move (1, 2), the firm's relations with the unions (6, 7), the number of jobs at risk (26), the union reaction (38, 39, 40 and 44) and NVT's attack on the Government (45).

In terms of coverage of these ten points, the newspapers rated as follows:

| 10/10 | 9/10 | 8/10 | 7/10 |
|---|---|---|---|
| *The Daily Telegraph* | *The Times* | *The Guardian* | *Daily Express* |
| | *Daily Mirror* | *Financial Times* | *Morning Star* |
| | | *Daily Mail* | *The Sun* |

The greatly varying size of news reports is not fully reflected in the differences in scores, but, as usual, the short reports have concentrated on a few main points.

(*b*) There are 21 points listed in Table C27 which were contained in only one news report. A number of these are peripheral, some are matters of opinion or judgement, but a few seem to be facts of substance which might have been expected to have wider coverage. Amongst the matters of interpretation are: the existence of a united front between management and workers (20, *The Daily Telegraph*); the conclusion that NVT is trying to pre-empt a sit-in (21, 22, *The Guardian*); the embarrassment caused to the Government (51, *The Guardian*). The points of substance might include: the references to Norton's success (19, *The Times* and 13, *Financial Times*); the signing of a Commons motion calling for action (34, *Morning Star*); the firm's talk of suing the Government (54, *The Guardian*); the disputed question of Meriden's responsibility for the crisis (47, *The Daily*

197

**TABLE C27**

**CHECKLIST OF MAIN POINTS**

**NORTON-VILLIERS LIQUIDATION DECISION, 2 AUGUST 1975**

| Main Points | The Sun | Daily Mirror | Daily Mail | Daily Express | Morning Star | Financial Times | The Daily Telegraph | The Guardian | The Times |
|---|---|---|---|---|---|---|---|---|---|
| **I. Liquidation at Norton, events and causes** | | | | | | | | | |
| 1. Liquidator to be called in next week at Wolverhampton factory of N.V. Ltd. | × | × | × | × | × | × | × | × | × |
| 2. The move follows Government decision not to continue financial backing | × | × |  | × | × | × | × | × | × |
| 3. Plans for reduced working will be explained to workers as soon as possible | | | × | | × | | × | × | × |
| 4. Lawyers advised urgent liquidation | | | × | | | | | × | |
| 5. NVT Chairman (Poore) says impossible to operate two plants | | | × | | | | | × | × |
| 6. Poore says it is up to unions to accept plan or bring pressure on Government | × | × | × | | × | × | × | × | × |
| 7. Firm will back union if they pressure the Government | | × | × | | × | | × | × | × |
| 8. Liquidation inevitable under Companies Act | | | × | | | × | × | | × |
| 9. Decision reversible | | | | | | | | × | |
| 10. Creditors owed £3.3m by Norton (£3.8m) | | | | | | × | | × | |
| 11. Judgement of insolvency of Wolverhampton is a fine one | | | × | | | × | | × | |
| 12. Work in progress at Norton valued at £2.3m | | | | | | × | | | |
| 13. No recent deterioration of NVT position | | | | | | | | | |
| 14. Some suppliers had already stopped supplies | | | | | | × | | | |
| 15. Norton is only one subsidiary out of nine | | | | | | | | | |
| 16. Norton plant has been operating without trouble for 55 years | | | × | | | | | | × |
| 17. Poore says his interests in manganese bronze not a factor in closure | | | | | | | | | |
| 18. Small Heath plant in better position | | | | | | | | × | × |
| 19. Norton plant was successful | | | | | | | | | × |
| 20. Management and workers united against Government | | | | | | | | × | |
| 21. Poore trying to pre-empt factory occupation | | | | | | | | × | |
| 22. Sit in by workers would mean less for creditors | | | | | | | | | |
| 23. Work force split evenly between the two factories | | | | | | | | | |
| **II. Consequences of liquidation decision** | | | | | | | | | |
| 24. Wolverhampton plant will have to close | | | | | | | × | × | × |
| 25. Small Heath plant will run at reduced scale (three day week) | | × | | | | | × | × | × |
| 26. Number of jobs will reduce from 3,000 (3,200) to 1,000 (or 1,600 jobs to go) | × | × | × | | | × | × | × | × |
| 27. No dismissals until consultation with unions | | | × | | | | | | |
| 28. Decision on loss of jobs left to liquidator | | | × | | | | | | |
| 29. Development of Wankel to be postponed | | | × | | | | | | × |

198

III. Response by union

(Table of newspaper coverage points — 9 columns with totals: 12, 16, 21, 10, 14, 23, 26, 39, 27)

30. NVT does not rule out keeping both plants open
31. Cannot say which plant would lose most jobs
32. Whole NVT group at risk if unions lose most jobs
33. Closure would affect suppliers of components
34. 53 Labour MPs sign Commons motion calling for action
35. Mrs Short trying to see P.M.

III. Response by union
36. Factory convenor shocked at lack of consultation
37. Shop-stewards at NVT ready to organise a sit-in against closure
38. Pickets set up to prevent removals from factory
39. Emergency plans laid for occupation of factory
40. Shop stewards and union officials consult Mrs Short, M.P.
41. Workers determined to resist closure
42. Workers angry at Government ("selling down drain")
43. Workers want £5m. loan from Government
44. Workers ready to run factory as workers' co-operative (like Meriden)

IV. Relations with Benn and Government
45. Varley statement on NVT prospects refuted by Poore
46. Government criticised for lack of encouragement
47. NVT blame Government, not Meriden
48. Letter from Benn to Small Heath shop stewards released (by unions)
49. Letter from Benn to Hattersley released
50. Text of Benn letters promising support for industry published in whole or part
51. Criticism is embarrassing to Government Ministers
52. Poore trying to make political capital out of Benn letter
53. Heseltine calls Benn pledge a "blunder"
54. Firm considering suing the Government

V. Meriden connection
55. Meriden may not be much affected
56. NVT still contracted to take bikes from Meriden
57. Benn gave £5m to Meriden co-operative
58. Workers want equal treatment with Meriden
59. NVT only received 15,000 bikes from Meriden
60. Two prototypes received from Meriden (with defects)
61. Meriden blamed for problems of NVT
62. NVT trouble creates new difficulties for Meriden

Total number of points: 12, 16, 21, 10, 14, 23, 26, 39, 27

199

*Telegraph* and 61, *The Guardian*). Apart from this, the occurrence of points in only one or two reports generally reflect the amount of space, rather than some distinctive kind of news coverage. Five of the 21 "singleton" points were in the *Financial Times*.

(*c*) The actual decision to liquidate and its immediate implication were quite fully reported, but the financial aspects and the context of the whole firm's operations were not generally well covered. Most full reporting went to response by the unions. (Section III in Table C27), with an average of five points out of nine being reported by each newspaper. Readers of the *Daily Mail*, *Daily Express*, *Daily Mirror* and *The Sun* would generally have been left without an idea of the involvement of Benn and the Government and the commercial involvement with the Meriden plant.

(*d*) The main evidence of diversity of treatment is implied in the previous paragraph, but it is something more than a matter of incompleteness. Basically, the pattern of omission follows the division established in headlines. For the *Daily Mail* especially, and to a lesser degree the *Daily Mirror* and *Daily Express*, the story is about actions by workers mainly contemplated rather than actual. The *Daily Mirror* story carries more content sympathetic to the workers' view. For *The Guardian* and *The Daily Telegraph* it is more of a political-economic story and for *The Times* and *Financial Times* rather less political and more economic and commercial.

These latter differences are reflected in some degree in Table C27, especially in Section IV and V where *The Times* and *Financial Times* score 5 and 7 respectively out of 18, compared to 11 and 9 by *The Guardian* and *The Daily Telegraph*. As with the Budget story (Case 4) we have a story where the content is not very clearly defined by specific *events*. Much lies in the future and the significance of the issue is not easy to convey except in terms of a threat to employment.

## 5. Accuracy

There are a number of financial particulars given by two or three newspapers and no important or evident discrepancies. The main other matters of factual detail seemed sufficiently consistent between papers—in particular the number of workers likely to be affected. The figure varied according to whether or not estimates given including workers in other industries supplying components, but all versions seemed consistent when all the information available was put together.

## 6. Attitude expressed in editorial comment

Both *The Sun* and *The Daily Telegraph* carry editorials. *The Sun*, under the heading "The lessons for Britain", criticises politicians for "throwing good money after bad" in supporting uneconomic industry. It blames the motor industry for failing against foreign competition. Its message is that we should make better cars with less manpower and treat strikes and go-slows as a self-destructive luxury. The Government is applauded for becoming more realistic.

*The Daily Telegraph* under the heading "The world is hard" takes a similar view, calling the Government action a "belated recognition of reality". It too criticises the Government for "pouring money down the drain" and Mr Shore for urging us to buy British. The general tenor of the leader is contained in the following statement:

"The irresponsibility involved in subsidising uneconomic industries, to be paid for out of taxes levied on the firms that actually earn our bread and butter, is staggering".

### 7. Editorial attitude or "colour" in news reports

(a) There are very few points of a non-factual kind, and those that occur have been mentioned in 4b above. *The Guardian* seems to offer most in the way of interpretation in points which are not always substantiated by reference to a source. It speaks of a "cliff-edge" attempt to change the Government's mind. It describes Mr Poore's offer to back the unions as a "clear attempt to pre-empt occupation of the factories" (point 21). It makes the point (51) that worker protests would be "carried out against a highly embarrassing barrage of accusations against Government Ministers". It is the only newspaper to say that the judgement of whether the Wolverhampton subsidiary is insolvent or not is a fine one (point 11). The factual basis for this judgement (value of work in hand) is also provided by the *Financial Times* (point 12) together with the assertion that Norton's financial position had been unchanged for several months (point 13). *The Times* (point 19) also refers to the healthy state of the order book and climbing sales to new markets. At the same time (point 8) the decision is said by *The Times* to be inevitable under the Companies Act. *The Guardian* thus seems to be the only paper trying to interpret Mr Poore's moves and it speaks of him as playing an "extremely complicated tactical game", following the lessons of Meriden. The implication gives a rather different cast to the story as generally presented, in which Government cuts off finance, closure of plant is inevitable and firm offers to back workers in their fight for their jobs.

(b) There are three parties to this as to some other industrial disputes: Government, Employer and Workers. It is not easy to represent this story as a clear conflict between management and workers, especially in the light of *The Guardian* interpretation of events. The party to emerge as potentially the villain is the Government, although, on the other hand, we have seen some guarded editorial praise for the Government's firm line. In the news reports, the main facts of the story seem to tell against the Government: it withdrew aid unilaterally; its grounds for doing so were challenged by the firm and in some financial reports; it was represented as an object of criticism by unions and workers; it was represented as renaging on commitments made to unions. An attempt to "score" newspapers according to their picking up of points potentially unfavourable to the Government produced a result which mainly reflected the degree of completeness of reports, in that *The Guardian* and *The Daily Telegraph* picked up more of the points involved than did other newspapers.

Given the general tenor of most reports, it is not fruitful to look for facts which tell against the firm or the workers, although a few might be found.

(c) There is little "colour", apart from headlines which emphasise confrontation, dramatic events (to come, in the main) and anger. *The Daily Telegraph* has a passage of comment in its financial pages which generally echoes the line taken in the editorial and concludes that the "choice lies between sliding back into

201

Mr Benn's socialist economy and a painful leap towards modernisation". Otherwise, there are words or phrases in several papers which heighten the impression of crisis and which usually occur early in the news report. *The Guardian* refers to "angry" workers who might "seize the plant", to jobs being "slashed", to the "wreck of the British Motor Cycle industry". In *The Sun*'s report, the motor-cycle group is "crisis-hit". The *Daily Mirror* speaks of a "desperate bid" to stop the plant closing as "angry shop stewards" order a "blockade" of the factory. Other reports were less strongly worded and what "colour" there is carries no clear evaluative implication.

# IX CASE 8: Hospital Doctors' Dispute, Tuesday, 18 November 1975

## 1. Introduction

The story concerns the decision at a meeting of the junior doctors' section of the BMA to recommend a 40-hour week limit on work in support of a claim for concessions on pay and contracts. Compared to some other cases looked at, a relatively simple news event is involved, although the causes of the dispute in detail are not simple.

## 2. Space allocation and prominence

*The Daily Telegraph* and *Daily Mail* both make this a main lead story and it is on page one of *The Times*, *Financial Times* and *The Guardian*. *The Sun*, *Daily Mirror* and *Morning Star* give the item rather little space, as Table C28 shows. The *Financial Times* has a substantial feature on the work of hospital doctors elsewhere in the paper, but this is not included in the study.

**TABLE C28**

**ALLOCATION OF NEWS SPACE TO HOSPITAL DOCTORS' DISPUTE, 18 NOVEMBER 1975**

| Title | Total news space (col.cms.) | Headlines as % of space | Presentation |
|---|---|---|---|
| The Times ... ... | 30 | 13% | 1 item |
| The Guardian ... ... | 45 | 25% | 1 item + picture |
| The Daily Telegraph ... | 60 | 33% | 1 item + picture |
| Financial Times ... ... | 43 | 22% | 1 item |
| Morning Star ... ... | 14 | 28% | 1 item |
| Daily Express ... ... | 51 | 29% | 2 items + picture |
| Daily Mail ... ... | 73 | 59% | 1 item |
| Daily Mirror ... ... | 18 | 27% | 1 item + picture |
| The Sun ... ... ... | 16 | 35% | 1 item |

Generally, the amount of news space allocated is rather small and only the *Daily Mail* gives great prominence to the story. The amount of illustration is unusual—all pictures of Dr Wasily Sakalo leaving the meeting and being kept quiet by his colleagues.

## 3. Headlines

**TABLE C29**

**HEADLINES IN HOSPITAL DOCTORS DISPUTE STORY, 18 NOVEMBER 1975**

| | |
|---|---|
| The Times ... ... | 51.7% OF DOCTORS IN POLL BACK INDUSTRIAL ACTION |
| The Guardian ... ... | BALLOT BACKS DOCTORS IN OVERTIME BAN THREAT |
| The Daily Telegraph ... | DOCTORS SET 10-DAY DEADLINE<br>Emergencies—only plan put to BMA |
| Financial Times ... ... | OFFICIAL BAN BY DOCTORS NEXT WEEK |
| Morning Star ... ... | JUNIOR DOCTORS DECIDE ON ACTION FOR PAY |
| Daily Express ... ... | SORRY, MY LIPS ARE SEALED<br>Militant gagged as doctors split over "industrial action" |

203

**TABLE C29**—*continued*

| | |
|---|---|
| *Daily Mail* ... ... | IT'S ALL-OUT WAR BY THE DOCTORS<br>Mrs Castle faces new challenge in hospitals |
| *Daily Mirror* ... ... | ANGRY DOCTORS GET TOUGH |
| *The Sun* ... ... ... | JUNIOR DOCTORS SACK THEIR LEADERS |

There are wide variations in tone and content. The "Popular" dailies generally diverge from the others by a greater emphasis on the conflict or by concentrating on personality aspects of the story.

### 4. Completeness and diversity

(*a*) Of the 48 points listed in Table C30, an average of 16 was included in each paper. No one point is common to all nine newspapers, mainly because certain key points are omitted or very obscure in one or two papers. *The Sun*, for instance, reports the facts of industrial action to come but implies it was a minority decision. The form of industrial action is not clear in the *Daily Mirror* report. Seven of the points, with six or more endorsements, account for 53 of 142 references (38%), which is a somewhat lower level of concentration than the average for other case studies. Nevertheless, the pattern of reporting shown in Table C30 suggest a good deal of agreement on main points.

If the two points with five references (30 and 28) are added to the seven mentioned to give a measure of completeness, the papers score out of nine as follows:

| 8/9 | 7/9 | 6/9 | 5/9 |
|---|---|---|---|
| *The Times* | *The Guardian* | *Morning Star* | *Daily Express* |
| *The Daily Telegraph* | *Financial Times* | *Daily Mirror* | |
| *Daily Mail* | *The Sun* | | |

(*b*) The different parts of the story are covered in varying degrees of thoroughness. The details of proposed action (Section III of Table C30) received most full coverage—with an average of 3·3 out of 8 points in each paper. The events of the doctors' meeting and ballot results are next in order of completeness across titles. The *aims* of the doctors' action seem to be rather under-reported with several papers either not stating the objectives or making very vague references to "pay" or "overtime". Perhaps this reflects the complexity of the argument over contracts. However, the contrast with the specificity of information on industrial action is very notable.

There are 14 points appearing in only one report (4, 10, 17, 18, 20, 21, 25, 27, 33, 35, 40, 42, 44, 47). A few are either minor details or alternative ways of putting other points. Those of more significance include: *The Guardian* conclusion (17) that the ballot gave "strong support" for industrial action (? consistency with points 18, 19, 20 in the *Daily Express*); point 25 on suspension of waiting lists (*Daily Mail*); the conclusion (*The Guardian*, 44) that there will be wide support.

(*c*) We are led by this to the question of diversity, since there seem to be alternative interpretations of what occurred, despite agreement on the facts, consequences and on Government reaction. The *Daily Express* report tends to emphasise the internal split between moderates and militants. This moderate/militant interpretation is also present in varying degrees in the *Daily Mirror* and *The Sun*. It is referred to in *The Times*, *The Guardian* and *Daily Mail* reports, but avoided by the *Financial Times*, *The Daily Telegraph* and *Morning Star*. The main alternative framework of interpretation (most strongly evident in *The Daily Telegraph*, *Daily Mail* and *Financial Times*, but also present in *The Guardian*), focuses on the clash with the Government and with Mrs Castle in particular (see Section V of table C30). The *Morning Star* report concentrates on the proposed action and on the claims being made. Apart from the general difference reported in this paragraph, diversity is otherwise more a matter of picking up or omitting sub-elements of the story. For instance, only three of the six papers make the connection with action announced by consultants.

## 5. Accuracy

There is scope for inaccurate reporting in this story and taken together the nine versions make confusing reading. However, more than one ballot and set of pay proposals is involved and it is difficult to make appropriate comparisons. The following figures can be assembled on the balloting:

| Title | No. of junior doctors | No. who voted in national ballot | No. voting for industrial action | No. voting against | No. voting to accept new contract |
|---|---|---|---|---|---|
| The Times ... ... | 19,000 | 14,400 | 7,355 | 5,336 | 12,009 |
| The Guardian ... | 19,000 | 14,400 | 7,300 | 5,300 | 12,000 |
| The Daily Telegraph | 19,000 | 14,440 | — | — | — |
| Financial Times ... | 15,000 | ? | half | — | — |
| (figure of 15,000 said to be number of full-time practising doctors) | | | | | |
| Morning Star ... | — | — | 7,355 | — | 12,000+ |
| Daily Express ... | 19,000 | 14,450 | 7,355 | 5,336 | 12,000 |
| Daily Mail ... ... | 19,000 | 12,691 | 7,335 | 5,336 | — |
| Daily Mirror ... | 19,000 | — | 7,355 | 5,366 | — |
| (this report adds that "6,400 were undecided" in the vote on industrial action) | | | | | |
| The Sun ... ... | 19,000 | — | 7,355 | — | — |

The figures are generally fully reported and consistent with each other. The *Daily Mirror* report seems to interpolate an "undecided" figure, by subtraction from 19,000. The *Daily Mail* report may involve a confusion between the vote on the contract and the vote on the industrial action. The *Financial Times* introduces a new figure for the total number of "effective" doctors.

## 6. Attitude expressed in editorial comment

*The Sun*, under the heading "Physician, heal thyself" calls the ballot result a "victory for apathy": "the abstainers have allowed the militants to sneak home by a mere 260 votes". The doctors are accused of putting patients' "lives at risk" of "recklessness" in sacking their chairman and executive committee ("a gesture expected from Young Liberals, but not from mature, trained and responsible people"). Generally, the editorial expresses little sympathy. The figure given as 7,095 for voting against industrial action is not borne out by any other paper.

**TABLE C30**

**CHECKLIST OF MAIN POINTS**

**HOSPITAL DOCTORS DISPUTE, 18 NOVEMBER 1975**

| Main points | The Times | The Guardian | The Daily Telegraph | Financial Times | Morning Star | Daily Express | Daily Mail | Daily Mirror | The Sun |
|---|---|---|---|---|---|---|---|---|---|
| **I. Events at Junior Doctors' Meeting** | | | | | | | | | |
| 1. Junior doctors' confrontation with government (challenge to pay policy) | × | × | × | × | × | × | × | × | × |
| 2. Committee recommended industrial action: 40 hour week/go slow/work to rule | × | × | × | × | × | × | × | × | × |
| 3. Negotiating committee (moderate) censured/voted out/sacked/resigned | × |  | × |  |  | × | × | × | × |
| 4. Sakalo proposed vote of censure |  |  |  |  |  |  |  |  |  |
| 5. Temporary chairman, militant Dr Mander, took over | × | × | × |  |  | × |  |  |  |
| 6. New committee under David Wardle elected | × | × |  |  |  | × | × | × | × |
| 7. Change of committee is victory of militants over moderates |  |  |  |  |  |  |  |  |  |
| 8. Dr Wardle describes himself as "angry moderate" |  |  | × | × |  |  |  |  |  |
| 9. Wardle said he accepts pay code, but needs flexible interpretation | × | × | × |  |  | × | × | × | × |
| 10. Dr Sakalo elected to executive |  | × |  |  |  |  |  |  |  |
| 11. Sakalo gagged to stop talking to reporters |  |  |  |  |  |  |  |  |  |
| 12. Peace deal (compromise) by Mrs Castle rejected |  |  |  |  | × |  |  |  |  |
| **II. Results of ballot on action** | | | | | | | | | |
| 13. Majority of votes cast in favour of industrial action (various figures) | × | × | × | × |  | × | × | × |  |
| 14. Votes cast were 14–15,000 out of 19,000 Junior Doctors (or 12,691) | × | × | × |  |  | × | × | × |  |
| 15. Majority accept concept of new contract | × | × |  |  |  |  |  |  |  |
| 16. Resolution passed highly critical of ballot wording and procedure |  | × |  |  | × | × |  |  |  |
| 17. Ballot gave strong support for industrial action |  |  |  |  |  | × |  |  |  |
| 18. Moderates claimed majority not large enough for effective action |  |  |  |  |  | × |  |  |  |
| 19. Ballot shows doctors split on question of action |  |  |  |  |  | × |  |  | × |
| 20. Row over interpretation of ballot results |  |  |  |  |  | × |  |  |  |
| 21. Ballot results given on three Government options within pay code | × |  |  |  |  | × |  |  |  |

206

|  | | | | | | | | | | | |
|---|---|---|---|---|---|---|---|---|---|---|---|
| **III. Details of industrial action and its effects** | | | | | | | | | | | |
| 22. Overtime beyond 40 hours to be banned | x | x | | | | x | x | | x | | x |
| 23. Ban to start in 9/10 days (or November 27) | x | x | | | | x | x | | x | | x |
| 24. Emergency cases only to be treated | x | x | | | | | | | | x | |
| 25. Waiting lists for non-urgent to be suspended | | | | x | | x | | | | | |
| 26. Work to rule will cause major disruption | | | | x | | | | | | | |
| 27. Most serious threat to hospitals since dispute began | | x | | | | | | | x | | |
| 28. Action extends present unofficial action | | x | | | | | | | | | |
| 29. Action to be flexible re local needs | | x | | | | | | | x | | |
| **IV. Objectives of Doctors' action (or causes)** | | | | | | | | | | | |
| 30. Aim is for basic salary for 40 hr, week | x | x | | | | x | | | x | | x |
| 31. Overtime rate for 40–80 hrs and locum rate for 80 hrs + | x | x | | | | x | x | | x | | x |
| 32. Demand is for new contracts | | | x | x | | | | | | | |
| 33. Anger that some doctors will lose under Castle proposals | | | | | | x | x | | | | |
| **V. Response by Mrs Castle or Government** | | | | | | | | | | | |
| 34. Mrs Castle deplores any industrial action | x | x | x | x | | x | x | | x | | x |
| 35. Castle appeals to doctors to consider carefully | x | x | | x | | x | x | | x | | |
| 36. Castle warns of consequences for patients | x | x | | x | | | | | x | | |
| 37. Castle says pay policy must be respected | x | x | | x | | x | x | x | x | | |
| 38. Government can go no further to meet demands (limit of £12m) | x | x | x | x | | x | | | x | | x |
| 39. Counter inflation policy necessary for NHS | x | x | | | | | | | x | | |
| 40. Government relaxation would influence other workers | | | | | | x | x | | | | |
| **VI. Next steps** | | | | | | | | | | | |
| 41. Action will have to be endorsed by BMA Council | x | x | | | | x | x | | x | | |
| 42. Committee will press Mrs Castle to reopen talks | x | x | | | | x | | | x | | x |
| 43. Unlikely to achieve a return to normal work on basis of Castle offer | | | | x | | | | | x | | |
| 44. Action likely to receive wide support | | | | | | | | | x | | |
| **VII.** | | | | | | | | | | | |
| 45. Hospital consultants decide on one day-stoppage | x | x | x | x | | x | x | | x | | x |
| 46. Their move relates to private medicine separation plans | x | x | | | | | | | x | | |
| 47. Other doctors to be asked to handle emergencies | | | | | | | | | | | |
| **Total number of points** | 18 | 20 | 22 | 17 | 9 | 17 | 16 | 9 | 19 | 9 | 12 |

*The Guardian* ("Doctors raise the temperature") is equally disapproving—an "infection of militancy" it is called. The dispute is described as a "pay policy dispute" with the Government, putting patients at risk, on the doctors' own admission. Apathy is blamed, Dr Sakalo is referred to, by implication, as an "irresponsible militant". The complaints about low pay are rejected.

### 7. Editorial attitude or "colour" in news reports

(*a*) Points of a non-factual kind implying the kind of attitude expressed in editorials are not easy to find. Perhaps the predictions about effects may be counted as examples—for instance point 26 on the "major disruption" which will ensue—picked up by the *Daily Express* and *Daily Mail*.

(*b*) The balance of reporting of points which might reflect more or less unfavourably on the doctors can be looked at, although, if industrial action (by doctors in particular) is assumed to be undesirable, then the whole story might be accounted as having this tendency. Nevertheless, the following points (in Table C30) seem especially likely to imply or provoke criticism:

( 1)  Challenge to pay policy (confrontation with Government);
( 7)  Victory of militants over moderates;
(12)  Peace deal rejected;
(24)  Emergency cases only to be treated;
(25)  Suspension of waiting lists;
(26)  Major disruption to ensue;
(27)  Most serious threat to hospitals;
(36)  Castle warns of danger to patients.

Points more favourable, supportive, or in mitigation include:

( 9)  Wardle accepts pay code in principle;
(15)  Majority accept concept of new contract;
(18)  Moderates say majority for action not enough;
(19)  Ballot shows doctors split on action;
(29)  Action to be flexible;
(33)  Doctors' anger that some lose under Castle proposals;
(44)  Action likely to receive wide support.

The balance of points "unfavourable" to "favourable" for the main daily newspapers is as follows:

TABLE C31

RATIO OF POINTS "UNFAVOURABLE" TO "FAVOURABLE" IN RELATION TO DOCTORS

| | | | | | | |
|---|---|---|---|---|---|---|
| *The Times* | ... | ... | ... 3:2 | *Daily Express* | ... ... | 3:3 |
| *The Guardian* ... | ... | ... 2:4 | *Daily Mail* | ... | ... 6:– |
| *The Daily Telegraph* ... | ... | 2:1 | *Daily Mirror* ... | ... | ... 3:– |
| *Financial Times* | ... | ... 4:1 | *The Sun* | ... ... | ... 3:1 |

208

(*c*) The main instances of "colour" can be found in the *Daily Express, Daily Mail* and *The Sun*, although, as noted above, references to "militants" and "moderates" occur in several other papers. The words and phrases which give colour in some reports emphasise either the conflict or the role of a prominent personality on the "militant" side (Dr Sakalo). The *Daily Mail* report says that doctors "threw out" a peace deal and "declared all-out war on the Government". The *Daily Express* report stresses conflict and the part played by the "bush-hatted Australian leader of the militant medicos". In both cases, the more extravagant expressions appear at the start of the article, following headlines in similar vein and later parts of the account are factual in content and more careful in style.

# X   Case studies: conclusions

1. In the course of dealing with each case, a number of points were made in assessment of the particular story. Because of the nature of the method and the limited evidence such conclusions were inevitably tentative. The purpose of this concluding section is to bring together some of these points and to attempt an overall assessment of the general character of industrial relations reporting and of the way in which national daily newspapers seem to differ, in terms of the criteria which have been applied. While the conclusions are still tentative, they will be stronger through drawing on a wider range of examples.

## 2. Form of presentation of industrial relations stories

The studies looked at were not typical of those which formed the bulk of items examined in the statistical study reported in Part B. In particular, they differ in being generally front page news and in their above average complexity. It is common for a single theme to unite two or more items of news and one of these often involves Government or politics in general. This complexity tends to be reflected in the form of presentation, with separate news items often dealing with different aspects of the story. This is marginally more likely to occur in the "Qualities" than in the *Daily Mail, Daily Express, Daily Mirror* or *The Sun*.

## 3. Use of headlines

Newspapers were seen to vary predictably in the extent of headlining. The following figures summarize the relative position of all titles across the eight case studies, showing the average proportion of relevant space given to headlines in the items studied.

| | | | | | | | | | |
|---|---|---|---|---|---|---|---|---|---|
| *The Times* | ... | ... | ... | 21% | *Daily Express* | ... | ... | 52% |
| *The Guardian* | ... | ... | ... | 26% | *Daily Mail* | ... | ... | ... | 41% |
| *The Daily Telegraph* | ... | ... | 20% | *Daily Mirror* ... | ... | ... | 43% |
| *Financial Times* | ... | ... | 23% | *The Sun* | ... | ... | ... | 35% |
| *Morning Star* ... | ... | ... | 33% | | | | |

Headlines in *The Times* were found to be longer and carry more information than those in other newspapers. A very approximate judgement made of the headlines in all papers for the eight stories suggests that *The Guardian, The Daily Telegraph, Financial Times, Morning Star* and *The Sun* generally provided headlines which gave the *main point of the item reported*. The *Daily Express* and *Daily Mail* were somewhat less inclined to do so and the *Daily Mirror* headlines seemed to be generally uninformative about what was to follow. In very few, if any, cases was a headline inconsistent with the news report, although this might be said of *The Daily Telegraph* headline in Case 1, where the story is very much as in other papers, but the headline draws a somewhat divergent conclusion about union response to Mr Benn's initiative on British Leyland.

In the cases looked at, the expression of direct editorial views in headlines was unusual. They were not generally tendentious, but they did on occasion contain words and phrases of an emotive kind which might influence reader interpretation. The general conclusion arrived at was that such headlines were designed to catch attention and to emphasize the dramatic nature of events rather than influence opinion. However, in a few cases, "colour" in headlines did imply an attitude with a particular direction. Examples include:

Case 2, reference in the *Daily Mail* to a "big scramble"; Case 4, *Daily Express* headline, "that's torn the contract"; Case 5, *Morning Star* headline " 'Stunt' fails to dissuade car workers"; Case 6, *Daily Express* on "Midsummer Misery". Perhaps the summary conclusion, on this evidence, should be that headlines are generally not tendentious, although they are sometimes vague and over-dramatic.

## 4. Completeness

The assessment of completeness is, of course, relative, in the absence of any source of information external to the newspaper reports examined. It was found possible to express the content of reporting in terms of a number of "points" or items of information drawn from the whole range of reports on the day in question. The total number of "points" in these eight cases ranged from 39 to 62, and in the "average" newspaper report the degree of coverage was 38% of all points listed. If minor details had been included as separate points, the percentage figure would, of course, be lower. It is also true that the difference between newspapers tends to be narrowed by the policy which was followed of concentrating on main points. For instance, some newspaper reports contained extensive details of pay claims or current wage rates which were not separately recorded. Even so, it is not too misleading to use the relative number of "points" as a basis for comparison. For instance, a low coverage paper like *The Sun* recorded 53% of the number of points recorded for *The Times*, while its non-headline space was 46% of that given by *The Times*. Thus, a comparison based on space would not have shown much larger *absolute* differences.

Newspapers varied in the degree of completeness attained, as the totals for frequency of references per paper indicate, in the third table of each case study. On the whole, such variation corresponds to the amounts of space allocated, especially non-headline space. An alternative way of assessing relative completeness of coverage is the one followed in each case study, where the key points of the story, as established by the consensus of reports, were used as a basis for comparing newspapers. A summary of the results for the eight cases takes the following form:

TABLE C32

RELATIVE COMPLETENESS OF COVERAGE OF KEY POINTS IN EIGHT CASE STUDIES

| | | | | | | |
|---|---|---|---|---|---|---|
| *The Daily Telegraph* | ... | ... | 93% | *Daily Express*... | ... | ... | 83% |
| *The Guardian* ... | ... | ... | 92% | *Daily Mirror* ... | ... | ... | 79% |
| *The Times* | ... | ... | 90% | *Daily Mail* | ... | ... | 73% |
| *Financial Times* | ... | ... | 83% | *The Sun* | ... | ... | 72% |
| | | | | *Morning Star* | ... | ... | 56% |

While this table under-represents the variation in extent of coverage between papers, it does reflect the fact that even small reports tended to concentrate on a few points which were also in other reports (whether smaller or large). The result seems to reflect a high measure of agreement on what is newsworthy or salient and, inevitably, implies some lack of diversity in reporting. It follows too, that a reader of a lower coverage paper would in general be somewhat worse off for learning about *alternative* or *different* versions or aspects of events, than a reader of a high coverage newspaper. The *Morning Star* is something of an exception. Its low rank position in Table C32 does indicate an orientation to

211

somewhat different news values since, in terms of space allocated to these stories and "points" covered, it was almost identical to *The Sun* newspaper.

## 5. Diversity

It follows from what has just been said that the daily newspapers do not offer a great deal of diversity, except as an aspect of varying completeness. The longer the report the more ground is covered, but despite differences of emphasis, the reports in different newspapers generally offer much the same version of events, derived from the same sources. The characteristic style of non-interpretive reporting tends to narrow the range of diversity still further.

Occasionally, there was some evidence of variation in the interpretive framework offered to the reader, although it is not possible to see a systematic difference between newspapers in this respect. Examples include: Case 1, the degree to which Mr Benn's actions and Mr Wilson's weekend attack on strikes were linked; Case 3, the varying extent to which the internal Labour Party dispute between Mr Foot and Mr Prentice figured in the report; Case 4, the presence or absence of the CBI view of the Budget; Case 7, the alternative between presenting the NVT news event as a broad political economic story or a fight by workers to save their jobs; Case 8, the varying degree to which the doctors' decision to strike was presented as an internal clash between militants and moderates. As these examples suggest, diversity usually involves changing or widening the context within which the same news event is reported.

## 6. Accuracy

Only the most tentative assessment of accuracy has been attempted, given the lack of external sources of information. As judged by internal consistency of reports, there is very little definite evidence of inaccuracy about checkable figures, facts or quotations. On the other hand, information is often so incomplete as to be of little use and there seems to be a scarcity of any clear conventions for presenting important facts about pay claims, wage rates and pay awards.

## 7. Editorial comment

There was at least one leader comment on each of the stories looked at. Almost invariably, the comments were strongly worded and had a clear direction—usually disapproving of industrial action and "social contract breaking", supportive of the Government and against public subsidy for, or control of, private industry. While this may not be surprising, the incidence of editorialising is high at 24% of all cases (17 out of 71). Only the *Morning Star* took a distinctively pro-union position. It should also be stressed that where leading articles did take a strong line, this did not appear to influence reporting.

## 8. Factualness

The principle of separating fact from comment does seem to have been observed quite faithfully in the cases examined. There are occasionally departures from the principle in all newspapers, but the great majority of points made are "factual" in the sense of being attributed to a source or being open to independent verification. The style of news reporting seems to involve an almost excessive devotion to the "fact" or quotation and continuity and sense sometimes

212

suffer as a result. The tables of main points in the case studies provide some examples of unverifiable judgement and interpretation on the part of the writer, and these have been commented on in the text. Sometimes, political "insider" information may be involved, but opinions are also expressed at times or predictions made about the future which may or may not be sound. However, the overall impression is of respect for "objectivity" as defined above.

## 9. Direction or bias in news reports

Little overt bias could be found in the sense of a clear tendency to favour one "side" over another. On the other hand, in the instances where such a tendency could be found, it was weighted against the union "side" or against workers deviating in a more militant way from union policy (as in case 3). In addition, it can be argued that some facts do tell more against one participant or side than another, and again the union side is most vulnerable to this tendency, if only because most industrial relations reporting is about unions, rather than about employers or Government. This is shown by the content survey evidence reported in Part B. In a number of the case studies, where it seemed appropriate, an attempt was made to classify some items according to whether they might reflect more or less favourably on unions. The very approximate character of the method has been stressed, but it provides one verifiable basis for comparing newspapers and reaching an overall assessment of the degree to which a negative "image" of union activity might be encouraged in the reports studied. It was in the nature of the value assumptions made that the overall balance should tell "against" unions (in particular that strike action is undesirable and co-operation with Government pay policy desirable). Here we can summarise the results for those five cases where an allocation of points telling "for" or "against" the union "side" seemed possible (Cases 1, 2, 4, 6, 8).

TABLE C33

SUMMARY COUNT OF FREQUENCY OF POINTS JUDGED LESS OR MORE "FAVOURABLE" TO UNION POSITION IN CASE STUDIES

| Title | Points "unfavourable" to union position | Points "favourable" |
|---|---|---|
| The Times ... ... | 23 | 13 |
| The Guardian ... ... | 17 | 17 |
| The Daily Telegraph ... | 24 | 12 |
| Financial Times ... ... | 20 | 11 |
| Daily Express ... ... | 18 | 15 |
| Daily Mail ... ... | 12 | 4 |
| Daily Mirror ... ... | 19 | 6 |
| The Sun ... ... ... | 13 | 7 |
| All ... ... ... | 146 | 85 |

The numbers are too small and variable between titles for a firm rank order to be based on these figures. On the basis of this calculation, however, *The Guardian* and *Daily Express* seem more inclined to have "favoured" union positions and *The Daily Telegraph*, *Daily Mail* and *Daily Mirror* seem to have been less inclined to do so. *The Sun*, *The Times* and *Financial Times* are close to the average position. It should be stressed that the "unfavourable" points constitute a small minority of all points. If the "unfavourable" points are expressed as percentages

213

of all points recorded for each newspaper in the five cases from which this particular evidence was taken, the results are as follows:

| | | | | | | | | |
|---|---|---|---|---|---|---|---|---|
| *The Times* | ... | ... | ... | 21% | *Daily Express* | ... | ... | 19% |
| *The Guardian* | ... | ... | ... | 15% | *Daily Mail* | ... | ... | 17% |
| *The Daily Telegraph* | ... | ... | 21% | *Daily Mirror* ... | ... | ... | 24% |
| *Financial Times* | ... | ... | 21% | *The Sun*... | ... | ... | 19% |

It would seem from this as if all newspapers are varying within a very narrow range.

## 10. "Colour" in news reports

The case studies produced some evidence of "colour" as an incidental aspect of news reporting, where emotive words and phrases were used which might affect the attitude of the reader and seem at least to reflect the attitude of the writer. Generally, such words or phrases occurred in the opening paragraph of the story, but the low incidence overall should be emphasised. As a rule of thumb, a count of references to "colour" in the eight case studies shows there to have been more examples in the *Daily Mail* and *The Sun* than in the *Daily Express* and *Daily Mirror* and only the *Morning Star* produced no examples for comment. A reference back to the case studies will show the use of "colour" to have been more associated with dramatisation than with a clear expression of editorial view. There is a notable absence of "personalisation" in reports, aside from an interest in the views of union leaders, and the only instance which can be cited is the case of the doctors and their "militant" leader Dr Sakalo (Case 8).

# Part D

**Social Welfare and Social Policy Content in National Daily
Newspapers, 1975: sample survey of 985 items**

# Main Tables

# I Aims and Methods

## 1. Introduction

The study reported here forms part of a larger content analysis of British newspapers for 1975. It deals with one of three areas of news and feature content chosen for more detailed examination, over and above the general description of content in terms of its main categories. The other two content areas studied in this way related to industrial relations and to foreign affairs respectively. The choice is to some extent arbitrary, although this particular area of news does form a relatively self-contained, clearly definable and large component of the important general category of "home social, economic and political" news. The precise calculation of proportionate size has not been made but it seems probable (in view of the numbers of items relative to those dealing with industrial relations) that it accounts, on average, for some 3-4% of news space in the National Daily Newspapers in 1975 and a correspondingly higher proportion of home news. Apart from its quantitative importance and representative character, it was felt that the area of social policy would be one of direct relevance to many newspaper readers as well as being important to the political process. Consequently, adequacy of newspaper coverage should be expected as a matter of good editorial policy.

## 2. Aims

The main objective of the analysis has been to provide a detailed systematic description of the relevant content, as it appeared in a sample of 24 days' issues of the National Daily Press in 1975. The study has been guided by the following general questions:

(i) How much space and prominence is given to the main areas of social policy?

(ii) What events or concerns form the substance of reporting in different areas of social policy?

(iii) In what events and sources does social policy news seem to originate?

(iv) How frequently do different sorts of participant feature in an active way in news reports?

(v) What general themes or news angles occur in reports?

(vi) How do different newspapers compare in the extent and kind of coverage on any of the above matters?

The choice of question has been guided by a broad concern with questions of completeness and diversity of coverage. In addition, there is some attempt to shed light on the principles underlying selection, insofar as this method and the rather small sample allows.

## 3. Social welfare and social policy content

While it has been claimed that such content is relatively self-contained and readily identifiable, it is also true that it is diverse and does contain material open to alternative forms of classification. In particular, some news falling under this heading could also be included as political news or as industrial relations news.

The extent of overlap with these other categories is known approximately, since it was found in the analysis of the 985 items sampled that 42 had a political character (see Col. 36 of coding frame in Appendix D1) and as many as 150 (15%) were classified as about "industrial relations and trade union matters". This overlap with other categories presents no particular problems but it is a useful reminder that no scheme of classification in content analysis can hope to achieve a set of substantive categories which are mutually exclusive. The diversity of content is more difficult to deal with since, despite a common relationship to the political and social system, the areas of activity involved are very different from each other. The similarity between education, sickness, unemployment and so on is a somewhat abstract one and newspapers are not primarily concerned with the abstract. It should be stated at the outset, consequently, that the analysis has tended to adopt one particular perspective on the material and it is a perspective which pays most attention to what is common to the different events and activities under the general heading of social policy. In particular, the focus is on administrative, political and financial matters. While it is true that this way of looking at such content is generally close to the press perspective and has been guided by the latter, it should be borne in mind that a content analysis is itself selective and could be guided by somewhat different concerns. Finally, the list of policy areas which, in practice, provided the criteria for deciding whether to analyse items or not, was constructed specifically for this investigation and does not represent any single official list of social services. There is a possibility, consequently, that some marginal kinds of social service have been arbitrarily excluded and others included.

## 4. Sampling

The items for analysis were chosen by taking the sample of 24 days used in the general content analysis of National Daily Newspapers and studying relevant items contained in the newspapers selected. The method of choosing the sample has already been described in some detail (Part A pp.[2-3] ). In brief, it involved a random choice of weekdays in 1975, after ensuring that the quarters of the year and, within those quarters, the different weekdays would be correctly represented. In each newspaper chosen, each item dealing with a social welfare matter was identified as a "case" for detailed study. A drawback of the method is that it does take a day's news in isolation from what preceded and might follow and consequently fails to capture important aspects of story development. Another effect of the method is that relatively few different news events get sampled, since the same story is being looked at over and over again in different newspapers. The sampling method is thus better suited to the purpose of comparing newspapers than to providing the widest range of different sorts of story. It is an intrinsic weakness of any such sampling procedure that significant and revealing cases of news events are liable to be omitted. The focus is, inevitably, on the *general* character of news reporting.

## 5. Design and Methods

In essence, the method is to apply normal sample survey techniques to newspaper content. A limited number of "questions" are asked about each newspaper item in a systematic way, in order to produce a standardised set of results and to minimise variations in the way the content of items is recorded. An important principle to be observed is that the study is confined to what is contained in an

218

**TABLE D3**—*continued*

| | |
|---|---|
| 13. Health: hospitals ... ... ... ... ... ... ... ... ... | 131 |
| 14. Health: GPs, medical, dental ... ... ... ... ... ... ... | 22 |
| 15. Health: handicapped ... ... ... ... ... ... ... ... | 20 |
| 16. Health: mental ... ... ... ... ... ... ... ... ... | 29 |
| 17. Community health ... ... ... ... ... ... ... ... ... | 7 |
| 18. Health: family planning, etc. ... ... ... ... ... ... ... | 25 |
| 19. Health: other ... ... ... ... ... ... ... ... ... | 75 |
| 20. National Insurance: general benefits ... ... ... ... ... ... | 3 |
| 21. Social security benefits ... ... ... ... ... ... ... ... | 22 |
| 22. National Insurance retirement, OAP ... ... ... ... ... ... | 3 |
| 23. Social work ... ... ... ... ... ... ... ... ... | 18 |
| 24. Legal and penal matters ... ... ... ... ... ... ... | 56 |
| 25. Minority groups ... ... ... ... ... ... ... ... | 29 |
| 26. Children ... ... ... ... ... ... ... ... ... | 45 |
| 27. Family matters ... ... ... ... ... ... ... ... | 26 |
| 28. Population ... ... ... ... ... ... ... ... ... | 4 |
| 29. Transport and communications ... ... ... ... ... ... ... | 7 |
| 30. Libraries, museums ... ... ... ... ... ... ... ... | 6 |
| 31. Occupational ... ... ... ... ... ... ... ... ... | 23 |
| 32. Youth services ... ... ... ... ... ... ... ... | 5 |
| 33. Youth employment ... ... ... ... ... ... ... ... | 9 |
| 34. Employment in general ... ... ... ... ... ... ... | 8 |
| 35. Misc. social problems ... ... ... ... ... ... ... | 7 |
| 36. Nationalised industries welfare ... ... ... ... ... ... | 7 |
| 37. Other ... ... ... ... ... ... ... ... ... | 18 |

*More detailed wording for items can be found in the coding frame, reproduced as Appendix D1.

## 2. Coverage of main social policy areas in different newspapers

The list of 37 main policy areas was reduced to one of 13 categories, by grouping matters in related social policy fields. The reduced list of topics is given in Table D4 and it will be fairly clear from the headings which items have been put together. In the same table, the percentage distributions for different newspapers are given. By and large, the newspapers differ rather little in the proportionate attention paid to the main policy areas, bearing in mind the small numbers on which some of the percentage figures are based. There is not, for example, any general tendency for "Qualities" and "Populars" to differ in their priorities, although the latter group of papers leave inevitable gaps in coverage. Several areas are, in effect, absent from *The Sun* and *Daily Mirror* as fas as this sample is concerned. One broad point distinguishing "Qualities" from the rest is the greater attention to higher education and non-school educational matters generally. Presumably this reflects, or corresponds with, differences of background and interests amongst readers of different sorts of newspapers. There is, however, no correlative greater attention in the large circulation papers to matters which might directly concern their readers as clients of welfare services. Some newspapers did have "special subjects": for instance the concentration on "other health" matters in *The Sun*, the attention of the *Financial Times* to housing and employment, school education in the *Daily Express*, universities in the *Morning Star*, children and family matters in the *Daily Mirror*. In general, the most distinctive pattern of attention, by comparison with the sample as a

TABLE D4

MAIN SOCIAL POLICY AREAS*: PERCENTAGE DISTRIBUTION OF ITEMS FOR EACH NATIONAL DAILY NEWSPAPER AND FOR THE SAMPLE AS A WHOLE

| Policy area | The Times % | The Guardian % | The Daily Telegraph % | Financial Times % | Morning Star % | Daily Express % | Daily Mail % | Daily Mirror % | The Sun % | All Newspapers % |
|---|---|---|---|---|---|---|---|---|---|---|
| 1. Housing ... (1–3) | 9 | 6 | 8 | 14 | 9 | 3 | 8 | 7 | 2 | 7 |
| 2. Pre-school and school education (5–6) | 17 | 20 | 24 | 9 | 24 | 32 | 20 | 16 | 18 | 20 |
| 3. Universities and Polytechnics, etc. (7–8) | 6 | 8 | 10 | 2 | 15 | 3 | 4 | — | 3 | 7 |
| 4. Other education ... (9–12) | 4 | 6 | 4 | 3 | 5 | 1 | 2 | | — | 4 |
| 5. Hospital services (13) | 13 | 7 | 11 | 25 | 13 | 15 | 17 | 28 | 15 | 13 |
| 6. Other health ... (14–19) | 15 | 18 | 19 | 11 | 14 | 19 | 16 | 19 | 36 | 18 |
| 7. National Insurance & Social Security (20–22) | 4 | 2 | 2 | 2 | 2 | 2 | 5 | 5 | | 3 |
| 8. Social work ... (23) | 2 | 3 | 1 | 2 | 3 | 1 | — | — | 3 | 2 |
| 9. Legal and penal matters (24) | 7 | 7 | 6 | 3 | 3 | 5 | 7 | 2 | 7 | 6 |
| 10. Minority groups (25) | 4 | 4 | 2 | 2 | 2 | 3 | — | | 3 | 3 |
| 11. Children and family matters (26–27) | 10 | 9 | 4 | 2 | 4 | 5 | 7 | 14 | 12 | 7 |
| 12. Youth and Employment services (32–34) | 2 | 4 | 6 | 14 | 4 | 7 | 7 | 5 | — | 5 |
| 13. Miscellaneous (4, 28–31, 35–37) | 7 | 6 | 3 | 11 | 2 | 3 | 7 | 5 | 2 | 5 |
| TOTAL% | 100 | 100 | 100 | 100 | 99 | 100 | 100 | 101 | 101 | 100 |
| Numbers of items | 186 | 231 | 160 | 63 | 93 | 73 | 75 | 43 | 61 | 985 |

*The numbers in brackets after each item relate to the fuller list in Table D3

224

whole, can be found in the *Financial Times*. It should also be remembered that actual *numbers* tell a somewhat different story so that a figure of 10% in *The Guardian* means 23 items, but only four in the *Daily Mirror*.

## 3. Main policy areas, type of item and prominence

Were some policy areas more likely than others to appear in editorials and features and to have more prominence in the newspaper? On the whole the division between news and features does not vary as between policy areas. The pattern for editorial comment is somewhat variable, however. Two points stand out: leading articles are differentially more concerned with social work and with minority groups than their overall frequency as subjects for news seems to warrant. Between them, the two account for 15% of editorials (six out of 40), but less than 5% of all items. An inspection of the relative length and prominence of news items for the different main policy areas suggests one very obvious conclusion: the tendency to concentrate on a small number of policy areas is even more noticeable. For example, if appearance as a large front page news item is taken as a criterion, we find that of the 40 so classified, 15 were concerned with hospitals, seven with other health matters and nine with education. Thus three topics accounted for 78% of the most prominent stories. Otherwise there is little to note.

# IV  Topics of Social Welfare content

1. In addition to a classification according to the area of social policy or the social service concerned, newspaper items were also coded according to the main general topic of the event or report. To some extent, the results are not meaningful without their being related to the particular policy area. However, on their own they give some further indication of the general subject matter of reports and the discussion in this section treats them both on their own and in relation to the actual social services concerned. Table D5 gives the complete list of general topics, with the actual number of cases so classified and the percentage distribution. Subsequent analyses are confined to the more frequently occurring topics. In Table D6, for instance, these are given in rank order of frequency. The total number of codings amounts to 1,633 as against a total of 985 items. This difference is due to the fact that coders were permitted to record up to three general topics, although they had been instructed to confine the policy area coding to one main category, with the possibility of a secondary allocation (see above p.222). Where percentage figures are given, they are calculated on the number of newspaper items in the sample and not on the number of codings, since this gives a truer indication of the nature of the content.

TABLE D5

GENERAL TOPICS OF SOCIAL WELFARE CONTENT: FREQUENCIES AND PERCENTAGES BASED ON THE TOTAL NUMBER OF ITEMS IN THE SAMPLE (N=985)

|  | N | % |
|---|---|---|
| 1. Level of provision, facilities, services, etc.: | | |
| (a) High, adequate, increasing | 18 | 1·8 |
| (b) Inadequate or falling | 106 | 10·8 |
| 2. Financial references: | | |
| (a) Financial problems or shortages | 137 | 13·9 |
| (b) Sufficient or more money | 11 | 1·2 |
| (c) Other financial | 15 | 1·5 |
| 3. Problems (other than financial): | | |
| (a) For service or personnel | 91 | 9·2 |
| (b) For clients of service | 141 | 14·3 |
| (c) Not specified or other problems | 33 | 3·4 |
| 4. Professional or occupational matters: | | |
| (a) Staffing cuts, shortages, levels | 18 | 1·8 |
| (b) Standards, training | 38 | 3·9 |
| (c) Other | 66 | 6·7 |
| 5. Industrial relations and trade union matters: | | |
| (a) Strikes or other disputes | 92 | 9·3 |
| (b) Pay negotiations | 34 | 3·5 |
| (c) Other | 24 | 2·4 |
| 6. Administration or policy-making | 251 | 25·5 |
| 7. Criminal, police or legal matters | 100 | 10·1 |
| 8. Research: plans or findings | 53 | 5·4 |
| 9. Participation or control by public, employee, client, etc. | 15 | 1·5 |

**TABLE D5**—*continued*

| | | |
|---|---|---|
| 10. Conflict: | | |
|     (*a*) Protest, sit-in or dispute (non-industrial) ... ... | 51 | 5·2 |
|     (*b*) Other conflict ... ... ... ... ... ... | 75 | 7.6 |
| 11. Reform or development: | | |
|     (*a*) Reform ... ... ... ... ... ... ... | 48 | 4·9 |
|     (*b*) Developments: positive, new initiatives ... ... | 69 | 7·0 |
|     (*c*) Developments: negative (banning, cutting, etc.) ... | 62 | 6.3 |
| 12. Specific topics: | | |
|     (*a*) Pay beds ... ... ... ... ... ... ... | 31 | 3.1 |
|     (*b*) Comprehensive education ... ... ... ... | 15 | 1·5 |
|     (*c*) Welfare rights ... ... ... ... ... ... | 6 | 0·6 |
|     (*d*) Public information ... ... ... ... ... | 7 | 0.7 |
|     (*e*) Other ... ... ... ... ... ... ... | 26 | 2·6 |

The four most frequent general topics were: administration and policy-making (26%); problems for clients of the service concerned (14%); financial shortages or problems (14%); and inadequate or falling levels of provision. Three of these topics have a mainly negative connotation and one way of expressing this result is to compare the overall frequency of items which are clearly "negative" with those which are "neutral" or "positive". The negative items might include 1*b*, 2*a*, 3, 4*a*, 5*a*, 7, 10 and 11*c*. Between them, these account for 906 topic references (54% of all). Positive topics include 1*a*, 2*b*, 11*a*, and 11*b* and amounts to 146 or 9% of all references. Consequently, 37% are "neutral". The observation is unsurprising and perhaps the proportion which seem to be "bad news" is not over-high. The balance between "negative" and "positive" news was not the same for all policy areas (see IV 3 below).

## 2. Comparisons between newspapers in terms of general topics

The main general topics (14 out of a possible 28) are listed in Table D6 in order of overall relative frequency, and with comparative percentage figures for each national daily newspaper, based on the number of items sampled from each title. While the order varies somewhat from title to title, the general impression, as with so many inter-paper comparisons, is of broad consistency. Perhaps even fewer exceptions than usual can be distinguished and there is little sign of any systematic difference between "Qualities" and "Populars". Some points to note include: the somewhat higher relative incidence of items about conflict in the "Populars" and their lower attention to positive or new developments; consistently with the data about "participants" (Section V below), the *Daily Mirror* gave a high proportionate allocation to "problems for clients of services". On the overall division between "positive" and "negative" news, there was little difference between newspapers, although specifically on matters classified as either to do with "reform" or "positive and new developments", *The Times* and *The Guardian* stand out. Between them, they account for 73% of all items coded under one or other heading.

## 3. General topics in relation to main areas of social policy

The analysis undertaken to relate topics to main policy areas produced a large number of new categories of social welfare items, since there were 13 main policy areas and 28 different main topics of coverage. It would be unhelpful to re-

## TABLE D6

COMPARISONS BETWEEN NEWSPAPERS IN TERMS OF THE MAIN GENERAL TOPICS OF SOCIAL WELFARE CONTENT: PERCENTAGE FIGURES BASED ON THE TOTAL NUMBER OF ITEMS SAMPLED FROM EACH NEWSPAPER, HENCE NOT ADDING TO 100%

| Main topics | The Times | The Guardian | The Daily Telegraph | Financial Times | Morning Star | Daily Express | Daily Mail | Daily Mirror | The Sun | All Newspapers |
|---|---|---|---|---|---|---|---|---|---|---|
| | % | % | % | % | % | % | % | % | % | % |
| 1. Administration or policy-making | 33 | 30 | 23 | 25 | 29 | 23 | 24 | 28 | 11 | 26 |
| 2. Problems for clients of service | 16 | 13 | 9 | 6 | 18 | 10 | 19 | 30 | 24 | 14 |
| 3. Financial problems or shortages | 12 | 14 | 15 | 13 | 18 | 7 | 20 | 12 | 11 | 14 |
| 4. Inadequate or falling levels of provision | 11 | 10 | 14 | 10 | 13 | 7 | 12 | 12 | 3 | 11 |
| 5. Criminal, police or legal matters | 13 | 11 | 11 | 0 | 5 | 10 | 11 | 14 | 11 | 10 |
| 6. Strikes or other disputes | 8 | 5 | 11 | 10 | 14 | 12 | 6 | 7 | 11 | 9 |
| 7. Problems for service or personnel | 6 | 21 | 9 | 3 | 2 | 6 | 15 | 12 | 5 | 9 |
| 8. Conflict (other than protests, sit-ins, or industrial disputes) | 2 | 7 | 14 | 8 | 5 | 10 | 0 | 0 | 2 | 8 |
| 9. Positive or new developments | 11 | 10 | 6 | 11 | 4 | 10 | 0 | 12 | 5 | 7 |
| 10. Professional or occupational matters (4c in Table 5) | 5 | 6 | 5 | 5 | 15 | 1 | 8 | 10 | 7 | 7 |
| 11. Negative developments, cuts, etc. | 5 | 7 | 8 | 10 | 2 | 8 | 8 | 0 | 13 | 6 |
| 12. Research plans and findings | 5 | 8 | 3 | 2 | 2 | 1 | 4 | 0 | 5 | 5 |
| 13. Conflict: protests, sit-ins, disputes (non-industrial) | 13 | 8 | 7 | 0 | 15 | 5 | 1 | 0 | 5 | 5 |
| 14. Reform | 8 | 6 | 3 | | 1 | 3 | 0 | 0 | 0 | 5 |
| Total number of items | 186 | 231 | 100 | 63 | 93 | 73 | 75 | 43 | 61 | 985 |

228

produce the whole set of data, but of some interest to reproduce a short list of the most important new categories which were formed by this cross-tabulation. For the most part, the new categories were numerically small and only those with 20 or more cases are listed in Table D7. In all, 451 out of the sample of 985 items are covered by taking the 15 new categories so established. One or two conclusions can be drawn from these figures—for instance the fact that the hospital doctors' dispute accounted for most industrial dispute items and a good part of all items about hospitals (70 out of 131). This in turn suggests that the particular events of 1975 (as in any other year) may have had a strong effect on the balance of press attention to different social services or policy areas. On the other hand, it would also seem from the fuller set of figures from which these data were extracted that many topics recur in their expected proportion over a wide range of policy areas. This is true, in particular, of "administration and policy-making", "problems for client or service", "financial problems", "falling levels of provision" and "conflict" generally. Each of these topics provides the subject matter of news about different social services.

The variation between policy areas in the incidence of more negative topics mentioned earlier can be expressed in the following way. If we take, as "negative" topics, "problems for clients or the service concerned", "financial shortage", "falling levels of provision", "negative developments and conflict" (not industrial conflict), the incidence of these topic codings, expressed as a percentage of the number of items in each policy area, is as follows (from more to less "negative", in order): social work, 133%; universities and polytechnics, 113%; housing, 100%; N.I.S.S., 93%; other education, 92%; children and family, 75%; youth employment, 73%; school education, 67%; minority groups, 48%; other health, 44%; legal and penal, 41%; hospitals, 31%. This is obviously a rather crude index but it does to some degree show the "image" presented of each main policy area in terms of the amount of "bad news" of all kinds associated with each service. More than likely, it does generally reflect the circumstances of the year reasonably well.

TABLE D7

SOCIAL WELFARE CONTENT: FREQUENCIES AND PERCENTAGES IN MAIN NEW CATEGORIES OBTAINED BY COMBINING GENERAL TOPIC WITH MAIN POLICY AREA: (PERCENTAGES BASED ON WHOLE SAMPLE OF 985)

|  | $N$ | % |
|---|---|---|
| 1. Topic: strike or dispute<br>   Policy area: hospitals (n = 131) ... ... ... ... ... | 70 | 7·1 |
| 2. Topic: administration and policy-making<br>   Policy area: school education (n = 201) ... ... ... ... | 46 | 4·7 |
| 3. Topic: administration and policy-making<br>   Policy area: health (non-hospital) (n = 175) ... ... ... ... | 43 | 4·4 |
| 4. Topic: problems for clients<br>   Policy area: school education (n = 201) ... ... ... ... | 35 | 3·6 |
| 5. Topic: criminal or police matters<br>   Policy area: legal or penal (n = 56) ... ... ... ... ... | 33 | 3·4 |
| 6. Topic: falling level of provision<br>   Policy area: housing (n = 74) ... ... ... ... ... ... | 25 | 2·5 |

229

**TABLE D7**—*continued*

| | | |
|---|---|---|
| 7. Topic: Administration and policy-making<br>Policy area: children and family (n = 72) ... ... ... ... | 25 | 2·5 |
| 8. Topic: problems for the service or personnel<br>Policy area: school education (n = 201) ... ... ... ... | 23 | 2·3 |
| 9. Topic: conflict—sit-in, dispute<br>Policy area: universities and polytechnics (n = 69) ... ... ... | 23 | 2·3 |
| 10. Topic: research<br>Policy area: other health (non-hospital) (n = 175) ... ... ... | 22 | 2·2 |
| 11. Topic: professional or occupational matters<br>Policy area: other health (non-hospital) (n = 175) ... ... ... | 22 | 2·2 |
| 12. Topic: administration and policy making<br>Policy area: hospitals (n = 131) ... ... ... ... ... | 21 | 2·1 |
| 13. Topic: financial shortage<br>Policy area: school education (n = 201) ... ... ... ... | 21 | 2·1 |
| 14. Topic: financial shortage<br>Policy area: other education (n = 38) ... ... ... ... ... | 21 | 2·1 |
| 15. Topic: positive developments<br>Policy area: school education (n = 201) ... ... ... ... | 21 | 2·1 |

# V  Sources of social welfare content and participants referred to

## 1. Sources of social welfare content

Wherever possible, each newspaper item was classified according to the main source from which the original news was acquired or to the kind of event which led to the matter involved becoming public. The list of possible sources and the percentage of items classified in relation to each source is given in Table D8. It should be emphasised that no information about source other than that available in the newspaper items themselves was made use of in the classification.

TABLE D8

MAIN SOURCE OR OCCASION OF NEWSPAPER REPORT: PERCENTAGE DIS-
TRIBUTION AGAINST 20 CATEGORIES* (n=985)

|  | % |
|---|---|
| Trade Union (official or leader) ... ... ... ... ... ... ... | 10·6 |
| Official (or quasi-official) report ... ... ... ... ... ... ... | 9·0 |
| Government (or party) report or bill ... ... ... ... ... ... ... | 7·6 |
| Local Government official source ... ... ... ... ... ... ... | 7·6 |
| Pressure or action group ... ... ... ... ... ... ... | 7·4 |
| Court case ... ... ... ... ... ... ... ... | 6·3 |
| Conference report ... ... ... ... ... ... ... ... | 5·9 |
| Ministerial or party speech ... ... ... ... ... ... ... | 5·7 |
| Parliamentary proceedings ... ... ... ... ... ... ... | 4·7 |
| Book, pamphlet, article ... ... ... ... ... ... ... ... | 3·9 |
| Director, chief executive of service, etc. ... ... ... ... ... ... | 3·4 |
| Investigation by newspaper itself ... ... ... ... ... ... | 2·6 |
| National Union of Students ... ... ... ... ... ... ... | 2·2 |
| Opposition speech or document ... ... ... ... ... ... ... | 2·0 |
| Research report ... ... ... ... ... ... ... ... | 2·0 |
| Trade Union—rank and file ... ... ... ... ... ... ... | 1·4 |
| Other political source ... ... ... ... ... ... ... ... | 1·2 |
| "Expert" ... ... ... ... ... ... ... ... | 1·0 |
| Other media ... ... ... ... ... ... ... ... | 0·3 |
| Not identifiable or other ... ... ... ... ... ... ... | 15·1 |
| TOTAL ... ... ... | 99.9% |

*For a more complete description of the source, see the coding frame in Appendix
D1 (Cols. 37–8).

In general, the table speaks for itself, with little need for comment. It is clear that a good deal of such news does originate in official sources—either administrative or political. The dominant position apparently occupied by trade unions is somewhat misleading, since more than half (58) of the 104 items involved related to hospitals and many concerned the Junior Hospital Doctors' dispute over pay and contracts. Leaving aside trade unions as source, approximately 41% of items originated in some official or political source. One might also note the low incidence of items originating with the opposition party, although some may have appeared as "parliamentary proceedings".

## 2. Source and policy area

The concentration of trade union-originated reports in the field of hospital services has already been mentioned. A complete cross-tabulation of sources against policy areas produced a few additional instances, where the general pattern of source origination did not apply in the expected way. For example:

231

70% of items originating with the opposition related to education; where a director or chief executive was given as source, it was mainly in the educational field; all but one of NUS-originated items related to higher education; of the 73 items originating with pressure or action groups, 14 related to school education, 12 to "other health" matters, ten to children and the family, nine to housing. The overall impression is that the different main policy areas are reported from very much the same range of sources, once allowance is made for the effect of the particular news events of the year sampled (1975).

### 3. Variations between newspapers in terms of source of items

A detailed comparison between newspapers in terms of the percentage distribution of items against the 20 categories of source shown in Table D8 shows that, with few major exceptions, the pattern of source origination was similar for all newspapers. When the distribution for each newspaper is compared with the overall pattern, the following points can be made, choosing only the largest deviations from the average (see Table D8 above). *The Times* differed in its greater attention to Government reports and bills (12·8%) and Opposition sources (3·7%) and in the non-use of its own investigative reporting (0%). *The Guardian* gave above-average attention to pressure and action groups (10·4%), to books (6·1%), and to research reports (4·3%). *The Daily Telegraph* drew more from directors of services (6·2%), Opposition sources (3·7%) and the NUS (3·7%) and less from pressure or action groups (3·7%). The *Financial Times* showed a very distinctive pattern, with no sampled items originating in court cases, pressure or action groups, the Opposition, or the NUS and very few (1·6%) with local government. The bulk of its content appeared to come from Government, parliamentary, official or party sources, books and conference reports. An above average number originated in research reports (4·8%) and its own investigative activity (6·3%). The *Morning Star* deviated sharply in giving high attention to pressure or action groups (20·4%), to the NUS (8·6%) and to union rank and file sources (4·1%). It was most notably low in attention to parliament (1·1%), local government (4·3%), court cases (2·2%) and the Opposition (0%).

The *Daily Express* drew notably on official reports (12·3%) and on its own investigation (8·2%) and was inclined to avoid pressure or action groups (2·7%), the NUS (0%) and research reports (0%).

The *Daily Mail* was also low in attention to pressure and action groups (2·7%) and also drew on its own investigative resources (6·7%).

The *Daily Mirror* was high in the proportion of local government sources (14%), court cases (9·3%), and investigative (7%) and trade union rank and file (7%) sources. It was generally less inclined than the average in use of Government and official sources.

*The Sun* showed a high inclination to use official reports (19·7%) and a disinclination towards local government sources, conference reports and parliamentary proceedings. The proportion of its reports coming from pressure or action groups was high at 8·2%.

Despite the number of apparent deviations from the average noted above, it should be recalled that the percentage differences involved are often not large and the number of cases involved also quite low, especially in the "Popular" newspapers. Consequently, the results should not be regarded as more than indicative and the similarity is more striking than the differences. There is little in the way of an overall differentiation between "Popular" and "Quality" press in respect of apparent source. The latter are, however, somewhat more inclined to draw on reports of conferences, on parliamentary proceedings, on books and on research reports. The "Popular" newspapers seem to make more use of their own investigative resources, although this should be taken in a rather loose sense, in the absence of further evidence.

## 4. Participants reported in social welfare content

A list of categories of participants was included in the coding scheme and coders were asked to record the occurrence of any quotation or direct report in a given item. In their original form, the data included a count of the number of such references, in each item, to each kind of participant, but this level of detail has been disregarded in the present discussion and the presence of a given reference might be a single or multiple occurrence of quotation or direct report. Table D9 gives first the overall frequency of occurrence of each category.

TABLE D9
PARTICIPANTS QUOTED OR REPORTED IN SOCIAL WELFARE CONTENT: FREQUENCY OF OCCURRENCE OF EACH OF NINE CATEGORIES AS A PERCENTAGE OF ALL ITEMS (n = 985).

| | % |
|---|---|
| 1. Director, chief of service or other principal | 18·1 |
| 2. Government Minister, MP, or official | 14·4 |
| 3. Lower level staff member (eg teacher, nurse) | 8·3 |
| 4. Spokesman for semi-official (non-government) body | 7·4 |
| 5. Client, recipient of service, consumer | 7·2 |
| 6. Spokesman for pressure or action group | 6·8 |
| 7. Opposition MP or politician | 6·0 |
| 8. Expert | 5·9 |
| 9. Other | 17·9 |

The figures show some tendency for direct quotations or reports to come differentially from the "top", although, without knowledge of the content of what was reported, little can be concluded from these data alone. Equally, it is not apparent how much "overlap" there was between participants in the items studied. The number of cases in which no participant featured was probably quite large.

There are certain differences between newspapers in the incidence of different kinds of participant and, despite the rather small numbers of cases, it is worth reporting some of the differences. Table D10 gives comparative figures for four categories of participant.

TABLE D10
SOCIAL WELFARE ITEMS: PERCENTAGE IN EACH NEWSPAPER CONTAINING A REPORT OF OR QUOTATION FROM: A GOVERNMENT MP OR OFFICIAL; AN OPPOSITION MP OR SPOKESMAN; A DIRECTOR OF SERVICE; AND A CLIENT, BENEFICIARY OR CONSUMER

| Participant Category | The Times | The Guardian | The Daily Telegraph | Financial Times | Morning Star | Daily Express | Daily Mail | Daily Mirror | The Sun | All |
|---|---|---|---|---|---|---|---|---|---|---|
| | % | % | % | % | % | % | % | % | % | % |
| 1. Government | 17 | 16 | 16 | 28 | 8 | 11 | 11 | 9 | 11 | 14 |
| 2. Opposition | 10 | 6 | 8 | 2 | 1 | 4 | 4 | 2 | 7 | 6 |
| 3. Director | 15 | 21 | 23 | 11 | 10 | 18 | 28 | 14 | 15 | 18 |
| 4. Client/ Consumer | 2 | 4 | 11 | 2 | 5 | 18 | 12 | 16 | 10 | 7 |
| Number of items | 186 | 231 | 160 | 63 | 93 | 73 | 75 | 43 | 51 | 985 |

The main point to emerge is a greater tendency for "Quality" newspapers to include "Government" participants than do "Popular" newspapers and a greater tendency for the latter to include clients or consumers in their news reports.

## 5. **Main policy area location of participants**

Some further information about the nature of "participation" in social welfare reporting can be obtained by looking at the location of categories of participants in different social policy areas. The complete data are too cumbersome and unrevealing to reproduce, but the following points can be made. Of those categorised as directors of services, etc, 42% were in education of one sort or another, 23% in health or hospitals and 8% in housing. Of Government participants, 31% were in health, 15% in education and 13% concerned with children and the family. Of "lower-level" staff members, 29% were in education and 35% in health. Clients or consumers were mainly either in higher education (21%) or health (23%). The Opposition voice was heard in school education especially (34%), on hospitals (17%) and on family matters (17%). Generally, the incidence of participants of different kinds was much the same in different policy areas. The evidence here is a corrective to supposing that the appearance of clients or consumers in reports necessarily shows that the underprivileged are being heard. More likely than not, they are students or parents of school children.

# VI   Themes in social policy content

The idea of a theme as distinct from a topic is discussed in Appendix D2, xi. Briefly, themes have been thought of as the underlying public concerns which at a given time provide either the criteria for selecting events as newsworthy or as the frame of reference for interpreting events and assessing their significance. They may be thought of as the "news angles" which give perspective and context to reports. The analysis reported here is based on what was anticipated as relevant to the content to be studied and another version of the relevant themes might have produced different results. The results give no indication of the importance of a theme in a given item, since the reference might have been short and incidental or quite central to the whole news item. This is a weakness of the method, which relies on the overall count to reflect relative salience. It should also be stressed that to record a reference to a theme is not necessarily to record the view of the *paper itself*, since generally the reference will be taken from some other attributed source.

The main purposes of recording and counting the occurrence of themes were: to pick up some of the more incidental aspects of news content; to "profile" different topics and different newspapers in terms of themes referred to; generally to try and extend the qualitative dimension of the study, without loss of objectivity.

## 2. Frequency of theme references

Table D11 gives the actual frequency of reference to each of the 24 themes, in rank order of occurrence. There is a fairly even spread of items and some

TABLE D11

**THEMES IN THE REPORTING OF SOCIAL WELFARE IN ALL NINE NATIONAL DAILY NEWSPAPERS: OVERALL FREQUENCY**

| Theme* | No. of references |
|---|---|
| 1. Criticism of Government or local authority | 122 |
| 2. Danger to public | 91 |
| 3. Good news, success, achievement | 70 |
| 4. Sex aspects | 68 |
| 5. Private vs. public provision | 53 |
| 6. Inhumanity towards "client" or beneficiary | 48 |
| 7. Violence, conflict | 42 |
| 8. Waste, profligacy, undue expense | 35 |
| 9. Deprivation, discrimination in general | 35 |
| 10. Colour bar, needs of immigrants (67) | 33 |
| 11. Scandal, misconduct (on part of service or personnel) | 31 |
| 12. Bureaucracy, "red tape" or inefficiency | 31 |
| 13. Tough line, clampdown, banning | 30 |
| 14. Left-wing activity, militancy | 24 |
| 15. Unequal treatment, social class differences | 16 |
| 16. Party political disagreement in general | 16 |
| 17. Welfare or client rights | 15 |
| 18. Worker control or direct action | 14 |
| 19. Public or user representation | 13 |
| 20. Crisis | 8 |
| 21. False claims, fiddling (55) | 6 |
| 22. Right-wing activity, reaction | 4 |
| 23. Over-generous treatment by authorities | 4 |
| 24. Welfare "scrounging" | 1 |
| Total: | 810 |

*Where a number is given in brackets, it refers to the column number in Appendix D1 and a fuller wording of the item.

diversity at the top of the table. Although two "negative" themes head the list ("criticism of Government" and "danger to the public"), second and third places are taken, respectively, by the general, "good news" theme and by references to "sex aspects". The items which seem *prima facie*, to have emotive or tendentious implications, are generally fairly low in order of occurrence. There is a relatively low incidence of themes altogether, with an average of less than one theme per item. This may in part be the result of a strict application of the coding rule that a reference should be clear and specific, but it can also probably be taken to reflect the factual character of reporting. Approximately a third of all references are taken up by points which involve a direct criticism of the services or public authorities (items 1, 6, 8, 11 and 12), although it is unclear from these data to what extent criticism is voiced on behalf of beneficiaries rather than others. The items which clearly involve criticism of welfare recipients (21, 23, 24 and perhaps 8) are seemingly little used.

## 3. Themes in relation to policy areas

The data in Table D11 become more meaningful when they are looked at in relation to the different social policy areas. In order to examine this inter-association, the five reference themes with lowest frequency of use have been ignored. Table D12 shows the distribution of 19 themes against 13 main policy areas. The data can be analysed in one of two ways—either by showing, for each policy area, what themes predominated; or by looking at the location in policy areas of the different main themes. First, we can learn from these data something of the overall use of themes in different policy areas. On average, 80% of all reports examined carried a theme reference (although, of course, some will have had more than one and more than 20% will have none), and we can use this average as a basis for comparing the main policy areas. In fact the range of use is not very wide, since all fall between 42% (University education) and 91% (Hospitals). The policy areas attracting most references are health and minority groups (90%) and those attracting least are non-school education, social work and legal and penal matters. We might interpret a high incidence of themes as evidence of a generally more interpretive style of reporting, with a greater tendency to employ a distinctive set of news values.

It is clear from table D12 that themes are not randomly distributed between policy areas and it would be surprising if it were otherwise, given the specific content of many themes. Some policy areas seem to be fairly clearly defined in terms of a set of themes, while others show no strong associations. The largest single policy area, school education, is linked with a number of themes, although no single one predominates. Of the total of 201 items on this subject, 12% were accompanied by a reference to "good news" and 12% by a reference to "sex aspects". There are several associations which were found to be statistically significant, at a confidence level of 5%. These include links with: "left wing activity"; "scandal and misconduct"; "party political disagreement"; "violence"; "sex aspects"; "good news". As the figures in Table D12 make clear, it is not that a large number of items about school education necessarily carry a reference to any one of these themes. Rather, we find that the references are concentrated on items about school education in a way which is dispro-portionate to their overall incidence.

236

**TABLE D12**

**INCIDENCE OF 19 MAIN THEMES IN RELATION TO 13 MAIN POLICY AREAS**

| Main Policy Area | Themes* | | | | |
|---|---|---|---|---|---|
| | Left-wing activity | Private vs Public provision | Party political disagreement | Waste; undue expense | Scandal; misconduct |
| Housing (n = 74) ... | 1 | 5 | 1 | 12 | 2 |
| School education (n = 201) ... ... | 12 | 7 | 7 | 3 | 12 |
| Universities & Polytechnics (n=69) | 2 | 0 | 0 | 4 | 1 |
| Other education (n = 38) ... ... | 0 | 0 | 1 | 2 | 0 |
| Hospitals (n = 131) ... | 7 | 28 | 3 | 2 | 2 |
| Other health (n = 175) | 1 | 10 | 0 | 4 | 7 |
| N.I. & Social Security (n = 28) ... ... | 0 | 0 | 0 | 2 | 0 |
| Social Work (n = 18) ... | 0 | 0 | 0 | 1 | 0 |
| Legal & Penal (n = 56) | 0 | 0 | 1 | 2 | 3 |
| Minority groups (n=29) | 0 | 0 | 0 | 0 | 0 |
| Children and Family (n = 72) ... ... | 0 | 1 | 1 | 2 | 3 |
| Youth; employment (n = 45) ... ... | 1 | 2 | 1 | 1 | 0 |
| Miscellaneous (n=49) | 0 | 0 | 1 | 0 | 1 |
| Total (n = 985) ... | 24 | 53 | 16 | 35 | 31 |

| Main Policy Area | Themes | | | | |
|---|---|---|---|---|---|
| | Bureau-cracy; red tape | In-humanity to client | Danger to public | Unequal treatment | Criticism of Govrnt. or L.A. |
| Housing ... ... | 3 | 3 | 2 | 2 | 16 |
| School education ... | 3 | 1 | 0 | 5 | 22 |
| Universities & Polytechnics ... | 0 | 1 | 0 | 1 | 8 |
| Other education ... | 1 | 0 | 1 | 2 | 5 |
| Hospitals ... ... | 10 | 2 | 33 | 0 | 19 |
| Other health ... ... | 3 | 12 | 40 | 0 | 19 |
| N.I. & Social Security | 0 | 2 | 0 | 2 | 7 |
| Social work ... ... | 2 | 2 | 0 | 0 | 2 |
| Legal & Penal ... | 1 | 11 | 6 | 1 | 7 |
| Minority groups ... | 1 | 1 | 1 | 0 | 4 |
| Children & Family ... | 6 | 9 | 4 | 1 | 5 |
| Youth; employment ... | 1 | 1 | 3 | 0 | 3 |
| Miscellaneous ... | 0 | 3 | 1 | 2 | 5 |
| Total ... ... | 31 | 48 | 91 | 16 | 122 |

*A more complete wording of these themes can be found in Table D11 or Appendix D1.

**TABLE D12** (*continued*)

## INCIDENCE OF 19 MAIN THEMES IN RELATION TO 13 MAIN POLICY AREAS

| Main Policy Area | Themes | | | | |
|---|---|---|---|---|---|
| | Worker Control | Welfare rights | Public/user representa-tion | Violence or conflict | Problems/ immigrants |
| Housing ... ... | 0 | 1 | 2 | 2 | 1 |
| School education ... | 3 | 1 | 6 | 16 | 5 |
| Universities & Polytechnics ... | 2 | 0 | 0 | 0 | 2 |
| Other education ... | 0 | 2 | 1 | 0 | 1 |
| Hospitals ... ... | 5 | 0 | 2 | 0 | 1 |
| Other health ... ... | 1 | 5 | 1 | 4 | 1 |
| N.I. and Social Security | 0 | 3 | 0 | 0 | 0 |
| Social work ... ... | 0 | 0 | 0 | 0 | 0 |
| Legal & Penal ... | 0 | 0 | 0 | 15 | 0 |
| Minority groups ... | 0 | 0 | 0 | 0 | 18 |
| Children and Family ... | 2 | 1 | 0 | 3 | 1 |
| Youth; Employment ... | 1 | 1 | 1 | 2 | 3 |
| Miscellaneous ... | 0 | 1 | 0 | 0 | 0 |
| Total ... ... | 14 | 15 | 13 | 42 | 33 |

| Main Policy Area | Themes | | | |
|---|---|---|---|---|
| | Deprivation/ discrimination | Tough line; clampdown | Sex aspects | Good news |
| Housing ... ... ... ... | 4 | 1 | 2 | 3 |
| School education ... ... ... | 11 | 6 | 24 | 25 |
| Universities & Polytechnics ... | 2 | 4 | 2 | 6 |
| Other education ... ... | 1 | 0 | 2 | 3 |
| Hospitals ... ... ... | 0 | 3 | 0 | 2 |
| Other health ... ... ... | 3 | 3 | 27 | 8 |
| N.I. & Social Security ... ... | 4 | 1 | 1 | 1 |
| Social work ... ... ... | 1 | 0 | 0 | 1 |
| Legal and Penal ... ... | 3 | 6 | 1 | 2 |
| Minority groups ... ... ... | 0 | 0 | 0 | 1 |
| Children and Family ... ... | 4 | 0 | 5 | 5 |
| Youth; employment ... ... | 1 | 2 | 1 | 9 |
| Miscellaneous ... ... ... | 1 | 4 | 3 | 4 |
| Total ... ... ... ... | 35 | 30 | 68 | 70 |

**TABLE D13**

**SOCIAL WELFARE CONTENT: INCIDENCE OF 19 MAIN THEMES IN NATIONAL DAILY NEWSPAPERS (ACTUAL FREQUENCIES)**

| Main Themes | All (frequency) | All (Per cent) | The Times | The Guardian | The Daily Telegraph | Financial Times | Morning Star | Daily Express | Daily Mail | Daily Mirror | The Sun |
|---|---|---|---|---|---|---|---|---|---|---|---|
| | | % | | | | | | | | | |
| 1. Criticism of Government or local authority | 122 | 16 | 31 | 32 | 19 | 5 | 17 | 3 | 8 | 5 | 2 |
| 2. Danger to public | 91 | 12 | 20 | 16 | 11 | 7 | 6 | 6 | 8 | 6 | 11 |
| 3. Good news, success, achievement | 70 | 9 | 10 | 25 | 7 | 7 | 6 | 6 | 5 | 2 | 2 |
| 4. Sex aspects | 68 | 9 | 4 | 11 | 7 | — | 3 | 12 | 12 | 8 | 11 |
| 5. Private vs. public provision | 53 | 7 | 8 | 7 | 18 | 9 | 1 | 5 | 2 | 2 | 1 |
| 6. Inhumanity towards "client" or beneficiary | 48 | 6 | 7 | 15 | 6 | — | 5 | 5 | 5 | 5 | 8 |
| 7. Violence, conflict | 42 | 5 | 7 | 9 | 9 | 2 | 1 | 1 | 2 | 1 | 3 |
| 8. Waste, profligacy, undue expense | 35 | 4 | 12 | 8 | 8 | 3 | — | — | 1 | — | 1 |
| 9. Deprivation, discrimination in general | 35 | 4 | 5 | 10 | 11 | 2 | — | 2 | — | 2 | 2 |
| 10. Colour bar, needs of immigrants | 33 | 4 | 7 | 9 | 5 | 1 | 9 | — | 3 | — | 5 |
| 11. Scandal, misconduct (on part of service or personnel) | 31 | 4 | 4 | 8 | 4 | 1 | — | 5 | 3 | 1 | 4 |
| 12. Bureaucracy, "red tape", or inefficiency | 31 | 4 | 12 | 5 | 4 | 1 | 1 | — | 5 | — | 2 |
| 13. Tough line, clampdown, banning | 30 | 4 | 5 | 5 | 2 | 2 | 5 | 3 | 3 | 1 | 3 |
| 14. Left-wing activity, militancy | 24 | 3 | 1 | 3 | 5 | 1 | 4 | 4 | 3 | 1 | — |
| 15. Unequal treatment, social class differences | 16 | 2 | 6 | 2 | 1 | 1 | 1 | — | 3 | — | — |
| 16. Party political disagreement in general | 16 | 2 | 2 | 4 | 3 | 3 | — | 1 | — | 2 | — |
| 17. Welfare or client rights | 15 | 2 | 4 | 7 | 4 | — | — | — | 1 | — | 1 |
| 18. Worker control or direct action | 14 | 2 | — | 2 | 3 | 1 | 3 | 1 | — | 1 | — |
| 19. Public or user representation | 13 | 2 | 2 | 3 | — | 2 | 3 | 1 | 1 | 2 | — |
| Totals | 787 | 101 | 147 | 182 | 127 | 48 | 65 | 58 | 64 | 40 | 58 |

The policy areas of health and hospitals together show a tendency to be significantly linked with references to "danger to the public" and "private versus public provision" as themes. The topic of hospitals is also linked with "bureaucracy" and other health matters with reference to "sex aspects". There are few other noteworthy associations to be identified in Table D12, although there is a link between the housing topic and "extravagance" theme.

## 4. Comparisons between newspapers in the incidence of themes

The overall use of these themes, paper by paper, closely matches the overall occurrence of social welfare items. It is not easy to perceive any general pattern in Table D13, although it is fairly clear that the order of frequency is not very different from one paper to another. A closer inspection reveals some differences, however. For instance, criticism of the Government or local authority which, at 16% of all references, leads in the sample as a whole is the leading item only in the "Qualities" and in the *Morning Star*. For the other four papers, references to "sex aspects" leads or is jointly first. If the four "Qualities" are considered as a group and compared in percentage terms to the four "Populars", certain other differences show up. The former are generally more attentive to the question of private or public provision, to financial waste, to colour and immigration, deprivation in general and to welfare or "client" rights. The latter group ("Populars") differentially notice scandal or misconduct and left-wing activity or militancy. Individual newspapers seem to have particular tendencies towards one theme or another, involving some deviation from the overall pattern. Thus, *The Times* has the most frequent number of references to financial waste and bureaucratic "red tape". *The Guardian* accounts for almost half the 16 references to welfare or client rights and has, proportionately, much the largest number of references to the theme of inhumanity towards the client. *The Daily Telegraph* would appear to have taken a special interest in the question of private versus public welfare provision. The figures for the *Financial Times* show a similar tendency. The *Morning Star* has most references to problems connected with immigration and colour. Apart from the points made already, the remaining newspapers have no very noticeable tendencies, apart from the number of references in *The Sun* to the theme of inhumanity towards welfare clients.

# VII    Summary and conclusions

(The numbers in brackets refer to the relevant sections of the report)

1. The analysis confirmed that social welfare and social policy related material is consistently a fairly important component of national daily newspapers, by the criteria of frequency, space, prominence and editorial comment (II, 2). The differences between "Quality" and "Popular" papers reflect differences of space available rather than news values, for the most part.

2. The analysis also showed, however, that coverage is very uneven as between different services or policy areas, with school education and health (especially hospitals) claiming a large part of the attention. As a result, many topics, such as social security matters, social work and retirement or pension subjects are relatively sparsely covered on a day-to-day basis. The same comments apply to race and community relations (III, 1). This is not to say that an important event on one of these topics would not be adequately treated, but it may mean that "newsworthy" events according to normal selection criteria are relatively unusual or that reader interest is judged to be low. There is not much to differentiate newspapers in their practice in this respect (III, 2). It should be added, however, that some "neglected" areas from a news point of view were attended to in editorials (III, 3).

3. There was some tendency to notice more "bad news" than good, in social policy matters (IV, 1) and the "Popular" dailies gave relatively more attention to conflict than the "Qualities" (IV, 3). The policy areas with most "negative" kinds of news were social work, universities, housing and social security, if industrial conflict is left out of account.

4. Material seems to come from a wide range of sources although "official" sources of one kind or another tend to predominate. About 41% of items originated with a political or Governmental source (V, 1). Newspapers differed relatively little, although there was some evidence of particular papers having preferred kinds of source (V, 3) and some variation between "Qualities" and "Populars".

5. The analysis of "participants" in news stories mainly went to confirm the view that the range of sources is somewhat "top-heavy". The "Qualities" seemed to show this tendency rather more than the "Populars" (V, 4).

6. While the occurrence of themes and "news-angles" reflected a generally "negative" orientation in content, the most important "negative" theme involved criticism of central or local government and the more seemingly "loaded" themes were little used (VI, 2). The main difference between newspapers, apart from minor variations, was a tendency for criticism of government to predominate in "Qualities" and themes classified as "sex aspects" to lead in the "Popular" dailies.

# Part E

**Foreign Affairs Content in National Daily and two Scottish Newspapers, 1975: sample survey of 2,520 items**

# Main Tables

# I  Aims and Methods

## 1. Introduction

This report forms one of three, each focusing on different kinds of news content, and all relating to the same sample of newspapers for 1975 on which the general description of newspaper content was based (Part A above). The other two studies (Parts B, C and D) related to industrial relations news and to news of social welfare and social policy matters. They have been intended to provide information in more depth about some of the categories of news which were quantified in the earlier study. This study differs in two respects from the other two: it is based on a sample of 12 issues, rather than 24, because of the amount of content involved and it includes some information about two Scottish newspapers: *The Scotsman* and *Glasgow Herald*.

## 2. Aims

The general objective was to provide a detailed and systematic description of the relevant content and the research was guided by the following more specific questions:

(i) What are the main topics and themes of foreign coverage and how much attention is given to each?

(ii) What countries or parts of the world are represented in news content and in what proportion?

(iii) How do different parts of the world compare in terms of the topics and themes of news coverage? Do different regions have different "news profiles"?

(iv) How much foreign news involves Britain or the United States?

(v) What can be learnt of the general character of foreign news in terms of such criteria as the degree of predictability, "excitement", or "negativity"?

(vi) What can be said about the sources of news and the main kinds of chief participants in events?

(vii) How do different newspapers compare in respect of any of these questions?

The choice of questions has been guided by a broad concern with issues of diversity and adequacy of foreign coverage and with the principles which under-lie selection of news.

## 3. The choice of content for investigation

The general study of newspaper content (Part A) employed a number of separate categories for identifying "external" content and the classification applied in that study has been used for the present purpose, although with some exclusions and additions. In brief, external news was originally classified, firstly, as either "international" or "foreign, domestic" and then further sub-divided according to whether content was either about political, social or economic matters, or not. A separate category for international sport news was included. This latter category included reports of any sporting event occurring abroad. In addition, there was a category for any foreign feature content, whether international or not. The category of "international" news applies to

245

any news in which more than one country is involved, including Britain. For that reason, it is possible for Britain to figure as the main country of location of an "external" news event. In the present study, for instance, 6 % of all items studied were coded as located in Britain.

The present study has adopted the same definitions of external content as briefly described, with two exceptions. Firstly, sport news has been excluded. There is a great deal of such content, it already has been counted and classified, and most of the more detailed classifications used in this study would be of little relevance to such news. Secondly, an addition has been made of editorial (opinion) content related to external affairs. Even so, the body of content so identified does not exhaust the full range of potentially relevant material. There are five other main kinds of content which might have been considered, and which were left out only because they posed difficulties of identification or were sufficiently different in kind to make their analysis with a coding scheme designed primarily for news somewhat inappropriate. Reasons of economy of effort also played some part in the decision to exclude, since it was already apparent that the amount of "straight" foreign news in the sample would, on its own, take up available resources. The main kinds of content excluded (somewhat arbitrarily) from consideration were: travel and holiday features; international business and financial (not economic) news; letters; parliamentary debates on foreign affairs; advertisements (eg placed by foreign organisations). The most difficult line to draw was between economic and financial or market news and the attempt to exclude the latter has led to some under-recording of the total amount of such content—though mainly in newspapers where the quantity recorded is in any case large. This discussion of the basis for selection is a reminder that even such apparently straightforward categories as this have considerable ambiguities. It also underlines the need for caution in assessing the significance of differences between newspapers, especially where sport and travel content is involved, since these may be important sources of impressions of foreign countries for some readers.

## 4. Sampling

The items for analysis were chosen by taking the sample used in the general analysis of national daily newspapers and studying relevant items in the newspapers selected on 12 days out of the original 24. The method of choosing the days by a quasi-random procedure has already been described (Part A, pp. 2-3). It was designed to ensure adequate representation of different days of the week and quarters of the year. The decision to reduce the sample size from 24 to 12 days was a matter of economy after work on the first quarter (six days) had begun. In order to include the two Scottish newspapers, which were available only in the second half of the year, the sample was completed by adding the six days from the third quarter of the year. The sample period thus relates to the periods January—March and July—September of 1975. An obvious drawback of the method is that the news of one day is taken in isolation from the rest of what may be a continuing or developing story. Secondly, relatively few different news events or stories get sampled, since the same event may be looked at several times in different newspapers. The method is thus better adapted to providing a general comparative view of press coverage than to providing information in depth about reporting or including a very wide range of different kinds of news stories for the same amount of effort. The latter could be achieved by choosing more days from fewer newspapers.

## 5. Design and methods of analysis

The method employed is an adaptation of normal social survey methods to the study of newspaper content. The "population" to be studied is not composed of people but of items in newspapers. A limited number of "questions", formulated in advance, are "asked" of each item in a systematic way and the results recorded in a standardised form. As far as possible the recording of "answers" is carried out in an objective way and requires a minimum of personal judgement on the part of the analyst, in much the same way as a survey interviewer is required to be neutral. An important principle observed in the study is that analysis should be confined to what is contained in an overt way in newspaper reports and does not take account of any information about events available from an external source. For instance, if a news item seems incomplete or inaccurate by comparison with other reports of the same event, no attempt should be made to add missing information.

The basic tool of such an investigation is the coding schedule or frame which has to be prepared in advance and which has to be applicable equally to all cases. The coding frame (Appendix E1) was designed on the basis of an early exploratory analysis of foreign news content, a pilot test of its feasibility, and the comments of other advisers. A detailed commentary on its composition is included as Appendix E3. The design benefited very much from the opportunity to see a coding schedule prepared for an earlier investigation of broadcast news carried out at the Centre for Mass Communication Research at the University of Leicester. The actual reading and coding of all items was the work of three experienced coding assistants who worked systematically through the sample of newspapers, conferring where necessary with each other, and with the main investigator. Certain unanticipated difficulties had to be resolved by making new rules as the work proceeded, and minor adjustments were made to the coding schedule as a result. A summary analysis sheet was completed for each item (Appendix E2) and the data on these sheets were then transferred on to punched cards and magnetic tape and analysed on the UCSS computer, using standards SPSS programs. Mr Derek Cox, research assistant to the project, was responsible for this aspect of the work and for producing tabulations of data. We are grateful for the opportunity to use additional computer facilities at the University of Strathclyde.

# II  Description of the results

## 1. Amount of foreign coverage

The general study of newspaper content showed the category of foreign *news* to account for a large, though variable, component of all *news* space in different newspapers. The proportion in *The Guardian* was 27% and, in the *Daily Mirror* and *The Sun*, 9% and 10% respectively. Other newspapers fell in between these extremes. The exact proportion of all *editorial* space devoted to all material about foreign or international matters cannot be calculated from the available data, since some kinds of "foreign" content have been left out of account (see I, 3 above). However, if we ignore all financial and business news and also that category of feature content most likely to contain travel features, we can estimate the proportions of remaining editorial content which could be labelled as "foreign" as follows, for the national daily newspapers:

| The Times | The Guardian | The Daily Telegraph | Financial Times | Morning Star | Daily Express | Daily Mail | Daily Mirror | The Sun |
|-----------|--------------|---------------------|-----------------|--------------|---------------|------------|--------------|---------|
| 24% | 30% | 17% | 15% | 18% | 11% | 11% | 5% | 6% |

These figures indicate approximately the proportions of editorial space which were examined in the present study. Given the exclusions mentioned, these are minimum estimates of the amount of "foreign" news and feature content. Although this is clearly an important component of all newspapers it is especially so in the "Qualities". The actual numbers of items included in the present study reflect this variation between papers. Table E1 shows the frequency of items in each paper according to several categories of content.

**TABLE E1**

**FOREIGN CONTENT ITEMS IN 12 ISSUES OF NATIONAL DAILY NEWSPAPERS: FREQUENCY ACCORDING TO FIVE CATEGORIES**

| Category | The Times | The Guardian | The Daily Telegraph | Financial Times | Morning Star | Daily Express | Daily Mail | Daily Mirror | The Sun |
|----------|-----------|--------------|---------------------|-----------------|--------------|---------------|------------|--------------|---------|
| Foreign News | 263 | 186 | 221 | 176 | 62 | 83 | 65 | 44 | 52 |
| International News ... | 165 | 143 | 149 | 154 | 57 | 43 | 40 | 26 | 21 |
| Other News ... | 32 | 58 | 16 | 20 | 5 | 25 | 6 | 3 | 3 |
| Features ... | 27 | 61 | 8 | 24 | 11 | 3 | 7 | 1 | 1 |
| Editorials ... | 17 | 13 | 10 | 9 | 3 | 4 | 4 | 2 | 1 |
| Total ... | 504 | 461 | 404 | 383 | 138 | 158 | 122 | 76 | 78 |

Of the 2,324 items in the National Dailies, 6% were features and 3% were editorials. The latter figure is similar to the percentage of industrial relations items appearing in editorial columns, but the proportion of features is a good deal higher than in the case of industrial relations. The relative preponderance of foreign news may also be indicated by the fact that a sample of half the size produced a total number of items which was 64% higher. On another point of comparison, it seems that the difference between "Quality" and "Popular" newspapers is greater in the amount of foreign news than it is in the amount of industrial relations news. The average ratio of four "Qualities" to four "Populars" in the amount of foreign content item is 4:1 and for industrial relations content it is 2·4:1.

The numbers of foreign content items in the *Glasgow Herald* and *The Scotsman* (six issues of each only) were as follows, in Table E2.

TABLE E2

FOREIGN CONTENT ITEMS IN SIX ISSUES OF TWO SCOTTISH NEWS-PAPERS: FREQUENCY ACCORDING TO FIVE CATEGORIES

| Title | Foreign News | International News | Other News | Features | Editorials | Total |
|---|---|---|---|---|---|---|
| The Scotsman ... | 64 | 32 | 19 | 1 | 3 | 119 |
| Glasgow Herald... | 25 | 27 | 19 | 2 | 4 | 77 |

The total number of items in the English dailies for the same six days were as follows: *The Times*, 255; *The Guardian*, 224; *The Daily Telegraph*, 195; *Financial Times*, 196; *Morning Star*, 75; *Daily Express*, 82; *Daily Mail*, 56; *Daily Mirror*, 38; *The Sun*, 34. The two Scottish papers thus fall midway between "Populars" and "Qualities" in amount of coverage.

Certain differences between newspapers are apparent in terms of the kind of foreign content. Generally, "Quality" newspapers have higher proportions of features (*The Daily Telegraph* is the exception) and *The Guardian* has an exceptionally large number (13% of all items). The frequency of editorialising generally reflects the amount of news, although *The Sun* figure seems low. The balance between foreign (one country) news and international (more than one country) news also varies as between "Qualities" and "Populars" and is to be explained by the lower attention of the latter to politics and economics. A separate classification of all items, in addition to that given in Table E1, showed that 41% of all items were "international" and 58% were "foreign domestic".

## 2. Prominence and space given to foreign content

Two measures were employed to assess the degree of attention to foreign content, apart from the frequency of items and the record of actual column centimetres devoted to it. One was an index of prominence, distinguishing according to location and amount of space. Another was a scale used to classify the actual measurements.

249

Table E3 shows the proportion of *news items* in each paper which were large (over 60 col. cm.) front page stories.

TABLE E3

**FOREIGN NEWS ITEMS: PERCENTAGES OF TOTALS WHICH WERE LARGE FRONT PAGE STORIES IN 11 NEWSPAPERS**

| | | | | | | | | |
|---|---|---|---|---|---|---|---|---|
| The Times | ... | ... | ... | 7% | Daily Mail | ... | ... | ... | 6% |
| The Guardian | ... | ... | ... | 5% | Daily Mirror | ... | ... | ... | 13% |
| The Daily Telegraph | ... | ... | 5% | The Sun | ... | ... | ... | 8% |
| Financial Times | ... | ... | ... | 3% | Glasgow Herald | ... | ... | 3% |
| Morning Star | ... | ... | ... | 7% | The Scotsman | ... | ... | ... | 4% |
| Daily Express | ... | ... | ... | 6% | | | |

There is some indication here that "Popular" newspaper, although taking a smaller number of foreign stories, do take the more important ones and treat them accordingly. The relative size of items in different papers is shown in Table E4. This probably reflects a similar tendency, since the *Daily Mail, Daily Mirror* and *The Sun* give a relatively large amount of space to a much higher proportion of their foreign content items than do *The Times* or *The Daily Telegraph*. The high figure for *The Guardian* may partly reflect its large number of feature articles on foreign matters, which would generally be long. Otherwise, the most noticeable deviation from the general pattern is shown by the *Daily Mail*, with its low proportion of very small foreign items.

TABLE E4

**FOREIGN CONTENT IN 11 DAILY NEWSPAPERS: PERCENTAGE DISTRIBUTION OF ALL ITEMS IN TERMS OF FOUR CATEGORIES OF SIZE**

| Title | Item size in standard col. cms.* | | | | |
|---|---|---|---|---|---|
| | 1–10 % | 11–20 % | 21–60 % | 61+ % | Total % |
| The Times ... ... ... | 29 | 21 | 42 | 8 = | 100 |
| The Guardian ... ... ... | 27 | 15 | 41 | 17 = | 100 |
| The Daily Telegraph ... ... | 41 | 13 | 38 | 8 = | 100 |
| Financial Times ... ... | 24 | 29 | 39 | 8 = | 100 |
| Morning Star ... ... ... | 40 | 25 | 21 | 14 = | 100 |
| Daily Express ... ... ... | 43 | 16 | 32 | 9 = | 100 |
| Daily Mail ... ... ... | 9 | 25 | 46 | 20 = | 100 |
| Daily Mirror ... ... ... | 36 | 17 | 29 | 18 = | 100 |
| The Sun ... ... ... ... | 35 | 28 | 20 | 17 = | 100 |
| Glasgow Herald... ... ... | 31 | 18 | 46 | 5 = | 100 |
| The Scotsman ... ... ... | 36 | 17 | 40 | 7 = | 100 |

*The standard column varies in width from paper to paper, within the range 4 cm. (eg *The Sun*) to 5 cm. (eg *The Daily Telegraph*), and this has not been adjusted for. Hence the figures are not strictly comparable and will tend to underestimate the "gap" between "Qualities" and "Populars".

# 3. Characteristics of items

All the items analysed were classified according to a number of general characteristics which were thought to reflect something of the nature of foreign news. Data about these characteristics will be introduced where it is relevant during the report in relation to other aspects of content. It may, however, be useful to present the basic findings on these measures, at this point, so that overall distributions can be seen and comparisons made between newspapers.

## (a) Type of event or report

The classification involved relates to the kind of action or event which forms the substance of a story. The categories are probably self-explanatory and the overall distribution for the complete sample is given in Table E5. See also Appendix E3, (vii).

**TABLE E5**

**PERCENTAGES OF ALL ITEMS, CLASSIFIED ACCORDING TO MAIN FEATURES OF REPORT (n=2,520)**

|  | % |
|---|---|
| 1. About an action or event, including travel or arrival   ...   ...   ...   ... | 59 |
| 2. About a statement, speech or announcement   ...   ...   ...   ...   ... | 26 |
| 3. Mainly background or description   ...   ...   ...   ...   ...   ...   ... | 14 |
| 4. Not so classifiable or uncertain   ...   ...   ...   ...   ...   ...   ... | 1 |
| Total ...   ...   ...   ...   ... | 100 |

Evidently most items do concern some action. An inspection of results for different newspapers showed the pattern to hold generally for all newspapers. However, there were some variations, especially as between "Qualities" and "Populars". For the latter, a higher overall proportion of items were classified as about an action or event—the average figure for the *Daily Express, Daily Mail, Daily Mirror* and *The Sun* was 69% and for the four national "Qualities" only 56%. The figure for *The Scotsman* was 60%, and for the *Glasgow Herald* 69%, and for the *Morning Star*, 59%. As between the four popular papers, the balance between "statements" and "background" varied a good deal—with the *Daily Mirror* having fewest background items—only two in number. This finding gives some indication as to how extra space for foreign content in the larger newspapers is allocated, since it seems to be used for background.

## (b) Predictability of news events

The findings on this point can only be treated as indicative since some subjective judgement must enter into the assessment. In brief, coders had to judge whether or not the event or statement was more or less expected, was likely to be in the advance "diary" of events or not. The large proportion of items recorded as "uncertain" reflects the difficulty of the task in the absence of external evidence. However, it also increases confidence in the measured difference between the proportions of "predictable" and "unexpected" events. The findings

251

can be simply given. Of all 2,520 items, 29% were recorded as "predictable", 36% as "unexpected" and 35% as uncertain or, in a few cases, as not relevant to this classification principle. Again, comparisons between newspapers reveal some points of interest, if the split between the expected and the unexpected is taken as the key indicator.

TABLE E6

FOREIGN CONTENT IN DAILY NEWSPAPERS: CLASSIFICATION OF EVENTS RECORDED AS EITHER PREDICTABLE OR UNEXPECTED (PERCENTAGES BASED ON TOTAL ITEMS FOR EACH TITLE)

| Title | % predictable | % unexpected |
|---|---|---|
| The Times ... ... ... ... ... ... ... | 36 | 31 |
| The Guardian ... ... ... ... ... ... ... | 29 | 39 |
| The Daily Telegraph ... ... ... ... ... ... | 20 | 36 |
| Financial Times ... ... ... ... ... ... | 30 | 32 |
| Morning Star ... ... ... ... ... ... | 48 | 25 |
| Daily Express ... ... ... ... ... ... ... | 23 | 41 |
| Daily Mail ... ... ... ... ... ... ... | 17 | 48 |
| Daily Mirror ... ... ... ... ... ... ... | 15 | 47 |
| The Sun ... ... ... ... ... ... ... | 21 | 47 |
| Glasgow Herald ... ... ... ... ... ... | 30 | 40 |
| The Scotsman ... ... ... ... ... ... | 34 | 35 |

Generally, the more "Popular" newspapers are relatively less reliant on "predictable" news stories. The figure for the *Daily Mirror* is only 15% of all stories compared, to 36% for *The Times*. Interestingly, the coverage of the *Morning Star* is most strongly weighted towards the "predictable".

### (c) Estimate of "excitement" factor

The degree to which events in news reports can be considered dramatic or undramatic is an even more subjective matter. The findings are at least consistent with the measure of predictability and the differences between newspapers (although not large) are in a direction which might have been predicted. In all, 73% of stories were judged to be "*undramatic*" (the estimate was applied to the subject not to the manner of treatment) and only 20% as "dramatic", "exciting", or "violent". The remaining 7% could not be clearly allocated to either category The lowest proportion of "dramatic" events was in the *Financial Times* (9%) and the highest in the *Daily Mail* (29%).

### (d) Whether story is about an individual or a collectivity

With the primary aim of distinguishing coverage according to the degree of personalisation and to help in identifying main participants, stories were classified as being mainly about either an individual or a "collectivity"—group, organisation, Government, etc. The overall finding was that 44% of stories primarily referred to an individual and 51% to a collectivity. A general difference between newspapers, according with the quality/popular dimension again showed up. The proportions of stories with a predominantly "individual" reference were as follows: *The Times*, 42%; *The Guardian*, 40%; *The Daily Telegraph* 47%; *Financial Times* 42%; *Morning Star*, 36%; *Daily Express*, 52%; *Daily Mail*, 54%; *Daily Mirror*, 61%; *The Sun*, 55%; *The Scotsman*, 40%; *Glasgow Herald*, 36%.

252

# III  Analysis of foreign content according to countries involved

## 1. The location of events in the news

Several pieces of information were recorded about the countries involved in news reports. These included the following: whether the item was international or "foreign domestic"; whether this item involved one, two, or three or more countries; the actual names of the countries involved as participants or mentioned in a significant connection; where *two* countries were involved, certain *country pairs* were looked for (see columns 47–8 of Coding Frame in Appendix E1); the main country or area where the event occurred or to which the report referred, grouped by continent; finally, whether or not Britain was involved in some way in an event occurring abroad, and similarly for the United States involvement outside the USA. The number of approaches mentioned reflects the complexity of what might seem a relatively simple task. In fact, it is not easy to give a picture of the geography of world events in the news except in approximate terms and there will always be alternative possibilities for expressing the result. Several difficulties are involved. Firstly, foreign news is frequently not a matter of a single discrete event occurring in a foreign country. Secondly, two or more countries are often involved. Thirdly, the "home" country (here Britain) is often a party to an event involving two or more countries. Fourthly, where more than one country is involved it is not always easy to judge which country is mainly involved. Fifthly, it is not always possible to say where an event occurs or which country a report mainly refers to; this is especially true of diplomatic events or news, which often seem to occur in the home country itself (eg ministerial statement on foreign affairs). Sixthly, when a discrete event occurs in a foreign country, there is often an indirect British involvement or a direct relevance to stated British interests or people (hence the coding for "British involvement").

As a result of all these difficulties, the findings have to be treated with caution, since more judgement (possibly subjective) is involved than appears likely at first sight. It is also difficult to give any straightforward account of the frequency of reference to different countries. While this would be possible by counting all references to named participant countries, this information is not conveniently available. Only data which could be transferred on to punched cards are dealt with in this report and the task of recording all country references exhaustively on punched cards was regarded as too time-consuming to be worthwhile. In the light of these comments, it is intended simply to report the findings as they have been recorded in their differing ways, adding explanations, where necessary, about limitations in the data.

For the sample, as a whole, as we have seen, the division between "international" and "foreign domestic" content was 41% to 58%, with 1% unclassifiable as either. The division according to number of countries involved was: one country, 60%; two countries, 19%; more than two countries, 15%; other and United Nations, 5%. The apparent small inconsistency between the number of "foreign domestic" stories and "international" stories arises because in some cases an event involving only one named country could have clear international implications or occur outside the country's territory (there were a number of "space" stories involving either USA or USSR which belonged to this category). The most central evidence comes from the recording of the main country involved, where the instruction was to code for the country or area of *occurrence* of the event, or to which the event *referred*. Where two or more countries were involved, not within the same region, the instruction was to record the country or region of primary reference. Of the 2,520 items in the sample as a whole, all but 57 have been allocated to a country or region. The 57 cases not so coded were all international stories involving a pair of countries and coded accordingly. They were mainly diplomatic stories and some difficulty had been experienced in giving a primary single country of reference. It should be emphasised that the coding scheme only allowed for *one* country or region to be recorded, thus involving an incomplete representation of international stories. Bearing this in mind, the overall results for the whole sample are given in Table E7 for the main continents or regions.

TABLE E7

LOCATION OF EVENTS, OR PRIMARY REFERENCE OF REPORT BY CONTINENTAL GROUPINGS (WHOLE SAMPLE, 2,520)

|  | % |
|---|---|
| Europe (including USSR) ... ... ... ... ... ... ... ... | 40 |
| Middle East ... ... ... ... ... ... ... ... ... ... | 10 |
| Africa ... ... ... ... ... ... ... ... ... ... ... | 12 |
| Asia ... ... ... ... ... ... ... ... ... ... ... | 11 |
| Latin America ... ... ... ... ... ... ... ... ... | 3 |
| North America ... ... ... ... ... ... ... ... ... | 18 |
| Australasia ... ... ... ... ... ... ... ... ... | 3 |
| Other ... ... ... ... ... ... ... ... ... ... | 2 |
| No country coded ... ... ... ... ... ... ... ... | 2 |
| Total ... ... ... ... | 101 |

The predominance of Europe and North America is very noticeable, as is the low position of South America. A separate analysis of these results according to prominence produced similar results. For instance, the percentages of stories occurring as large frontpage news, by continental grouping, closely matched the figures in table E7, although it was noticeable that items relating to Asia got much less prominent treatment—only 2% of large front page items were about Asia, while 15% of stories under 10 col. cms. were so classified. Items relating to Latin America were also given relatively low prominence. Of all such items, 46% were under 10 col. cms. in length, while the corresponding figure for North American stories was 29% and for the sample as a whole, 30%.

In table E7, we can see a further degree of concentration on some areas in particular. The relatively high number of "foreign" news events apparently occurring in the British Isles are mainly accounted for by matters of diplomacy or international trade and economics. The United States and EEC countries between them account for 32% of all foreign stories. Generally, the smaller and/ or more remote the country or region, the less the coverage. The distribution does, however, also strongly reflect the happenings of the period:—the political changes in Portugal; the continuing security crisis in the Middle East and the oil situation; the conflict in Southern Africa; the last stages and aftermath of the

254

Vietnam war; the Stonehouse affair in Australia. Generally, there is a relative lack of attention to former colonies and dominions. Further, it would seem that the *routine* coverage of much of the world is very sparse (although it should be recalled that only twelve days' news are involved). One might interpret this pattern of coverage as suggesting that outside the EEC and USA it takes very significant and dramatic events or crises to qualify as newsworthy.

TABLE E8

LOCATION OF EVENTS, OR PRIMARY REFERENCE OF REPORT, BY COUNTRIES AND REGIONS WITHIN CONTINENTAL GROUPINGS (FREQUENCIES)

| 1. Europe | | | | n | 4. Asia | | | | | n |
|---|---|---|---|---|---|---|---|---|---|---|
| British Isles | ... | ... | ... | 154 | China | ... | ... | ... | ... | 32 |
| Scandinavia | ... | ... | ... | 45 | Japan | ... | ... | ... | ... | 34 |
| EEC country | ... | ... | ... | 358 | South East Asia | ... | ... | ... | 109 |
| Iberia | ... | ... | ... | 155 | India, Pakistan Sri Lanka | | ... | 69 |
| | | | | | Other Asian | | ... | ... | 25 |
| USSR | ... | ... | ... | 98 | | | | | | |
| Other East Europe | | ... | ... | 37 | | Total | ... | ... | 269 |
| Cyprus | ... | ... | ... | 44 | | | | | | |
| Other Europe | ... | ... | ... | 112 | | | | | | |
| | | | | | 5. South and Central America | | | | |
| | Total | ... | ... | 1,003 | | | | | | |
| | | | | | Chile | ... | ... | ... | ... | 13 |
| | | | | | Mexico | ... | ... | ... | ... | 4 |
| | | | | | Brazil | ... | ... | ... | ... | 7 |
| 2. Middle East | | | | | Argentina | ... | ... | ... | ... | 27 |
| | | | | | Caribbean | ... | ... | ... | ... | 11 |
| Israel | ... | ... | ... | 60 | Other | ... | ... | ... | ... | 19 |
| Egypt | ... | ... | ... | 28 | | | | | | |
| Israel's neighbours | | ... | ... | 61 | | Total | ... | ... | 81 |
| Other Middle East | | ... | ... | 105 | | | | | | |
| | | | | | 6. North America | | | | |
| | Total | ... | ... | 254 | | | | | | |
| | | | | | USA | ... | ... | ... | ... | 441 |
| | | | | | Canada | ... | ... | ... | ... | 18 |
| 3. Africa | | | | | Other | ... | ... | ... | ... | 1 |
| | | | | | | | | | | |
| North Africa | | | | | | Total | ... | ... | 480 |
| (exc. Egypt) | ... | ... | ... | 15 | | | | | | |
| West Africa (Br.) | ... | ... | ... | 13 | 7. Australasia | | | | |
| West Africa (Fr.) | ... | ... | ... | 13 | | | | | | |
| East and Central Africa | ... | ... | 102 | | Total | ... | ... | 63 |
| Southern Africa | ... | ... | ... | 128 | | | | | | |
| Other African | ... | ... | ... | 20 | 8. Other | | | | |
| | | | | | | | | | | |
| | Total | ... | ... | 291 | | Total | ... | ... | 42 |

## 2. Links between pairs of countries

A record was made of the occurrence of a number of specified links between countries. The record was made only for cases where no more than the two countries concerned were involved, in order to reduce ambiguity and the need for double counting. However, as a result, the absolute frequencies underestimate the extent of certain links. For instance, the United States was often involved with two foreign countries at one time (eg Israel and Egypt) and this would not be recorded. Consequently, the results should only be regarded as giving a relative idea of the importance of particular joint relationships in news reports. Table E9 gives the actual frequencies for the pairs which occurred most often. In all, 133 items were recorded as involving the specified pairings.

TABLE E9
FREQUENCY OF MAIN LINKS BETWEEN PAIRS OF COUNTRIES

| | |
|---|---|
| Great Britain—Soviet Union ... ... ... ... ... ... ... ... ... | 35 |
| Israel—Arab country ... ... ... ... ... ... ... ... ... | 25 |
| Great Britain—EEC as a whole ... ... ... ... ... ... ... ... | 21 |
| Great Britain—Africa ... ... ... ... ... ... ... ... ... ... | 21 |
| USA—Soviet Union ... ... ... ... ... ... ... ... ... | 17 |
| USA—Israel ... ... ... ... ... ... ... ... ... ... | 15 |
| Great Britain—USA ... ... ... ... ... ... ... ... ... | 14 |
| USA—Middle East ... ... ... ... ... ... ... ... ... | 14 |
| Great Britain—France ... ... ... ... ... ... ... ... | 13 |
| Great Britain—Eastern Europe ... ... ... ... ... ... ... ... | 11 |
| Great Britain—Middle East... ... ... ... ... ... ... ... | 10 |

The set of contacts between nations seems to predominantly involve the Middle East, Russia, East Europe and the United States. The figures themselves are an underestimate but they probably represent the true picture fairly well. The leading position of "contacts" between Britain and the Soviet Union is surprising and hard to account for in terms of any major event of 1975.

## 3. Home news abroad

Finally, there is the question of foreign news in which Britain or the USA is involved. The overall figures produced by the analysis show 321 items to have occurred abroad and to have involved Britain or British people or interests in some direct way. These items we might classify as "home news abroad". If we add to this 321 the 154 items located in the British Isles ("foreign news at home") the total for "British" news comes to 475, or 19% of the whole sample. A similar exercise for United States' involvement shows there to have been 214 items occurring outside the United States but directly involving that country. If this figure is added to the figure for occurrence in the USA (441), the total represents another 26% of all stories. Thus, in all, 45% of foreign news stories involved either Britain or the USA in some direct way.

The geographical distribution of British and United States' involvement is of some additional interest. For Britain, the main locations of the "home news abroad" items were: Europe, 38%; East, Central and South Africa, 14%; USA, 11%; all Asia, 10%. For the United States, the main locations were: Middle East, 35%; Europe, 32%; Asia 16%. The largest single case recorded was the United States' involvement with Israel, at 15% of all the United States' news abroad cases.

## 4. Comparisons between newspapers

The main features of each paper's coverage, according to different parts of the world can be derived from Table E10. While there is an overall similarity between titles there are also some fairly large variations. Thus, while all newspapers give the bulk of attention to Europe and North America jointly (ranging from 49% in *The Scotsman* to 64% in the *Daily Mirror*), the balance between these two main areas varies a good deal. Thus, the proportion of "European" items ranges from 47% in the *Morning Star* to 28% in the *Daily Mirror* and of North American items from 11% in the *Morning Star* and 13% in *The Scotsman* to 34% in the *Daily Mirror*. There is a general tendency for "Popular" papers to give rather more attention to North American news, relative to news from Europe. The same papers show less attention to Third World areas—South and Central America and Asia especially. The same papers also seem marginally more attentive to the former "white" colonies or dominions.

A closer examination of the "component parts" of the continental groupings did not add a great deal to these points, especially in view of the small numbers involved. In the reporting of European countries, we find *The Times* very high in reporting about EEC countries (43% of its European coverage) and the *Morning Star* very low (8%). The *Morning Star* was noticeably high in attention to the Soviet Union and Eastern Europe. Only the *Financial Times* gave any significant attention to West Africa, accounting for seven out of 26 items. A closer inspection of the coverage of Asian and Latin American countries confirms what has been suggested above. The coverage of Asia in the *Morning Star* was almost entirely concentrated on South East Asia.

## 5. The "news image" of different parts of the world

The study was designed to give some indication of the kind of picture of other parts of the world which might be conveyed in the press. This was to be achieved by comparing, in aggregate, the stories occurring or originating in one part of the world with those in others, in terms of a number of characteristics of the stories, including their main subject matter. The possibilities for comparative analysis are restricted by the limited sample size for some parts of the world and, of course, the restriction to the news on 12 particular days in the

TABLE E10

**FOREIGN CONTENT ITEMS, BY CONTINENTAL GROUPINGS: PERCENTAGE DISTRIBUTION IN 11 DAILY NEWSPAPERS***

| Title | Europe | Middle East | Africa | Asia | South & Central America | North America | Austra-lasia | Total |
|---|---|---|---|---|---|---|---|---|
| | % | % | % | % | % | % | % | % |
| The Times ... (n=504) | 45 | 8 | 12 | 11 | 4 | 17 | 2 | 99 |
| The Guardian ... (n=461) | 39 | 10 | 11 | 14 | 2 | 16 | 3 | 95 |
| The Daily Telegraph ... (n=404) | 33 | 13 | 11 | 14 | 3 | 19 | 2 | 95 |
| Financial Times (n=383) | 46 | 9 | 11 | 9 | 5 | 15 | 2 | 97 |
| Morning Star ... (n=138) | 47 | 10 | 13 | 10 | 5 | 11 | — | 96 |

257

| Title | Europe | Middle East | Africa | Asia | South & Central America | North America | Austra- lasia | Total |
|---|---|---|---|---|---|---|---|---|
| | % | % | % | % | % | % | % | % |
| Daily Express ... (n=158) | 38 | 12 | 11 | 6 | 1 | 25 | 6 | 99 |
| Daily Mail ... (n=122) | 30 | 10 | 11 | 4 | 1 | 30 | 6 | 92 |
| Daily Mirror ... (n=76) | 28 | 7 | 12 | 1 | 1 | 34 | 3 | 86 |
| The Sun ... (n=78) | 40 | 8 | 12 | 5 | 1 | 24 | 6 | 96 |
| The Scotsman** (n=119) | 36 | 8 | 15 | 17 | 3 | 13 | 3 | 91 |
| Glasgow Herald** (n=77) | 43 | 14 | 12 | 5 | 4 | 18 | 1 | 97 |

*Percentages add across rows. The shortfall from 100% is explained by lack of a specific country allocation in 4% of cases.

**Only one quarter (six issues) analysed.

year 1975. However, a few points can be made to help answer the question about tendencies in the news. It has been argued that people rely on the media for their impressions or images of foreign countries and that the press can give a mis-leading or unfavourable picture of other countries, either because of the in-fluence of news values which favour bad news or because of an editorial attitude of approval or disapproval, usually the latter. The same standard of objective reporting may be expected in respect of foreign news, but in practice the sanctions against partiality are much weaker than is the case with domestic news.

The results of this part of the enquiry are given in two parts: in Section IV, below, where the topics of news are looked at in relation to geographical area and here, where a number of news story characteristics are looked at in relation to the main location of events. The data discussed here, in brief, are somewhat less objective than on the question of story subject matter, since the assessments have to be approximate and involve some personal judgement. The relevant criteria had to do with whether stories were: action-orientated; predictable; dramatic; or generally "positive" or "negative" in the sense of being about good, beneficial or constructive events as against harmful, violent, or problematic matters (see Appendix E3 for a further discussion of the criteria). It should be mentioned that coders were also asked to make an overall assessment of each item in terms of whether it was clearly favourable or clearly unfavourable and critical of any country or main participant in a story. The fact that only 2·2% could be classified as favourable and 2·8% as unfavourable is a reflection of the general absence of overt value judgements.

The results of three indicators of story characteristics for the main continental groupings are given in Table E11, in summary form.

TABLE E11

COMPARISON BETWEEN CONTINENTAL GROUPINGS IN TERMS OF THREE
CHARACTERISTICS OF NEWS ITEMS: PERCENTAGE OF STORIES, BY REGION,
WHICH WERE (a) ACTION-ORIENTATED; (b) PREDICTABLE; (c) DRAMATIC

| Groupings | | | | | (a)<br>Action-<br>orientated | (b)<br>Predictable | (c)<br>Dramatic |
|---|---|---|---|---|---|---|---|
| | | | | | % | % | % |
| All Europe ... | ... | ... | ... | ... | 56 | 31 | 13 |
| Middle East | ... | ... | ... | ... | 62 | 28 | 29 |
| Africa | ... | ... | ... | ... | 64 | 35 | 32 |
| Asia | ... | ... | ... | ... | 64 | 21 | 31 |
| South America | ... | ... | ... | ... | 68 | 28 | 27 |
| North America | ... | ... | ... | ... | 54 | 25 | 19 |
| Australasia | ... | ... | ... | ... | 58 | 28 | 20 |

The three indices all tell much the same story, and the result would not be
materially altered by giving figures for the rest of the classification. Essentially,
we find a tendency for content relating to Europe, and to lesser extent North
America, to be less dramatic and exciting, more likely to consist of "diary"
events, known in advance, and to be less concerned with action. The higher the
proportion of economic and diplomatic news, the more likely this is to be the
case as can be seen from IV, 6(c) below. News from Asia and Latin America
is most likely to show the reverse characteristics to these mentioned.

The same general tendency is reflected in the results of the classification of
stories according to their predominant character as "good" or "bad" news. For
the most part, we might expect the dramatic and unexpected to be more "negative" than news which is predictable and undramatic. The results of the comparison are given in the following table.

TABLE E12

ASSESSMENT OF STORY CONTENT AS PREDOMINANTLY POSITIVE ("GOOD
NEWS") OR NEGATIVE ("BAD NEWS"): PERCENTAGE OF STORIES, BY REGION,
CLASSIFIED IN THIS WAY

| Groupings | | | | Positive<br>(Good news) | Negative<br>(Bad news) | Ratio |
|---|---|---|---|---|---|---|
| | | | | % | % | |
| All Europe ...<br>(exc. Britain) | ... | ... | (n=847) | 35 | 44 | 1:1.3 |
| Middle East | ... | ... | (n=254) | 25 | 51 | 1:2.0 |
| Africa | ... | ... | (n=291) | 29 | 49 | 1:1.7 |
| Asia | ... | ... | (n=269) | 25 | 48 | 1:1.9 |
| South America | ... | ... | (n=81) | 19 | 63 | 1:3.3 |
| North America | ... | ... | (n=460) | 21 | 52 | 1:2.5 |
| Australasia | ... | ... | (n=63) | 10 | 68 | 1:6.8 |
| All items | ... | ... | (n=2,520) | 26 | 48 | 1:1.8 |

If the figures given for the ratio of "positive" to "negative" reporting are
taken as an indication of position on a single dimension, then Europe represents
one pole (positive) and the pattern of reporting for South America the other
(leaving Australasia aside as a special case, since it is effectively only one country).

The other continental groupings are close enough to the average, apart from North America, where the balance of reporting is "unduly" weighted towards "negative events". It seems clear that Europe has the most evenly balanced reporting in terms of this criterion and it does not seem to be merely a function of frequency of items, so that the more the number of items, the higher the proportion of those which are positive. In general, the conclusion that news from nearer home is less likely to be characterised by "bad" news, is in line with findings just presented about story characteristics.

A more detailed analysis of individual countries within the main continental groupings adds a few points of interest to this conclusion, especially in relation to Europe, where the numbers are large enough to justify sub-comparisons. First, it is noticeable that in stories involving Britain (not included in figures in Table E12), the balance actually favours "positive" news over negative to a small degree. Secondly, Scandinavia has the highest ratio of "positive" to "negative" stories and Spain and Portugal the lowest. Thirdly, stories about the USSR and Eastern Europe report predominantly positive news. Jointly, the ratio is 36% positive to 29% negative, and for the Soviet Union alone it is 41% to 22%. Evidently, there are quite large variations between countries which reflect the events of the period and probably (as in the case of the Soviet Union) the kind of news which is most available. In the case of the Middle East, it is Syria and Jordan which had the most negative pattern of reporting. For other continental groupings, the figures are less reliable, but, not surprisingly, Southern Africa and South-East Asia contribute heavily to a "negative" tendency in news pattern. Within the "Asia" category, however, it is really only China and Japan which are exceptions to the strongly negative balance. In South America, Chile and Argentina receive the most "bad news" reporting.

These findings are only indicative, but they support the conclusion that news is more likely to be negative than positive and that, other things being equal, the more distant and the lower the level of economic development, the more likely are events reported to be negative. For whatever reason, Communist countries have a more balanced reporting according to the criterion discussed here. There is little sign of overt "bias", as this last point helps to demonstrate, but it is possible that a negative "image" of certain parts of the world is inadvertently created in a fairly systematic way.

# IV    Main topics of foreign content

## 1.  General coverage

In advance of the analysis, a set of 29 categories or sub-categories of subject matter was devised and coders were instructed to allocate each item to a topic heading, and if necessary to a second heading if no main topic could be established. Obviously, the complexity of many stories is not adequately reflected by this simple categorisation, but it is a way of indicating approximately the nature of content. In the event, very few items were allocated to more than one topic and the total number of topic codings, at 2,557, only exceeds the number of cases by 37. The full details of topic codings are given in Table E13. In some cases it seems that sub-categories have not been sufficiently detailed. For instance, more than half of the foreign (domestic) political stories and of the economic stories are in residual categories. The familiar difficulty of a classification scheme which is intended to provide a set of exclusive categories can also be noted. The distinction between "international" and "foreign domestic" content which has already been made, does not apply in the same way to the data discussed here. It has only been used to differentiate political content. Content in any of the other topic categories could be either "domestic" or involve more than one country.

In order of importance, the main general areas of coverage were: foreign political, 21%; international diplomatic, 20%; economic, 20%. Of the items categorised as "foreign political", almost half dealt with conflict or crisis.

## 2.  Topics and location

The purpose in looking at the relationship between geographical area and topic is to assess the balance and diversity of reporting of different regions and to shed light on the factors which make some parts of the world newsworthy. In the limited time period represented by this sample we would expect coverage to reflect only the particular events of the period, but some indications of general tendencies can be obtained from this limited evidence. Table E14 shows the comparative percentage figures for each main area according to seven main categories of content. The only topics not accounted for in the table are "aid" and the residual category, accounting for seven and 93 items, respectively.

TABLE E13

MAIN TOPICS OF FOREIGN CONTENT IN COMPLETE SAMPLE, FREQUENCIES AND PERCENTAGES BASED ON n=2,520

| Main topics | n | % |
|---|---|---|
| 1. International, political or diplomatic    ...    ...    ...    ... | 502 | 20 |
| 2. Foreign, domestic, political | | |
|    (a) Non-violent, constitutional, conflict or crisis...    ...    ... | 101 | 4 |
|    (b) Violent or revolutionary conflict    ...    ...    ...    ... | 131 | 5 |
|    (c) Elections, campaigns, appointments ...    ...    ...    ... | 46 | 2 |
|    (d) Other political matters ...    ...    ...    ...    ... | 262 | 10 |
| Sub total:    ...    ... | 540 | 21 |

261

| Main topic | | | | | | | *n* | % |
|---|---|---|---|---|---|---|---|---|
| 3. Military and defence | | | | | | | | |
| (a) Armed conflict ... | ... | ... | ... | ... | ... | ... | 81 | 3 |
| (b) Peace moves ... | ... | ... | ... | ... | ... | ... | 35 | 1 |
| (c) Other military and defence | ... | ... | ... | ... | ... | 89 | 4 |
| Sub total: | | | | | ... | ... | 205 | 8 |
| 4. Economic, trade, financial, industrial | | | | | | | | |
| (a) Agreements on trade, tariffs, etc. | | ... | ... | ... | ... | 74 | 3 |
| (b) Industrial projects | ... | ... | ... | ... | ... | ... | 33 | 1 |
| (c) Agricultural matters | ... | ... | ... | ... | ... | ... | 27 | 1 |
| (d) Industrial disputes | ... | ... | ... | ... | ... | ... | 64 | 3 |
| (e) Other industrial relations | ... | ... | ... | ... | ... | 33 | 1 |
| (f) Other economic ... | ... | ... | ... | ... | ... | ... | 258 | 10 |
| Sub total: | | | | | ... | ... | 489 | 19 |
| 5. Aid and development | ... | ... | ... | ... | ... | ... | 17 | 1 |
| Sub total: | | | | | ... | ... | 17 | 1 |
| 6. Crime and legal matters | | | | | | | | |
| (a) Ordinary civil crime | ... | ... | ... | ... | ... | ... | 147 | 6 |
| (b) Crime and punishment, political or military | | | | ... | ... | 189 | 8 |
| (c) Other ... | ... | ... | ... | ... | ... | ... | 38 | 2 |
| Sub total: | | | | | ... | ... | 374 | 16 |
| 7. Social welfare | | | | | | | | |
| (a) Problems ... | ... | ... | ... | ... | ... | ... | 16 | 1 |
| (b) Achievements | ... | ... | ... | ... | ... | ... | 14 | 1 |
| (c) Other ... | ... | ... | ... | ... | ... | ... | 12 | 1 |
| Sub total: | | | | | ... | ... | 42 | 3 |
| 8. Culture, arts ... | ... | ... | ... | ... | ... | ... | 31 | 1 |
| 9. Scientific, technical, medical | ... | ... | ... | ... | ... | 55 | 2 |
| 10. Student matters | ... | ... | ... | ... | ... | ... | 8 | — |
| 11. Entertainment, show business | ... | ... | ... | ... | ... | 15 | 1 |
| 12. Personalities—show business | ... | ... | ... | ... | ... | 36 | 1 |
| 13. Personalities—other... | ... | ... | ... | ... | ... | ... | 28 | 1 |
| 14. Human interest, sex news ... | ... | ... | ... | ... | ... | 108 | 4 |
| 15. Ecology, environment | ... | ... | ... | ... | ... | ... | 24 | 1 |
| 16. Other (including natural disasters) | ... | ... | ... | ... | 93 | 4 |
| Total: | | | | | ... | ... | 2,557 | 103% |

There are some important differences between the "topic profile" of different countries. Firstly, Europe, the most extensively covered area, seems also to have the most "balanced" coverage in terms of these seven broad subjects. About a fifth of the items are devoted to each of diplomatic, foreign political, and economic and trade matters. Crime accounts for 16% and welfare and human interest for 7% each. The distribution for North America differs only in the much lower attention to diplomatic news (understandable since fewer separate countries are involved) and the higher proportion to human interest and show business content. Of Middle East news, 58% is accounted for by diplomatic and military news. Africa is "dominated" in the news by international or domestic politics—mainly a reflection of the importance of Rhodesia, Angola and South Africa. There is a notable lack of human interest or show business content from any of the Third World areas. In general, the lower the total coverage the more it seems to concentrate on a few topic areas, reflecting the specific events of the time sampled.

TABLE E14

RELATIONSHIP BETWEEN MAIN TOPICS AND LOCATION OF EVENT:
PERCENTAGES OF ITEMS IN EACH CONTINENTAL GROUPING ACCORDING TO
SEVEN MAIN TOPIC AREAS

| Topic | LOCATION | | | | | | |
| --- | --- | --- | --- | --- | --- | --- | --- |
| | Europe | North America | Middle East | Africa | South America | Austral-asia | Asia |
| | % | % | % | % | % | % | % |
| 1. International diplomatic ...    ... | 21 | 7 | 32 | 35 | 16 | 6 | 12 |
| 2. Domestic political... | 20 | 17 | 14 | 35 | 35 | 28 | 27 |
| 3. Military, defence  ... | 4 | 5 | 26 | 7 | — | — | 13 |
| 4. Economic trade   ... | 24 | 24 | 13 | 9 | 25 | 10 | 14 |
| 5. Crime, police    ... | 16 | 20 | 6 | 10 | 16 | 30 | 15 |
| 6. Welfare, culture, science    ...    ... | 7 | 5 | 4 | 4 | — | 19 | 5 |
| 7. Show business, personalities, human interest    ...    ... | 7 | 17 | 4 | 1 | 4 | 32 | 4 |
| Total % *     ... | 99 | 95 | 95 | 101 | 96 | 125 | 90 |
| Base for %    ... | 1,003 | 460 | 254 | 291 | 81 | 63 | 269 |

*The percentages do not add up to 100% for two reasons: (1), they are based on the total number of items per country, not the total of topic codings; (2), double coding of topics was permitted, although unusual. In the case of Australia, however, there was extensive double coding, mainly because of the Stonehouse case.

## 3. Sub-topic and location

A more detailed examination of sub-topics within the categories shown in Table E13 reveals some further differences according to location.

(a) The balance between "crisis-related" and other foreign domestic political content varies somewhat from location to location. Overall, the balance between

263

"crisis" and other content is 43%: 57%. For Europe, the ratio is almost identical, but for North America it is 23%: 77%. For the Middle East, it is 80%: 20%.

(*b*) The balance between "non-violent" and "violent" political conflict also varies a good deal from area to area. For Asia, Africa and the Middle East, the balance is strongly weighted towards violent conflict, while for Europe there is a predominance of non-violent conflict and this is markedly so for North America.

(*c*) News of industrial relations is "concentrated" in Europe (46% of all such items) or in North America (35%).

(*d*) The balance between "ordinary" or civil crime and crime matters with a political or military reference also differs significantly as between Europe and North America, with a predominance of civil crime in North American news.

## 4. Comparisons between individual countries

Within some continental groupings, differences between individual countries in their content profiles can also be identified. Since only Europe provides sufficient numbers for a detailed comparison, Table E15 relates only to some national areas within Europe.

TABLE E15

RELATIONSHIP BETWEEN TOPICS AND LOCATION: PERCENTAGES OF ITEMS IN EACH OF FOUR EUROPEAN AREAS ACCORDING TO SELECTED TOPICS

| Topic | Area in Europe | | | |
|---|---|---|---|---|
| | EEC (excl. G.B.) (n=358) | USSR & E. Europe (n=135) | Spain & Portugal (n=155) | Scandinavia (n=45) |
| | % | % | % | % |
| 1. International, diplomatic ... ... | 12 | 21 | 10 | 44 |
| 2. Political, conflict/crisis ... ... | 4 | 1 | 34 | — |
| 3. Political, other ... ... ... | 10 | 12 | 27 | 11 |
| 4. Military, defence ... ... ... | 3 | 7 | 1 | 4 |
| 5. Economic ... ... ... ... | 40 | 16 | 5 | 24 |
| 6. Crime, police, military or political | 8 | 9 | 10 | 2 |
| 7. Crime, police, other ... ... | 10 | 4 | 5 | — |
| 8. Culture, art, science ... ... | 4 | 11 | — | 7 |
| 9. Human interest ... ... ... | 5 | 5 | 2 | — |
| Total % ... | 96 | 86 | 94 | 92 |

If coverage of EEC countries is taken as the norm, then coverage of Socialist countries is characterised by a high attention to diplomatic news and a low attention to economic news. There is also relatively more attention to political as against ordinary crime. There is a notable absence of crisis or conflict-related political news, but more about defence matters. The coverage of Spain and Portugal is much more divergent, with high attention to domestic political news

264

(61% of items), much of it conflict-related, and little attention to economic news. We should probably regard the news pattern in relation to the Socialist countries as, of the four areas, the most "normal" in 1975, in view of the referendum over EEC entry in Britain and the political crisis in Portugal. Scandinavia figures in British newspapers primarily for its role in international diplomacy (especially the Helsinki Security Conference).

## 5. Comparisons between newspapers on topics of foreign coverage

The data on which to make comparisons are given in Appendix E4. The most evident pattern of differentiation is between "Qualities" and "Populars". The former (*The Times, The Guardian,* and *The Daily Telegraph*) give relatively more attention than the populars (*Daily Express, Daily Mail, Daily Mirror* and *The Sun*) to news about diplomatic matters, non-crisis foreign political news, economic news and news of welfare, culture and the arts. They give relatively less news of matters connected with show business, personalities and human interest generally, and also less to crime news. The comparison is summarised in the following figures, averaging the percentages for the two groups mentioned and grouping the categories mentioned. (The summary data are derived from Appendix E4).

Within these two groups of newspapers there is not a great deal of variation, although *The Guardian* and *The Sun* would stand out as most opposed in respect of the balance of content between the two broad groupings of "heavier" and

TABLE E16

**SUMMARY COMPARISON OF THREE "QUALITY" NATIONAL DAILIES AND FOUR "POPULARS" ON TWO MAIN GROUPS OF FOREIGN CONTENT TOPICS**

| Topics | Three "Qualities" (ave.) | Four "Populars" (ave.) |
|---|---|---|
| | % | % |
| A. Diplomatic; "foreign political"; economic-welfare, culture, science ... | 64 | 44 |
| B. Show business; personalities; human interest; crime news ... ... ... | 20 | 47 |
| C. Other ... ... ... ... ... | 16 | 13 |
| | 100% | 100% |

"lighter" foreign content. *The Guardian* ratio is 70%:17% and *The Sun* ratio, 39%:52%. Other points to note about individual newspapers include the following. Both *The Scotsman* and *Glasgow Herald* are close to the "quality" average, with the former even more inclined towards "serious" coverage than *The Guardian*. *The Times* has notably high coverage of economic news (19%). Such news also accounts for 42% of *Financial Times* items, with diplomatic news following at 20% and welfare, culture and art at 11%. The *Morning Star* concentrates on diplomatic news (33%) and foreign political economic content, but also has a largish component of welfare, culture and art news (11%). The balance between "crisis" or "conflict" political news and other sorts of political news tends to favour the latter in the "Qualities" and is evenly divided in the "Populars". Similarly, there is a difference in the kind of crime and police news.

265

The "Populars" tend to emphasise ordinary crime or police action, while the "Qualities" tend to divide attention evenly between "ordinary" and "political" crime.

## 6. Other aspects of the topics of foreign content

### (a) British involvement

The extent to which foreign news content involved Britain or the United States has been described in Section III, 3 above. Here we can note the kind of foreign news most likely to have been reported as involving Britain. The total number of items coded in this way was 405, or 16% of the whole sample of items. With two main exceptions, "British involvement" was observed to occur in an expected amount in the main topic categories. The exceptions were the high concentration in diplomatic news and the low occurrence in respect of foreign domestic political news. A similar pattern was noted for items coded as involving the USA.

### (b) Collective or individual reference of news items

The classification of each item according to whether the reference was primarily to a person or to an organisation was made partly to provide some measure of "personalisation" of news. We can see how different topics emerged according to this criterion. In the sample as a whole, 44% were classified as primarily about individuals and 51% about "collectivities" (see Section VI, 2 below for more details). The breakdown varied, however, according to topics as follows: diplomatic, 57%; "individual" and "collective" 41%; foreign political, 45%/54%; military, 24%/59%; economic, 31%/66%; crime and police, 50%/46%. The category most likely to be dealt with in terms of individual actors is that of international diplomacy. The reverse is true of defence and economic news.

More interesting, perhaps, is the variation between newspapers on this matter. Generally, the "Popular" papers are somewhat more likely to deal with all news in individual terms (see Section VI below) but the difference is very marked in relation to international and diplomatic news. This tendency can be seen clearly from the following figures which show the proportion of "*international diplomatic*" items classified as having a mainly "individual" reference (the calculations exclude items of uncertain classification):

| | | | | | |
|---|---|---|---|---|---|
| *The Times* ... | ... 45% | *Morning Star* | ... 47% | *The Sun* ... | ... 86% |
| *The Guardian* | ... 59% | *Daily Express* | ... 73% | *Glasgow Herald* | ... 65% |
| *The Daily Telegraph* | ... 64% | *Daily Mail* ... | ... 89% | *The Scotsman* | ... 48% |
| *Financial Times* | ... 56% | *Daily Mirror* | ... 83% | | |

### (c) Story characteristics according to topic

Each item was classified according to a number of characteristics already described in Sections II and III. The evidence from this analysis sheds some further light on the differences of content indicated by the broad topic categories. Three indicators showed most tendency to discriminate: whether an item was about an *action* rather than a statement or background matter; whether the event was *predictable* or not; whether the item was judged *dramatic* or not. The following is a summary of the divergences from the average for each main category of content: diplomatic stories are more predictable and less dramatic;

266

economic stories are also undramatic and less action-orientated; crime and police stories are very action-orientated and unpredictable; cultural news is more predictable and less dramatic. To some extent, these variations may be helpful in accounting for the difference between newspapers described in 5 above.

### (d) Prominence accorded to different topics

An analysis of relative space and prominence given to different types of subject matter showed these to be largely reflective of the order of frequency. In general, the three most frequent topics—international politics, domestic politics and economic matters—each had lower proportions of very small items (0–10 col. cms.), while minority topics (numerically), such as social welfare and cultural matters, had much higher proportions of brief items. The category of "other" foreign news is very heavily composed of small items—70% are under 11 col. cms. and 87% under 21 col. cms. Similarly prominence, as reflected in front page location, follows an identical pattern. It is interesting to note, however, that "personality" and "human interest" stories have an above average tendency to appear prominently on front pages despite their being mainly short news items. This probably reflects a different policy on the part of "Popular" newspapers.

# V Themes of foreign news content

## 1. Introduction

The inclusion in the coding scheme of a number of possible themes of news reporting was originally intended to capture some aspects of news reporting which might "cut across" the topic classification. Certain recurrent "news-angles", which provide the background to the news and the basis for selecting an event for report, might be reflected in these themes, a full list of which is given in the coding scheme (Appendix E1, cols. 57 to 75). In the event, the results suggest that such themes are either in general not very much in evidence, or that the particular themes anticipated were not especially appropriate to the brief periods analysed. This comment is based on the rather low frequency of references to the themes actually recorded even allowing for some under-recording (on average only one theme was recorded for every two items). The second explanation suggested is very plausible, since only 12 days in two separate quarters were studied and foreign news is probably more likely to reflect, in its incidence, the specific events of a period than is domestic news which gives coverage on a more continuous basis to some general kinds of subject matter, irrespective of peaks and troughs of activity. In the circumstances, it seems best to treat the evidence as indicating something more about the specific sub-topics of foreign reporting, within the more general categories already discussed. The overall results of this part of the analysis are given in Table E17.

TABLE E17

MAIN THEMES OF FOREIGN REPORTING, TO WHICH A CLEAR AND SPECIFIC REFERENCE WAS IDENTIFIED, IN ORDER OF RELATIVE FREQUENCY (% BASED ON WHOLE SAMPLE OF 2,520).

| Themes | No. of references | % |
|---|---|---|
| 1. Economic problems ... ... ... ... ... ... ... | 195 | 7·7 |
| 2. Internal political instability ... ... ... ... ... ... | 180 | 7·1 |
| 3. Oil... ... ... ... ... ... ... ... ... | 120 | 4·8 |
| 4. Internal left-wing activity ... ... ... ... ... ... | 85 | 3·4 |
| 5. The media-TV, press, etc. ... ... ... ... ... | 82 | 3·3 |
| 6. Détente, East-West coexistence ... ... ... ... ... | 81 | 3·2 |
| 7. Soviet and other Communist external involvement ... ... ... | 81 | 3·2 |
| 8. Economic success ... ... ... ... ... ... | 80 | 3·2 |
| 9. Apartheid, colour bar, black power, anti-white feeling ... ... | 68 | 2·7 |
| 10. Autocracy, repression, torture ... ... ... ... ... ... | 60 | 2·4 |
| 11. Secession (as internal problem) ... ... ... ... ... | 55 | 2·2 |
| 12. Sex aspects ... ... ... ... ... ... ... | 49 | 1·9 |
| 13. Royalty ... ... ... ... ... ... ... ... | 41 | 1·6 |
| 14. Espionage ... ... ... ... ... ... ... | 41 | 1·6 |
| All other references ... ... ... ... ... ... ... | 286 | 11·3 |

In summary, the main concern of external news seems to be with foreign domestic, economic and political problems, with oil, with internal left-wing or external Communist activity, with détente and with problems of race and racial conflict. Amongst the themes included in the coding scheme which apparently received minimal attention, one might particularly note: dissidence in the USSR; coloured immigration; Ulster and the IRA; poverty and famine; East-West conflict. These omissions may be a matter of sampling accident. The general framework for news in this period seems to be shaped by a concern with relations between the Communist and non-Communist world and with world economic recession or recovery. Within this framework, various specific kinds of "bad news" take precedence over good news.

## 2. Themes and topics

By cross-tabulating theme references against topics we can learn a little more about the latter and vice versa, but the data are either too fragmentary or too self-evident to be worth detailed reporting. A few points can be added to what has been already said about topics. Firstly, a fair amount of "international diplomatic" news was evidently concerned with East-West relations. Secondly, a rather high proportion of internal political news was concerned with internal problems and instability. Thirdly, economic news was more likely to be about problems than successes, since 31% of economic items carried a reference to problems and only 12% to success. Fourthly, 28% of items categorised as "military or defence" matters contained a reference to Soviet or other Communist involvement in other countries.

## 3. Themes and location

As a contribution to further clarifying the meaning and context of themes we can look at their incidence in relation to different geographical areas, much as in sections IV 2 and 3 above, where topics were examined according to location. At first sight there seems a fair amount of similarity between different parts of the world in terms of general news themes. However, there are also important variations and certain themes are more likely than others to characterise different parts of the world. The evidence can best be reported by describing the main departures from the average pattern shown in Table E17. The pattern for Europe is very close to that average, although it is also apparent that news of Portugal and Spain has a very distinctive characterisation, since together they account for 24% of all references to "political instability" and 38% of all references to "internal left-wing activity". The balance between "economic problems" and "economic success" is also more weighted towards success than the average and distinctly more so than in the case of North America. Middle East news strongly emphasises the themes of "Soviet involvement", "oil" and "instability" in equal degree. African news is dominated by "apartheid" and related issues, with "instability" and "secession" as secondary themes. Reference to "economic problems" exceed references to success by 11 to 1. The secession theme relates mainly to Central Africa. For Asia, the themes of "political instability" and "Communist involvement" lead, but the Vietnam war news largely accounts for this. For North America, the themes of "economic problems", "oil" and "sex" lead, in that order. The only three references to "national stereotypes" all relate to Australia.

## 4. Comparisons between newspapers

When allowance is made for the variation in numbers of items between different newspapers, the general distribution of themes is very similar. There are, however, some exceptions which suggest, firstly, a general difference between "Quality" and "Popular" newspapers and, secondly, some particular tendencies on the part of individual newspapers. On the first point, the four

"Popular" national dailies are characterised by a disproportionate tendency to refer to the themes of sex and royalty and to avoid references to: autocracy and torture, fascist activity, left-wing activity, apartheid and Soviet or Communist involvement. On the whole, this only reflects their lower proportions of political news. Taking each paper in turn, particular features of coverage include the following (the complete table is in Appendix E5): *The Times* refers to oil relatively more than other newspapers (27% of references, 20% of items) apart from the *Financial Times* (22% of references, 15% of items). It also accounts for 28% of references to autocracy/torture. *The Guardian* also differentially refers to internal left-wing activity (31% of all references); to autocracy and torture (28%); to apartheid and fascist activity.

*The Daily Telegraph* refers relatively more to détente (25% of references) and less to apartheid or colour bar generally. The *Financial Times* concentrates more on economic themes. The *Morning Star* differentially notices the same four themes which appeared relatively more in *The Guardian*. The numbers of theme references in popular papers are generally too small to allow much useful comment beyond the general differentiation from quality papers. Comment on *The Scotsman* and *Glasgow Herald* is less useful, for similar reasons. Their most noticeable feature is the absence of any references to economic *success*, although it should be remembered that only six issues of each were analysed.

One might discern a slight tendency or pattern in these results, along the following lines: *The Times* and *Financial Times* share a more economic orientation; *The Guardian* and *Morning Star* share a greater attention to seemingly "liberal" concerns or to themes which involve political conflict between left and right. The two papers together account for: 42% of references to internal left-wing activity; 50% of references to autocracy or torture; 44% of references to apartheid; and 50% of references to fascist activity. On each of these, *The Daily Telegraph* has a lower proportion of references than its share of all items. Otherwise, the latter paper has no very distinctive inclination to a particular theme, apart from détente. The distinction mentioned here can only be regarded as a rather shadowy tendency which would need much more extensive research for confirmation.

# VI Sources and participants

Only limited data could be collected about either source or participant, in the absence of external information and in view of the complexity of many stories. The results of this analysis can only give a very approximate indication of the kinds of source referred to in news reports.

## 1. Sources

Three main questions about source were asked: whether a report was based on a direct report, on a quotation, or simply on an attribution to a source, or was not attributed; whether the media (of the country concerned) were the source or not; whether a report was attributed to a news agency or similar news service, to a correspondent or to some other specified source. The results for the whole sample of 2,520 items can be summarised as follows:

| (a) | | |
|---|---|---|
| Reported from a specified source | ... ... ... ... ... ... | 14% |
| Quoted from a specified source | ... ... ... ... ... ... | 9% |
| Attributed to a specified source | ... ... ... ... ... ... | 50% |
| Not attributed | ... ... ... ... ... ... ... | 5% |
| Other/mixed ... ... ... | ... ... ... ... ... | 23% |
| | Total ... ... | 101% |

(b) The local media were given as source in 7% of cases.

| (c) | | |
|---|---|---|
| Credited to a news agency ... | ... ... ... ... ... ... | 15% |
| Credited to own correspondent | ... ... ... ... ... ... | 20% |
| Credited to other source ... | ... ... ... ... ... ... | 38% |
| No source given, unsure ... | ... ... ... ... ... ... | 25% |
| | Total ... ... | 98%. |

The main conclusions to be drawn from these overall results are, firstly, that items are not generally based on direct reports or quotations and, secondly, that relatively few items are specifically attributed to news agencies.

A separate analysis of these results for individual newspapers showed up some apparent differences of policy or practice. On differences in respect of reporting or quoting from sources, there is little that can reliably be said. On the use of local media as source, it was the "Quality" papers who were most inclined to credit local media as source. Of the English papers, *The Daily Telegraph* led in this matter, with 10% of its reports so attributed. More differences showed up between papers in the matter of attribution to a news agency or not. Most striking is the virtual absence of attributions to news agency sources from the *Daily Express*, *Daily Mail*, *The Sun* and *Daily Mirror*. Of the other papers, *The Scotsman*, at 51%, is the most inclined to credit items to agency sources (or *The Times* foreign news service), followed by the *Morning Star* at 27%. Variation between newspapers on types or attribution to sources cannot be reported because of some apparent differences of coding practice. In some cases "own correspondent" has been taken to refer to a named correspondent not, as intended, to the appearance of that particular phrase or its equivalent. For this reason the figures in (c) above will over-represent the "own correspondent" attributions. Even so, it is the case that, in general, *The Times* and *The Daily Telegraph* were most inclined to make this kind of attribution.

## 2. Participants

The analysis of story participants could only be accomplished in the most general terms, given the diversity of subject matter. The main aim was to identify the main kinds of "actors" (in terms of their social position) in stories and the main sorts of institution figuring prominently in news content. The initial distinction between an "individual" and "a collective" actor has already been discussed in Section IV, 6 above. Following that division, items were then classified according to sub categories under each of the two headings. The results for the sample as a whole are given in Table E18.

**TABLE E18**

DISTRIBUTION OF ITEMS (a) ACCORDING TO 11 CATEGORIES OF MAIN INDIVIDUAL PARTICIPANT AND, (b) ACCORDING TO NINE CATEGORIES OF TYPE OF COLLECTIVITY PRIMARILY INVOLVED (n=2,520)

| (a) Type of individual participant | % | (b) Type of Collectivity | % |
|---|---|---|---|
| Official, diplomat, foreign minister | 14 | Executive or legislature ... | 21 |
| Prime Minister, elected leader | 7 | Police or army ... ... | 7 |
| Head of State or representative | 5 | Business firm ... ... ... | 3 |
| Celebrity, star or "personality" | 4 | Political Party ... ... | 2 |
| Opposition leader, politician ... | 3 | Trade Union ... ... ... | 2 |
| Military leader ... ... | 2 | Legal body ... ... ... | 2 |
| Business leader ... ... | 2 | City or town ... ... ... | 1 |
| Artist, intellectual ... ... | 1 | Religious body ... ... | * |
| Religious leader ... ... | 1 | Other ... ... ... ... | 14 |
| Trade union leader ... ... | * | Not about collectivity ... | 47 |
| Other, not classified ... ... | 6 | | |
| Not mainly about individual ... | 55 | Total ... | 99% |
| Total ... | 100% | | |

*Indicates entry below 0·5%

One should view the figures as approximations, given the requirement to confine the recording to only *one* main individual or collectivity. This will have tended to reduce the apparent representation of subsidiary organisations or less "important" kinds of participant. Even so, the general impression is of a very high concentration on "official" activities and established institutions. The figures seem to confirm that news does concentrate most heavily on the powerful and on those aspects of the exercise of power which are relatively public. This is not difficult to understand and is consistent with the evidence about topics of coverage already discussed. However, it does also confirm that foreign coverage is not in general likely to tell us a great deal about the views and activities of those outside official or established circles or in institutions which are not politically central. The analysis of topics of news coverage in Section IV showed that 41% of items were primarily about international or domestic politics. If we add together the categories in Table E18 which relate directly to political actors or political institutions the total for the six categories is 52%, which suggests that the news is even more "political" than the earlier figure indicated.

The general difference between newspapers in their seeming preference for individual or collective actors has already been discussed (IV, 6) and it was noted that "quality" newspapers seemed less likely to deal with stories in individual

272

terms. A comparison between newspapers in respect of categories of individual or collectivity adds little to that, since papers did not generally vary a great deal in the distribution between categories. However, a few points can be noted. The *Financial Times* had the highest proportion of items featuring officials or diplomats (22%) and *The Sun* the lowest (4%). The popular papers generally had higher proportions of stars or celebrities (eg *The Sun* and *Daily Mirror* both at 15%). *The Guardian* accounted for seven out of all 21 items with artists or intellectuals as main participant. *The Guardian* also accounted for a third of all references to political parties as the main collectivity involved.

# VII  Summary and Conclusions

(The numbers in brackets refer to the relevant sections of the report)

## 1. Quantity and distribution of foreign content

Even according to the relatively narrow definition of foreign content adopted for this study, the amount is generally very high. In none of the National Dailies was the proportion of *news* space given to foreign news less than 9% and in one case it was as high as 27%. Generally the "Quality" papers gave proportionately more space to foreign news than did the "Popular" papers and the "gap" between the two sorts of paper was wider in this respect than, for example, was the case with home industrial relations news. Even so, the "Popular" papers gave, on average, approximately twice as much space to external news as to news of industrial relations at home. Generally, when comparisons were made, the two Scottish papers examined fell midway between "Qualities" and "Populars". There were quite wide variations in the number of feature articles, giving background to news, with *The Sun* and *Daily Mirror* providing least and *The Guardian* most. The relative prominence of foreign news, as indicated by the amount of front page treatment, was much the same in the different titles examined.

## 2. Characteristics of news stories

An attempt was made to classify all items studied according to a number of general characteristics. The results showed, firstly, that the majority (58%) of items were about an action or event rather than about a statement or background information (II, 3, a). An assessment of the level of "predictability" of news showed 29% of items to be classifiable as about "predictable" events and 36% about "unexpected" events (II, 3, b). On the other hand, only 20% of items could be classified as having a "dramatic" character and 73% were judged "undramatic" (II, 3, c). Fourthly, a general assessment of whether items involved "good news" (eg constructive, positive) or "bad news" (negative, violent, etc) showed the largest proportion (48%) to be assignable to the latter category and only 26% to be judged as positive. On all four indicators, the "Popular" dailies tended to differ from the "Qualities" in the same direction: their stories were more likely to be "action-orientated", less "predictable", more "dramatic" and less positive.

## 3. Geography of foreign coverage

The majority of stories (60%) were about events occurring in a single foreign country, rather than having an "international" character (III, 1). Europe (including USSR) and the USA predominate as the regions most involved in foreign news, accounting for 40% and 18%, respectively, of the allocations of all items to regions. The EEC countries and the USA on their own account for 32%. Australia and Latin America get least attention and the relatively low position of Third World regions in terms of numbers of items is accentuated when prominence and space allocation of news are taken into account. Thus, Asia and Latin America receive a disproportionately low number of front page stories and a high number of very brief items. News coverage is evidently much more closely related to "nearness to home" and level of economic development than to the population or size of regions. One could interpret the evidence as indicating that the routine coverage of normal activities in much of the world is thin: outside Europe and the USA, it takes a major event to make news (III, 1). The Soviet Union accounted for 4% of all items (as primary reference or location of event) and the single most frequently occurring link between *pairs* of countries involved Britain and the USSR (III, 2). If account is taken of evidence of British or US involvement abroad, one can estimate the proportion of all items involving this country as 19%, and all involving the USA as 26% (III, 4). A comparison between regions of the world in terms of the kinds of story reported showed news events in Europe and, to a lesser extent, in North America to be less "predictable" and less dramatic than events elsewhere. Europe provided the most "balanced" news in terms of the ratio between "positive" and "negative" news and generally, the nearer home the news and the more "developed" the region involved, the more positive the news (III, 6). News concerning the USSR was found to be unusually "positive" in character. The findings as a whole lend support to the view that some parts of the world might tend to have a consistently more negative "news image" than other regions. On two points, a general difference showed up between "Qualities" and "Populars", with the latter giving relatively more space to North America and less to the Third World (III, 5).

## 4. Topics of foreign coverage

Most news or features concern either international diplomatic events, foreign domestic political matters or economic and trade matters (each about 20% of all items). The next largest categories are crime and human interest, at 15% and 4% respectively (IV, 1). Different regions show different "topic profiles". For instance, Third World regions are lacking in "human interest" and generally have more news of political violence. The USA has an above average proportion of news of crime, showbusiness and human interest and least "crisis" news. The Middle East leads in the latter respect (IV, 2 and 3). Despite an overall similarity between newspapers, the "Popular" titles do vary in a predictable direction, having relatively less political, diplomatic and economic news (IV, 5). Of news, 44% is mainly about individuals and 51% about "collectivities", although the popular newspapers are generally more inclined to individualise, especially on diplomatic topics (IV, 6, b).

## 5. Themes of coverage

Generally, the main themes of news on the days examined were concerned with economic and domestic political problems, with left-wing or Communist activity in the world, with détente and with matters of race (V, 1). Some differences between "Popular" and "Quality" titles show up, especially in the differential attention by the former to sex and royalty and by the latter to the more negative aspects of foreign internal politics (V, 4). There was also some (rather faint) indication of another dimension differentiating between papers in terms of more "liberal" or more "conservative" concerns (or left versus right wing) (V, 5).

## 6. Sources and participants

News reports are nearly always attributed to some source, although not usually as a direct report or quotation. Little credit is given to news agencies (only 15% of items state a news agency origin) but there is considerable variation between titles in this respect (VI, 1). Evidence about participants suggests news to be heavily weighted towards reporting from and about official and political figures or institutions.

# Analysis of Newspaper Content

## APPENDICES

**Coding reliability**

(i) There are three main sources of error in the work described in this report. One is sampling error, which is discussed in Appendix A2. Another is measurement error, which can be discounted as insignificant since all totals and sub-totals for pages, papers and categories can be and have been checked. Such errors as remain are too small to affect the calculated percentage figures. There remains a third and most serious potential for error—in the allocation of items to categories of the coding frame. This is more serious because it is extremely difficult to estimate the margins of variability with accuracy and because there is no absolute standard of correct coding in using many of the categories. The only way to reduce such error is by initial training and cross-checking, but they have a limited value, especially in solving the problem of allocating ambiguous or mixed content to an appropriate category. The only measure of successful coding and of a good coding scheme is the extent to which subsequent coding by others conforms with earlier decisions. This appendix reports a limited coding check based on this principle. The results can only be regarded as indicating very approximately the level of confidence which can be placed on the results and in identifying the most doubtful areas of coding decisions. The method employed was to take one sample issue of each of the nine National Dailies, acquire a second copy and have the second copy recoded and remeasured by a different coder and checked by a different member of the research group. Since the second copy was in some cases a different edition, it was necessary to eliminate from the comparisons any item which did not appear, or was differently printed in one issue. The results which follow are thus based on less than the total amount of space in the sample issue, although the difference between editions was not substantial. A second restriction was that some parts of the sample issue were coded in blocks and not item by item (financial, sport and advertising content). The effect of this is to reduce the number of items available for comparison. An additional effect is to generally magnify the coding differences, since such block coded content is normally the least ambiguous. The main procedure in making the "code-recode" comparison has been to calculate the proportion of items in the set of newspapers taken as a whole which were identically coded on different occasions and by different people.

(ii) There are two main sources of coding divergence. One is human error—the mistaken allocation of an item to an inappropriate code. Another arises from differences of judgement about where an item in dispute should be located. A clear line cannot, of course, be drawn between the two. In reporting on divergences, this distinction has been noted and applied according to the subjective judgement of the main investigator. That is, he has decided whether a mistake is involved or where a case could reasonably be made out for alternative allocation. As we might expect, the latter source of error is the most frequent one, especially given the fact of a second inspection of all coded newspapers. In the recoding exercise, the coders knew that a check was involved, although the originally coded sample issues were taken in no systematic way from the stock of completed newspapers. Several, but not all, have the same date of issue.

**TABLE I**

**PROPORTION OF ITEMS IDENTICALLY CODED ON TWO OCCASIONS**

| Result | N | % |
|---|---|---|
| Same coding ...        ...        ...        ...        ...        ...        ...        ... | 944 | 85·4 |
| Different coding because of ambiguity        ...        ...        ...        ... | 112 | 10·1 |
| Different coding because of error ...        ...        ...        ...        ... | 50 | 4·5 |
| Total no. of items available for recoding ...        ...        ...        ... | 1,106 | 100 |

(iii) The results of the first main comparison are given in Table I. The total number of pairs of identical items are divided into those identically coded on two occasions, those differing because of uncertainty of category boundaries or item ambiguity and complexity and those differing because of a mistaken coding on one or other of the two occasions.

Across the set of nine national newspapers we can conclude that 10% of coding decisions may be inherently doubtful. Where human error is involved the actual error rate to be expected if this pattern were to be repeated is less than the figure of 4·5%, since it arises from two sets of processing. The average error rate is thus half the figure shown for any given set of coding decisions—approximately 2·5%. It might be added that the final error rate in the whole set of newspapers is probably lower than this estimate, since subsequent operations with the coded newspapers and some further routine checking have led to a number of mistakes being rectified before tabulation. It is probably safe to conclude that the main source of doubt over the content distribution figures contained in this report is attributable to ambiguity in particular items and in coding categories. The general level of such error is probably not less than 10%, tlthough this estimate cannot be used in any precise way.

(iv) Table II gives the results of comparisons for each individual title of a Daily Newspaper.

TABLE II

CODE-RECODE COMPARISONS, TITLE BY TITLE

| Result | The Times | The Guardian | Daily Telegraph | Financial Times | Morning Star | Daily Express | Daily Mail | Daily Mirror | The Sun |
|---|---|---|---|---|---|---|---|---|---|
| | % | % | % | % | % | % | % | % | % |
| Same coding | 89 | 83 | 86 | 84 | 88 | 86 | 77 | 87 | 88 |
| Different, ambiguous | 8 | 12 | 11 | 11 | 11 | 8 | 17 | 6 | 7 |
| Different, error | 3 | 5 | 3 | 5 | 1 | 6 | 6 | 7 | 5 |
| Total items compared | 180 | 148 | 166 | 122 | 77 | 132 | 104 | 83 | 94 |

The main conclusion to be drawn from Table II is that the incidence of error is very similar in coding different newspapers. This across-title consistency should increase confidence in the estimated measure of coding error as a whole and suggests the problems to lie in the nature of the coding task and the coding frame and not in the coders themselves or the general method adopted.

Some indication of the overall effect of discrepant coding on the estimation of space allocation to categories is given in Table III where the alternative space allocations produced by the original coding and the check coding are reproduced. For this purpose the results for all nine title have been averaged. It should also be noted that the difference between editions has not been allowed for in these comparisons and some (small) part of the discrepancy in percentages is accounted for by this fact.

(v) While the discrepancy in relation to news and features is quite large it should be noted that one or two large items can be responsible for big percentage changes and, as can be seen below, the boundary between sport news and features was the one most frequently involved in discrepant coding. No systematic distorting factor could be identified.

**TABLE III**

ANALYSIS OF AVERAGE SPACE OF ONE DAY'S ISSUES OF NINE NATIONAL
DAILY NEWSPAPERS INTO SEVEN CATEGORIES, ACCORDING TO ORIGINAL
CODING AND SECOND CODING

| Category | Original coding | Second coding | Difference |
|---|---|---|---|
| | % | % | % |
| Home news ... ... ... ... | 24·9 | 22·8 | +2·1 |
| External news ... ... ... ... | 6·0 | 6·4 | −0·4 |
| Other news ... ... ... ... | 8·6 | 7·7 | +0·9 |
| Features ... ... ... ... ... | 18·8 | 20·8 | −2·0 |
| Other editorial ... ... ... | 10·4 | 10·8 | −0·4 |
| Advertisements and headings ... ... | 31·4 | 31·5 | −0·1 |
| Total ... ... ... ... ... | 100·0 | 100·0 | +0·1 |
| Picture content ... ... ... ... | 7·9 | 7·8 | +0·1 |

A detailed inspection of the cases of discrepancy produced further evidence of the
ambiguities built into the coding frame. Since mistaken coding tends to be random and
idiosyncratic it is most useful to look at discrepancies which arise from uncertainty.
There were 112 such cases out of 1,106 pairs examined. Table IV shows the "boundaries" most frequently involved in discrepant coding.

**TABLE IV**

CATEGORY PAIRS MOST FREQUENTLY INVOLVED IN DISCREPANT CODING

                                                                           *N*

1. Sport news/sport features ... ... ... ... ... ... ... 8
2. Financial features/consumer, price features ... ... ... ... ... ... 7
3. Other regular features/other features ... ... ... ... ... ... 6
4. Home, political social and economic news/financial, market news ... ... ... 6
5. International political news/international "other" ... ... ... ... ... 6
6. Home sport news/international sport news ... ... ... ... ... ... 4
7. Home political news/home "other" news ... ... ... ... ... ... 4

Some other points to emerge from this analysis include the following:

(a) 58% of discrepant cases are *inside* the main category boundaries of home news
external news, other news, features, other editorial space and advertising. Of
the 47 cases which cross main class boundaries, 26 involve either sport or
financial news or features.

(b) Of the 112 discrepant cases, 23 involve financial news or features and 16
involve sport. In all, 32 involve one or other of the residual categories and
have mainly arisen where this allocation has been chosen in place of a more
specific category.

(c) Of the 14 cases which involve crossing the news/features boundary, 11 relate to
financial or sport content.

(vi) The main lessons to be learnt from this analysis are that the most reliable
distinctions are being made between advertising and editorial matter, between home
and foreign content, between sport and non-sport categories. In addition, it is clear that
specific subject exclusive categories, compared with general format categories, are
more reliable. This is evidenced, for example, by the reliable coding of items relating to
the Ulster Crisis, to industrial relations and to legal or police matters. Despite the
ambiguity in the concept of sex-related content, this did not show up as a major

problem in the check coding, although the number of items is, in any case, not large. It is apparent, from the evidence cited already, that the overall amount of unreliability in the results, arising from the source of error discussed here, would be much reduced if all sport, whether news or features, were to be grouped together and if financial and market news and features were to be grouped together along with features on consumer/ price matters. An additional increment of reliability would be obtained by treating all political, social, economic news and features along with financial and market news, but this would involve abandoning the separation between home and external news which has other advantages. In so far as this exercise increases confidence in the results, then it reflects the attainment of consistency within a group of workers trying to apply a common set of conventions and definitions.

It should be said that a further proportion of coding unreliability could and should have been avoided by the preparation of a more elaborate code book and making more specific "rules of precedence" for ambiguous cases of classification. This would have improved the measured reliability, although it would have been to some extent an arbitrary procedure in the sense that an alternative set of rules of precedence would have achieved a different result. There is no way of eliminating the *cause* of the problem which is the inherent ambiguity and complexity of newspaper content. The only reason for not preparing a more elaborate set of rules was pressure of time, in that such rules have to be prepared in advance on the basis of a longer pilot study than had been allowed for.

## Accuracy of the estimates

### Introduction

(i) The percentage figures in the main tables of this report are all subject to sampling error, in the sense that they are only estimates of the true figures of distribution of space into various categories for the whole of the year. The method of sampling was designed to reduce the error in the estimates, especially by taking account of weekday and seasonal variations. It is, however, possible to calculate the margins of error within which the figures presented can be accepted and, following statistical convention, this has been carried out with reference to the 95% confidence limits. That is, we can give limits on either side of the measured proportion within which the true figure would fall with a probability of 19 times out of 20 or greater. Tables I, II and III give the results for several such calculations. Since each figure would require its own calculation, it is not possible to give complete results and a small number of cases have been chosen from tables which relate the National Daily analysis. The intention is to give a general impression of the level of statistical accuracy, though it should be borne in mind that error from other sources has also to be taken into account (see Appendix A1). The examples chosen relate to different categories and different magnitudes of space and are some guide to what might be expected if the analysis were to be pursued.

### Statistical note*

(ii) The method used for computing variances is that of "collapsed strata". We have originally made one selection in each of 24 strata for each newspaper. No unbiased estimate of variance is available in this situation. However, by pairing what are thought in advance to be similar strata, we calculate an estimate of variance as if there had been two selections from each 24 strata. This method, of course, overestimates the variance by an amount equal to the gains made by the aditional stratification. This bias is probably not serious and may compensate for the additional non-sampling variance due to coders, which has not been measured.

### Comment

(iii) The measured errors are not large and we can assume a similar range of variance for other figures obtained with the National Daily sample. It should also be noted that in comparing percentage figures as between different newspapers the margins of error will be lower than the joint variance suggests. That is, the error of a difference between two estimates is less than the sum of the errors of the individual estimates.

Few other conclusions can be drawn from the results, although it seems as if the estimates for tabloid newspapers (*Daily Mirror* and *The Sun*) are subject to rather larger margins of error and the *Financial Times* estimates are generally least subject to error. Picture estimates are generally very accurate.

---

*We are very grateful to Dr T. J. Tomberlin of The Department of Social Statistics, University of Southampton for advice in the calculation of measures of variance, and to Dr J. Fields of the same Department for computing advice.

TABLE I

STANDARD ERROR OF THE ESTIMATES OF SPACE DEVOTED TO THREE CATEGORIES OF NEWS SPACE AS A PROPORTION OF ALL NEWS SPACE IN NATIONAL DAILIES, 1975

| Category | The Times | The Guardian | The Daily Telegraph | Financial Times | Morning Star | Daily Express | Daily Mail | Daily Mirror | The Sun |
|---|---|---|---|---|---|---|---|---|---|
| | % | % | % | % | % | % | % | % | % |
| All home news ... ... ... ... | 47·2±1·1 | 57·7±1·7 | 59·2±1·2 | 18·2±0·9 | 76·8±2·7 | 74·5±3·4 | 73·7±2·1 | 88·7±2·3 | 89·8±2·3 |
| Industrial relations ... ... ... | 3·9±0·7 | 5·4±0·7 | 4·4±0·7 | 4·7±0·3 | 18·5±3·9 | 4·6±1·0 | 6·2±1·6 | 3·9±1·2 | 4·4±1·2 |
| Home sport news ... ... ... | 14·2±1·3 | 18·7±1·2 | 22·6±1·3 | 1·5±0·2 | 23·1±1·9 | 33·7±3·6 | 32·4±1·8 | 49·5±3·0 | 45·1±3·2 |

TABLE II

STANDARD ERROR OF THE ESTIMATES OF TWO CATEGORIES OF NEWSPAPER SPACE AS A PROPORTION OF ALL SPACE IN THE NATIONAL DAILIES, 1975

| Category | The Times | The Guardian | The Daily Telegraph | Financial Times | Morning Star | Daily Express | Daily Mail | Daily Mirror | The Sun |
|---|---|---|---|---|---|---|---|---|---|
| | % | % | % | % | % | % | % | % | % |
| All news ... ... ... ... | 39·1±1·1 | 37·3±1·5 | 36·1±1·9 | 44·2±1·3 | 52·5±1·3 | 32·0±2·3 | 29·8±1·1 | 28·4±1·5 | 31·2±2·4 |
| All features ... ... ... | 15·6±0·9 | 25·4±1·6 | 11·5±0·6 | 16·3±0·8 | 26·8±1·9 | 15·8±1·3 | 23·7±0·9 | 19·7±1·6 | 18·6±1·6 |

TABLE III

STANDARD ERROR OF THE ESTIMATE PICTURE CONTENT AS A PROPORTION OF ALL EDITORIAL SPACE, NATIONAL DAILIES, 1975

| Category | The Times | The Guardian | The Daily Telegraph | Financial Times | Morning Star | Daily Express | Daily Mail | Daily Mirror | The Sun |
|---|---|---|---|---|---|---|---|---|---|
| | % | % | % | % | % | % | % | % | % |
| Picture content ... ... ... | 6·4±0·6 | 9·5±0·7 | 9·6±0·4 | 3·3±0·2 | 14·5±1·8 | 15·3±0·8 | 13·4±0·7 | 16·7±1·0 | 17·1±1·0 |

284

## Coding Frame reproduced from report of Royal Commission on the Press 1947-9

### 1.0 HOME NEWS

News relating to events which occurred in the British Isles, excluding Eire.

### 1.1 Political, social and economic

Political news and appointments; parliamentary news, excluding reports of debates on imperial, foreign and international affairs; taxation; rationing; food news; housing; social services; education; communications; travel; employment; wages, disputes and settlements; strikes; planning; production; retail prices; crop reports and news; news of the fighting services (other than promotions and appointments); etc.

### 1.2 Law and police

News of and reports on proceedings in all courts of law; legal news (other than appointments); police news; crime reports.

### 1.3 Accidents

Accidents involving death or injury to persons.

### 1.4 Personalities

Court news; promotions and appointments (not political); wills and bequests; university news; news of functions when the guests were the main interest of the news item; biographical notes on people in the news (not connected with sport); etc.

### 1.5 Sport

Reports on, and news of, all kinds of sport and games; programmes and fixtures; race cards; racing news; horse shows; dog shows etc; news of well known personalities, players and teams connected with sport, etc.

### 1.9 Other home news

Home news in brief; state of roads; weather news not included elsewhere; theatre and film news not included elsewhere; accidents not involving injury or loss of life; examination results; and all other home news which cannot be classified under 1.1-1.5 above.

### 2.0 EXTERNAL NEWS

#### Imperial

News of events which occurred in the Dominions, colonies, mandated territories and Eire.

### 2.1 Political, social and economic

Imperial news of the same type as the news included in category 1.1.

### 2.2 Other

All other imperial news.

#### Foreign

News of events which occurred in any one country not within the British Commonwealth and Empire. The dependencies, etc, of any other country were considered as part of that country.

### 2.3 Political, social and economic

Foreign news of the same type as the news included in category 1.1.

### 2.4 Other

All other foreign news.

### International

News of events which concerned more than one country. The British Commonwealth and Empire was considered as one country, and similarly the dependencies of other countries were considered as parts of those countries. News of the League of Nations, etc, is included in this category. Events on the oceans and high seas outside territorial limits are also covered. News of Germany, Austria and Japan involving the occupying powers was treated as international.

### 2.5 Political, social and economic

International news of the same type as the news included in category 1.1.

### 2.6 Other

All other international news.

### 2.9 Miscellaneous

External news in brief; news of oceans and high seas not involving shipping or aircraft; external news not falling under classifications 2.1-2.6.

## 3.0 OTHER NEWS

News of events which were neither specifically home or external.

### 3.1 Financial and commercial

Financial and market news and reports from all countries; crop and mining reports affecting market prices, etc.

### 3.2 Scientific and technical

News of scientific and technical events from all countries when such news was not primarily political, social or economic.

### 3.9 Miscellaneous news

Shipping news; shipping casualties affecting the movement of ships.

## 4.0 FEATURES

Articles whose primary purpose was to give, not current news, but background material to the news, general information, or entertainment. This excludes leading articles (ie editorial comment) and fiction.

4.1 Women's features.

4.2 Children's features (including children's cartoons).

4.3 Theatre, film, radio, art, music and literary criticism.

### 4.4 Political columns

### 4.5 Light columns

Gossip columns (home and abroad). Beachcomber, Timothy Shy and similar columns.

### Special articles:

### 4.6 Political, social and economic

Relating to topics such as those included in category 1.1.

4.7 **Other**

4.9 **Other features**

Obituaries; radio and other programmes; weather forecasts; nature notes; historical items; horoscopes; gardening; etc.

5.0 **OTHER EDITORIAL SPACE**

5.1 **Leading articles (editorial comment)**

5.2 **Correspondence**

5.3 **Pictures**

5.4 **Topical cartoons**

5.5 **Strip comic cartoons**

5.6 **Fiction**

5.7 **Puzzles and competitions**

Crosswords; anagrams; bridge and chess problems; children's competitions; etc.

5.9 **Miscellaneous editorial space**

Index; order forms; advertisement index; news in all advertisements; publication particulars; subscription and advertising rates; blank spaces (eg empty stop press column).

6.0 **OTHER SPACE**

6.1 **Advertisements**

Items which were considered to have been paid for by outside firms or individuals, including: display and classified advertisements; notices of births, deaths and marriages: company reports; pool results.

6.2 **Margins and titles**

7.0 **PARLIAMENTARY NEWS**

8.0 **NEWS AND FEATURES OF SEX INTEREST**

Comment on application of 1975 Coding Frame

The purpose of these comments is to give some indication of the conventions adopted in coding and also of the experience obtained in trying to apply them to a range of different newspapers. This aim is best achieved by briefly commenting on each category in turn, at the risk of some tedium. The full list of categories is given in Section II 1 of the text. Where no comment is made below, it can be taken that nothing can usefully be added to the rubric in the coding frame itself.

(a) **Home Political, social and economic news**

This is a large and disparate category, but not difficult to identify reliably, except where a judgement has to be made of the significance of the news report rather than the subject and where a line has to be drawn between economic news and financial or market news (see Appendix A1 on coding reliability). The greater part of such news has a political character, deriving from parliament or relating to the main political parties. Otherwise, news of the social services is an important component and this has been separately studied (Part D of this Report).

(b) **Industrial relations and trade union matters**

This has also been separately studied and is reported elsewhere (Part B). In practice, it proved easy to identify reliably and any central reference to trade union matters qualified an item for inclusion.

(c) **Ulster crisis-related news**

Again, this presented no problems of classification, except that reports involving the Irish Republic had to be coded as international (Ulster-related) news.

(d) **Law and police news**

A large and heterogenous category since it includes court news of all kinds: inquests, divorce proceedings, magistrate's court proceedings, *The Times* law reports, etc, as well as all crime and police matters. Any significant legal aspect in an item qualified it for inclusion here. Separate categories for legal aspects of the Ulster crisis, industrial relations and sex cases or crimes were used in order to solve conflicts of priority on these specific subjects. The category of sex-related legal news was not easy to apply, since it required a judgement of the centrality of the sexual aspect. Some divorce proceedings were included, others not, and the same court case or crime might be treated differently in different newspapers. In general, we would expect the result of our coding of sex-related news to have under- rather than over-estimated sex content and we have tended to adopt a conventional view of what is of mainly sex interest and what might be regarded as titillating by readers or be intended as such. These remarks apply in much the same way to all the separate sex news and feature categories.

(e) **Accidents**

Some difficulty was experienced in deciding on the gravity of the accidents and in deciding whether the news was reported as accident news *per se* or as police news or personality news. Generally, accident news is very brief.

(f) **Personalities**

This is an especially heterogeneous category as we have used it and its meaning tends to vary between different newspaper titles. Basically, there are three types of news under this heading. One consists of regularly appearing news of social events as found mainly in *The Times* and *The Daily Telegraph*. Another includes news of appointments, promotions and achievements mainly in business, politics or public life. In some cases, obituaries fall in this category where they are of an occasional and unusual kind, but otherwise they are coded as "regular information". Thirdly, there is news of stars, entertainers, sportsmen etc. This third group includes news items which could not otherwise have news interest but for the involvement of a famous person—eg minor accidents, conflicts, financial matters.

## (g) Sport

All home sport of all kinds is included here. The main coding difficulties arising related to the boundary with international sport and some uncertainty as to whether fringe leisure activities should count as sport or not. In addition, it was not always easy to draw a line between sports news and features (see Appendix A1). The result of this, since sport content is so large, is to cast some doubt on the general and rather basic distinction between news and feature content of the press.

## (h) Other home news

This is both a residual category for the otherwise unclassifiable and a place for very small items. In general, a space allocation of under five standard column centimetres justified inclusion here. Some difficulty was experienced in dealing with cases where a front page index gives small items of news as a trailer to later more substantial treatment. Normally, where there was a trailer, it was coded separately as index.

## (j) External news

In general, these categories proved easy to apply, although it was a matter of judgement whether an item should be regarded as "political, social or economic" or "other". Usually, the seriousness of the item was taken into account. Another problem of interpretation was raised by the need to distinguish external news from financial and market news, much of which is international in origin or reference. Location on financial or foreign news pages was a guide to classification, but could not be taken as a firm rule. We can only report the fact of overlap.

## (k) Other news

Several comments have already been made about financial news. It is a large category in modern daily newspapers and overlaps with economic news. The most useful guideline in making the distinction was the common reference to prices of commodities or stocks or the financial performance of firms and industries. The "economic" category generally involved a reference to the wider context of trade and industry and often to political aspects. At the extreme points, the two categories are clearly different and most content can readily be categorised in ways justified by treatment and placement. Nevertheless, we cannot be very confident about decisions in the fringe areas. Another difficulty with this category is the occasional lack of clear distinction between news and feature treatment. Some items mix news reports and background comment quite inextricably.

Scientific, technical and medical news presented some difficulties of identification because of varying treatment between newspapers. In addition, there is an overlap between news and feature treatment, since scientific events usually occur on a different time-scale than normal news events.

### (*l*)  Features

The allocation of particular articles to feature categories was guided, in many cases, by the identifying criteria already mentioned and subject to similar problems. Our chief guideline in allocation between news and features, was the extent to which the item related to a particular "news" event or not and the extent to which treatment was in the nature of background discussion. Location in the newspaper was a useful guide, but not taken as a fixed rule. In particular, on financial and sports pages, news and features, by our criteria, tended to be inter-mixed. It should be stressed that our criteria of allocation are not necessarily those of the press organisation, although we expect them to be close. It would not have been possible to discover and apply the internal criteria for the number of different titles involved.

The main problems experienced in distinguishing features from news related, as has been noted, to the categories "financial", "sport" and "personalities". In addition, the following particular difficulties were experienced. Consumer/ price content tended to overlap with financial content. The distinction between "political" "mixed" and "light" columns presented some problems, and was intended mainly to reflect the varying degree of levity and of mis-cellaneousness. Features, or pages for women, are less easy to identify than was once the case and it was a matter of judgement whether material was intended primarily for women. The general guidelines, apart from joint location of similar content, had to do wtih specific subject matter. Thus cooking, needlework, child-rearing, housekeeping and women's fashion were the staple content together with articles for social and personal problems experienced by women in particular.

The category of "other regular features" was originally established to cover the area of content, not yet accounted for, which is predictable on a daily or weekly basis, although diverse in subject matter. In the outcome, we would probably not regard it as very usefully distinct from the residual category of "other" features or from the category of "other regular information", except that the latter does not have the characteristics of feature treatment, and relates to very specific matters. The bulk of "other regular features" in most papers consists of (usually weekly) columns on motoring, gardening, property, natural history, etc. Where a topic has a specific category of its own such as finance, politics, arts, consumer matters etc, it would be so coded.

Picture-features relate mainly to photographic content and the space so coded includes captions or other text. Occasional difficulties of allocation were involved in judging the substantive importance of the text and hence a possible alternative coding by topic.

### (*m*)  Other editorial space

The headings in the coding frame are largely self explanatory and the categories themselves derive largely from 1947. Few problems of allocation were experienced, although occasionally an item was coded as a competition or offer when it might well have been differently placed. For instance, some offers, illustrated by pin-ups, might otherwise have attracted a sex-related coding.

### (*n*)  Advertisements

The allocation between classification and display was guided mainly by the criterion of grouping and labelling, aided by the different newspapers' own index and published definitions. In terms of format, some classified content has a display or semi-display appearance, although generally the two types of advertising are distinctive in appearance. The practice of newspapers varies, however. For instance there is a major difference between *The Guardian* and *The Daily Telegraph*, in that the former invariably classifies display format advertisements for situations vacant, while a large proportion of situations vacant advertising in *The Daily Telegraph* is not given any heading and we have included it as display advertising, apparently following newspaper policy. Thus it is important to remember that the distinction is somewhat conventional and not a good guide to actual subject matter. We would not regard the distinction made in our coding as having a very high degree of validity, because of insufficient evidence.

## ( *p* ) Parliamentary debate reports

This category was used only for items where verbatim reports of speeches were systematically given, although some of the space so classified would also contain comment and summary by political correspondents.

## (*q*) Sex-related

This exclusive category has been used mainly for pin-ups or pictures of sex interest where no "news" is involved.

**Evidence of trends from 1965 to 1975**

The untypical character of the immediate post-war period makes the comparison between 1947 and 1975 less useful than it might otherwise have been. Fortuitously, an analysis using a similar sampling scheme and a version of the same coding frame (as for 1947) was carried out by C. Seymour-Ure for the year 1965. This is reported in *The Press, Politics and the Public, Methuen, 1968*. While that set of findings is not strictly comparable with our own, there is a sufficient basis for making some broad comparisons and Tables I and II bring together some of the most relevant figures.

The following points emerge:

 (i) Between the two points in time, the proportion of space devoted to advertising overall remained broadly constant, although *The Guardian* seemed to have lost ground in advertising space and *The Sun* to have gained significantly.

 (ii) Features generally have increased in importance relative to news, although the apparent relative decline in news for several papers (*The Times*, *The Guardian* and *Daily Mail*) probably reflects the use of different criteria for allocation to the features category.

 (iii) The proportion of editorial space given to pictures shows a small decline for four papers and no increase for anyone.

 (iv) The most significant developments can probably be seen in Table ii, where it seems as if the three "Quality" papers have each increased their attention to news from overseas, while, with the exception of the *Daily Express*, the "Popular" papers have either not changed or moved towards more Home news coverage. For three "Qualities", the Home/Overseas balance has moved from an average of 59% : 17% to 53% : 22%. For four "Popular" papers the balance has moved from 77% : 13% to 82% : 13%. Since attention to external news is in general a mark of the "Quality" press, this tendency, if it is occurring might indicate a widening of the "gap" between these two sets of papers. Another sign of the same phenomenon seems to be the greater attention to Financial and business news (since 1947) and (since 1965) its apparent decline in the popular press.

The most significant conclusion to emerge from this comparison over a ten year period links with earlier remarks about the loss of titles since 1947. The titles which have dropped out, especially the *News Chronicle* and *Daily Herald*, represented a section of the press with "Quality" features (according to the criteria used here) and reasonably large circulation. The "replacements" in the range of national newspapers, especially *The Guardian* and *The Sun* have each represented a rather "pure type" of quality and popular paper respectively, thus serving to accentuate the gap rather than to increase the diversity of what is available. Of course, these remarks do not relate to the question of political diversity nor to other qualitative differences which have not been examined.

# TABLE I

## SOME COMPARISONS OF SPACE ALLOCATION FOR EIGHT NATIONAL DAILY NEWSPAPERS, 1965 AND 1975

### (a) TOTAL SPACE BETWEEN EDITORIAL AND ADVERTISING

| Content | The Times 1965–1975 | | The Guardian 1965–1975 | | The Daily Telegraph 1965–1975 | | Morning Star 1965–1975 | | Daily Express 1965–1975 | | Daily Mail 1965–1975 | | Daily Mirror 1965–1975 | | The Sun 1965–1975 | |
|---|---|---|---|---|---|---|---|---|---|---|---|---|---|---|---|---|
| | % | % | % | % | % | % | % | % | % | % | % | % | % | % | % | % |
| Editorial ... ... ... ... | 66 | 65 | 62 | 74 | 48 | 54 | 92 | 91 | 60 | 58 | 61 | 65 | 64 | 63 | 75 | 64 |
| Advertising ... ... ... ... | 34 | 35 | 38 | 26 | 52 | 46 | 8 | 9 | 40 | 42 | 39 | 35 | 36 | 37 | 25 | 36 |
| | 100 | 100 | 100 | 100 | 100 | 100 | 100 | 100 | 100 | 100 | 100 | 100 | 100 | 100 | 100 | 100 |

### (b) ALL NEWS, ALL FEATURES, AND ALL PICTURE CONTENT AS A PROPORTION OF ALL EDITORIAL SPACE

| | The Times 1965–1975 | | The Guardian 1965–1975 | | The Daily Telegraph 1965–1975 | | Morning Star 1965–1975 | | Daily Express 1965–1975 | | Daily Mail 1965–1975 | | Daily Mirror 1965–1975 | | The Sun 1965–1975 | |
|---|---|---|---|---|---|---|---|---|---|---|---|---|---|---|---|---|
| | % | % | % | % | % | % | % | % | % | % | % | % | % | % | % | % |
| News ... ... ... ... | 69 | 59 | 61 | 48 | 64 | 63 | 54 | 50 | 53 | 47 | 52 | 40 | 46 | 39 | 40 | 42 |
| Features ... ... ... ... | 17 | 21 | 23 | 21 | 18 | 17 | 23 | 23 | 22 | 21 | 26 | 28 | 18 | 22 | 17 | 18 |
| Picture content ... ... ... | 8 | 6 | 9 | 9 | 12 | 9 | 16 | 14 | 15 | 15 | 14 | 14 | 23 | 17 | 17 | 17 |

*Notes:*

1. The figures for 1965 are taken from an analysis carried out with a similar sample and similar coding frame, reported by C. Seymour-Ure in *The Press, Politics and the Public*, Methuen, 1968, p. 62. Exact comparability cannot, however, be assumed.

2. In order to make the comparison, picture content has been excluded from the 1975 data, hence the difference between figures here and in some other tables for 1975.

3. The figures in the second half of the table do not add to 100% because they do not include all categories of editorial space, especially those that have been categorised elsewhere as "other editorial space".

TABLE II

A COMPARISON OF SPACE ALLOCATION OF THREE MAIN NEWS CATEGORIES FOR EIGHT NATIONAL DAILY NEWSPAPERS, 1965* AND 1975:

| Content | The Times | | The Guardian | | The Daily Telegraph | | Morning Star | | Daily Express | | Daily Mail | | Daily Mirror | | The Sun | |
|---|---|---|---|---|---|---|---|---|---|---|---|---|---|---|---|---|
| | 1965 | 1975 | 1965 | 1975 | 1965 | 1975 | 1965 | 1975 | 1965 | 1975 | 1965 | 1975 | 1965 | 1975 | 1965 | 1975 |
| | % | % | % | % | % | % | % | % | % | % | % | % | % | % | % | % |
| Home News ... ... ... ... ... | 49 | 47 | 59 | 54 | 68 | 58 | 83 | 75 | 77 | 75 | 71 | 73 | 84 | 89 | 76 | 90 |
| External News ... ... ... ... | 17 | 21 | 18 | 26 | 14 | 18 | 16 | 24 | 13 | 17 | 15 | 16 | 12 | 10 | 12 | 9 |
| Financial and Business News ... | 33 | 30 | 21 | 16 | 17 | 23 | 1 | — | 10 | 9 | 13 | 10 | 3 | 1 | 10 | — |

*Source: Seymour-Ure, 1965. Notes 1 and 2 from Table I also apply to this Table.

294

**Picture content in National Dailies**

(i) Only editorial space has been considered in coding for picture content. Generally, pictorial matter is photographic, but it also includes cartoons, line drawings, graphs, maps, etc.

(ii) Since 1947, there has been a general increase in the proportion of picture content (Table I), although figures for 1965 taken from Seymour-Ure (*The Press, Politics and the Public*, Methuen, 1968) suggest that the increase had been largely accomplished by that date. Only *The Times* seems to have been fairly consistent in its proportion of picture content since 1947.

(iii) The "Quality" papers, as a group, give approximately half the amount of space, in relative terms, as do the "Popular" Dailies.

(iv) The analysis of picture content relies mainly on three pairs of comparison Tables, one pair relating to all news content, another to news space and a third to features. The first Table in each pair gives a distribution of picture content by sub-category, the second gives a comparable distribution of space excluding pictures. Differences between comparable figures in the two Tables show whether particular sub-categories are more or less likely to be illustrated.

(v) In general, features space receives a disproportionate amount of illustration compared with news.

(vi) Of news categories, "other news" (mainly business and financial) receives least illustration. Home news is relatively less illustrated than external news. This is true quite generally of all titles (Tables II A and II B). Variations in picture content for all categories of editorial space quite closely reflect the variations between newspapers in their attention to different categories.

(vii) Within the Home News category, there are few variations in relative amounts of illustration for sub-categories, although it is clear that news of personalities and "other" home news (often "human interest") both receive an above-average degree of illustration. In the treatment of sports news, the "Quality" papers (here including the *Morning Star*) give relatively more picture content than do the "Popular" papers. This may simply reflect the different quantitative significance of this category in the two groups of papers. In all but *The Times*, *Financial Times* and *Morning Star*, law and accident news received a higher than proportionate share of picture content. Home political, social and economic news has a consistently low proportionate share of pictures across the complete range of daily newspapers.

(viii) Within feature content, the sub-category of picture-features is predictably prominent. In the "Quality" papers, the "arts and entertainment" category contributes a high proportion of picture content. The same is generally true for all papers of the category for "personalities" and that relating to women and children.

(ix) In general, we should conclude from the comparison Tables that relative incidence of illustration is determined more by subject matter than by differences of policy between newspapers.

**TABLE I**

**NATIONAL DAILIES, 1947, 1965 AND 1975:**

**PICTURE CONTENT AS A PROPORTION OF EDITORIAL SPACE**

| Title | 1947* | 1965** | 1975 |
|---|---|---|---|
| The Times ... ... ... ... ... ... | 5 | 8 | 6 |
| The Guardian ... ... ... ... ... ... | NA | 9 | 9 |
| The Daily Telegraph ... ... ... ... ... | 3 | 12 | 9 |
| Financial Times ... ... ... ... ... ... | NA | NA | 3 |
| Morning Star/Daily Worker ... ... ... ... | 4 | 16 | 14 |
| Daily Express ... ... ... ... ... ... | 8 | 15 | 15 |
| Daily Mail ... ... ... ... ... ... | 9 | 14 | 14 |
| Daily Mirror ... ... ... ... ... ... | 12 | 23 | 17 |
| The Sun ... ... ... ... ... ... | NA | 17 | 17 |

*Source: Royal Commission on the Press 1947–9
**Source: C. Seymour-Ure *Press Politics and Public*, Methuen, 1968

**TABLE IIA**

**NATIONAL DAILIES, 1975:**

**ANALYSIS OF PICTURE CONTENT INTO SEVEN CATEGORIES**

| Category | The Times | The Guardian | The Daily Telegraph | Financial Times | Morning Star | Daily Express | Daily Mail | Daily Mirror | The Sun |
|---|---|---|---|---|---|---|---|---|---|
| | % | % | % | % | % | % | % | % | % |
| Home news ... | 21 | 17 | 36 | 7 | 42 | 42 | 28 | 34 | 35 |
| External news | 14 | 10 | 18 | 2 | 9 | 11 | 7 | 4 | 6 |
| Financial news | 1 | 1 | — | 17 | — | 1 | — | — | — |
| Features ... | 59 | 68 | 44 | 73 | 46 | 39 | 60 | 48 | 33 |
| Other editorial | 5 | 4 | 2 | 1 | 3 | 5 | 4 | 5 | 5 |
| Headings and titles ... | — | — | — | — | — | 2 | — | 1 | — |
| Sex features ... | — | — | — | — | — | — | 1 | 8 | 21 |
| TOTAL ... | 100 | 100 | 100 | 100 | 100 | 100 | 100 | 100 | 100 |

**TABLE IIB**

**NATIONAL DAILIES, 1975:**

**ANALYSIS OF ALL NON-PICTORIAL EDITORIAL SPACE INTO SEVEN CATEGORIES**

| Category | The Times | The Guardian | The Daily Telegraph | Financial Times | Morning Star | Daily Express | Daily Mail | Daily Mirror | The Sun |
|---|---|---|---|---|---|---|---|---|---|
| | % | % | % | % | % | % | % | % | % |
| Home news ... | 26 | 29 | 39 | 11 | 44 | 41 | 35 | 41 | 45 |
| External news | 14 | 14 | 13 | 8 | 14 | 10 | 8 | 5 | 5 |
| Financial news | 19 | 9 | 16 | 48 | — | 5 | 5 | 1 | — |
| Features ... | 21 | 31 | 19 | 23 | 27 | 24 | 32 | 25 | 22 |
| Other editorial | 15 | 13 | 10 | 7 | 13 | 19 | 17 | 25 | 25 |
| Headings and titles... ... | 2 | 2 | 1 | 2 | 2 | 1 | 3 | 2 | 1 |
| Sex features ... | — | — | — | — | — | — | — | — | — |
| TOTAL ... | 97 | 98 | 98 | 99 | 100 | 100 | 100 | 99 | 98 |

## TABLE IIIA
## NATIONAL DAILIES, 1975:
## ANALYSIS OF PICTURE CONTENT OF NEWS SPACE INTO NINE CATEGORIES

| Category | The Times | The Guardian | The Daily Telegraph | Financial Times | Morning Star | Daily Express | Daily Mail | Daily Mirror | The Sun |
|---|---|---|---|---|---|---|---|---|---|
| **Home news** | % | % | % | % | % | % | % | % | % |
| Political, social and economic | 11 | 14 | 10 | 12 | 45 | 9 | 11 | 7 | 6 |
| Law and accidents ... | 5 | 8 | 10 | — | 2 | 21 | 24 | 17 | 20 |
| Personalities ... | 9 | 9 | 11 | 5 | 1 | 13 | 17 | 18 | 19 |
| Sport ... | 23 | 17 | 30 | 2 | 27 | 14 | 15 | 30 | 22 |
| Other ... ... | 11 | 11 | 6 | 5 | 7 | 21 | 13 | 17 | 18 |
| Total ... | 59 | 59 | 67 | 24 | 82 | 78 | 80 | 89 | 85 |
| **External news** | | | | | | | | | |
| Political, social and economic | 25 | 26 | 23 | 7 | 15 | 8 | 8 | 3 | 5 |
| Sport ... ... | 6 | 3 | 3 | 1 | 3 | 2 | 5 | 3 | 1 |
| Other... ... | 8 | 8 | 7 | 1 | — | 11 | 7 | 5 | 9 |
| Total ... | 39 | 37 | 33 | 9 | 18 | 21 | 20 | 11 | 15 |
| All other news | 2 | 3 | — | 64 | — | 1 | — | — | — |
| TOTAL... | 100 | 99 | 100 | 97 | 100 | 100 | 100 | 100 | 100 |
| Mean news picture content per sample issue (col.cms.) | 158 | 176 | 353 | 66 | 134 | 329 | 200 | 220 | 239 |

## TABLE IIIB
## NATIONAL DAILIES, 1975:
## ANALYSIS OF NEWS SPACE (EXCLUDING PICTURES) INTO NINE CATEGORIES

| Category | The Times | The Guardian | The Daily Telegraph | Financial Times | Morning Star | Daily Express | Daily Mail | Daily Mirror | The Sun |
|---|---|---|---|---|---|---|---|---|---|
| **Home news** ... | % | % | % | % | % | % | % | % | % |
| Political, social and economic | 16 | 22 | 19 | 12 | 46 | 14 | 16 | 13 | 14 |
| Law and accidents ... | 6 | 7 | 7 | — | 6 | 12 | 14 | 13 | 16 |
| Personalities | 4 | 1 | 4 | 1 | — | 3 | 2 | 3 | 3 |
| Sport ... ... | 14 | 19 | 22 | 1 | 20 | 37 | 34 | 52 | 49 |
| Other ... | 3 | 5 | 5 | 2 | 3 | 8 | 7 | 8 | 9 |
| Total ... | 43 | 54 | 57 | 16 | 75 | 74 | 73 | 89 | 91 |
| **External news** | | | | | | | | | |
| Political, social and economic | 16 | 20 | 13 | 12 | 19 | 7 | 7 | 3 | 3 |
| Sport ... ... | 4 | 3 | 3 | — | 4 | 4 | 3 | 4 | 2 |
| Other... ... | 3 | 4 | 2 | 1 | 2 | 6 | 6 | 3 | 4 |
| Total ... | 23 | 27 | 18 | 13 | 25 | 17 | 16 | 10 | 9 |
| **Other news** All other news | 30 | 17 | 23 | 69 | — | 9 | 10 | 1 | — |
| TOTAL... | 96 | 98 | 98 | 98 | 100 | 100 | 99 | 100 | 100 |

**TABLE IV A**

NATIONAL DAILIES, 1975:

ANALYSIS OF PICTURE CONTENT OF FEATURES SPACE INTO TEN
CATEGORIES

| Category | The Times | The Guardian | The Daily Telegraph | Financial Times | Morning Star | Daily Express | Daily Mail | Daily Mirror | The Sun |
|---|---|---|---|---|---|---|---|---|---|
| | % | % | % | % | % | % | % | % | % |
| Political, social and economic | 12 | 33 | 5 | 43 | 35 | 7 | 15 | 6 | 3 |
| Scientific/ Consumer ... | 4 | 2 | 3 | 9 | — | 2 | 2 | 1 | 2 |
| Columns ... | 1 | 1 | 3 | — | — | 14 | 7 | 9 | — |
| Personalities ... | 5 | 10 | 7 | 4 | — | 19 | 18 | 19 | 10 |
| Sports ... | 5 | 4 | 1 | — | 7 | 10 | 9 | 10 | 9 |
| Arts and Entertainments | 22 | 16 | 13 | 29 | 25 | 9 | 8 | 3 | 10 |
| Women and Children ... | 7 | 8 | 26 | 8 | 5 | 13 | 19 | 14 | 5 |
| Picture features | 24 | 16 | 33 | 1 | 25 | 6 | 3 | 13 | 12 |
| Sex features ... | — | — | — | — | — | 5 | 1 | 14 | 39 |
| Other features | 20 | 10 | 9 | 6 | 3 | 15 | 18 | 11 | 10 |
| TOTAL... | 100 | 100 | 100 | 100 | 100 | 100 | 100 | 100 | 100 |
| Mean features picture content per sample issue (col.cms.) | 266 | 443 | 287 | 186 | 115 | 241 | 349 | 325 | 317 |

**TABLE IV B**

NATIONAL DAILIES, 1975:

ANALYSIS OF FEATURES SPACE (EXCLUDING PICTURES) INTO TEN
CATEGORIES

| Category | The Times | The Guardian | The Daily Telegraph | Financial Times | Morning Star | Daily Express | Daily Mail | Daily Mirror | The Sun |
|---|---|---|---|---|---|---|---|---|---|
| | % | % | % | % | % | % | % | % | % |
| Political, social and economic | 40 | 44 | 31 | 58 | 35 | 20 | 25 | 10 | 8 |
| Scientific/ Consumer ... | 8 | 4 | 2 | 11 | — | 3 | 4 | 6 | 6 |
| Columns ... | 5 | 5 | 11 | 4 | 1 | 14 | 11 | 19 | 6 |
| Personalities ... | 4 | 4 | 1 | 1 | — | 11 | 9 | 7 | 7 |
| Sports ... | 5 | 6 | 3 | — | 8 | 14 | 10 | 11 | 22 |
| Arts and Entertainments | 20 | 23 | 26 | 17 | 27 | 12 | 13 | 10 | 15 |
| Women and Children ... | 2 | 4 | 12 | 1 | 8 | 10 | 7 | 12 | 8 |
| Picture features | 1 | 1 | 1 | — | 1 | 1 | 1 | 2 | 2 |
| Sex features ... | — | — | — | — | — | 1 | 1 | 3 | 9 |
| Other features | 14 | 9 | 13 | 7 | 6 | 14 | 18 | 20 | 17 |
| TOTAL... | 99 | 100 | 100 | 99 | 86 | 100 | 99 | 100 | 100 |

## Headline space of Home News in the National Dailies

(i) A short study was undertaken of the headline space of Home News content, which accounted for a sizeable and fairly consistent proportion of editorial space, as well as being presented in a fairly standard fashion. It was expected that such a study could reveal any major differences or similarities in styles of headlining. Consequently, the headline content of Home News was studied for the 23 April and 27 November, two sample days chosen at random.

(ii) It was further decided that Home Sports news should be excluded from the study as sports news in all the newspapers is normally clearly distinguished from the rest of Home News.

(iii) Headlines were defined, for this purpose, as the summary of a story in a type face or type faces of much larger pointage than the bulk of the story. By this definition cross-headings were ignored, but multiple headlines of the type common in the tabloid papers were included and treated as being a single headline.

(iv) Where a story carried over from one page to another, the pertinent headlines on both pages were counted as part of headline space. The headline space was then counted in terms of standard column centimetres and classified by item type in the conventional way.

TABLE I

## HEADLINES AS PROPORTION OF NEWS SPACE

| Title | 1947* | 1975** | |
|---|---|---|---|
| | | 23 *April* | 27 *November* |
| *The Times* ... ... ... ... ... | 13 | 15 | 14 |
| *The Guardian* ... ... ... ... | NA | 25 | 21 |
| *The Daily Telegraph* ... ... ... | 15 | 18 | 16 |
| *Financial Times* ... ... ... ... | NA | 21 | 27 |
| *Daily Worker/Morning Star* ... ... | 22 | 20 | 22 |
| *Daily Express* ... ... ... ... | 27 | 27 | 28 |
| *Daily Mail* ... ... ... ... ... | 23 | 28 | 32 |
| *Daily Mirror* ... ... ... ... | 27 | 35 | 33 |
| *The Sun* ... ... ... ... ... | NA | 39 | 34 |

*Source:* Royal Commission on the Press 1947–9: Analysis of headline space as proportion of news space.

**Proportion of Home news space as headlines.

(v) From Table I, it appears that the proportion of news space for headlines has not increased across the range of National Daily newspapers, though there is relatively more in what are now the tabloid papers. For six newspapers, where comparisons with 1947 are possible, the proportion of Home News space as headlines for *The Times*, *The Daily Telegraph*, *Morning Star* and *Daily Express* has remained much the same. The main differences are to be seen in the *Daily Mail* and *Daily Mirror*, both of which have increased the proportion of headline to news by something like one quarter. In the case of the *Daily Mail* this has probably been due in some part to its change to a tabloid format.

(vi) As between the newspapers, *The Times* and *The Daily Telegraph* devote least home news space to headlines (under 20%) followed by the *Morning Star*, *Financial Times* and *The Guardian*. The remaining four "popular" papers had a higher percentage again.

(vii) The allocation of headline space to categories within home news varied according to type of newspaper. Headline space in the "Quality" papers tended to be dominated by the "Political, Social and Economic" categories. This reflects not only the higher amounts of such news in these newspapers, but also the fact that these subjects are the ones more likely to be given prominence in these newspapers.

(viii) For the "Popular" papers, the Law and Police news categories generally had the largest absolute and proportionate amounts of headline space, followed closely by the "Political, Social and Economic" categories and Other Home News.

This reflects the larger importance of Law and Police News in these newspapers as well as the more even spread of Home News space between the "Political", "Law" and "Other" news categories.

(ix) As far as "Political, Social and Economic news" is concerned, the "Quality" and "Popular" papers adopt different approaches to headlining. The load of Political Social and Economic headlines in the "Quality" papers is spread between several pages, often fairly evenly. This tends not to be so for the "Popular" papers, where one page, and often one item, accounts for the bulk of the "Political, Social and Economic" headlines. In such a circumstance it is often the front page lead story that is concerned, and a very large percentage of this story may simply be headline. For example, approximately ¾ of the lead story of *The Sun* on 23 April, dealing with the proposed nationalisation of British Leyland was headline space. This is compounded by the fact that this story accounted for 60% of the Political News reported in *The Sun* on that day. In other words, half of the total Home Political news in the paper was the headline of the lead story—a headline which gave but two "facts". As a contrast, on the same day, headlines to Political, Social and Economic articles (admittedly a broader category than the Political News referred to in the case of *The Sun*) could be found on six pages in *The Times* and headlines only accounted for 17% of the total 1·1 category news space.

(x) Aside from this qualification about the "headlineability" of certain Political, Social and Economic lead stories, it does not seem as if some types of news were more likely than others to receive headline treatment. In fact, for each of the newspapers, most of the main news categories had roughly equivalent proportions of space devoted to headlines.

## Advertising content in National Dailies

(i) This brief analysis of display advertising has been carried out to indicate the main types of goods and services which are advertised and to show some broad patterns of difference between newspapers. Since only one quarter (April–June) has been looked at and only six issues of each paper (one from each weekday) the findings may not be representative of the full year and the percentage figures are subject to rather high margins of sampling error.

(ii) A broad difference between "Quality" and other newspapers is very noticeable, with the latter heavily weighted towards advertisements for consumer goods and services and the former towards business, finance and industry. The *Daily Mail* comes nearer to the "Quality" papers in this respect, than does the *Daily Mirror* or *The Sun*. *The Guardian* is "nearer" to the "Popular" papers in this respect than the other "Qualities".

(iii) Within the "consumer" sector, there are further marks of differentiation. For instance, the group of "Quality" papers gave disproportionate attention to travel and holidays and to alcoholic drinks, while the "Popular "group was differentially inclined to carry advertisements for tobacco products, shops and mail order goods. Amongst consumer goods, products related to motoring were most prominent and food products as such come low down. While *The Daily Telegraph* seems to under-represent motoring products it should be remembered that its weekend magazine gives much space to this form of advertising as well as other consumer goods (see Appendix L).

(iv) The categories of public service and political advertising include a high proportion of content paid for by government and local authorities. Virtually all category 11 appears to be so financed and it is noticeably more present in the "Popular" newspapers. Charity appeals gravitate towards the "Quality" press and political advertising is fairly evenly distributed. The period sampled includes the most active period for the EEC Referendum Campaign.

(v) A separate identification was made of advertising originating in central or local government, nationalised industries or other public bodies (including armed services and police). The figures are not given in Table I, but the results can be summarised, firstly by showing the percentage of display advertising from such sources for each title (Table II) and, secondly, by noting that almost all is accounted for by categories 1, 11, 14, 16 and 22 of Table I.

TABLE I

ANALYSIS OF DISPLAY ADVERTISING CONTENT OF NATIONAL DAILIES INTO 20 CATEGORIES: SECOND QUARTER OF 1975 (SIX ISSUES OF EACH TITLE)

| Category | The Times | The Guardian | The Daily Telegraph (1) | *The Daily Telegraph (2) | Financial Times | Morning Star | Daily Express | Daily Mail | Daily Mirror | The Sun |
|---|---|---|---|---|---|---|---|---|---|---|
| | % | % | % | % | % | % | % | % | % | % |
| **Consumer goods and services:** | | | | | | | | | | |
| 1. Travel, holidays, air-lines ... | 4 | 7 | 5 | 7 | 7 | — | 4 | 3 | 3 | 2 |
| 2. Cars, Motoring accessories etc. ... | 18 | 11 | 6 | 8 | 10 | 34 | 15 | 9 | 9 | 9 |
| 3. Alcoholic drink (non-retail) ... | 3 | 2 | 1 | 2 | 1 | — | — | 1 | — | — |
| 4. Tobacco products ... ... | — | 4 | 2 | 2 | — | — | 10 | 9 | 13 | 15 |
| 5. Food, other drink, medicines ... | 3 | 2 | 1 | 1 | — | — | 3 | 1 | 4 | 4 |
| 6. Clothing fashion, toilet, jewellery ... | 1 | 5 | 1 | 2 | — | — | 3 | 2 | 4 | 5 |
| 7. Books, magazines, theatre, arts ... | 4 | 7 | 3 | 4 | 1 | 17 | 3 | 4 | 5 | 3 |
| 8. Direct retail distributive ... | 2 | 2 | 4 | 6 | — | — | 18 | 13 | 23 | 17 |
| 9. Other consumer goods ... ... | 2 | 7 | 5 | 6 | 4 | 32 | 10 | 10 | 6 | 12 |
| 10. Mail Order consumer goods... ... | 4 | 3 | 4 | 5 | — | — | 9 | 12 | 11 | 6 |
| Total ... ... | 41 | 50 | 32 | 43 | 23 | 83 | 75 | 64 | 78 | 73 |

**Public service and opinion:**

| | | | | | | | | | | |
|---|---|---|---|---|---|---|---|---|---|---|
| 11. Social Welfare, health, safety, employment ... ... ... | 4 | 4 | 2 | 2 | 2 | — | 6 | 5 | 6 | 6 |
| 12. Charity appeals, religion ... | 3 | 3 | 3 | 4 | 1 | — | 1 | 1 | 1 | 1 |
| 13. Political and foreign policy ... | 3 | 5 | 1 | 1 | — | 16 | 2 | 3 | 1 | 3 |
| Total ... ... | 10 | 12 | 6 | 7 | 3 | 16 | 9 | 9 | 8 | 10 |

**Company, business financial:**

| | | | | | | | | | | |
|---|---|---|---|---|---|---|---|---|---|---|
| 14. Company and financial reports ... | 24 | 9 | 11 | 16 | 36 | — | — | 2 | — | — |
| 15. Banks, insurance and related financial, including P.O. savings ... | 9 | 23 | 11 | 16 | 17 | — | 8 | 13 | 6 | 7 |
| 16. Other company advertising ... ... | 9 | 1 | 3 | 6 | 8 | — | 3 | 6 | 1 | — |
| 17. Products and services for business or industry ... ... ... ... | 1 | 3 | 7 | 10 | 10 | — | 3 | 2 | — | — |
| Total ... ... | 43 | 36 | 32 | 48 | 71 | — | 14 | 23 | 7 | 7 |

**Other:**

| | | | | | | | | | | |
|---|---|---|---|---|---|---|---|---|---|---|
| 18. Sport, football, pools, racing ... | — | — | — | — | — | — | 2 | 2 | 3 | 3 |
| 19. Jobs ... ... ... ... | — | — | 29 | — | — | — | — | 2 | 4 | 4 |
| 20. Miscellaneous ... ... | 6 | 2 | 2 | 2 | 3 | 1 | 2 | — | — | 3 |
| Total ... ... | 6 | 2 | 31 | 2 | 3 | 1 | 2 | 4 | 7 | 10 |
| TOTAL ... ... | 100 | 100 | 101 | 100 | 100 | 100 | 100 | 100 | 100 | 100 |
| Mean display advertising per sample issue —second quarter only (col.cms.) ... | 2,097 | 1,634 | 4,757 | 3,343 | 3,511 | 72 | 2,455 | 1,751 | 1,803 | 1,784 |

303

*Two alternative sets of figures are given for *The Daily Telegraph*, the first based on a total in which much "situations vacant" advertising has been included, the second excluding this type of advertising. All other figures in the report relating to *The Daily Telegraph* follow the former policy, but since this is divergent from other quality papers, the second set of figures is more comparable.

**TABLE II**

| The Times | The Guardian | The Daily Telegraph | Financial Times | Morning Star | Daily Express | Daily Mail | Daily Mirror | The Sun |
|---|---|---|---|---|---|---|---|---|
| 10% | 13% | 7% | 3% | — | 10% | 13% | 11% | 11% |

The average for all eight titles is 8·8% of display advertising space. A larger sample would probably reduce some of the differences, suggesting a fairly even distribution of expenditure between titles by public bodies.

(vi) Other points to note include: the importance (in space terms) of advertisements for banks and insurance; and the incidence of sport-related advertising in the popular press.

(vii) In summary, we can see a number of the main aspects of reader and editorial content profile reflected in a consistent way in the advertising of products. It also seems that different sorts of newspapers have rather different sources of advertising revenue and may be, consequently, subject to different kinds of commercial risk. A more extended and representative study would be needed to confirm the stability of the pattern which is revealed here. In fact, the distribution of display advertising space for the second quarter does exactly match the pattern for the year as a whole in quantitative terms. The internal composition might, however, be different in different quarters.

# Special supplements in the National Daily Newspapers

(i) Supplement material—sections of pages on some subject or subjects added to the normal layout of a newspaper—exists in three main forms in the national daily newspapers:

(a) The Special Report: a report prepared by the editorial staff of a newspaper on some subject and backed up by advertising by parties interested in the subject matter of the report.

(b) The Advertising Supplement: prepared by an advertiser or advertisers; this is simply a very long display advertisement, using editorial-like lay-out devices.

(c) The Pseudo-Supplement: where a newspaper has a great deal of copy on one topic, it might collect all this together to create a kind of supplement but here any advertising space will be unconnected with the subject of the supplement. The only example in our sample was the Sportsmail Derby Special and this has been included in the regular analysis since the copy would have gone into the newspaper anyway and printing it in supplement form is largely an editorial device. In the case of the other two categories, the content would not have been included if it had not been in this supplement form.

(ii) *The Advertising Supplement.* While this type of supplement is common in the provincial newspapers (see Appendix A13), in the full national daily sample only one occurred, in the *Financial Times* for 17 April, on Rolatruc Limited.

(iii) *The Special Report.* This category covered all the other special supplements found in the sample of national daily newspapers. A full list of these, categorised by subject matter, is found in Table I. The *Financial Times* has 68% of the supplements, followed by *The Times* with 21% and *The Guardian* with 11%. The dominance of the special report supplement is attributable to the fact that such supplements concern broad subjects—usually either an industry, unit of local government or foreign country and advertising can be sought from many sources. This makes the floating of a special report a viable proposition, whereas the finding of an advertising supplement of four or even eight pages is a heavy commitment to the display advertising budget of a company. The cost of a special report is borne by both newspaper and advertisers, and as the advertisers pay only for their particular advertisement space, the load on their advertising budget may not be heavy.

(iv) When counted as part of newspaper space, the special supplements make a significant difference to issue size of the newspapers involved. For the sample studied, the special supplements added, on average, 15·4% to the size of the *Financial Times*, 6·6% to the size of *The Times* and 1·3% to the size of *The Guardian*. Although special supplements were not counted as part of newspaper content for the main analyses of the national daily papers, the inclusion of the supplement content affects the relative sizes of the newspapers involved, as shown in Table II.

These increases are equivalent to 4½ pages per issue in the *Financial Times*, 1¾ pages in *The Times*, and 1¼ pages in *The Guardian*. They mean that the *Financial Times* takes over from *The Daily Telegraph* as the newspaper with the largest average size, and that *The Times* comes much closer than before to *The Daily Telegraph* in terms of mean size per issue.

(v) However, the inclusion of supplements does not greatly affect the ratio of editorial to advertising space in the relevant newspapers, although there is a slight tendency towards an increase in the proportionate share of advertising space as Table III shows.

Similarly, comparison of the various percentages of editorial and advertising space in Table I shows that, for the bulk of the special report supplements, the space given to editorial and advertising content is divided roughly 50-50.

SPECIAL SUPPLEMENTS

TABLE I

SPECIAL SUPPLEMENTS IN NATIONAL DAILIES: SIZE, SUBJECT AND SPACE
ALLOCATION

| Subject | Total space s.c. cm. | Editorial space % | Advert space % | Title | No. of pages |
|---|---|---|---|---|---|
| **Foreign Countries** | | | | | |
| Hong Kong ... ... ... | 5280 | 53 | 47 | FT | 12 |
| Australia ... ... ... | 3520 | 47 | 53 | T | 8 |
| Portugal ... ... ... | 2640 | 51 | 49 | FT | 6 |
| Brazil ... ... ... ... | 3520 | 43 | 57 | FT | 8 |
| Qatar ... ... ... ... | 3520 | 44 | 56 | FT | 8 |
| Oman ... ... ... ... | 6160 | 43 | 57 | T | 14 |
| Japan ... ... ... ... | 1760 | 68 | 32 | T | 4 |
| Yugoslavia ... ... ... | 880 | 48 | 52 | FT | 2 |
| Kenya ... ... ... ... | 2200 | 59 | 41 | FT | 5 |
| **Commercial: Manufacturing** | | | | | |
| Movable Buildings ... ... | 880 | 48 | 52 | G | 2 |
| Offshore Oil Exploration ... | 5280 | 49 | 51 | FT | 12 |
| Cranes ... ... ... ... | 1320 | 52 | 48 | FT | 3 |
| Tin ... ... ... ... | 880 | 50 | 50 | T | 2 |
| Batteries ... ... ... | 1320 | 47 | 53 | FT | 3 |
| Building Industry ... ... | 3520 | 42 | 58 | FT | 8 |
| Italian Building ... ... | 1320 | 50 | 50 | FT | 3 |
| *Rolatruc ... ... ... | 1760 | 0 | 100 | FT | 4 |
| **Commercial: Service Industries** | | | | | |
| Computing Services ... ... | 1760 | 47 | 53 | FT | 4 |
| Word Processing ... ... | 880 | 50 | 50 | FT | 2 |
| Franchising ... ... ... | 880 | 57 | 43 | FT | 2 |
| Data Processing ... ... | 2200 | 46 | 54 | FT | 5 |
| **Commercial: Consumer** | | | | | |
| Books for Christmas ... ... | 5280 | 54 | 46 | T | 12 |
| **Municipal** | | | | | |
| Basildon ... ... ... | 880 | 51 | 49 | FT | 2 |
| Basildon ... ... ... | 880 | 61 | 39 | T | 2 |
| Midland New Towns ... ... | 1320 | 54 | 46 | G | 3 |
| Greater Manchester ... ... | 1760 | 47 | 53 | FT | 4 |
| **Political** | | | | | |
| Pre-Referendum Supplement | 5280 | 46 | 54 | FT | 12 |
| **Other** | | | | | |
| International Coin and Stamp Fair ... ... ... ... | 440 | 60 | 40 | FT | 1 |
| Outward Bound Courses ... | 880 | 57 | 43 | G | 2 |

*The Rolatruc supplement is an advertising supplement, whereas the other 28 are all special
report supplements.

**TABLE II**

**MEAN NEWSPAPER SIZE INCLUDING AND EXCLUDING SUPPLEMENTS**

|  | The Times | The Guardian | The Daily Telegraph | Financial Times | Morning Star | Daily Express | Daily Mail | Daily Mirror | The Sun |
|---|---|---|---|---|---|---|---|---|---|
| Mean newspaper size excluding supplements (col.cms.) ... | 10,944 | 9,433 | 12,655 | 11,957 | 1,954 | 6,917 | 6,546 | 5,367 | 5,333 |
| Mean newspaper size including supplements (col.cms.) ... | 11,658 | 9,952 | 12,655 | 13,785 | 1,954 | 6,917 | 6,546 | 5,367 | 5,333 |

**TABLE III**

**EDITORIAL AND ADVERTISING SPACE INCLUDING AND EXCLUDING SUPPLEMENTS**

|  | Financial Times | | The Times | | The Guardian | |
|---|---|---|---|---|---|---|
|  | Adverts | Editorial | Adverts | Editorial | Adverts | Editorial |
|  | % | % | % | % | % | % |
| Excluding supplements ... | 34 | 66 | 35 | 65 | 26 | 74 |
| Including supplements ... | 37 | 63 | 36 | 64 | 26 | 74 |

**A comparison between item-counting and space-counting as a method of measurement**

(i) The method used in this study has been to measure space allotted to different categories in terms of standard column centimetres. An alternative, giving the same results, would have been to measure area in square centimetres or inches. A third possibility, which has sometimes been used in previous studies, is to count items and to percentage sub-totals for each category. The apparent disadvantages of this method are: firstly, the inappropriateness of the "item" unit for some kinds of newspaper space (eg large display advertisements or articles spreading across several pages); secondly, the possibility that very different styles of newspaper format would reduce the comparability of the "item" as a unit of measurement. On the other hand, it might be argued that measurements of space give an undue advantage to the larger papers and the "Quality" papers and implicitly put a value on space, irrespective of the fact that reading patterns may actually favour smaller items. Thus, a paper with a lot of small items of "serious" news may be undervalued by comparison with a paper with much longer items on the same or fewer topics.

(ii) In order to test for the difference between methods, an analysis was made of the space given to all home news (apart from sport) in six issues of nine National Dailies. The results are summarised in Table I, first by averaging the percentage distributions of all nine titles together, secondly by making a comparison between the two titles which showed most evidence of divergence when the alternative measures are used.

TABLE I

COMPARISON OF DISTRIBUTION OF HOME NEWS SPACE FOR NATIONAL DAILIES, 2nd QUARTER OF 1975, ACCORDING TO MEASURES OF ITEM—COUNTS AND TOTAL SPACE

| Category | All Titles | | The Times | | The Sun | |
|---|---|---|---|---|---|---|
| | Item-count method | Space measure | Item-count method | Space measure | Item-count method | Space measure |
| | % | % | % | % | % | % |
| 1. All political social, economic ... ... | 50 | 54 | 54 | 58 | 28 | 34 |
| 2. Crime, police accidents | 19 | 17 | 17 | 16 | 37 | 34 |
| 3. Personalities ... ... | 7 | 9 | 10 | 13 | 8 | 13 |
| 4. Other ... ... ... | 24 | 20 | 19 | 13 | 27 | 20 |
| TOTAL ... ... ... | 100 | 100 | 100 | 100 | 100 | 100 |

(iii) The full set of figures from which these data are extracted tell a story of high correlation between the item-count measure and the space measure and of very great consistency between newspapers in the relationship between the two measures. Table I also shows the two titles for which space and item-count measures produced the most divergent results in the sense that the ratio of categories to each other was internally most affected by the use of alternative measures. This was more apparent on smaller news categories and less so in the grouped figures in the total. It can be concluded that all nine titles were very similar and all exhibited one same basic tendency: for the "miscellaneous" or residual category to "gain" from the item-count measure purely because very small items were often placed here.

(iv) Two main conclusions can be drawn from these data. One is that the "Popular" papers would not show up as relatively "better" or even significantly different if an item count measure was used. In fact, the space measure brings *The Sun* "closer" to *The Times* than does the item count measure. Secondly, we might also conclude that for relatively homogeneous categories of newspaper space, like news content, an analysis of space by item counts would be a reliable method of proceeding. It would certainly be much quicker and less laborious and would lend itself more readily to analysis by computer. The objection to it as a method for analysis of all newspaper space remains, but an acceptable strategy could be to employ a mixture of space and item count methods. This should certainly be considered if research of this kind is undertaken again.

(v) As a by-product of this analysis, figures were produced showing the average space per item for the home news categories in different newspapers. The results are predictable from data presented earlier in this section and in main Table A7 showing the distribution of news space. It is worth emphasising, however, that, on average, the space given to an item of political, social or economic news is not generally smaller in a "Popular" than in a "Quality" paper. Summary statistics for two home news categories are given in Table II.

TABLE II

ADJUSTED MEAN SPACE PER ITEM FOR TWO CATEGORIES OF HOME NEWS (COL. CMS.)

| Category | The Times | The Guardian | The Daily Telegraph | Financial Times | Morning Star | Daily Express | Daily Mail | Daily Mirror | The Sun |
|---|---|---|---|---|---|---|---|---|---|
| Political, social and economic news (Home)... | 24 | 30 | 25 | 28 | 24 | 26 | 37 | 25 | 33 |
| Industrial relations, Labour news... | 28 | 34 | 24 | 26 | 19 | 28 | 20 | 22 | 20 |

Similarity of size in the top row results mainly from the greater size of the "Qualities", on the one hand and, on the other, the tendency of "Populars" to give extensive, front-page treatment (with large headlines) to major political news items of the day.

**Weekend Magazines: summary analysis**

A basic comparison of content of these publications is given in Table I. Since only small samples were involved, the reliability of estimates is limited, and the classification of editorial content is subject to an inevitable degree of error. The dates chosen for the Sunday magazines were the same as for the sample of Sunday newspapers. The *Sunday Telegraph* magazines were taken from six dates: September 12, 19 and 26, November 28, December 5 and 12, 1975.

**TABLE I**

**ANALYSIS OF CONTENT OF WEEKEND MAGAZINES: THE OBSERVER, THE SUNDAY TIMES, SUNDAY TELEGRAPH (SIX ISSUES OF EACH)**

(a) Analysis of content into editorial and advertising space

| Content | The Observer | The Sunday Times | Sunday Telegraph |
|---|---|---|---|
| | % | % | % |
| Editorial ... ... ... ... ... | 43 | 38 | 36 |
| Advertising ... ... ... ... | 57 | 62 | 64 |
| TOTAL ... ... | 100 | 100 | 100 |

(b) Analysis of editorial content into seven categories

| Category | The Observer | The Sunday Times | Sunday Telegraph |
|---|---|---|---|
| | % | % | % |
| Cover, index, miscellaneous ... ... | 12 | 5 | 27 |
| Personalities, biography ... ... ... | 14 | 19 | 11 |
| Sport, leisure, motoring, food, d.i.y., consumer matters ... ... ... | 24 | 21 | 15 |
| Art, entertainment, design, photography, architecture ... ... ... ... | 4 | 26 | 10 |
| Puzzles, competitions, children ... ... | 16 | 4 | 9 |
| Nature, travel, science, history, anthropology ... ... ... ... ... | 14 | 10 | 4 |
| Political, social and economic ... ... | 16 | 15 | 24 |
| TOTAL ... ... | 100 | 100 | 100 |

(c) Analysis of advertising into eight categories

| Category | The Observer | The Sunday Times | Sunday Telegraph |
|---|---|---|---|
| Travel, motoring ... ... ... ... | 10 | 13 | 16 |
| Drink, tobacco ... ... ... ... | 33 | 21 | 30 |
| Food, fashions, clothes ... ... ... | 5 | 5 | 12 |
| Mail order ... ... ... ... ... | 8 | 8 | 3 |
| Company advertising, banks, insurance | 10 | 9 | 13 |
| Other consumer goods ... ... ... | 24 | 32 | 21 |
| Business, industrial ... ... ... | 1 | 5 | 1 |
| Other ... ... ... ... ... | 11 | 7 | 6 |
| TOTAL ... ... | 102 | 100 | 102 |

Only a few points need be added to the tabular picture. First, advertising content is high, though not above the normal level for the Sunday Press and there is a large quantity of non-advertising content. (The average sizes of *The Observer*, *The Sunday Times*, and *Sunday Telegraph* sample issues were 51, 66 and 54 pages respectively). Advertising content in all three is dominated by drink, tobacco and consumer goods advertisements. Editorial content is dominated by leisure, arts and entertainment, and political, social and economic content, but personality and biography is important in each of the three. Despite some characteristic differences, the overall impression is of similarity.

**Comments on coding frame applied to Provincial Morning and to Provincial Evening Newspapers**

(i) The analysis of provincial newspapers presented some new problems as well as new opportunities and the set of categories which has been devised is a compromise between the wish to retain the possibility of comparison with the national press and the wish to explore some types of local news in more detail. For the most part the innovations relate to national and provincial news, although the set of feature content categories has also been rewritten. The basic strategy has been to introduce a division between news and features relating to the circulation area of the paper and those items having mainly non-local or "national" reference, and to categorise the former in greater detail. At the same time, a lower emphasis has been placed on external news and on non-local features. In general, the separation of the two main categories of content did not prove difficult to put into practice, although there are evidently cases where an event occuring locally may also be of national interest. Where this occurred coders were instructed to code the material as non-national. This makes very little difference to the results especially since the issue arose most frequently for sport news.

(ii) In so far as problems in coding occurred which are different from those discussed already in relation to the National Dailies, they mainly concerned the distinction between political, social and economic aspects of local and regional news. Some aspects of coding difficulties and conventions are discussed in the following paragraphs.

(a) Category P1.11 (local Political news) was taken to include references to the region in National politics, and statements by regional politicians in London as well as locally.

(b) While the coding frame contained a category 1.2S for non-local law news with a sexual component, there was not a similar P1.2S for Provincial News. This was something of an omission and certainly there was a component of slightly salacious regional court cases, although most of the Provincial mornings also covered the more lurid cases that featured in the national press eg the "Playland" homosexual vice-ring in September.

(c) Category P1.3 ("Accidents") was made more inclusive than 1.3 in the National Daily Frame, and included some sorts of property destruction—specifically that which could not be attributable to criminal action. In the National Daily study, only personal accidents were included.

(d) Categories P1.4 and P1.6 ("Personalities" and "Events" and "Activities") contain items which could have either codings. For instance, pictures of local firms or associations' dinner-dances were coded as P1.6, whereas weddings were coded P1.4. Pictures and treatment were often the same, perhaps the only difference being the use of names in wedding photos and not for dinner-dances, etc. The convention hinged around this distinction, however, so whenever the main focus of the story was the people concerned it was coded P1.4 and where the *event* was of greater prominence it was P1.6. However, certain difficulties remained and some coding inconsistency can be expected to have occurred. A related difficulty emerged if the photo content of a P1.6 report was very large, and there was some confusion over leaving the coding as P1.6 or "upgrading" it to P4.8, local picture features. By and large, the conflict was resolved by leaving the coding P1.6.

(e) Category 4.1 (Non-local Political, Social and Economic features) only covers developments in the rest of Great Britain. Features of P.S.E. content concerning foreign events were coded 4.9. This decision was taken to allow comparability with category 4.1 in the National Daily study (when combined with category P4.1L), but it does mean that the 4.9 categories in the two studies are not comparable, and that the "serious" feature coverage for the Provincial mornings will be slightly underestimated.

(*f*) Category P1.6 was also taken to include reports of ordinary club meetings and events.

(*g*) Categories P1.5 and 1.5 created problems when sporting events involving local teams or sportsmen were involved. Generally speaking, the geographical rule was applied—if the event happened within the newspaper's catchment area the event was regarded as local. However, there were two exceptions to this rule.

   (i) Racing news and racing form was coded as 1.5 even when the meeting was local.

   (ii) Football and rugby reports were given opposite treatment and where a local team was concerned reports of its fortunes were given the local "P" prefix even if the team was playing at the other end of the country. It was felt in this case that such reports *were* mainly motivated by regional considerations.

(*h*) The 4.6 and P4.6 categories in the Provincial Mornings frame (Arts and Entertainment Features) cover previews as well as reviews, and have been treated as being more inclusive than the category 4.6 in the National Daily coding frame. In the latter case, previews were treated as being Other Regular Features (4.81), but this category disappeared for the Provincial Mornings, and previews were coded into 4.6. This may give the erroneous impression of greater weight being given to entertainment features than in the National Daily papers.

(*i*) Difficulty was experienced in allocating financial and market news between category 3.1 and P1.12 (local economic). As far as possible, the rubric written into the coding frame was followed but, inevitably some, inconsistency has resulted. A certain proportion of material classified as 3.1 (financial news) does in any case relate to local firms and business. An additional category for agricultural market and price news, with mainly local references, was devised and applied.

(*j*) The category P4.3 (provincial consumer news) only concerns "matters of *local* consumer interest" and hence prices and shops in the circulation area. However, much of the information about prices and consumer affairs in many of the papers was couched in *national* terms and was therefore lost to this category. Thus P4.3 only tells one how much *provincial* consumer news was given, and not how much *total* consumer news there was.

(iii) The Scottish newspapers presented some distinctive coding problems. As has been said, there was very little difficulty in setting boundaries around the catchment area of the newspaper—that is, in distinguishing between local and non-local content—in the case of English and Welsh newspapers. Because of Scotland's quasi-national status, however, its newspapers cannot be treated as equally "provincial" and certain conventions were adopted that were not followed when dealing with the English and Welsh papers.

As far as the "Non-Local" *vs* "Provincial" News distinction was concerned, the six Scottish Daily papers were divided into two groups; those "National" Scottish papers that might claim to cover Scotland as a whole, *The Scotsman, Glasgow Herald, Daily Record* and *Scottish Daily News*, and those serving a "city-region" like the English Provincial Mornings; the *Courier and Advertiser* from Dundee, and *The Press and Journal* from Aberdeen. The former group were coded so that everything reported as happening in Scotland had the "P" prefix, whereas for the latter pair, only events in

313

their respective "city regions" were so coded. This probably resulted in an overestimate of the "Provincial" content of the four "national" Scottish papers, while underestimating the amount for the others. For the English papers, events may truly be said to be simply either Provincial or National, but in the Scottish papers a further step is observable, making a gradation of "Provincialness" of news from "provincial" to "Scottish" to "National". In order to identify those contents of the Aberdeen and Dundee papers which related to Scotland rather than the United Kingdom or their own city regions, a suffix "E" was applied. Apart from this, the only variation in practise called for in coding the Scottish newspapers was to treat all sports news relating to Scotland as P1.5, regardless of the distinction between the "national" and "provincial" Scottish newspapers described above.

**Special supplements in the Provincial Morning Newspapers**

(i) The sample of 12 issues of 17 titles yielded 15 special supplements, of which nine were special reports and six were advertising supplements. In the case of the National Dailies, all but one of the 29 supplements sampled were special reports (see Appendix A9). However, the line between the two types is less clearly drawn in the Provincial newspapers, since, in some cases it was hard to distinguish editorial matter from content directly related to advertising.

(ii) The Provincial papers with special supplements tended to be of the "metropolitan" type (See Section IV, 3 of Part A of the report), that is, papers with more national and financial news.

(iii) The presence of supplements makes some difference to the average size of the different newspapers, as these were recorded in Table 18 of the main report. *The Birmingham Post* increases by an average of 2·6 pages, the *Morning Telegraph* (Sheffield) by 2·2 pages and the other titles, where applicable, by less than a page.

**TABLE I**

## SPECIAL SUPPLEMENTS IN THE PROVINCIAL MORNING NEWSPAPERS

| Supplement Titles | Supple-ment* Type | Title of Newspaper | Space s.c.cms. | Editorial Space % | Advert Space % | Number of full pages |
|---|---|---|---|---|---|---|
| Lombard—RAC Rally ... | SR | The Birmingham Post | 3890 | 42 | 58 | 10 |
| National Exhibi-tion Centre... | SR | The Birmingham Post | 4712 | 50 | 50 | 8 |
| Buck and Hickman Ltd. | A | The Birmingham Post | 2356 | 34 | 66 | 4 |
| Midlands Indus-trial Property Survey ... | A | The Birmingham Post | 5890 | 31 | 69 | 10 |
| Homemaker ... | A | Morning Telegraph | 5890 | 5 | 95 | 14 |
| Homemaker ... | A | Morning Telegraph | 6048 | 12 | 88 | 12 |
| Shopabout ... | SR | The Journal | 4032 | 9 | 91 | 8 |
| Christmas ... | SR | Eastern Daily Press | 1892 | 58 | 42 | 4 |
| Kingston-upon-Hull ... | A | Yorkshire Post | 1288 | 29 | 71 | 2½ |
| Hirst Buckley Ltd. ... | SR | Yorkshire Post | 2016 | 29 | 71 | 4 |
| Welsh Rugby Review ... | SR | Western Mail | 2688 | 52 | 47 | 8 |
| Building and Civil Engineering | SR | The Scotsman | 1792 | 47 | 53 | 4 |
| Advertising Review ... | SR | The Scotsman | 1792 | 53 | 47 | 4 |
| Scottish Motor Show ... | SR | Glasgow Herald | 2745 | 35 | 65 | 5 |
| Fife Review ... | A | The Courier and Advertiser | 2490 | 22 | 78 | 4 |

*SR = Special Report
A = Advertising Supplement

## Note on the Scottish Daily News

(i) Six issues of the *Scottish Daily News* were analysed and the results were available for comparison with a sample of six issues of other Scottish papers from the same dates. Data comparing the *Scottish Daily News* with two other papers published in Glasgow, the *Daily Record* and the *Glasgow Herald*, are given in Tables I and II.

### TABLE I

COMPARISON BETWEEN SCOTTISH DAILY NEWS AND TWO OTHER SCOTTISH NEWSPAPERS IN TERMS OF PROPORTION OF TOTAL SPACE GIVEN TO NEWS, FEATURES, OTHER EDITORIAL SPACE, ADVERTISING AND OF PICTURE CONTENT AS A PROPORTION OF EDITORIAL SPACE

| Category | Daily Record | Scottish Daily News | Glasgow Herald |
|---|---|---|---|
| | % | % | % |
| Editorial Space: | | | |
| News ... ... ... ... ... | 33 | 49 | 30 |
| Features ... ... ... ... ... | 15 | 19 | 13 |
| Other ... ... ... ... ... | 11 | 14 | 8 |
| Total ... ... | 59 | 82 | 51 |
| Advertising... ... ... ... ... | 41 | 18 | 49 |
| TOTAL ... ... | 100 | 100 | 100 |
| Mean space per sample issue: (Col. cms.) | 5,817 | 4,438 | 9,264 |
| Pictures as % of editorial space ... | 20 | 17 | 10 |

(ii) In terms of this basic comparison, the *Scottish Daily News* differs most evidently in having been smaller on average than either the *Glasgow Herald* or *Daily Record*, in its markedly lower proportion of advertising and its higher pictorial content. Some more detailed comparisons of news coverage are given in Table II.

(iii) This table does not indicate any great difference of profile between the *Scottish Daily News* and the *Daily Record* and *Glasgow Herald*, although the former did give relatively more news space to non-Scottish news than either of the others, much of it being sport news. Its allocation of space to sport was high (50%). It gave a relatively high proportion of space to external news, but the distribution of space between headings of local regional and provincial news is unexceptional. The overall allocation of news space to political, social and economic news, at 14%, was lower than that of the *Daily Record* (18%) or the *Glasgow Herald* (26%).

(iv) Feature and other editorial space distributions are not tabulated here for the *Scottish Daily News*, but the following points can be noted. Firstly, the fact that a higher proportion of feature space (62%) was given to non-local features. Secondly, that 7% of feature space was coded as "sex-related". Thirdly, that features on local places or topography or local personalities were completely absent—although both are a distinctive feature of the provincial newspaper and between them accounted for 10% of the *Daily Record* and 8% of the *Glasgow Herald*. By these criteria, the *Scottish Daily News* seems to have been more like a national UK paper than either a Glasgow or a Scottish paper.

**TABLE II**

**COMPARISON BETWEEN SCOTTISH DAILY NEWS AND TWO OTHER SCOTTISH NEWSPAPERS IN TERMS OF ALLOCATION OF ALL NEWS SPACE BETWEEN 12 CATEGORIES**

| Category | Daily Record | Scottish Daily News | Glasgow Herald |
|---|---|---|---|
| | % | % | % |
| National Home News: | | | |
| 1. Political, social and economic, including labour, Ulster news parliament ... ... ... ... | 6 | 4 | 9 |
| 2. Law, police, accident ... ... | 5 | 4 | 2 |
| 3. Sport ... ... ... ... ... | 28 | 34 | 8 |
| 4. Other ... ... ... ... ... | 4 | 6 | 1 |
| Total ... ... | 43 | 48 | 20 |
| 5. External News ... ... ... | 6 | 12 | 13 |
| 6. Financial News ... ... ... | 1 | 1 | 30 |
| Total ... ... | 7 | 13 | 43 |
| Provincial, regional and local news: | | | |
| 7. Political ... ... ... ... | 4 | 4 | 6 |
| 8. Economic (including labour) ... | 5 | 4 | 8 |
| 9. Social, planning ... ... ... | 3 | 2 | 3 |
| 10. Law, police, accident ... ... | 10 | 6 | 5 |
| 11. Sport ... ... ... ... ... | 14 | 16 | 10 |
| 12. Other ... ... ... ... ... | 13 | 7 | 5 |
| Total ... ... | 49 | 39 | 37 |
| TOTAL ... ... | 99 | 100 | 100 |
| Mean news space (Col. cms.) ... | 1897 | 2179 | 2758 |

## Comment on the coding frame applied to the Local Weekly Newspapers

(i) Because of the particular character of the local weekly newspaper, a different coding frame was applied to those in our sample so as to give an adequate descriptive account of their content. The Provincial morning and evening newspapers had needed a separate coding frame in order to explore local news in more detail than was possible with the national daily newspapers, and the local weeklies needed a further step to be taken in the same direction. Thus, all non-local news is placed in one residual category. Similarly, all non-local features are allocated to one category.

The following paragraphs deal with ways in which new categories were interpreted especially when the rubric or category itself left room for discretion.

(ii) Local News.

    (*a*) Category 1.12L—Local trade union matters were only to be placed in this category when concerned with industrial relations or the general pursual of union members' interests. Peripheral activities of trade unions, such as trips, social evenings etc, were coded according to the nature of the activity.

    (*b*) Category 1.13P (Local Social Problems) was given a broad interpretation. Any local social problem could be included here, from hooliganism to environmental concerns.

    (*c*) There was some overlapping between categories 1.4 and 1.6—(Personality news and news of local events), especially where part of a local event report focussed attention on individuals. For instance, events such as school prize-givings or local association A.G.M.s were more like personality reports. By and large, the local event category 1.6 was given precedence in such cases.

    (*d*) Category 1.7—Local information. The boundaries of this category remained somewhat indistinct, although it was intended to cover content dealing with the simple and factual presentation of useful local information—often in list form. The main difficulty was to separate this from news of local events (1.6) and there could have been some inter-coder inconsistency in making the distinction.

    (*e*) Category 1.91—"*Around the Districts column*". This category covered columns giving a detailed coverage of events in a small part of the newspapers' catchment area. Where longer pieces were included as part of such columns, or where the news concerned local politics, social services etc, the items were coded separately by their subject matter, leaving the rest of the column as 1.91.

(iii) National or external news. Category 2.0 was used even when foreign news covered such subjects as a local sports team playing abroad eg Wrexham Football Club's matches on foreign soil were coded as 2.0.

(iv) Local features.

    (*a*) Category 4.4—*Personality features* was taken to include a particular form of composite feature consisting of a series of reports of local funerals, giving background information about those deceased. The category was also interpreted as having precedence over Womens features (4.71), so that a personality feature on what was ostensibly a women's page would be coded as 4.4.

    (*b*) Where competitions occurred in a *Children's feature* (4.72) they were separately coded as *Puzzles, Competitions and Offers* (5.7).

    (*c*) Category 4.8—*Local picture features* mainly covered photographs unrelated to any news event and often consisted of local scenic attractions. Even where very large pictures were included, if they were connected with a news story, they were coded as part of the story.

**A note on the balance of content favourable to, or unfavourable to, Britain's continuing membership of the EEC: National Daily Newspapers, May 1975.**

A very brief study of content relating to the EEC Referendum was undertaken during one complete week of the period of the official campaign. The dates were from Monday, May 26 to Saturday, May 31 and six issues of each of nine National Daily Newspapers were looked at for the purpose (apart from the *Financial Times*, for which one day's issue was missing from the sample).

The method adopted was to identify any item relevant to the campaign, whether news, feature, editorial, letter or advertisement and to classify each item according to its general *direction* in respect of the issue. Four categories were available for this classification: for the Common Market; against the Common Market; mixed or neutral; other. The latter category was mainly designed to cover material relating to the procedure of the Referendum or matters of a humourous, "human interest" or peripheral kind which would give no direct indication of position on the issue. The main aim was to reach approximate conclusions about the distribution of overall *space* against these four categories and especially the balance between "pro" and "anti". Obviously a degree of subjective judgement is involved, although generally it was felt not to be a difficult task to take decisions about categories, given the availability of a category to cover cases of uncertainty or neutrality. On the whole, the direction implied or intended by the source of a report of news or background information was fairly clear. Nevertheless, it should be remembered that the indication of direction varies according to the kind of content item. For instance, it might come from an editorial opinion, or a reader's letter, or a report of a politician's or other campaigner's speech, or from a feature article giving information telling for or against the EEC, explicitly or implicitly. Briefly, in interpreting the percentage figures for the allocation of space, the approximate, summarising and general character of the assessment has to be borne in mind. The main findings are given in Table I.

**TABLE I**

**PERCENTAGE DISTRIBUTION OF SPACE (EDITORIAL AND ADVERTISING) IN ONE WEEK OF THE NATIONAL DAILIES RELEVANT TO THE EEC REFERENDUM, ACCORDING TO FOUR CATEGORIES OF DIRECTION IN RESPECT OF THE ISSUE OF CONTINUING MEMBERSHIP**

| Titles | For EEC | Against EEC | Mixed/ Neutral | Other | Total Space (col.cms.) | Nos. of Items |
|--------|------|--------|---------|-------|-------|-------|
| | % | % | % | % | | |
| *The Times* ... ... ... | 42 | 29 | 11 | 18 | 3,613 | 97 |
| *The Guardian* ... ... ... | 27 | 20 | 28 | 25 | 4,166 | 105 |
| *The Daily Telegraph* ... ... | 53 | 11 | 15 | 21 | 3,602 | 80 |
| *Financial Times* ... ... ... | 31 | 19 | 26 | 24 | 4,267 | 95 |
| *Morning Star* ... ... ... | 1 | 94 | 2 | 3 | 2,821 | 73 |
| *Daily Express* ... ... ... | 43 | 14 | 26 | 17 | 1,281 | 23 |
| *Daily Mail* ... ... ... | 46 | 13 | 20 | 21 | 1,702 | 28 |
| *DailyMirror* ... ... ... | 64 | 15 | 13 | 8 | 2,083 | 36 |
| *The Sun* ... ... ... ... | 40 | 16 | 23 | 21 | 2,375 | 59 |

The overall picture shows the *Daily Mirror* to have been most strongly inclined towards the EEC in the period looked at and the *Morning Star* most opposed. Both *The Guardian* and *Financial Times* seem to have provided the most evenly balanced content, while the remaining five papers have a definite tendency in the "Pro" direction, especially *The Daily Telegraph*. The exclusion of paid advertising content from the calculation does not greatly change the overall position, or the relative position of different newspapers, although it has a fairly notable effect on the figures for the *Daily Express*. For the latter the ratio of content FOR to AGAINST becomes 23%:18%, (with advertising included).

As well as measuring space, a count was made of the number of separate items in the four categories. If the percentages had been based on these data, the results would have been very similar for all newspapers, except the *Daily Express*, where only 23 items were involved and the percentages would have been: For, 26%; Against, 17%; Mixed, 26%; Other, 30%. In order to indicate approximately the amount of space given to the referendum in an average issue, the average amount of space in each paper can be expressed as a percentage of the average editorial space in each paper (taking this average figure from the sample of 24 titles for the year 1975). Campaign advertising is left out of account in this calculation. The results are as follows:

## TABLE II

**AVERAGE OF ALL EDITORIAL SPACE PER ISSUE DEVOTED TO REFERENDUM CAMPAIGN**

| The Times | The Guardian | The Daily Telegraph | Financial Times | Morning Star | Daily Express | Daily Mail | Daily Mirror | The Sun |
|---|---|---|---|---|---|---|---|---|
| 8% | 10% | 9% | 11% | 17% | 5% | 6% | 8% | 10% |

In addition to measuring space in terms of direction, an attempt was made to allocate each item to the main campaign issue with which it dealt. For this purpose, a set of 14 issues, plus four additional categories, was formulated in advance of the analysis. The proportion of all relevant space distributed against these 18 categories is shown in Table III.

## TABLE III

**PERCENTAGE DISTRIBUTION OF RELEVANT SPACE AGAINST 14 ISSUES IN THE REFERENDUM CAMPAIGN AND FOUR OTHER CATEGORIES**

| | | |
|---|---|---|
| 1. | *Economic* (Prospects in or out of Europe) ... | 29% |
| 2. | *Domestic politics* (Splits, coalitions, left vs right) ... | 13% |
| 3. | *Prices* (food and living costs) | 8% |
| 4. | *International politics* (Voice in Europe, Defence) ... | 5% |
| 5. | *Sovereignty* | 4% |
| 6. | *Trade unions* (Views of unions, industrial relations) | 3% |
| 7. | *Regions* (Prospects for Scotland, Wales) ... | 2% |
| 8. | *Farming* ... | 2% |
| 9. | *Oil* (control of North Sea fuel) ... | 1% |
| 10–14. | *Social welfare, Culture/Education, Communism. Terms of the deal, Commonwealth* | 2% |
| 15. | *Procedural matters* | 15% |
| 16. | *Multiple issues* | 10% |
| 17. | *Personalities* ... | 3% |
| 18. | *Other* ... | 5% |
| | | 102% |

It is clear that, apart from campaign procedure, press content was predominately about either economic matters or the domestic political implications of the choice. Between them these matters accounted for 50% of all space. In general, individual newspapers deviate rather little from the overall order of frequency.

**Summary comparison of contents of Provincial Morning, Provincial Evening and Local weekly newspapers**

In order to assist the comparison of the possible functions of three different kinds of local newspaper, a summary has been made of the results for the different samples of non-national papers examined in this report, according to some of the categories which were common to the two different coding frames. The comparison is between eleven English Provincial Morning newspapers (the *Leamington and District Morning News* has been omitted because of its very small size), 12 Evening newspapers and 28 weekly papers. The figures are arrived at by averaging percentage figures in relevant tables, hence giving equal weight to each title.

TABLE I

ANALYSIS OF TOTAL SPACE OF THREE GROUPS OF NEWSPAPERS INTO THREE CATEGORIES OF EDITORIAL AND TWO CATEGORIES OF ADVERTISING SPACE

| Category | Provincial Mornings | Provincial Evenings | Local Weeklies |
|---|---|---|---|
| | % | % | % |
| Editorial Space: | | | |
| News ... ... ... ... ... | 37·6 | 25·3 | 29·3 |
| Features ... ... ... ... | 11·8 | 10·4 | 7·4 |
| Other ... ... ... ... ... | 10·2 | 10·5 | 6·0 |
| Total ... ... | 59·6 | 46·2 | 42·7 |
| Advertising: | | | |
| Classified ... ... ... ... | 26·5 | 29·5 | 25·2 |
| Other ... ... ... ... | 13·9 | 24·3 | 32·0 |
| Total ... ... | 40·4 | 53·8 | 57·2 |
| Mean space per sample issue (col.cms.)... | 6,809 | 7,419 | 9,888 |

The figures in Table I show the Morning papers to have a significantly higher proportion of *news* content, accounted for by the higher proportion of advertising in the Evening and Weekly papers. The additional advertising in the latter two kinds of newspaper is apparently non-classified. One other general point of difference, not shown in the Table, is in the degree of illustration. On average, 21% of editorial content in the Weekly paper consists of pictures, against 16% in the Evening paper and 12% in the Provincial Morning.

TABLE II

ANALYSIS OF ALL NEWS SPACE IN THREE GROUPS OF NEWSPAPERS INTO FOUR CATEGORIES

| Category | Provincial Mornings | Provincial Evenings | Local Weeklies |
|---|---|---|---|
| News: | % | % | % |
| National Home ... ... ... | 33·7 | 23·5 | 0·4 |
| External ... ... ... ... | 6·8 | 6·6 | — |
| Local ... ... ... ... ... | 49·7 | 67·3 | 99·6 |
| Financial* ... ... ... ... | 10·1 | 2·5 | — |
| TOTAL ... ... | 100·3 | 99·9 | 100·0 |

*News about *local* business will also be found in the financial category.

**TABLE III**

**ANALYSIS OF ALL LOCAL AND REGIONAL NEWS SPACE INTO EIGHT CATEGORIES**

| Category | Provincial Mornings | Provincial Evenings | Local Weeklies |
|---|---|---|---|
| | % | % | % |
| Political ... ... ... ... ... | 7·5 | 7·7 | 7·6 |
| Economic/Industrial ... ... ... | 10·8 | 6·1 | 4·6 |
| Social services ... ... ... ... | 4·9 | 5·0 | 7·1 |
| Planning ... ... ... ... ... | 6·8 | 6·1 | 6·4 |
| Crime/accidents ... ... ... ... | 16·4 | 17·2 | 7·5 |
| Sport ... ... ... ... ... | 26·5 | 28·3 | 23·0 |
| Personalities and Events ... ... ... | 14·1 | 16·5 | 40·5 |
| Other ... ... ... ... ... | 13·0 | 13·1 | 3·3 |
| TOTAL ... ... | 100·0 | 100·0 | 100·0 |

The analysis of news space shows an increasing degree of local concentration, as one moves from the Morning to the Evening, to the Weekly. In terms of specific content of local news, there is some overall similarity between the types of newspaper. Not dissimilar proportions of space are given to political, social, planning and sport news. The main differences are the greater attention to economic news by the Mornings especially, and the low attention to crime and high attention to personalities of the Weekly newspaper.

Comparisons on some other matters of content, not tabulated, showed the Provincial morning newspaper to give significantly higher proportions of space to editorial comment (9% of "other" space) than did either the average evening or weekly newspaper (both 3%). The Morning papers apparently gave more attention to features dealing with political, social and economic matters. On this comparison, the typical Evening newspaper allocated more space to local consumer and price matters than did either the Morning or Weekly paper (3% of feature space, compared to 1% and 1% respectively).

## PRESS COVERAGE OF INDUSTRIAL RELATIONS: CODING FRAME

*Columns*

1    *Title of newspapers*

    T  G  DT  FT  MS  DE  D.Ma  D.Mi  S
    1  2  3   4   5   6   7    8    9

2–4    *Serial number of item:* runs from 001 upwards for each title

5–6    *Sample day number*

    01(7/1) 02(15/1) 03(3/2) 04(15/2) 05(21/2) 06(6/3) 07(17/4) 08(23/4)
    09(9/5) 10(12/5) 11(3/6) 12(28/6) 13(7/7) 14(2/8) 15(21/8) 16(5/9)
    17(10/9) 18(23/9) 19(18/10) 20(29/10) 21(10/11) 22(18/11) 23(27/11) 24(12/12)

7–8    *Page Numbers*

9    *Item type*

    1  News (1.1L or 1.2L)
    2  Feature (4.1L)
    3  Leader (5.1)
    0  Other

10–12    *Space in s.c.cm*

13–14    *Headline space in s.c.cm*

15    *Item size scale*

    1   0–10 s.c.cm
    2  11–20  ,,
    3  21–40  ,,
    4  41–60  ,,
    5  61–80  ,,
    6  80 s.c.cm+

16–17    *Branch of Industry* (see separate list for standard classification)

    Code: 01  02  03  04  05  06  07  08  09  10  11  12
            13  14  15  16  17  18  19  20  21  22  23  24
            25  26  27
    If not applicable, code 00

## MAIN TOPIC(S)

Normally only one main topic will be coded, but occasionally it is necessary to code for two main topics. More than two codes should be avoided

18    Main topic: *Disputes, stoppages, industrial action generally*

    0  Does not apply
    1  Type of action: strike
    2  Type of action: work to rule/overtime ban
    3  Type of action: blacking
    4  Type of action: lockout
    5  Type of action: picketing/lobbying/demonstrations
    6  Type of action: token stoppage
    7  Type of action: unspecified industrial action
    8  Other

If *dispute* coded as main topic: check for applicability of cols. 19–30. If dispute not main topic code 0 for cols. 19–30

19   (i) Timing of dispute

     0 Does not apply—not coded for dispute or not mentioned
     1 Past
     2 Current
     3 Future: date specified
     4 Future: no date specified
     5 No time indicated

20   (ii) Status of dispute

     0 Does not apply—not coded for dispute or not mentioned
     1 Unofficial
     2 Official
     3 Not known/other

21   (iii) Settlement reported

     0 Does not apply—not coded for dispute or not mentioned
     1 Applies

22   (iv) Causes of dispute

     0 Does not apply—not coded for dispute or no cause mentioned
     1 Cause(s) mentioned

If causes mentioned check cols. 23–30. If does not apply code 0 for cols. 23–30

23  Cause: Pay

     0 Does not apply—not coded for dispute or not mentioned as cause
     1 Applies

24  Cause: Hours/conditions

     0 Does not apply—not coded for dispute or not mentioned
     1 Applies

25  Cause: Redundancy/laying off

     0 Does not apply—not coded for dispute or not mentioned
     1 Applies

26  Cause: Manning/demarcation

     0 Does not apply—not coded for dispute or not mentioned
     1 Applies

27  Cause: Union matters (eg sympathy/victimisation/inter-union dispute)
     0 Does not apply—not coded for dispute or not mentioned
     1 Applies

28  Cause: Dismissal

     0 Does not apply—not coded for dispute or not mentioned
     1 Applies

29  Cause: Political

     0 Does not apply—not coded for dispute or not mentioned
     1 Applies

30  Cause: Other

     0 Does not apply—not coded for dispute or not mentioned
     1 Applies (write in on coding sheet)

*Columns*

31        Main topic: *Negotiations between unions and employers over pay*
Where no dispute is yet in progress or threatened. Includes pay claims, arbitration proceedings, offers, settlements, awards etc

        0  Does not apply
        1  Settled
        2  Current
        3  Future

32        Main topic: *Actions or statements by Government*, ministers, political parties or politicians, with reference to particular disputes or any industrial relation matters including wage settlements, pay policy, social contract etc, occasional employment matters where particular case concerns union specifically will be included

        0  Does not apply
        1  Directed at TUC or workers in general
        2  Directed at particular union or groups of workers
        3  Directed at employers in general
        4  Directed at particular employers or industry
        5  Directed at employers and employees jointly
        6  No particular direction

33        Main topic: *Action or statements by TUC, particular unions, professional association, or union leaders.* Includes union conferences reports, safety and welfare matters

        0  Does not apply
        1  Directed at Government
        2  Directed at employer(s)
        3  Other

34        Main topic: *Union elections, other internal union matters* and inter-union relations

        0  Does not apply
        1  Union elections
        2  Other internal union matters
        3  Inter-union relations
        4  Other

35        Main topic: *Actions or statements jointly from both "sides" of industry directed at Government*

        0  Does not apply
        1  Applies

36        Main topic: *Actions or statements by employers or their organisations*

        0  Does not apply
        1  Directed at Government or politicians
        2  Directed at unions or workers
        3  Other

37        Main topic: *Industrial, commercial or technical developments* affecting unions and members, eg employment prospects, pay. Includes news of closures, redundancy, changes in skill, new orders, increases in production, etc

        0  Does not apply
        1  Developments mentioned are beneficial to workers
        2  Developments mentioned are harmful
        3  Other

38        Main topic: *General economic context to industrial relations*

        0  Does not apply
        1  Applies

39        Main topic: *Worker control, participation, profit sharing, work-in etc*

        0  Does not apply
        1  Applies

40        Main topic: *Legal action.*

        0  Does not apply
        1  Against employer
        2  Against union
        3  Against workers
        4  Other

41        *Other main topic*

        0  Does not apply
        1  Applies (write in)

### PARTICIPANTS

42

| *Mentioned* 43 | *Reported* 44 | *Quoted* | |
|---|---|---|---|
| 0 | 0 | 0 | Does not apply |
| 1 | 1 | 1 | Government Minister, MP, Official |
| 2 | 2 | 2 | Opposition MP, spokesman |
| 3 | 3 | 3 | TUC leader or spokesman |
| 4 | 4 | 4 | CBI leader or spokesman |
| 5 | 5 | 5 | Expert |
| 6 | 6 | 6 | Management, employer |
| 7 | 7 | 7 | TU Official, local or national |
| 8 | 8 | 8 | Shop steward, convenor |
| 9 | 9 | 9 | Worker or member of public |

### THEMES OR "NEWS ANGLES" TO WHICH THERE IS A CLEAR AND SPECIFIC REFERENCE

*Notes*—1.  The headings are simply a convenience for classifying the references and are not alternative to the set of "main topics" outlined above.

        2.  Any number of themes (or none at all) may be coded, although generally no more than two or three will be found.

        3.  The distinction from "main topic" lies in one or other of the following: the briefer and more incidental character of the reference; the evaluative connotation usually present.

      (i) Pay claim or settlement

45        1  Claim or award very large or excessive
        2  Claim or award low, or inadequate
        3  Claim in line with pay policy, social contract etc
        0  Does not apply

      (ii) Relations between unions, Government and employers

46        1  Union or TUC *discord* with Government over policy
        2  Union or TUC *accord* with Government over policy
        0  Does not apply

47          1  Employer—Government *discord* over pay, industrial relations or policy

             2  Employer—Government *accord* over pay, industrial relations or policy

             0  Does not apply

(iii) Effects of industrial action or settlement

48          1  Inconvenience, danger etc to public

             0  Does not apply

49          1  Damage or threat to economy, international confidence, exports: also increased inflation, spurring other large claims

             0  Does not apply

50          1  Loss of output or money to firm or industry

             0  Does not apply

51          1  Loss of work by non-disputants in same or other firm

             0  Does not apply

52          1  Financial danger to firm or industry, including any threats to employment prospects

             0  Does not apply

(iv) Employer faults

53          1  Undue obstinancy or unreasonable behaviour by employers, incompetent handling of dispute

             0  Does not apply

54          1  Resentment at, or criticism of, employer/management perks or priveleges

             0  Does not apply

55          1  Anti-union activities by employers or employer organisations, victimisation of worker representative

             0  Does not apply

(v) Union faults

56          1  Criticism of unions, "wildcat" strikes, unreasonable behaviour

             0  Does not apply

57          1  Alleged political motivation by unions or workers, left-wing activity, militant actions and attitudes where criticism of this is implied

             0  Does not apply

(vi) Government pay policy

58          1  Success of, conformity with, support for, pay policy, social contract etc

             2  Weakness, failure, challenge or opposition to, pay policy, social contract, etc

             0  Does not apply

(vii) Conflict or violence

59          1  Conflict within union, especially left vs right, moderates vs extremists (militants)

             0  Does not apply

*Columns*

60      1   Intimidation or violence by strikers, pickets vs public or other workers
            0   Does not apply

61      1   Inter-union disputes, local-national union, or TUC vs union conference
            0   Does not apply

62      1   The class struggle
            0   Does not apply

(viii) Sex aspects

63      1   Women's work and equal pay and discrimination aspects
            0   Does not apply

64      1   Sex aspects generally, male or female
            0   Does not apply

(ix) Additional references evaluative of particular disputes

65      1   Dispute unnecessary, absurd or irresponsible
            0   Does not apply

66      1   Public sympathy or support for disputants or aims
            2   Lack of public sympathy or support
            0   Does not apply

67      1   Objections to strike by family members of strikers (eg wives)
            0   Does not apply

68      1   Solidarity of workers in dispute
            2   Lack of solidarity
            0   Does not apply

(x) Miscellaneous

69      1   Welfare costs, "fiddles", subsidies (to strikers)
            0   Does not apply

70      1   Workers participation, control, profit-sharing
            0   Does not apply

71      1   Public ignorance or misunderstanding
            0   Does not apply

72      1   Blacklegs, lump, non-union labour etc
            0   Does not apply

73      1   Strike-proneness of firm or country or particular site/contract etc
            0   Does not apply

74      1   Closed shop reference
            0   Does not apply

75      1   Good news in industrial relations
            0   Does not apply

**Comment on Coding Frame**

The following points correspond to particular sections of the coding schedule. The numbers in brackets relate to "column numbers" of the coding frame (Appendix B1).

(i) *Item type* (Col. 9). The distinction between types of item are the same as those employed in the general newspaper content analysis. A "feature" is recognisable by its concentration on background information and comment although it will generally be about a matter of topical interest. The great majority of all cases studied (95%) were news items. Letters were not examined.

(ii) *Total space and headline space* (Cols. 10–14). These were recorded in the standard column centimetre measure used in the main content analysis (see Part A p. 5). In the present report, the results of this measurement have not been used, since they would probably not add very much to what can be learnt from looking at frequency distributions and using the index of item size and the "measure of prominence" described in (iv) below. A further analysis could indicate precisely what proportion of space was devoted to headlines for different topics and different newspapers.

(iii) *Item size scale* (Col. 15). On the basis of a sub-sample analysis, six categories of item size were established and this scale has been used in preference to the exact measure of space.

It should be stressed that in this study, *all* items concerning industrial relations were coded and no minimum size requirement was applied.

(iv) *Measure of prominence.* To provide an appropriate indication of prominence, an index was prepared, designed to reflect the approximate salience of presentation and with the following categories, from greatest to least: (1) Front page, main lead; (2) Other large front page (over 20 col. cms); (3) Major feature (eg on leader page); (4) Editorial; (5) Other feature; (6) Other news over 20 col. cms; (7) Other news, over 10 col. cms; (8) News under 11 col. cms. This scale is not reproduced in the coding schedule, but its use can be seen, in an abbreviated form, in Table B9.

(v) The *main topics* and *sub-topics* are self-explanatory. In coding, an effort was made to place a single item under one topic heading only and in the event there were only 32 cases where a second topic code was used. In the analysis the second topic code has been disregarded (see p. 112).

(vi) In addition to classifying *participants* according to their status and the way in which they figured in the story, actual names were recorded. None of these data were, however, recorded on punched cards. Although the results of the counts are reported, the data cannot easily be analysed in relation to other matters in the study.

(vii) *Themes or news angles* (Cols. 45–75). A more detailed discussion of this aspect of the coding scheme appears as para. 6 of Section I above.

(viii) Other data recorded during coding included the name of the union mainly involved in a story and whether or not the story was illustrated.

## APPENDIX B3
## PRESS COVERAGE OF INDUSTRIAL RELATIONS: ANALYSIS SHEET

| | | |
|---|---|---|
| 1-4 | Serial No. | ☐☐☐☐ |
| 5-6 | Sample Day No. | |
| 7-8 | Page No. | |
| 9 | Item Type | |
| 10-12 | Space | ☐☐☐ |
| 13-14 | Headline Space | |
| 15 | Item Size Scale | |
| 16-17 | Branch of Industry | ☐☐ |

**PARTICIPANTS**

42 Mentioned

43 Reported

44 Quoted

**MAIN TOPIC**

| | | |
|---|---|---|
| 18 | Disputes | ☐ |
| 19 | Time | ☐ |
| 20 | Status | ☐ |
| 21 | Settlement | ☐ |
| 22 | Cause | ☐ |
| 23 | Pay | ☐ |
| 24 | Hours/Conditions | ☐ |
| 25 | Redundancy | ☐ |
| 26 | Manning | ☐ |
| 27 | Union Matters | ☐ |
| 28 | Dismissal | ☐ |
| 29 | Political | ☐ |
| 30 | Other | ☐ |
| 31 | Pay Negotiations | ☐ |
| 32 | Government Actions | ☐ |
| 33 | Union Actions | ☐ |
| 34 | Inter Union Affairs | ☐ |
| 35 | "Industry" vs Government | ☐ |
| 36 | Employers Actions | ☐ |
| 37 | Developments | ☐ |
| 38 | Economic Context | ☐ |
| 39 | Worker Participation | ☐ |
| 40 | Legal Action | ☐ |
| 41 | Other | ☐ |

**THEMES**

| | | | | | | | |
|---|---|---|---|---|---|---|---|
| 45 ☐ | 53 ☐ | 61 ☐ | 68 ☐ |
| 46 ☐ | 54 ☐ | 62 ☐ | 69 ☐ |
| 47 ☐ | 55 ☐ | 63 ☐ | 70 ☐ |
| 48 ☐ | 56 ☐ | 64 ☐ | 71 ☐ |
| 49 ☐ | 57 ☐ | 65 ☐ | 72 ☐ |
| 50 ☐ | 58 ☐ | 66 ☐ | 73 ☐ |
| 51 ☐ | 59 ☐ | 67 ☐ | 74 ☐ |
| 52 ☐ | 60 ☐ | | |

**HEADINGS**

**INDUSTRY INVOLVED**

**UNIONS NAMED**

**MEASURE OF PROMINENCE**

**PHOTO CONTENT**

331

APPENDIX B4

## INDUSTRIAL RELATIONS THEMES: FREQUENCY IN NATIONAL DAILIES†

| Themes | The Times | The Guardian | The Daily Telegraph | Financial Times | Morning Star | Daily Express | Daily Mail | Daily Mirror | The Sun | All newspapers |
|---|---|---|---|---|---|---|---|---|---|---|
| 1. Union or TUC discord in relations with Government (46) | 19 | 14 | 18 | 32 | 40 | 12 | 18 | 15 | 5 | 173 |
| 2. Loss of output or money by firm or industry as effect (50) | 22 | 10 | 14 | 24 | 5 | 2 | 1 | 10 | 3 | 91 |
| 3. Conflict within union, especially left vs right (59) | 15 | 10 | 13 | 16 | 6 | 4 | 7 | 3 | 3 | 77 |
| 4. Inconvenience or danger to public as effect (48) | 12 | 11 | 13 | 11 | — | 5 | 11 | 5 | 5 | 73 |
| 5. Weakness or failure of Government pay policy (58) | 6 | 8 | 6 | 16 | 4 | 3 | 5 | 5 | 5 | 58 |
| 6. Loss of work by non-disputants as effect (51) | 15 | 7 | 4 | 11 | 9 | 1 | 2 | 3 | 4 | 56 |
| 7. Success of, support for, Government pay policy (58) | 9 | 7 | 9 | 11 | — | 4 | 2 | 4 | 5 | 50 |
| 8. Worker participation, profit-sharing (70) | 9 | 7 | 5 | 11 | 1 | 5 | 1 | 3 | 3 | 47 |
| 9. Alleged political motivation, left-wing militancy (57) | 7 | 2 | 10 | — | 6 | 2 | 5 | 2 | 6 | 43 |
| 10. Solidarity between workers in dispute (68) | 3 | 5 | 3 | 5 | — | 5 | 5 | 4 | 3 | 43 |
| 11. Inter-union disputes or TUC vs union (61) | 5 | 9 | 5 | 12 | 16 | 2 | 5 | 2 | — | 43 |
| 12. Unreasonable behaviour by employers (53) | 7 | 9 | 7 | 3 | 2 | 5 | 3 | 1 | 3 | 38 |
| 13. Anti-union activity by employers (55) | — | 3 | 5 | 5 | — | 3 | 5 | — | 2 | 36 |
| 14. Employer discord in relations with Government (47) | 6 | 6 | 4 | 8 | 8 | 3 | 3 | 1 | — | 41 |
| 15. Pay claim or award large or excessive (45) | 10 | 11 | 4 | 5 | 2 | 2 | 2 | 2 | 4 | 29 |
| 16. Union or TUC accord in relations with Government (46) | 8 | 4 | 1 | 9 | — | 5 | 7 | — | — | 28 |
| 17. Closed shop references (74) | 8 | 4 | 10 | 2 | 4 | 2 | — | 1 | — | 26 |
| 18. Damage or threat to economy, as effect (49) | 2 | — | 3 | 7 | 3 | — | 2 | — | — | 25 |
| 19. Financial danger to firm or industry, as effect (53) | 1 | 5 | 3 | 6 | — | 2 | 5 | 1 | 1 | 20 |
| 20. Criticism of unions, unreasonable, "wildcat" strikes | 1 | 2 | 7 | 3 | 1 | — | 5 | 1 | — | 18 |
| 21. Blacklegs, lump, non-union labour | 2 | 3 | 1 | 2 | 9 | — | — | 1 | 1 | 18 |
| 22. Intimidation or violence by strikers, pickets (60) | 1 | 1 | 2 | — | — | — | 3 | — | — | 16 |
| 23. Women's work, equal pay (63) | — | 2 | 3 | 6 | 1 | 1 | — | — | 1 | 16 |
| 24. Lack of solidarity of workers (68) | 1 | 3 | 1 | 4 | 3 | 3 | 11 | 1 | — | 15 |
| 25. "Good news" in industrial relations (75) | — | 2 | 2 | 5 | 1 | — | — | — | — | 14 |
| 26. Pay claim or settlement in line with policy (45) | 1 | 2 | 1 | 6 | — | 1 | 2 | 3 | — | 13 |
| 27. Pay claim or settlement low or inadequate (45) | 2 | — | — | 2 | 1 | 2 | 2 | — | 1 | 13 |
| 28. The class struggle (62) | 1 | 1 | 2 | — | 8 | — | 2 | 1 | — | 12 |
| 29. Sex aspects generally | 2 | — | — | 2 | 2 | — | — | 1 | 1 | 11 |

| No. | | | | | | | | | | Total |
|---|---|---|---|---|---|---|---|---|---|---|
| 30. | Strike—proneness ... | 3 | — | — | 3 | — | 2 | — | 2 | 11 |
| 31. | Public ignorance or misunderstanding (71) | — | 1 | 1 | 2 | — | 1 | 2 | — | 7 |
| 32. | Public sympathy or support for disputants (66) | — | 1 | 1 | 1 | 1 | 1 | — | — | 4 |
| 33. | Dispute unnecessary or absurd (65) ... | — | 1 | 2 | 1 | 1 | — | — | — | 4 |
| 34. | Welfare costs, "fiddles" and subsidies ... | — | — | — | — | — | — | — | — | 3 |
| 35. | Lack of public sympathy (66) ... | 1 | 1 | 1 | 1 | — | — | — | — | 2 |
| 36. | Employer *accord* in relations with Government (47) | — | — | — | — | — | — | — | — | 2 |
| 37. | Resentment at, or criticism of, employer privileges | — | — | — | 1 | — | — | — | — | 1 |
| 38. | Objections to strike by family of strikers ... | — | — | — | — | — | — | — | — | 1 |

† The numbers in brackets refer to column numbers in Appendix B1

333

## STANDARD INDUSTRIAL CLASSIFICATION

### Agriculture, forestry, fishing
Agriculture and horticulture
Forestry
Fishing

### Mining and quarrying
Coal mining
Stone and slate quarrying and mining
Chalk, clay, sand and gravel extraction
Petroleum and natural gas
Other mining and quarrying

### Food, drink and tobacco
Grain milling
Bread and flour confectionery
Biscuits
Bacon curing, meat and fish products
Milk and milk products
Sugar
Cocoa, chocolate and sugar confectionery
Fruit and vegetable products
Animal and poultry foods
Vegetable and animal oils and fats
Food industries not elsewhere specified
Brewing and malting
Soft drinks
Other drink industries
Tobacco

### Coal and petroleum products
Coke ovens and manufactured fuel
Mineral oil refining
Lubricating oils and greases

### Chemicals and allied industries
General chemicals
Pharmaceutical chemicals and preparations
Toilet preparations
Paint
Soap and detergents
Synthetic resins and plastics materials and synthetic rubber
Dyestuffs and pigments
Fertilisers
Other chemical industries

### Metal manufacture
Iron and steel (general)
Steel tubes
Iron castings, etc
Aluminium and aluminium alloys
Copper, brass and other copper alloys
Other base metals

334

## Mechanical engineering

Agricultural machinery (excluding tractors)
Metal-working machine tools
Pumps, valves and compressors
Industrial engines
Textile machinery and accessories
Construction and earth-moving equipment
Mechanical handling equipment
Office machinery
Other machinery
Industrial (including process) plant and steelwork
Ordnance and small arms
Other mechanical engineering not elsewhere specified

## Instrument engineering

Photographic and document copying equipment
Watches and clocks
Surgical instruments and appliances
Scientific and industrial instruments and systems

## Electrical engineering

Electrical machinery
Insulated wires and cables
Telegraph and telephone apparatus and equipment
Radio and electronic components
Broadcast receiving and sound reproducing equipment
Electronic computers
Radio, radar and electronic capital goods
Electric appliances primarily for domestic use
Other electrical goods

## Shipbuilding and marine engineering

Shipbuilding and ship repairing
Marine engineering

## Vehicles

Wheeled tractor manufacturing
Motor vehicle manufacturing
Motor cycle, tricyle and pedal cycle manufacturing
Aerospace equipment manufacturing and repairing
Locomotives and railway track equipment
Railway carriages and wagons and trams

## Metal goods not elsewhere specified

Engineers' small tools and gauges
Hand tools and implements
Cutlery, spoons, forks and plated tableware, etc
Bolts, nuts, screws, rivets, etc
Wire and wire manufactures
Cans and metal boxes
Jewellery and precious metals
Metal industries not elsewhere specified

## Textiles

Production of man-made fibres
Spinning and doubling on the cotton and flax systems
Weaving of cotton, linen and man-made fibres
Woollen and worsted
Jute
Rope, twine and net
Hosiery and other knitted goods
Lace
Carpets
Narrow fabrics (not more than 30 cm wide)
Made-up textiles
Textile finishing
Other textile industries

## Leather, leather goods aud fur

Leather (tanning and dressing) and fellmongery
Leather goods
Fur

## Clothing and footwear

Weatherproof outerwear
Men's and boys' tailored outerwear
Women's and girls' tailored outerwear
Overalls and men's shirts, underwear, etc
Dresses, lingerie, infants' wear, etc
Hats, caps and millinery
Dress industries not elsewhere specified
Footwear

## Bricks, pottery, glass, cement, etc

Bricks, fireclay and refractory goods
Pottery
Glass
Cement
Abrasive and building materials, etc, not elsewhere specified

## Timber, furniture etc

Timber
Furniture and upholstery
Bedding, etc
Shop and office fitting
Wooden containers and baskets
Miscellaneous wood and cork manufactures

## Paper, printing and publishing

Paper and board
Packaging products of paper, board and associated materials
Manufactured stationery
Manufactures of paper and board not elsewhere specified
Printing, publishing of newspapers
Printing, publishing of periodicals
Other printing, publishing, bookbinding, engraving, etc

**Other manufacturing industries**

Rubber
Linoleum, plastic floor-covering, leathercloth, etc
Brushes and brooms
Toys, games, children's carriages, and sports equipment
Miscellaneous stationers' goods
Plastics products not elsewhere specified
Miscellaneous manufacturing industries

**Construction**

**Gas, electricity and water**

Gas
Electricity
Water supply

**Transport and communication**

Railways
Road passenger transport
Road haulage contracting for general hire or reward
Other road haulage
Sea transport
Port and inland water transport
Air transport
Postal services and telecommunications
Miscellaneous transport services and storage

**Distributive trades**

Wholesale distribution of food and drink
Wholesale distribution of petroleum products
Other wholesale distribution
Retail distribution of food and drink
Other retail distribution
Dealing in coal, oil, builders' materials, grain and agricultural supplies
Dealing in other industrial materials and machinery

**Insurance, banking, finance and business services**

Insurance
Banking and bill discounting
Other financial institutions
Property owning and managing, etc
Advertising and market research
Other business services
Central offices not allocable elsewhere

**Professional and scientific services**

Accountancy services
Educational services
Legal services
Medical and dental services
Religious organisations
Research and development services
Other professional and scientific services

337

**Miscellaneous services**
  Cinemas, theatres, radio, etc
  Sport and other recreations
  Betting and gambling
  Hotels and other residential establishments
  Restaurants, cafes, snack bars
  Public houses
  Clubs
  Catering contractors
  Hairdressing and manicure
  Private domestic service
  Laundries
  Dry cleaning, job dyeing, carpet beating, etc
  Motor repairers, distributors, garages and filling stations
  Repair of boots and shoes
  Other services

**Public administration and defence**
  National Government service
  Local Government service

**Ex-service personnel not classified by industry**

**Adult students**

**Other persons not classified by industry**

Source: *DOE Gazette.*

**Press Coverage of Social Welfare and Social Policy**

*Columns*

1    *Title of newspapers*

| T | G | DT | FT | MS | DE | D.Ma | D.Mi | S |
|---|---|----|----|----|----|------|------|---|
| 1 | 2 | 3  | 4  | 5  | 6  | 7    | 8    | 9 |

2–4    *Serial number of items:* runs from 001 upwards for each title

5–6    *Sample day number*

    01(7/1) 02(15/1) 03(3/2)   04(15/2) 05(21/2) 06(6/3)   07(17/4) 08(23/4)
    09(9/5)  10(12/5) 11(3/6)    12(28/6) 13(7/7)   14(2/8)    15(21/8) 16(5/9)
    17(10/9) 18(23/9) 19(18/10) 20(29/10) 21(10/11) 22(18/11) 23(27/11) 24(12/12)

7–8    *Page Numbers*

9–11    *Story Number*

12    *Item Type*
    1  News
    2  Feature
    3  Leader
    0  Other

13–15    *Space in S.C.Cm.*

16–17    *Headline space in S.C.Cm*

18    *Item size scale*
    1   0–10 s.c.cm
    2  11–20  ,,
    3  21–40  ,,
    4  41–60  ,,
    5  61–80  ,,
    6  80 s.c.cm +

19–20    *Main Social Service or policy area referred to*
01    *Housing:* Planning, land, development, enquiries, new towns, urban renewal
02    *Housing:* Conditions, improvements, rents and finance, supply of housing,
        building starts (applies to public and private sector, and "social" but not
        financial aspects of mortgage finance)
03    *Housing:* Homeless, squatting, housing action
04    *Community:* Action, development, associations etc
05    *Education:* Pre-school
06    *Education:* School
07    *Education:* University
08    *Education:* Polytechnic and other further and higher
09    *Education:* Adult, non-vocational
10    *Education:* Open University
11    *Education:* In general
12    *Education:* Other
13    *Health:* Hospital services
14    *Health:* General practitioner, medical and dental
15    *Health:* Handicapped, including blind, deaf, physically disabled
16    *Health:* Mental and psychiatric specifically (takes precedence over other health
        categories)

*Columns*

| | |
|---|---|
| 17 | *Health:* Community health services, including schools, health visiting, midwives, maternity services |
| 18 | *Health:* Abortion, family planning, vasectomy, etc |
| 19 | *Health:* General or other |
| 20 | *National Insurance:* Retirement, old age pensions, widows' pensions |
| 21 | *National Insurance:* Income maintenance-unemployment, sickness, industrial injury benefits |
| 22 | *Social Security matters:* Supplementary benefits, FIS, family allowance, etc Includes problems of poverty and destitution in general |
| 23 | *Social work* and personal welfare services not coded elsewhere |
| 24 | *Legal* and penal matters, legal aid, prisons, after care, probation, delinquency as social problem, tribunals of various kinds |
| 25 | *Minority* groups: race and community relations, immigration |
| 26 | *Children:* Care, adoption, fostering, neglect, rights of children, baby-battering |
| 27 | *Family matters:* Marriage guidance, one-parent families, custody, maintenance, social aspects of divorce |
| 28 | *Population:* Size, immigration, trends |
| 29 | *Transport* and communications: *subsidies, social aspects, including free TV licences etc.* |
| 30 | *Libraries*, museums, information services, leisure, arts |
| 31 | *Occupational* welfare matters not otherwise covered, including pensions, work conditions etc |
| 32 | *Youth* Services |
| 33 | *Employment* unemployment, retraining and job creation: Youth |
| 34 | *Employment* unemployment, retraining and job creation: Other |
| 35 | *Misc. social problems:* drugs, alcoholism |
| 36 | *National industries*—social welfare aspects of services to customers |
| 37 | *Other*, including forces welfare, charity matters etc |

21–22   *Secondary social service or policy area referred to* (if applicable)
Code as for 19–20

23   *Status of service*
0   Not applicable
1   Public
2   Private or voluntary
3   Mixed or not known

MAIN GENERAL TOPIC(S) (Code no more than three)

24   Level of provision, facilities, services, supply
0   Does not apply
1   High, adequate, increasing
2   Inadequate, falling

25   Financial
0   Does not apply
1   Problems, shortage
2   sufficient or more money, good news
3   Other

26   Problems (other than financial)
0   Does not apply
1   For service or its personnel

340

*Columns*

26    2  For "clients"—patients, students, inmates, victims, consumers, recipients, etc

        3  Not specified or other

27    Professional/occupational matters

        0  Does not apply
        1  Staffing—cuts, shortages, levels
        2  Standards, training, etc
        3  Other

28    Industrial relations and trade union matters

        0  Does not apply
        1  Strike or other dispute
        2  Pay negotiations, claim, award, etc.
        3  Other

29    Administration and policy-making

        0  Does not apply
        1  Applies

30    Criminal, police, legal matters

        0  Does not apply
        1  Applies

31    Research: plans, findings, medical, technical

        0  Does not apply
        1  Applies

32    Participation or control, by public, employee, clients, etc

        0  Does not apply
        1  Applies

33    Conflict

        0  Does not apply
        1  Protest, sit-in, dispute, etc (other than industrial)
        2  Other

34    Reform and development

        0  Does not apply
        1  Reform
        2  Developments: positive-initiation, new
        3  Developments: negative-banning, cutting, stopping

35    Specific topics

        0  Does not apply      4  Public information
        1  Pay beds      9  Other
        2  Comprehensive education
        3  Welfare rights

36    *Item political or not in treatment*

        0  Not political
        1  Political (eg reference to political party, ideology etc)

37–38 MAIN SOURCE OR OCCASION OF STORY

    00 Not identifiable
    01 Government or ruling party document, report, statistics, white paper, parliamentary bill etc
    02 Ministerial or ruling party speech, statement
    03 Opposition document, statement, bill, speech
    04 Other political or politician sources
    05 Local government official source, administration or political
    06 Official or quasi-official report or statement, including as source independent national councils, review bodies, enquiries, official reports of institutions
    07 Director, chief executive or high level member of service or institution e.g. Director of Education, Prison Governor, Head Teacher, Chairman of Governors, Vice-Chancellor etc.
    08 Court case
    09 Research report
    10 Book, pamphlet or article
    11 Trade union leader or official or collective statement
    12 Rank and file member of relevant union
    13 NUS
    14 Pressure or action group—Age concern, CPAG, CEA, etc
    15 Conference speech or report
    16 Parliamentary proceedings
    17 Other media
    18 "Expert"
    19 Newspaper's own investigation or sources of information
    20 Other


PARTICIPANTS QUOTED OR REPORTED (N.B. *not* mentioned alone)

39    1 Minister, government MP or official
      0 Does not apply

40    1 Opposition MP, politician or party spokesman
      0 Does not apply

41    1 Director, chief of service or other principal
      0 Does not apply

42    1 Expert
      0 Does not apply

43    1 Client, recipient of service, consumer (includes students and parents or relatives)
      0 Does not apply

44    1 Lower-level staff member—eg social worker, teacher, nurse, junior doctor etc
      0 Does not apply

45    1 Spokesman for semi-official (but non-governmental) body
      0 Does not apply

46    1 Spokesman for pressure or action group
      0 Does not apply

47      1  Trade Union spokesman or official (incl. Professional Associations)
         0  Does not apply
         9  Other

## THEMES

Particular aspects of the story or "news angles" to which there is a clear
and specific reference. Any number may be coded, or none. The distinction
from "main topic" (Cols 24–35) lies in one or other of the following: the
briefer and more incidental character of the reference; the evaluative connotation usually present.

N.B.—The headings are a convenience for classifying themes and are not
themselves alternative to the set of main topics.

    (i) Political
48        1  Left-wing activity, militancy
          0  Does not apply
49        1  Right-wing activity, reaction
          0  Does not apply
50        1  Private *vs* public provision
          0  Does not apply
51        1  Party political disagreement in general
          0  Does not apply

    (ii) Waste in or abuse of public services
52        1  Over-generous treatment by public authorities
          0  Does not apply
53        1  Welfare "scrounging"
          0  Does not apply

54        1  Waste, profligacy, undue expense, misapplied resources
          0  Does not apply

55        1  False claims, fiddling, dodging payments, mis-use of service by
             clients or recipients
          0  Does not apply

    (iii) Faults of service or personnel
56        1  Scandal, misconduct
          0  Does not apply

57        1  Bureaucracy, "red tape", inefficiency
          0  Does not apply

58        1  Inhumanity towards "client" or beneficiary
          0  Does not apply

59        1  Danger to public
          0  Does not apply

60        1  Unequal treatment, social class differences
          0  Does not apply

61        1  Criticism of government or local authority in general, failure of
             policy
          0  Does not apply

    (iv) Participation, consumer, client, or worker control and representa-
         tion
62        1  Worker control or direct action (eg over pay beds)
          0  Does not apply

| | | |
|---|---|---|
| 63 | 1 | Welfare, client, rights |
| | 0 | Does not apply |
| 64 | 1 | Public or user representation |
| | 0 | Does not apply |

(v) Problems

| | | |
|---|---|---|
| 65 | 1 | Crisis |
| | 0 | Does not apply |
| 66 | 1 | Violence, conflict |
| | 0 | Does not apply |
| 67 | 1 | Colour bar, special needs or disadvantages of immigrants and coloured community or problems alleged caused by immigrants |
| | 0 | Does not apply |
| 68 | 1 | Deprivation, discrimination in general |
| | 0 | Does not apply |
| 69 | 1 | Tough line, clampdown, banning |
| | 0 | Does not apply |

(vi) Miscellaneous

| | | |
|---|---|---|
| 70 | 1 | Sex aspects |
| | 0 | Does not apply |
| 71 | 1 | Good news aspects, success story, achievement generally |
| | 0 | Does not apply |

**Comment on coding frame**

This commentary deals only with points which seem to need explanation, and reference to the appropriate section of the coding scheme will be made by quoting the column numbers on the left-hand margins of Appendix D1. The numbers only signify the columns on punched cards.

(i) *Story number* (Cols. 9–11) A list was compiled of all separate stories covered by the analysis and an index number given to each story. Thus where, as frequently happened, the same story was covered in different newspapers, it is possible to identify all cases relating to that story. By recording this information it is also possible to discover what kinds of story are likely to get multiple coverage. In the event, little use has been made of the information, but it could be of use for more detailed analyses than have been attempted and it helps in comparing newspapers in terms of some data which were not punched onto cards (eg headlines).

(ii) *Item type* (Col. 12) The distinction between news and features is the same as that applied in the general content analysis of newspapers. Letters were not included in the analysis.

(iii) *Space and headline space* (Cols. 13–17). Measurements were recorded in the standard column centimetre study used in the main content analysis of newspapers (Part A). No direct use has been made of the information in this report since the scale of item size (iv below) and a measure of prominence (see Part D, II, 2) were simpler to use in the analysis and gave broadly the same results.

(iv) *Item size scale* (Col. 18). Six categories of item size were established on the basis of a pilot analysis.

(v) *Main and secondary social service or policy areas* (Cols. 19–20 and 21–22). The purpose of this basic classificatory scheme is self-evident, since it is clearly necessary to be able to classify the rather heterogeneous material for analysis purposes. The list is a very long one, but the greater detail at the outset makes for more reliable coding. For most purposes of analysis, the list of 37 categories was subsequently reduced to 13. The provision for a secondary coding was made because of a tendency for policy areas to overlap in places—eg health and education or social work and family matters.

(vi) *Status of service* (Col. 23). The analysis was meant to cover welfare activities of a non-statutory kind, hence this code category. In the event, no separate analysis has been made according to this variable. Of the 855 cases where a definite allocation could be made, only 69 were recorded as in the private or voluntary sector and 88 as "mixed" or "uncertain".

(vii) *Main general topics* (Cols. 24–34). The intention is to provide a basis for classification "cutting across" and independent from the social service or policy area classification. The set of categories listed reflects the fact that a similar range of general topics may be relevant to different policy areas—for instance: financial shortage; strikes and disputes; levels of provision; industrial relations, and so on. The freedom to code up to three such topics for any one item reflects the fact that a news report often has multiple topics with no single one encompassing the whole story or necessarily predominating. As a crude index of this it can be reported that each item was recorded as having an average of 1·6 general topics. Some of the topics are more specific than others and more likely to occur in relation to one policy area than others (eg criminal and legal matters in the sphere of penal policy).

(viii) *Item "political or not in treatment"* (Col. 36). As a matter of interest, it was thought useful to know whether the item concerned was dealt with in the context of party politics or political debate in the conventional sense. This would have included local as well as national party politics.

(ix) *Main source or occasion of story* (Cols. 37–8). The set of categories is self-explanatory. The inclusion of this variable is guided by an interest in where social welfare news generally originates and what sort of events give rise to social policy reporting. Only information in the news report itself was used in classification. However, in coding the same day's news in several different newspapers, coders had access to some relevant information and at times this source has been used to supplement what was in the item itself. In general, this practice has to be guarded against in content analysis of this kind. In the case of this particular variable, it was thought better to reduce the uncertainty of classification, since the item does not relate directly to the substance of the report.

(x) *Participants quoted or reported* (Cols. 39–47). Wherever one of the listed categories of people was represented in the form of a quotation or direct report (speech or statement), the information was recorded.

(xi) *Themes or "news angles"* (Cols. 48–71). Two main independent classificatory schemes have already been mentioned (social policy areas and general topic). This is a third and also independent scheme of classification. It is devised on the underlying assumption that news reports, as well as having an identification in terms of overt subject matter and specific events, also frequently allude to certain recurring themes. These themes do not generally provide the definition of content but are ideas, points of interest, or frames of reference, which help to make sense of isolated facts and may serve to structure the bare facts for the reader. Sometimes the themes provide images, sometimes they draw on stereotypes. Quite often there is some evaluative connotation in the allusion to a theme. In trying to capture this aspect of news content it is important to proceed very carefully and the method itself is barely adequate to the task since it requires a minimum reliance on interpretation and is not easy to apply to complex matters. All that can be done is to specify themes and instruct coders to record any instances where a clear and unambiguous reference to the theme specified seems to have occurred. The method is extremely mechanistic and the results are often fragmentary. Nevertheless, it was believed that the approach could add something to the other information recorded and, in conjunction with other data, could help to shed some light on the more evaluative and qualitative aspects of news reporting. Some of the main themes included: political militancy; waste and extravagance; bureaucracy or red tape; inhumanity towards "clients"; criticism of local or national government; violence or conflict; discrimination or deprivation; sex angles; "good news", success. The list of themes is diverse and varying in specificity, but based also on a prior reading of content. Nevertheless, such a list can itself risk imbalance and incompleteness and cannot be free from the investigator's own values and possible bias. Care was taken to instruct coders to record a reference to a theme only where this was clear and specific and as a result there has probably been a general tendency to err on the side of *under-recording*. This would seem desirable, given the risk of unreliable interpretation.

## Social welfare and social policy analysis sheet

| | | | |
|---|---|---|---|
| **THEMES** | | 1–4 | Serial No. |
| | | 5–6 | Sample day No. |
| 48 | 61 | 7–8 | Page No. |
| 49 | 62 | 9–11 | Story No. |
| 50 | 63 | 12 | Item type |
| 51 | 64 | 13–15 | Space |
| 52 | 65 | 16–17 | Headline space |
| 53 | 66 | 18 | Item size scale |
| 54 | 67 | 19–20 | Main social service/policy ref. |
| 55 | 68 | 21–22 | Secondary service/policy ref. |
| 56 | 69 | 23 | Status |
| 57 | 70 | | |

MAIN GENERAL TOPIC(S)

| | |
|---|---|
| 58 | 71 |
| 59 | |
| 60 | |

| | |
|---|---|
| 24 | Level of provision |
| 25 | Financial |
| 26 | Problems |
| 27 | Occupational |
| 28 | Industrial relations |
| 29 | Administrative |
| 30 | Criminal, legal |
| 31 | Research |
| **HEADLINES** | |
| 32 | Participation |
| 33 | Conflict |
| 34 | Reform |
| 35 | Specific/other |
| 36 | Political or not |
| **MEASURE OF PROMINENCE** | |
| 37–38 | Main source |

PARTICIPANTS

| | |
|---|---|
| 39 | Minister |
| 40 | Opposition |
| 41 | Director |
| 42 | Expert |
| 43 | Client |
| 44 | Rank and file |
| 45 | Semi-official |
| 46 | Pressure group |
| 47 | Other, d.n.a. |

**PHOTO CONTENT**

347

**Coding frame**

## PRESS COVERAGE OF FOREIGN NEWS AND FEATURES.

*Columns*

1      *Title of newspapers*

| T | G | DT | FT | MS | DE | D.Ma | D.Mi | S | Sc | GH |
|---|---|----|----|----|----|------|------|---|----|----|
| 1 | 2 | 3  | 4  | 5  | 6  | 7    | 8    | 9 | 0  | X  |

2–4      *Serial number of item:* runs from 001 upwards for each title

5–6      *Sample day number*
         01(7/1) 02(15/1) 03(3/2) 04(15/2) 05(21/2) 06(6/3) 07(17/4) 08(23/4)
         09(9/5) 10(12/5) 11(3/6) 12(28/8) 13(7/7) 14(2/8) 15(21/8) 16(5/9)
         17(10/9) 18(23/9) 19(18/10) 20(29/10) 21(10/11) 22(18/11) 23(27/11) 24(12/12)

7–8      *Page number*

9–11      *Story number*

12      *Item code*
         1   2.1
         2   2.2
         3   2.3
         4   2.4
         5   2.5 or 2.5U
         6   2.6
         7   2.9
         8   4.2
         9   5.1
         0   Other

13–15      *Space in s.c.cm*

16–17      *Headline space*

18      *Item size scale*
         1   0–10 s.c.cm
         2   11–20   ,,
         3   21–40   ,,
         4   41–60   ,,
         5   61–80   ..
         6   81+   ,,

19      *Whether international or foreign domestic*
         1   International (more than one country, at sea, in space etc)
         2   Foreign domestic
         0   Not classifiable

MAIN TOPIC(S)
     (Generally only one topic to be coded, but if necessary code a second topic)

20      Diplomatic/political (international stories only)
         1   Applies
         0   Does not apply

21        Political (foreign-domestic only)

       1   Conflict or crisis — non-violent/constitutional.
       2   Conflict or crisis — violent, revolutionary. Includes language and culture based conflict as well as political
       3   Elections, campaigns, results, appointments
       4   Other political, including legislation, changes of Government
       0   Does not apply

22        Military and defence

       1   Armed conflict, or threat of
       2   Peace moves, negotiations, settlements
       3   Other military and defence, including arms deals, nuclear weapons, NATO, bases, exercises etc
       0   Does not apply

23        Economic, trade, financial, industrial and agricultural (except aid)

       1   Agreements on trade, tariffs etc
       2   Major industrial projects, dams, ports, factories, roads, etc
       3   Agricultural matters in particular
       4   Industrial relations and labour: disputes and settlements
       5   Industrial relations and labour: all other matters
       6   Other, including references in general to problems, crises, success, failures
       0   Does not apply

24        Aid, development

       1   Disaster or famine relief
       2   Other development or aid matters
       0   Does not apply

25        Crime, police, judicial, legal and penal matters

       1   Non-political or non-military-crime, punishments, court proceedings of all kinds
       2   Crime, punishment, court proceedings with political or military aspects
       3   Penal policies, reforms, systems, projects of a constructive kind
       4   Other crime police and legal matters and those not classifiable under 1, 2 or 3
       0   Does not apply

26        Social services and welfare, including education (except students)

       1   Social problems of all kinds: bad housing, health, illiteracy, poverty, prostitution, etc (excluding police and crime matters)
       2   Achievements, progress, reforms and developments in social policy, social services
       3   Other social service and social welfare matters
       0   Does not apply

27        Culture, arts, archaeology, history, religion
       1   Applies

       Scientific, technical, medical (including nuclear energy)
       2   Applies
       0   Neither applies

28        Student matters
       1   Applies
       0   Does not apply

29      Entertainment, show business (except personalities)

       1  Applies
       0  Does not apply

30      Personalities, including appointments (other than political)

       1  Show-business, entertainment, arts
       2  Other
       0  Does not apply

31      Human interest, bizarre happenings, sex news not otherwise coded (eg prostitution as social problem)

       1  Applies
       0  Does not apply

32      Ecology, environment, pollution

       1  Applies
       0  Does not apply

33      Other (including natural disasters): 1, Applies, 0, Does not apply

34      *British involvement*

       1  Britain or Britons abroad — individuals in trouble or danger, commercial success or failure, tourist matters, scientific or cultural, achievements by British subjects
       0  Does not apply

35      *US involvement*

       1  US or US citizens abroad (similar to above)
       0  Does not apply

## STORY CHARACTERISTICS

36      Type of event or report

       1  Mainly about an action(s) or event(s) (includes travel, arrival, etc)
       2  Mainly about a statement, speech, announcement
       3  Mainly background, descriptive
       4  Not classifiable, uncertain
       5  Other

37      Predictability

       1  Planned, predictable (diary event)
       2  Unplanned, unexpected
       3  Not classifiable, uncertain
       4  Other

38      Estimate of "excitement" factor

       1  Dramatic, exciting, violent
       2  Undramatic, non violent
       3  Uncertain, not classifiable
       4  Other

39      Status of event or report

       1  Official or semi-official
       2  Unofficial or
          uncertain, not classifiable
       3  Other

40      Attribution to source (of significant part of story)

      1   Reported from identified person or source
      2   Quoted from identified person or source
      3   Attributed to identified source or person
      4   No attribution, not checkable
      5   Other


41      Time references

      1   Past
      2   Present or past/continuing
      3   Future
      0   Uncertain/not classifiable


42      Local media as source or not

      1   Local media as source (TV, radio, press)
      2   Not applicable, uncertain


43      Individual or collective reference

      1   Mainly refers to an individual
      2   Mainly refers to collectivity — group, organisation, government, whole society, nation etc
      3   Uncertain, not classifiable, mixed
      4   Other


44      If story refers to individual, status of main participant or chief actor

      1   Prime minister or chief elected leader
      2   Head of state
      3   Opposition leader or politician
      4   Religious leader
      5   Military leader or police
      6   Official, civil servant, ambassador, diplomat, minister
      7   Business or industrial leader
      8   Trade union leader
      9   Artist, intellectual, writer
      x   Celebrity, star
      y   Other
      0   Does not apply


45      If story refers to collectivity, type of collectivity involved

      1   Legislature, parliament, executive body, administration
      2   Political party
      3   Legal body
      4   Church body
      5   Police or army
      6   Trade union
      7   Business firm
      8   City, town
      9   Other
      0   Does not apply

### COUNTRY(IES) REFERRED TO IN REPORT EITHER AS LOCATION OR EVENT OR SOURCE OF REPORT, OR AS PARTICIPANT IN LINK BETWEEN TWO OR MORE COUNTRIES

46        (i) Number of countries involved

            1  One country
            2  Two countries
            3  More than two countries
            4  Other—eg UN or international body

        (ii) Write in name of country(ies)

47–48   (iii) Main *pairs* of countries and of *country-regions* where only *two* are involved

           00  Does not apply
           01  Britain—US
           02  Britain—EEC (as an entity)
           03  Britain—USSR
           04  Britain—France
           05  Britain—Germany
           06  Britain—Italy
           07  Britain—Benelux
           08  Britain—Rhodesia
           09  Britain—Ireland
           10  Britain—Spain or Portugal
           11  Britain—Japan
           12  Britain—Israel
           13  Britain—Australasia
           14  Britain—African country
           15  Britain—M. East country or area
           16  Britain—E. European country
           17  US—USSR
           18  US—Israel
           19  US—Arab country
           20  US—Middle East country or area
           21  US—China
           22  Israel—Arab country
           23  USSR—China
           24  US—Vietnam or Cambodia

        (iv) Main countries and region(s) to which report refers or where event occurred. Where report or event involves two or more countries not within same region, code region to which there is a primary reference. For example for US involvement in Vietnam, code for Vietnam unless it is an issue of US domestic politics. In some cases no specific region can be indicated.

49      *Europe*

      1  British Isles
      2  Scandinavia (Norway, Finland, Sweden)
      3  EEC country (Denmark, Germany, Benelux, Italy, France)
      4  Iberian peninsular
      5  USSR
      6  E. European (Socialist, incl. Yugoslavia)
      7  Other Europe and Europe generally
      0  Does not apply

50    *Middle East*

    1   Israel
    2   Egypt
    3   Israel's other neighbours—Jordan, Lebanon, Syria
    4   Other M. East, including Turkey, Iran, Iraq, Saudi Arabia etc also M. East
        in general
    0   Does not apply


51    *Africa*

    1   N. Africa, except for Egypt
    2   West Africa, English speaking
    3   West Africa, French speaking
    4   East and Central Africa
    5   South Africa, Rhodesia, Angola
    6   Other African and Africa generally
    0   Does not apply


52    *Asia*

    1   China
    2   Japan
    3   S. E. Asia (Indo China, Malaysia, Korea, etc)
    4   India, Pakistan, Ceylon
    5   Other Asian and Asia generally
    0   Does not apply


53    *South and Central America*

    1   Chile
    2   Mexico
    3   Brazil
    4   Argentina
    5   Other and Latin America generally
    6   Caribbean
    0   Does not apply


54    *N. America*

    1   USA
    2   Canada
    3   Other and N. America in general
    0   Does not apply


55    *Australasia*

    0   Does not apply
    1   Applies


56    *Other*

    0   Does not apply
    1   Other
    2   Unidentifiable, unspecific

## THEMES TO WHICH THERE IS A CLEAR AND SPECIFIC REFERENCE

These themes or news angles either represent recurring topics of a specific kind or imply some value judgement. The headings under which themes are grouped are intended only as a general guide and are not to be taken as a limitation on the use of particular items. A reference theme differs from a main topic by its more incidental or subsidiary character.

*Columns*

          (i) Communism and east-west relations

57                Internal left-wing activity

               1  Applies
               0  Does not apply

58                Détente, co-existence

               1  Applies
               0  Does not apply

59                East-west conflict, military threat etc

               1  Applies
               0  Does not apply

60                Soviet or other external communist involvement

               1  applies
               0  Does not apply

61                Splits in western alliance, weakness of NATO etc

               1  Applies
               0  Does not apply

62                Berlin wall, iron curtain

               1  Applies
               0  Does not apply

63                Dissidence in USSR, E. Europe

               1  Applies
               0  Does not apply

64                Soviet-China quarrel

               1  Applies
               0  Does not apply

         (ii) Internal political problems and undesirable aspects of domestic politics

65                1  Instability and violence
               2  Autocracy, arbitrary personal whim, lack of democracy
               3  Repression of own citizens, inhumanity, torture
               4  Corruption, venality, waste, extravagance, inefficiency
               5  Secession
               0  Does not apply

66                Cultural or language conflict

               1  Applies
               0  Does not apply

(iii) Economic or industrial matters

67         Economic problems or successes
- 1  Problems, failures, recession, inflation
- 2  Success, achievement, good news
- 0  Does not apply

68         Consumer shortages, economic inefficiency
- 1  Applies
- 0  Does not apply

69         Oil
- 1  Applies
- 0  Does not apply

(iv) Race relations, colour

70         Apartheid, colour bar, racism
- 1  Applies
- 0  Does not apply

71         Anti-white feeling, black power, Black/White conflict
- 1  Applies
- 0  Does not apply

72         Coloured immigration
- 1  Applies
- 0  Does not apply

(v) Other themes

73         Ecology
- 1  Good news
- 2  Bad news
- 3  Other ecology
- 0  Does not apply

74         Sex aspects
- 1  Applies
- 0  Does not apply

75         Miscellaneous
- 1  Fascist, right-wing activity
- 2  Famine, poverty
- 3  Drugs, drug traffic
- 4  Royalty or aristocracy
- 5  Mercenaries
- 6  Espionage
- 7  National stereotypes
- 8  The media—TV, radio, press, film
- 9  Ulster troubles, IRA
- 0  Does not apply

76         *Attributed source*
- 1  Specified news agency or news service (eg US newspaper)
- 2  Own correspondent
- 3  Other specified sources
- 4  Not given or not classifiable
- 0  Does not apply

*Columns*

77          *Is event or report in general negative or positive?*

            1  Judged mainly negative (eg critical, "bad news" relating to
               conflict or problems)
            2  Mainly positive
            3  Neutral or mixed
            0  Not classifiable or Does not apply

78          *Direction* (assessed)

            1  Mainly unfavourable to or critical of foreign country or partici-
               pant
            2  Mainly favourable
            3  Neutral or mixed
            4  Not classifiable or applicable

79          Measure of prominence

80          1  Illustrated
            0  Not illustrated

**Foreign news and features analysis sheet**

| | | | |
|---|---|---|---|
| 46 (i) | No. of countries | 1–4 | Serial No. |
| 47–48 | Country pairs | 5–6 | Sample Day No. |
| 49 | Europe | 7–8 | Page No. |
| 50 | Middle East | 9–11 | Story Number |
| 51 | Africa | 12 | Item Code |
| 52 | Asia | 13–15 | Space |
| 53 | S. and C. America | 16–17 | Headline space |
| 54 | N. America | 18 | Item size scale |
| 55 | Australasia | 19 | International/Foreign |
| 56 | Other | | |

46 (ii) **NAME OF COUNTRY(IES)**
(write in)

**MAIN TOPICS**

| | |
|---|---|
| 20 | Diplomatic/political (Int) |
| 21 | Political (domestic) |
| 22 | Military |
| 23 | Economic |
| 24 | Aid, development |
| 25 | Crime, legal |
| 26 | Social services |
| 27 | Culture, religion, scientific |
| 28 | Students |
| 29 | Entertainment |
| 30 | Personalities |
| 31 | Human interest |
| 32 | Ecology |
| 33 | Other |
| 34 | British involvement |
| 35 | US involvement |

**THEMES**

| | |
|---|---|
| 57 | |
| 58 | 67 |
| 59 | 68 |
| 60 | 69 |
| 61 | 70 |
| 62 | 71 |
| 63 | 72 |
| 64 | 73 |
| 65 | 74 |
| 66 | 75 |

**STORY CHARACTERISTICS**

| | |
|---|---|
| 36 | Type of event |
| 37 | Predictability |
| 38 | Excitement |
| 39 | Official or not |
| 40 | Attribution |
| 41 | Time |
| 42 | Local media |
| 43 | Individual/collective |
| 44 | Status of main actor |
| 45 | Type of collectivity |

**HEADLINE**

| |
|---|
| 76 |
| 77 |
| 78 |
| 79 |

**Comment on Coding Frame applied to Foreign News and Feature Content National Daily Newspapers, 1975**

The purpose of this commentary is to explain why particular forms of classification were chosen and to shed some light on the criteria which were applied and on the instructions given to coders. The order of discussion follows the order of items in the coding frame (Appendix E1) with references to the column numbers for identification.

(i) *Story Number* (cols. 9–11)

A serial number was allocated to any "story" or event which was reported in more than one newspaper on the same day. The original intention of this procedure was to allow comparison in treatment as between different newspapers and to investigate the factors which were associated with varying degrees of duplicate reporting.

(ii) *Item Code* (col. 12)

The categories represent the main types of foreign content as recorded in the general content analysis. In essence, they involve a distinction between "international", "commonwealth" and "foreign domestic" events, and between political, social and economic news and "other" news. They also identify feature and editorial content.

(iii) *Whether international or foreign domestic* (col. 19)

The main criterion for allocation was whether or not the event involved two or more countries (Britain counting as one country).

(iv) *Main Topics* (cols. 20–33)

Most of these topic headings will be self-explanatory and comments are only necessary in explanation of a few items. The intention was, in general, to provide a set of mutually exclusive subject categories and to allocate each newspaper item to one main category. This is not difficult in practice, although it involves some element of judgement and the possibility of variable decisions about which category should take precedence where more than one seems applicable. Normally, a more specific category takes precedence over a general one.

The main purpose in distinguishing between different kinds of domestic political stories (col. 21) was to separate the violent, dramatic and unexpected from the routine, predictable and institutionalised.

In the case of crime and police news (col. 25) the main distinction was between ordinary civil crime and police matters and those with political connotations. As an example of the specific having precedence over the general a political crime item could be coded under this heading rather than as political or both.

Social services and social welfare content (col. 26) would, similarly, be coded here rather as domestic politics.

In the analysis, "culture, art, etc", and "scientific, technical and medical" topics were treated together as a single category, in view of the small numbers involved (cols. 27, 28).

No separate category was allowed for in the original coding scheme for natural disasters and they were included in the residual (other) category (col. 33).

(v) *British involvement* (col. 34)

Any item involving Britain, British interests or citizens was so coded, even where the item was primarily a "foreign domestic" story. For a story to be coded as "international", a higher level of official British participation would be called for than was needed for recording some British involvement.

(vi) *US involvement* (col. 35)

Similar criteria were applied to assessing American involvement.

(vii) *Story characteristics* (cols. 36–45)

Much of what was intended will be apparent from the categories in this section. Broadly, the aims were, firstly, to provide an overall impression of the kind of story involved according to such evaluative criteria as the degree of "sensationalism" or "personalisation". Secondly, the aim was to assess, in broad terms, how much the news is "new". Thirdly, it was intended to discover something about the kind of attribution to sources and the kind of participant individual or group.

The following provide some examples of stories fitting the alternative classification categories. All are taken from *The Times*, using headlines only to indicate the story.

(a) *Type of event or report.*
1. Action or event:
   "Callaghan visit fills gaps in relations with Poland".
2. Statement, speech, announcement:
   "Mr Simon predicts stronger dollar".
3. Mainly background:
   "How our European partners choose their parliaments".

(b) *Predictability*
1. Planned, predictable:
   "Heads of 35 nations sign declaration" (Helsinki Conference).
2. Unplanned, unexpected:
   "200 homosexuals are arrested".

(c) *Estimate of "excitement"*
1. Dramatic, violent:
   "French wine protest hits holiday traffic".
2. Undramatic, non-violent:
   "Senora Peron takes rest to recover after illness".

These illustrative examples suggest some of the possibilities and limitations of the approach. Some element of judgement is involved, but in many cases there is little ambiguity. The emphasis was placed on only coding for a definite category where there was least doubt and using the "uncertain" category as extensively as necessary. There is no advantage in trying to classify all cases, only in having an index of the way different topics, newspapers, or countries might be ranked, for purposes of comparison.

The attempt to code for "official or unofficial status" of events or reports (col. 39) was found to be unsuccessful (after the event) because, of low reliability, and the information obtained has been disregarded. Similarly, the distinction between past and present events (col. 41) could not be made reliably, largely because of the failure to distinguish between the immediate (eg previous day) and more distant past. Reports about future events can also take the form of statements made in the past.

A reference to "local media as source" (col. 42) occurred where a report from the press or a broadcast in the foreign country concerned provided the substance of an item.

The classification according to whether a reference was to an individual or a "collectivity" (cols. 43–45) was partly made in order to assist sub-classification of main participant and partly to assess the extent to which news deals with personalities rather than institutions.

(viii) *Pairs of countries* (cols. 47–48)

The restriction of pairings to cases where only *two* countries is involved has led to some under-representation of important connections between states—especially those internal to the EEC and between the US and the Middle East. The results are thus of limited value.

(ix) *Themes* (cols. 57–75)

The purpose of recording themes has been briefly explained in the text (p. 268) and there is little to add. The potentially great variety of foreign news events makes it difficult to provide any comprehensive set of themes or news angles. The original intention was to reflect the general concerns underlying the selection of news in the period, cutting across the specific subject matter. Examples include the concern with relations between Western and Eastern power blocs, or with relations between races or with economic depression. However, in practice, many of the points looked for are in the nature of sub-topics of news and the level of generality varies a good deal.

(x) *Attributed source* (col. 76)

In order to be coded as originating with a news agency, an item would have required an attribution to an identified news agency. For coding as "own correspondent", the intention was to take account only of cases where this phrase was used. There was, however, some variation of practice in interpreting references to named correspondents and the line between categories in the results cannot be relied on.

(xi) *Assessment of whether event is positive or negative* (col. 77)

The intention was basically to distinguish "good news" from "bad news", with the emphasis in the news event itself and not on the imputed *intention* of the news item (thus "bad news" for a foreign country might conceivably be "good news" for Britain). Any story with an "objectively" negative component would be so coded.

(xii) *Direction* (col. 78)

The attempt to identify favourability or its opposite was not successful, partly because of difficulties of assessment, partly because such attitudes are rarely explicit.

## APPENDIX E4

### COMPARISON BETWEEN NEWSPAPERS IN TERMS OF MAIN TOPICS OF FOREIGN COVERAGE: PERCENTAGE DISTRIBUTION OF ITEMS IN EACH PAPER BY TOPICS

| Topic | The Scotsman** | Glasgow Herald** | The Times | The Guardian | The Daily Telegraph | Financial Times | Morning Star | Daily Express | Daily Mail | Daily Mirror | The Sun | All papers |
|---|---|---|---|---|---|---|---|---|---|---|---|---|
| | % | % | % | % | % | % | % | % | % | % | % | % |
| 1. International political, diplomatic | 18 | 22 | 19 | 20 | 23 | 20 | 33 | 17 | 15 | 16 | 9 | 20 |
| 2. Foreign domestic political—conflict or crisis—related | 13 | 12 | 9 | 12 | 7 | 8 | 15 | 6 | 8 | 8 | 8 | 9 |
| 3. Foreign domestic political—other | 19 | 10 | 13 | 15 | 14 | 15 | 9 | 7 | 8 | 7 | 5 | 12 |
| 4. Military and defence | 6 | 8 | 8 | 11 | 13 | 4 | 8 | 10 | 7 | 4 | 7 | 8 |
| 5. Economic, trade, financial | 22 | 16 | 19 | 16 | 14 | 42 | 15 | 13 | 11 | 11 | 9 | 19 |
| 6. Aid and development | — | 1 | 1 | 1 | 1 | 1 | — | — | 1 | 1 | — | 1 |
| 7. Crime, police and legal—military, political | 10 | 7 | 8 | 6 | 10 | 4 | 7 | 6 | 12 | 8 | 12 | 8 |
| 8. Crime, police and legal—other | 3 | 9 | 9 | 7 | 6 | 4 | 1 | 10 | 13 | 17 | 21 | 8 |
| 9. Welfare, culture, art, science | 2 | 3 | 8 | 4 | 3 | 2 | 11 | 3 | 3 | 4 | 8 | 4 |
| 10. Show business, personalities, human interest | 3 | 3 | 7 | 4 | 4 | 1 | 1 | 23 | 21 | 25 | 19 | 6 |
| 11. Other | 7 | 5 | 3 | 6 | 6 | 1 | 3 | 5 | 4 | 5 | 5 | 5 |
| TOTAL %* | 103 | 101 | 104 | 105 | 101 | 105 | 103 | 100 | 103 | 106 | 103 | — |
| Total No. of items: | 119 | 77 | 504 | 461 | 404 | 383 | 138 | 158 | 122 | 76 | 78 | 2,520 |

*The excess of totals over 100% is partly due to rounding errors and partly to the fact that more than one topic could be coded for a given item.

**Six issue only analysed.

## MAIN THEMES OF FOREIGN COVERAGE IN NATIONAL AND TWO SCOTTISH DAILY NEWSPAPERS: ACTUAL FREQUENCY OF COVERAGE

| Theme | Total | The Scotsman | Glasgow Herald | The Times | The Guardian | The Daily Telegraph | Financial Times | Morning Star | Daily Express | Daily Mail | Daily Mirror | The Sun |
|---|---|---|---|---|---|---|---|---|---|---|---|---|
| 1. Economic problems | 195 | 14 | 9 | 39 | 29 | 23 | 57 | 6 | 8 | 2 | 3 | 5 |
| 2. Internal political instability and violence | 180 | 15 | 8 | 39 | 36 | 30 | 20 | 12 | 9 | 3 | 1 | 7 |
| 3. Oil | 120 | 4 | 2 | 32 | 21 | 19 | 26 | 3 | 6 | 4 | 1 | 2 |
| 4. Internal left-wing activity | 85 | 7 | 2 | 12 | 26 | 10 | 14 | 10 | 1 | 2 | — | 1 |
| 5. The media—TV, Press, etc | 82 | 6 | 2 | 20 | 18 | 17 | 9 | 2 | 4 | 2 | 2 | 1 |
| 6. Détente, East-West co-existence | 81 | 5 | 3 | 14 | 15 | 20 | 11 | 3 | 5 | 2 | 1 | 1 |
| 7. Soviet and other Communist external involvement | 81 | 5 | 1 | 8 | 18 | 16 | 19 | 5 | 7 | — | 3 | — |
| 8. Economic success | 80 | — | 3 | 19 | 17 | 8 | 24 | 3 | 2 | 4 | 1 | 3 |
| 9. Apartheid, colour bar, plus black power etc | 68 | 3 | — | 19 | 12 | 7 | 5 | 10 | 4 | 1 | — | — |
| 10. Autocracy, repression, torture | 60 | 3 | 3 | 17 | 18 | 7 | 1 | 12 | — | 2 | 1 | 2 |
| 11. Secession (as internal problem) | 55 | 1 | 1 | 9 | 14 | 12 | 4 | 1 | 6 | 2 | 7 | 7 |
| 12. Sex aspects | 49 | 1 | — | 8 | 7 | 8 | — | — | 6 | 5 | 3 | 3 |
| 13. Royalty | 41 | 1 | 1 | 8 | 6 | 4 | 2 | 6 | 7 | 6 | 3 | — |
| 14. Espionage | 41 | — | 1 | 8 | 8 | 7 | 2 | 1 | 2 | 3 | — | — |
| 15. Ecology | 34 | 3 | — | 8 | 10 | 8 | 3 | 9 | 1 | 2 | — | 2 |
| 16. Fascist, right-wing activity | 33 | 3 | 1 | 5 | 5 | 3 | 2 | 1 | 3 | 3 | 1 | 1 |
| 17. Internal political corruption | 30 | — | — | 10 | 6 | — | 1 | 1 | 1 | 5 | — | 3 |
| 18. Cultural or language conflict | 27 | 3 | 3 | 5 | 1 | 6 | — | — | 3 | 9 | 3 | — |
| 19. Drugs | 24 | 1 | 1 | 5 | 4 | — | 8 | 1 | 1 | 2 | 1 | — |
| 20. Consumer shorts | 23 | — | 2 | 4 | 4 | 6 | — | — | 1 | — | 1 | — |
| 21. Ulster troubles or IRA | 20 | — | 1 | 3 | 4 | 6 | 1 | — | — | — | 2 | 1 |
| Percentage Share of all 2,520 items (for comparison) | 100% | 5 | 3 | 20 | 18 | 16 | 15 | 6 | 6 | 5 | 3 | 3 |

**Main foreign news events on days sampled**

This appendix is designed to provide a very brief reminder of the substantive content of world news in the periods studied. It does so by reproducing the headlines of main *front page* news stories (up to three), in order of length, appearing in *The Times* on the 12 days sampled. *The Times* has been chosen, partly because of the fullness of its news coverage, partly because its headlines are generally long and informative.

*January 7, 1975*

1. Mr. Hattersley on free trade pact with EEC "if we are lucky"
2. "Honourable settlement" on Rhodesia in sight
3. Dr. Kissinger suggests preliminary oil talks

*January 15, 1975*

1. Russia rejects trade pact with US in blow to détente
2. Group of ten agree two schemes for re-cycling petrodollars
3. Negotiations on sugar again deadlocked

*February 3, 1975*

1. Five year deal agreed between EEC and former colonies
2. Irish Government to risk death of IRA hunger-striker
3. Turks lose soldier in Nicosia flare-up

*February 15, 1975*

1. President Makarios says Greek Cypriots will resist partition
2. Mr Wilson's Kremlin talks centre on détente
3. Dr Kissinger fails to breach logjam

*February 21, 1975*

1. Troops executed for excesses in Asmara

*March 6, 1975*

1. Rockets cut American air links with Phnom Penh
2. Palestinian guerillas hold Tel Aviv seafront hotel in fierce battle
3. Herr Lorenz tells of his ordeal in hands of anarchist gang

*July 7, 1975*

1. Mr Callaghan flying for Mobutu meeting
2. Israelis raid Lebanon camp "by sea and air"
3. Independence from France declared in Comoros

*August 2, 1975*

1. Ford plea for Helsinki promises to be kept
2. OAU rejects Arab-backed move to expel Israel from UN
3. Concessions to Africans by Mr Smith

*August 21, 1975*

1. CIA "gave technological support to Israel to make atomic bomb after 1956 Suez war"
2. The British lesson how to ruin a country
3. Dr Kissinger likely to get hostile reception in Israel

*September 5, 1975*

1. Revised forecasts on World trade cast gloom on Britain's recovery plans
2. France puts millions into reflation plan

*September 10, 1975*

1. Tripoli fighting threatens to start civil war in Lebanon
2. £16.6m plan to rebuild quake town (Turkey)

*September 23, 1975*

1. Two arrested after shot is fired as he leaves hotel in San Francisco
2. Ford plan to free US from oil producers
3. US suggests new peace moves in the Middle East

Printed in England for Her Majesty's Stationery Office by Harrison & Sons (London) Ltd.

21714   Dd 290763   K40   7/77